D0229013

ONE WEEK LOAN
UNIVERSITY OF GLAMORGAN
TREFOREST LEARNING RESOURCES CENTRE
Pontypridd, CF37 1DL
Telephone: (01443) 482626
Books are to be returned on or before the last date below

3 0 NOV 2004

1 4 JAN 2005

1 5 APR 2005

0 9 NOV 2005

- 6 OCT 2006

1 2 JAN 2007

2 5 OCT 2007

0 NOV 2008

1 2 JAN 2009

THE LABOUR GOVERNMENTS 1964–70
volume 1

MANCHESTER
UNIVERSITY PRESS

THE LABOUR GOVERNMENTS 1964–70

Series editors   Steven Fielding and John W. Young

volume 1   *Labour and cultural change*   Steven Fielding
volume 2   *International policy*   John W. Young
volume 3   *Economic policy*   Jim Tomlinson

THE LABOUR GOVERNMENTS 1964–70

volume 1

Labour and cultural change

Steven Fielding

Manchester University Press

Manchester and New York

distributed exclusively in the USA by Palgrave

Copyright © Steven Fielding 2003

The right of Steven Fielding to be identified as the author of this work
has been asserted by him in accordance with the Copyright, Designs and
Patents Act 1988.

Published by Manchester University Press
Oxford Road, Manchester M13 9NR, UK
and Room 400, 175 Fifth Avenue, New York, NY 10010, USA
www.manchesteruniversitypress.co.uk

Distributed exclusively in the USA by
Palgrave, 175 Fifth Avenue, New York,
NY 10010, USA

Distributed exclusively in Canada by
UBC Press, University of British Columbia, 2029 West Mall,
Vancouver, BC, Canada V6T 1Z2

British Library Cataloguing-in-Publication Data
A catalogue record for this book is available from the British Library

Library of Congress Cataloging-in-Publication Data applied for

Learning Resources
Centre

12624535

ISBN 0 7190 4364 6   *hardback*

First published 2003

11 10 09 08 07 06 05 04 03   10 9 8 7 6 5 4 3 2 1

Typeset by R. J. Footring Ltd, Derby
Printed in Great Britain by CPI, Bath

For my parents with love.

Contents

List of tables   *page* viii
Series foreword   ix
Acknowledgements   x

1 Introduction. Cultural and political change in 1960s Britain   1
2 Labour's organisational culture   35
3 Responding to affluence   61
4 Reconciling the classes   86
5 Appealing to women   113
6 Integrating black immigrants   139
7 Instilling 'responsibility' in the young   165
8 Engaging with participation   191
9 Conclusion. The 1970 general election   217

Bibliography   236
Index   252

Tables

1.1 The distribution of economically active men by occupational
    category, 1951 and 1971   6
1.2 The distribution of economically active women by
    occupational category, 1951 and 1971   6
1.3 Labour and Conservative votes compared, 1950–70   21
2.1 Labour's official membership, 1955–70   43
2.2 Proportion of constituency Labour parties affiliating the
    minimum number of members, revised membership and
    average CLP membership, by region, 1965   44
2.3 Proportion of constituency Labour parties affiliating the
    minimum number of members, revised membership and
    average CLP membership, by region, 1968   45
2.4 Official and 'actual' memberships compared in the South
    West Region, 1965   46
2.5 Numbers of members and activists in Glasgow, 1961
    and 1968   49
3.1 Labour's vote by social category, 1955–66   63
5.1 Labour's official female membership, 1960–70   115
5.2 Women's section delegates attending the national
    conference of Labour women, 1960–70   117
7.1 Labour's youth and student organisations: numbers of
    branches, members and officers, 1955–70   170
9.1 The composition of the Labour vote, 1964–70   222
9.2 Women and Labour voting, by social class and age,
    1964–70   225
9.3 Men and Labour voting, by social class and age, 1964–70   225

Series foreword

Before the Labour Party entered government in October 1964 its leader, Harold Wilson, raised hopes of creating a 'new Britain', based on furthering the 'white heat' of technological change and aiming to pursue egalitarianism at home and abroad. In June 1970 Labour was ejected from office having lived up to few of these aspirations. Most analysts of the party's period in power consequently characterise it as a miserable failure. The majority focus on the Labour leadership's lack of ambition and reserve much of their censure for Wilson's strategic shortcomings. Present-day 'New' Labour, for which the 1960s are clearly an embarrassment, effectively endorses this glum assessment.

The three volumes in this series tackle different aspects of the 1964–70 Wilson governments' record and assume contrasting approaches to their subjects. Each, however, benefits from access to recently released government files housed in the Public Record Office, as well as other documents lately made available to historians. Together the volumes constitute the most complete record of these governments currently obtainable. While not denying Labour in office was a disappointment when measured against party rhetoric, the authors assume a more nuanced view compared with most previous accounts. In particular, they highlight a wider range of reasons for the governments' relative lack of achievement. If the disposition of Labour's leaders played its part, so did the nature of the party, the delicate state of the economy, the declining place of Britain in the world order and the limited ambitions of the British people themselves.

In testing some well entrenched assumptions about these governments in light of new evidence, the authors dispute their status as the black sheep of Labour history and establish some new perspectives. In this respect, these volumes therefore mark an important stage in the permanent revisionism to which all historians should subject the past. It is hoped they will encourage more research on Labour's period in office and challenge their overly grim reputation among both academics and lay readers alike.

Acknowledgements

This book has been a long time in the making, considerably longer, in fact, than the duration of the 1964–70 Wilson governments. During the course of the research and writing I have incurred debts, too many to fully recall and mention here. I would therefore like to take the opportunity to thank everybody who helped me on the way. In particular, I want to record my appreciation for the help, advice, knowledge and/or accommodation provided by Lindsay Abbott, Alan Bell, Stephen Bird, Lawrence Black, John Bochel, Stephen Brooke, John Callaghan, David Coates, Andy Davies, Pat Fielding, John Garrard, Andrew Geddes, Iain Maciver, Janette Martin, Chris Nicholls, Nigel Parker, Judith Read, Susan Sims, Jill Spellman, Jeremy Stokes, Duncan Tanner, Richard Temple, Jane Thorniley-Walker, Nick Tiratsoo, Jim Tomlinson, Richard Weight, Mark Wickham-Jones, Christine Woodland and John Young. I should also apologise to Abby, Jack, Tom and Anna for being such a pain while finishing this book, and thank them for their support.

For permission to cite from the John P. Mackintosh papers I should thank Una Maclean-Mackintosh; similarly, I need to thank the Scottish National Party for allowing me to refer to their papers. Every effort has been made to obtain permission to reproduce copyright material in this book. If any proper acknowledgement has not been made, copyright holders are invited to contact the publisher.

I received invaluable financial assistance from the British Academy in undertaking my archival work; the Arts and Humanities Research Board's research leave scheme helped me finalise my research and writing; and Salford University enabled me to purchase a laptop PC that is now due for early retirement.

1

Introduction. Cultural and political change in 1960s Britain

If they are to prosper, political parties must successfully engage with change. For the British Labour Party during the 1960s, this imperative seemed especially acute because, like other advanced capitalist societies, the country underwent what has been described as a 'cultural revolution'. The viability of what many took to be immutable identities and divisions based on class, gender, generation and ethnicity was widely questioned; in addition, the relationship between individuals and political authority was subject to sweeping critique. This book examines the nature of Labour's response during the 1964–70 governments led by Harold Wilson. Yet, while a work of history, it views its subject with one eye on the debate that began in the 1990s regarding how parties should react to what was believed to be another period of flux. By establishing how Labour thought and acted during the 1960s, it is hoped this work will put into perspective certain issues currently preoccupying those interested in the viability of representative politics.

The purpose of this introductory chapter is to clarify and contextualise issues that will be later investigated in greater depth and to outline the author's approach to the subject. Taking the second concern first, the critic Raymond Williams long ago remarked that, because there are so many ways in which it can be defined, 'culture' is one of the most difficult words in the English language.[1] To avoid later confusion, it is therefore necessary to clarify what in this work 'cultural change' implies. Following Williams, 'culture' here means 'relationships between elements in a whole way of life', something including not only the actions of individuals but also what those actions were taken to signify – because thoughts and feelings influence activity. Consequently, 'culture' embraces not just what individuals did, but what they imagined they were doing and what impact they believed their actions would have. 'Cultural change' therefore comprises both 'objective' transformation and what contemporaries – specifically members of the Labour Party – thought those changes were and how they should react to them. The work is particularly interested in what Williams described as the 'felt sense of the quality

1

of life ... a sense of the ways in which particular activities combined into a way of thinking and living', what he called the 'structure of feeling', comprising 'the most delicate and least tangible parts of our activity'. This focus is due to the assumption that the 'structure of feeling' sustained by Labour's organisation helps account for its members' understanding of cultural change. While that does not hold the key to explaining Labour's electoral performance – something due to other factors, many of which were beyond its control – it nonetheless illuminates the rationale for the party's actions.

Given this concern with culture, the work casts its net wider than most studies of contemporary British political history.[2] The actions of the Labour governments are placed in a milieu that includes more than Cabinet ministers, top civil servants and members of the National Executive Committee, as a focus on the workings of Whitehall and Transport House tends to abstract politics from society. For one of the purposes here is to establish the extent to which Labour was a cultural entity as much as – to take an almost random selection of 1960s artefacts – the television soap opera *Coronation Street*, Anthony Burgess's novel *The Clockwork Orange*, the pop group Herman's Hermits and Manchester United Football Club. Nonetheless, albeit embedded in time and place, Labour – in contrast to the likes of Herman and his Hermits – sought to change the society that produced it. In particular, members of the party talked of building 'socialism' and viewed cultural change with that aim in mind. Leaders and members could not, however, agree what form 'socialism' should take and so disputed the impact it might exert on their party's fortunes: more than a few in fact denied society was transforming on any substantive scale.

One of the aims of this chapter is to establish that cultural change provoked contrasting, and often flawed, readings. Given that contemporaries necessarily lacked the benefit of hindsight, they sometimes questioned the existence of what would later be thought critical trends – and occasionally exaggerated the importance of what would subsequently prove to be fads. Nonetheless, how change is first conceived can be of critical importance and so the main emphasis here is not on establishing the actuality of change but on what Labour members understood it to be. This means taking account of party thinking since at least 1945. For just as all armies prepare to fight only the last war, so civil institutions look to the future through preconceptions cast from past experience. In this regard, Labour was no different, except perhaps in the especially pronounced respect that many members paid to the party's history.

The 'Golden Age'

The 1960s fall within what Eric Hobsbawm has termed 'a sort of Golden Age', which began with Western Europe's recovery from the Second World War in the early 1950s and ended with the onset of global recession two decades later. Hobsbawm saw this as a time of 'extraordinary economic growth and social transformation' within advanced capitalist societies, 'which probably changed human society more profoundly than any other period of comparable brevity'.[3] That which Arthur Marwick called a 'cultural revolution' was not limited to a politically radical or socially privileged elite but affected the 'material conditions, lifestyles, family relationships, and personal freedoms' of 'the vast majority of ordinary people'.[4] According to Ronald Inglehart, unprecedented growth encouraged voters to embrace 'post-material values', such as a concern for the environment, and to demand a more direct say in decision-making.[5] Yet, if all authorities agree that the decade saw marked change, not all think it was a Golden Age.

Most historians believe that during the first half of the twentieth century Britain was a singularly stable society, such that, be it in the parlour, factory or polling booth, those in power were rarely challenged.[6] The most developed expression of what sociologists Edward Shils and Michael Young described as Britain's 'moral unity' was thought to have been the 1953 Coronation of Queen Elizabeth II. This caused two million subjects to express their devotion on the streets of London while thirty million more watched events unfold on television or listened to their description on radio. Even the politically progressive *Manchester Guardian* believed this ceremony saw 'the unity of a people expressed more convincingly than ever'.[7]

The indigenous view that Britons were happy with their political system was reinforced by US social scientists who, during the Cold War, searched for viable models of liberal democracy.[8] To Gabriel Almond and Sidney Verba, the country's 'civic culture' was exemplary, being 'neither traditional nor modern but partaking of both'. It was a 'pluralistic culture based on communication and persuasion, a culture of consensus and diversity, a culture that permitted change but moderated it'. Most notably, it had allowed the working class to enter mainstream politics and, 'in a process of trial and error, find the language in which to couch their demands and the means to make them effective'. Almond and Verba were confident that Britain's civic culture could easily accommodate any new political forces on the same basis.[9]

Almond later admitted that this conceptualisation of civic culture was both an independent and dependent variable: that is, it was thought to be an influence on, as well as subject to, more intractable structural factors.[10] Thus, it was unclear how far Britain's civic culture created the country's stability or was itself a product of the country's relatively placid history. Just because Britain had enjoyed political constancy for much of the twentieth century did not mean it would do so if its foundations crumbled: and to the alarmed eyes of many transatlantic observers, during the 1960s this began to happen. What Samuel Beer described as the 'romantic revolt' gave rise to a new 'populism' – evident in sex, music, clothing, marriage, the family, work, crime, sport, education, religion and race relations – that infected the body politic. Beer blamed the 'counterculture' for this, especially pop music: the Beatles, he wrote, were the 'unacknowledged legislators' of the decline of that deference which had underpinned the country's civic character.[11]

Contemporary British observers, such as the journalists Christopher Booker and Bernard Levin, also thought the decade undermined all that was once good about their country. As Levin put it:

> There was a restlessness in the time that communicated itself every-where and to everyone, that communicated itself to the very sounds in Britain's air, the stones beneath Britain's feet. These stones shifted as she walked ahead with her once-purposeful stride, so that she began to stumble, then to stagger, then to fall down.[12]

Expressed in less vivid terms, much subsequent academic analysis accepted that Britain's civic culture had been destroyed during this period, in-augurating what historian Kenneth Morgan described as a 'grim period of dissolution and indiscipline'.[13]

This negative assessment is, however, not the only one on show. There is, in fact, a school of thought that is its exact opposite, one that presents post-war Britain as defined by repression and tired conformity. Advo-cates of this view see change as heralding a much-needed liberation for hitherto excluded groups, such as the young, women, workers and ethnic minorities. According to them, instead of loss, the 1960s brought considerable gains and on that basis should be celebrated rather than mourned.[14]

Rather than seeing the period in zero-sum terms, others focus on how Britain after 1945 engaged with 'modernity'. Within this frame of reference, even the emblematic Coronation can be seen not as the glori-ous expression of an entrenched civic culture, but as one of a number of 'extraordinarily contradictory impulses towards the modern'.[15] This accords to some degree with the perceptive but neglected view of the historian Henry Pelling, that the 1960s did not mark a decisive break with the past but instead enjoyed an essential continuity with the late nineteenth century.[16]

In light of such contrasting viewpoints, we should accept that, during the 1960s, Britain experienced significant cultural changes that had important political consequences – even if they had different causes and were more uneven, less dramatic and not as dire as some conceived them. Thus, Britain's civic culture was not so much destroyed as reconfigured and placed on a more 'modern' or, as Anthony Giddens has it, 'post-traditional' basis, one notably bereft of deference.[17] It was undoubtedly an invigorating moment for those individuals challenging the status quo and a painful one for figures in authority. The period should, however, cease to be the occasion for further emotion and become subject to a sober analysis of its wider significance. That, at least, is the perspective adopted here.

Having established the work's overall approach, it is now appropriate to survey those subjects usually seen as critical to Britain's mid-century transformation. The review is not exhaustive: in particular, it does not directly deal with 'permissiveness', which fortunately has been very ably tackled by others.[18] This is because the purpose here is to address issues both of intrinsic cultural importance and of great significance to Labour, inasmuch as they brought some of the party's long-standing electoral, ideological and organisational problems to an uncomfortably sensitive point.

Workers

However important were other forms of cultural change, contemporaries were most preoccupied by the transformation of the working class, as the days of the class-conscious worker appeared numbered. While still forming a majority, the manual working class was undeniably contracting in size, from about two-thirds of the workforce in 1951 to somewhat over half by 1971. Decline was, moreover, steepest in unskilled and semi-skilled occupations – those with the lowest pay and most insecure conditions (see Tables 1.1. and 1.2). Observers believed this meant the future lay with administrators, technicians and secretaries, those who thought of themselves as middle class – even when their incomes were often inferior to those of skilled manual workers.

On the eve of the 1960s, the working class was richer than ever before. Between the mid-1950s and mid-1960s, a male workers' average income rose by a third in real terms; the proportion of households owning fridges went from one in ten to one in three; and those with a television set increased from two-fifths to two-thirds. In this context it was not unreasonable for the Conservative Prime Minister, Harold Macmillan, to declare that 'most of our people have never had it so good' and to urge his audience to go 'round the country, go to the industrial towns, go to the farms and you will see a state of prosperity such as we have never had in my life-time – nor indeed ever in the history of this country'.[19] Rising incomes were thought to be so altering

Table 1.1 The distribution (%) of economically active men by occupational category, 1951 and 1971

	1951	*1971*	*Difference*
Self-employed and higher-grade			
salaried professionals	2.8	6.1	+3.3
Employers and proprietors	5.7	5.2	−0.5
Administrators and managers	6.8	9.9	+3.1
Lower-grade salaried professionals			
and technicians	3.0	5.5	+2.5
Inspectors, supervisors and foremen	3.3	4.5	+1.2
Clerical workers	6.0	6.1	+0.1
Sales personnel and shop assistants	4.0	3.9	−0.1
Skilled manual	30.3	29.4	−0.9
Semi-skilled manual	24.3	21.2	−3.1
Unskilled manual	13.8	8.2	−5.6
Total active male population (in 1,000s)	15,584	15,609	

Source: A. H. Halsey, *Change in British Society* (Oxford, 1985), Table 2.1.

Table 1.2 The distribution (%) of economically active women by occupational category, 1951 and 1971

	1951	*1971*	*Difference*
Self-employed and higher-grade			
salaried professionals	1.0	1.4	+0.4
Employers and proprietors	3.2	2.9	−0.3
Administrators and managers	2.7	3.3	+0.6
Lower-grade salaried professionals			
and technicians	7.9	10.8	+2.9
Inspectors, supervisors and forewomen	1.1	1.2	+0.1
Clerical workers	20.3	28.0	+7.7
Sales personnel and shop assistants	9.6	9.4	−0.2
Skilled manual	12.7	9.3	−3.4
Semi-skilled manual	33.6	27.3	−6.3
Unskilled manual	7.9	6.4	−1.5
Total active female population (in 1,000s)	6,930	8,762	

Source: A. H. Halsey, *Change in British Society* (Oxford, 1985), Table 2.1.

lifestyles that, according to the social investigator Ferdynand Zweig, 'a deep transformation' in workers' values was in process: they were 'on the move towards new middle-class values and [a] middle-class existence'.[20] Yet how many workers could be described as 'affluent' and the consequences of this condition were keenly debated.

As early as 1951, the researchers Seebohm Rowntree and G. R. Lavers claimed full employment and the welfare state meant poverty afflicted only one in twenty households.[21] Some thought this meant poverty was virtually a thing of the past, although others believed Rowntree underestimated the problem; by the mid-1960s this latter view was taken more seriously.[22] Later studies suggested that poverty was three times more prevalent than noted by Rowntree; it certainly remained easy to find families for whom the world of televisions and fridges remained an exotic ideal.[23] Recent analysis indicates that poverty was neither as low as suggested by Rowntree nor as extensive as critics alleged.[24] Thus, if poverty remained a feature of working-class life, for most the threat of becoming poor had largely lost its sting.

Some believed rising working-class wages were accompanied by a redistribution of wealth: workers were not only better off in absolute terms but also catching up with middle-class incomes. The welfare state and the higher taxes required to finance it were, as one observer had it, 'relentlessly, year by year … pushing us towards collectivism and propertyless uniformity'.[25] Others were less sure, if only because assessing the extent of redistribution was bedevilled by contentious concepts and partial data.[26] By the end of the 1960s, however, it was generally accepted that while there had been a modest redistribution as a consequence of policies introduced during and immediately after the Second World War, the process had ended in the 1950s.[27] Similarly, the much-made claim that class barriers had broken down, allowing unprecedented social mobility, was subsequently shown to be wide of the mark.[28]

Even so, some thought rising incomes had by themselves called an end to the established collectivist proletarian way of life. In particular, ill-provided – but 'neighbourly' – working-class districts were broken up as residents decamped to socially mixed housing estates or were placed in high-rise tower blocks to live more isolated lives.[29] While it is unquestionable that what social historians term the 'traditional' working class began to fragment during the 1950s and 1960s, observers exaggerated the extent to which workers had ever shared a common way of life.[30] Social patterns were highly differentiated well before the advent of 'affluence': class was never more than one influence on a worker's identity, as status, gender, generation and ethnicity also played their part – and sometimes the dominating one.[31] In particular, there had always been elements within the working class – at the start of the twentieth century they were called 'labour aristocrats' – whose incomes enabled them to ape traits associated with their social superiors.[32] Contemporaries in addition underestimated how far new private housing estates remained marked by class differences.[33] Nonetheless, while changes promoted by affluence were not exactly novel, their scale was such that many *felt* they were – and that was significant enough.

If extensive, the impact of affluence was uneven: rising incomes were concentrated in particular industries located in the South East and the West Midlands. Unemployment, especially in the North, Scotland and Wales, where heavy manufacturing was in decline, remained an issue. There was, nonetheless, superficial evidence of affluence in such places – like the virtual disappearance of the wearing of clogs and shawls in Bolton.[34] However, 'traditional' workers did not experience so much cultural disruption as did employees in the more favoured parts of the country. Thus, while miners, of whom there were still half a million in 1960, enjoyed historically unprecedented standards of living, many remained in the same village, went to the same pubs and clubs, and worked in the same pit as their grandfathers. They consequently experienced a sense of continuity with the past.[35] In contrast, as many of Coventry's 'affluent' car factory workers were émigrés drawn from towns in Britain's former industrial heartlands, to them more or less everything appeared new.[36]

As the sociologists John Goldthorpe and David Lockwood discovered during their study of Luton car workers, even the lives of the affluent remained bounded by class.[37] While some shopfloor workers enjoyed higher incomes than white-collar employees, their jobs were more insecure and there was little chance of promotion. Moreover, even if they thought themselves to be individuals and were preoccupied with purchasing an expanding array of consumer goods, affluent workers could not afford to be entirely individualistic. In order to maintain their standard of living, they still needed shared institutions – most notably a trade union.

The number of trade unionists rose during the 1960s: at the start of the decade they accounted for 44.2 per cent of the workforce but by its end this share had reached 48.5 per cent.[38] If some took this to be sufficient refutation of the claim that workers had become middle class, the fact that the 1960s saw a steep rise in the number of industrial disputes appeared to settle the argument. Indeed, far-left observers believed that by the end of the decade workers had embraced a militant class consciousness.[39] The number of strikes certainly rose, from the 2,832 called during 1960 to 3,906 in 1970, resulting in three million and eleven million days lost, respectively. The majority of conflicts were, however, short and located in a small number of industries – the most prominent being car manufacturing.[40] That affluent workers were among those most inclined to industrial action led some, for example the journalist Alan Watkins, to assert that such strikes were expressions of middle-class individualism.[41] Certainly, the parochial nature of most disputes meant they did not represent a concerted assault on the status quo. They did, nonetheless, confirm that the workplace remained a place of conflict where, however much money they might earn, workers were unhappily subject to managerial authority. Even in industries untouched by strikes, the incipient hostility between manager and worker was evident to those who took the time to look.[42]

Given this, it is probable that the historian Nick Tiratsoo reached the right conclusion – that, while rising living standards enabled workers to abandon some of the characteristics associated with the 'traditional' proletariat, it did not make them any more middle class. Instead, he suggested, it allowed them to pursue 'different ways of being working-class'.[43]

Women

The 1960s is often associated with militant feminism – a not entirely accurate impression, for the first British women's liberation group was founded in 1968. Moreover, the preoccupation of feminists, generally young and middle class with backgrounds in the far left, with what they supposed was an inherent gender conflict meant little to most women.[44] The period nonetheless saw changes to many women's lives, although their impact needs to be understood in relation to the fact that the overwhelming majority were married with children and looked on their domestic role as life's priority.

Ironically, given what was to follow, affluence helped consummate the Victorian 'cult of domesticity', based on the notion that men and women operated in separate spheres.[45] This was partly due to the desire of policy-makers to reinforce family life after the disruption of the Second World War. Thus, while the welfare state improved the quality of women's lives, it proceeded from the assumption that they should remain at home, bringing up children.[46] Child psychologists also emphasised the importance of mothers staying at home, some suggesting that working mothers were responsible for juvenile delinquency.[47] In this climate, few found it remarkable that the 1956 Royal Commission on Marriage and Divorce urged wives to take their responsibilities seriously and warned them against exploiting their rights.[48] Popular women's magazines also promoted the idea that their readers' lives were rightly defined by homemaking and depicted the domestic sphere as a major source of pleasure.[49]

Historically, women had never fully lived up to their role as 'angels in the house': necessity meant some were forced to seek paid work. During the 1960s, the dissonance between ideal and reality became especially keen. First, greater access to sophisticated birth control meant women could have fewer children and better regulate when they gave birth, meaning they had offspring during a much shorter period than hitherto. Accordingly, if earlier marriages and births took women out of the labour market at younger ages than previously, mothers could then re-enter the workforce much sooner.[50] Rising real wages, moreover, gave married women with children an incentive to seek employment outside the home, while the expansion of the service sector created a greater demand for their skills. More women entered the world of work as a result: in 1951 one-quarter were in employment but by 1971 this figure had reached two-fifths, with much the greatest part of this growth occurring in part-time work.[51] The late 1960s also saw a rapid rise in the number of women enrolling in trade unions, from 26.3 per cent of female workers in 1965 to 31.5 per cent five years later – although that was still half the rate evident among men.[52]

Women had always operated in a gendered labour market, receiving less pay than men for similar work, a position that had not much changed by 1960. Those in authority, however, began to see women workers as an important means of overcoming the labour shortages created by full employment. The Royal Commission on Trade Unions and Employers' Associations, chaired by Lord Donovan, which reported in 1968, predicted that women would 'provide the only substantial new source from which extra labour and especially skilled labour can be drawn'. If women were not fully utilised, the nation's future growth would be placed in jeopardy. Some believed the national interest now dictated that women should be helped to escape low-skilled occupations and be paid more for the work they performed.[53]

Given these contradictory impulses, the 1960s was a time of some confusion. However, if women came to terms with the fact that they could be wives, mothers *and* workers, in their own minds the role of homemaker predominated.[54] Surveys undertaken during the period proved depressing reading for feminists. In her 1957 study, Viola Klein claimed working women were so preoccupied with being wives and mothers that they made only the weakest of claims to a 'right to work'. Not much had changed by the mid-1960s, when Nancy Seear bemoaned the lack of any female protest against sexual inequality.[55] Towards the end of the decade, a few working-class women did claim equal pay with men but they formed a small minority.[56] This lack of overt radicalism did not necessarily mean women willingly accepted their subordination: it is possible they considered it futile to focus on something they felt unable to change. In any case, some found being a housewife a fulfilling experience. Older married women, in particular, could establish a pre-eminent domestic position that gave them a powerful role, not just in their own home but also in the wider neighbourhood.[57] To them, feminism threatened a satisfactory way of life. Even female trade union-ists criticised feminists for thinking freedom could be obtained only through paid employment rather than homemaking.[58]

In understanding women's lives, it is important to appreciate that a higher proportion entered matrimony during the 1960s than at any other time in history. The greater prominence of wives at the workplace only slowly challenged the strict gender division upon which most marriages were established. In 'traditional' working-class households, where working wives were less common, such differentiation remained as profound as ever.[59] Some contemporaries believed, however, that in more recently established, affluent households, roles were less demarcated, so husbands spent a greater part of their time at home and assumed a more active domestic role.[60] A number also thought such relationships were based on more fulfilling sexual relationships and a more intense emotional bond.[61] A few even claimed men and women were finding marriage more enjoyable, as it became more like an equal partnership than a master–servant relationship.[62]

The extent of 'companionate' marriages remains uncertain. While contemporary investigators Peter Wilmott and Michael Young were con-vinced they detected its emergence, those who came later were less sure. According to the latter, the 'companionate' concept glossed over the majority of marriages, in which wives remained subject to their husbands' will.[63] There were in any case limits to companionship – even in affluent Luton, wives and husbands participated in distinct social networks, the former mainly based around neighbours and family, the latter origin-ating at work. While nearly a third of Luton wives worked outside the home – half full time – less than one in twenty husbands took primary responsibility for shopping or washing up. Perhaps an indication of better things to come, just over one in five husbands claimed they shared some responsibility for child care.[64]

Black immigrants

When the *Empire Windrush* docked in London from the West Indies in 1948 it opened a new chapter in the history of immigration to Britain, albeit one reiterating familiar themes.[65] Since industrialisation, immi-gration had formed an integral, if controversial, part of British life. Irish Catholics, who arrived in significant force during the mid-nineteenth century, and Eastern European Jews, who entered at the turn of the twentieth, generated much hostility.[66] Zealots believed both were racially inferior to those derived from Anglo-Saxon stock, but most were agitated by their cultural differences, specifically ones based around religion. In addition, immigrants settled in areas characterised by grim housing and insecure occupations; their presence only made matters worse. Yet, while first-generation settlers were often subject to violence, the passage of time saw their offspring secure a niche in many towns and cities, although tensions based on supposed racial and actual cultural differences never completely disappeared.

Post-war immigration formed part of this continuum, inasmuch as most immigrants were white and came from Ireland or Commonwealth countries like Australia and Canada. What made it distinct was that an increasing proportion originated from undeveloped parts of the Commonwealth, mainly the West Indies and the Indian sub-continent: and they were black. Figures vary, but in 1951 there were probably 100,000 non-white Commonwealth natives resident in Britain; by 1961 this number had risen to something over 400,000; and by 1971 had reached about 700,000, meaning they represented not much more than 1 per cent of the population.[67] Few considered immigration a problem if – as the 1949 Royal Commission on Population put it – newcomers 'were not prevented by their religion or race from intermarrying with the host population and becoming merged into it'.[68] Contemporaries became obsessed with the small number of black immigrants because it was believed they could never be 'merged' into that vague but evocative entity known as the 'British way of life'. National identity at this point was exclusively associated with whiteness, so many took it for granted that blacks could never properly become Britons.

Colour prejudice existed well before 1939; imperial propaganda had long emphasised the backwardness of native peoples.[69] During the Second World War many found themselves face to face with non-whites for the first time, although as these were usually US servicemen responses were muted because they did not threaten to leave a permanent mark. Just to make sure, the authorities discouraged women from forming relationships; they also did their best to segregate black members of the Empire who filled vacancies in British factories or served in uniform.[70]

In 1948 the Labour administration introduced a Nationality Act, which gave those born in the Empire and Commonwealth an equal legal status to that of Britons: government became obliged to allow the free movement of all those now effectively designated British subjects.[71] Few officials anticipated blacks would want to take advantage of the Act and settle in Britain, so the arrival of the *Empire Windrush* came as an unpleasant surprise; but it was something they could do nothing about. Doubts about black immigration were apparently confirmed when West Indians became quickly associated with a variety of social problems.[72] As with earlier waves, these difficulties were largely due to the poverty of those districts in which immigrants settled and the fact that established inhabitants imagined their new neighbours threatened their own precarious position.

The situation was most acute in London, where, during the 1950s, up to half of West Indian immigrants settled.[73] As the capital was experiencing a severe housing shortage, decent accommodation was hard to find. Local authorities lacked the resources to overcome the problem, while Conservative ministers made matters worse with their 1957 Rents Act. Believing privately rented accommodation was scarce because of statutory limitations on how much landlords could charge, the government deregulated new tenancies. In their pursuit of a higher income, unscrupulous landlords pressured tenants to quit, so they could be replaced with those no longer subject to controls. Many of these new tenants were black; in fact, some landlords moved blacks next to sitting white tenants, expecting the latter's own prejudices would force them to leave. In addition, black immigrants pooled their resources to buy properties to rent out in the hope that this would give them financial security. Not only did they pay over the market price but they also borrowed from disreputable figures levying exorbitant interest rates. Having purchased overpriced (and often run-down) properties, these new owners were keen to replace tenants with those willing to pay higher rents. Thus, while only some employed intimidation to secure their tenants' exit, prevailing bigotry meant it was generally viewed as a problem caused by wicked blacks forcing out noble whites.

Racially motivated attacks had long punctuated immigrants' lives but it was only when disturbances broke out in the St Ann's district of Nottingham and Notting Hill in London during August and September 1958 that the issue gained prominence.[74] Having thus been alerted to this problem, the public decided the best solution was to end unrestricted black immigration. This led to the Conservative government's 1962 Commonwealth Immigration Act, which introduced a system of vouchers to regulate the immigration of members of the Commonwealth who lacked a skill or were not guaranteed a job on entry.[75] Ministers were embarrassed to admit it but these controls were designed to cut black immigration while leaving white immigration unhindered. These controls were extremely popular: 70 per cent of those polled supported the Act.[76] Yet, while it curtailed primary (and largely male) immigration, the Act permitted the entry of dependants. The Conservative victory at Smethwick in the 1964 general election with a candidate backed by the slogan 'If you want a nigger for a neighbour vote Labour' suggested the issue had not gone away.

Students of white opinion believed 'education' held the key to overcoming prejudice. Writing in 1958, the sociologist Michael Banton stated that white hostility was based on the belief that immigrants' very colour denoted their 'strangeness'. Once they got to know individual black immigrants, Banton expected these associations would disappear, as white people came to appreciate any differences were outweighed by compelling similarities.[77] A 1966 survey by the Institute of Race Relations (IRR) endorsed this perspective: it indicated that while 53 per cent of white people considered black immigrants inferior, only 5 per cent said this was due to colour, the single most important reason being their supposed lack of education, followed by general 'cultural differences'.[78] As a Smethwick housewife interviewed in 1964 stated, when justifying her antipathy to Asian neighbours: 'they just don't seem to know how to hang curtains', which, she believed, made her street look 'awful'.[79] Superficially, this woman formed part of what the IRR calculated was just over half the public, in that she adhered to a 'conditional' type of hostility. In contrast to the 10 per cent of whites deemed irredeemably prejudiced, the IRR believed such people could be encouraged to look on immigrants more generously.[80]

It was, however, possible that what appeared conditional hostility was a polite expression of intractable chauvinism. It is straining credibility to accept that the Smethwick interviewee's support for controls was based on immigrants' incompetence with curtains. In this case, at least, it more likely denoted unbridgeable differences that followed from her perception of blackness.[81] Surveys can tell us only so much and the balance between conditional hostility and outright racism will never be truly established. In any case, white prejudice of whatever sort inhibited the kind of interaction Banton hoped for. As one mid-1960s survey conducted in north London discovered, while two-fifths of respondents claimed some sort of personal acquaintance with a black person, one-fifth still objected to working with blacks; half did not want to live next door to them; and nine-tenths disapproved of mixed marriages.[82] Ironically, these attitudes threatened to bring about that which opponents of immigration said they feared most: black ghettoes cut adrift from the British way of life.[83] If dominant assumptions about blackness gave minor cultural distinctions an inflated significance, they also meant that even when non-whites acted in the approved manner they might still be viewed as alien. As the experience of subsequent decades was to suggest, it would take more than 'education' to overcome hostility, while even those adopting the most archetypal 'British' ways remained vulnerable to abuse.[84]

During the 1960s, white attitudes appeared immutable: after 1964 never fewer than 80 per cent of those polled believed too many blacks were entering the country. If anything, opinion hardened: by 1970 over one-fifth wanted blacks repatriated and just under half wanted all non-white immigration stopped.[85] Support for Enoch Powell after his 1968 'rivers of blood' speech illustrated the entrenched nature of attitudes.[86] Powell painted a picture of a white population who had become 'strangers in their own country', their neighbourhoods having been changed beyond recognition by blacks, who also jumped to the front of the queue for social goods such as hospital beds and school places.

Unlike previous immigrants, Powell asserted, few blacks wanted to belong to mainstream society and their numbers were such they could ignore pressure so to do. Thus, he concluded by saying that, looking to the future, he was 'filled with foreboding' as '[l]ike the Roman, I seem to see "the River Tiber foaming with much blood"'. If few appreciated the classical allusion, most understood Powell was predicting a race war, one that could be prevented only by drastic action. Although he was sacked from the Conservative front bench and condemned by the great and the good, Powell won massive public support – especially among the working class.[87]

The young

'Youth culture' – a distinct way of life embracing recent school-leavers who had yet to marry – is generally taken to have first emerged in a developed form during the 1960s. As Hobsbawm has it, the period marked 'a profound change' in relations between the generations, as the young asserted their autonomy.[88] This was a sometimes violent process, with manifestations ranging from, at the start of the decade, the formation of street gangs to, at its end, university students demanding greater control of their curriculum. Some saw these expressions of inter-generational conflict as of great moment: a few suggested the 'generation gap' had even replaced class as the most important social cleavage.[89]

Tension between young and old was not new. The former had long socialised separately and created ways to emphasise their distinctiveness, and some authorities believe a fully formed youth culture was established during the inter-war decades.[90] The 1960s nonetheless represented a distinct stage in generational relations. First, if historically nothing special, the post-war 'baby boom' increased the proportion of those aged between 15 and 19 compared with earlier decades, from 6.8 per cent in 1951 to 7.8 per cent in 1966.[91] Second, improvements to diet meant children physically matured earlier than hitherto, so, biologically, adulthood came more quickly. Third, young workers' real wages rose steeply, such that those steering clear of marriage and children enjoyed a disposable income possibly double that of the 1930s.[92] Finally, affluence encouraged the unparalleled expansion of the commercial youth market, which in turn allowed the young to express their identity through consuming particular magazines, television programmes, films, music and clothes.

The development of youth culture was popularly associated with rising crime, so older contemporaries viewed it with apprehension, but closer inspection suggested working-class youths were no more inclined to delinquency than in the past.[93] While later analysts believed working-class youth culture contained anti-capitalist values, this was not apparent at the time.[94] Instead, it seemed that youngsters were increasingly immersed in lifestyles dominated by commercialised pursuits, and that this encouraged antisocial activity and spawned groups such as the Mods and Rockers.[95] Commentators already convinced of the degeneration of working-class culture cited the young as evidence. Thus, Richard Hoggart thought that those he termed 'juke box boys' were 'portents' of how others would fall victim to the pursuit of 'sensation without commitment' through lives dedicated to consumption.[96] Others thought commercialism had reduced the young to passive consumers, whose politics – if they had any – expressed material contentment and led to Conservative voting.

Middle-class youths were considered to be travelling in the opposite direction: for them, generational conflict was believed to be assuming an overtly politicised form, albeit one consciously rejecting the 'middle-aged game of politics'.[97] An early manifestation of bourgeois youth's supposed new orientation was the Campaign for Nuclear Disarmament (CND), established in 1958. CND was novel in a number of ways, not the least being the prominence of young people on its annual Easter marches. How far this represented a new level of political awareness is open to question. As one Young CND branch secretary complained, many joined just because it 'was the thing to do' and would 'annoy the grown-ups'.[98]

Many of CND's younger members were students and this group became the focus of increasing attention as the 1960s progressed. In the late 1930s, there were only 70,000 students; by the later 1950s, their number had reached 150,000 and the expansion inaugurated by the 1963 Robbins report saw the total reach 400,000 in 1970. Yet, while their numbers increased, students remained middle class: less than one-third came from working-class backgrounds. Moreover, even by the end of the decade, students accounted for no more than 10 per cent of those in their late teens and early twenties.[99]

British students were not famous for their revolutionary fervour – as late as 1963 they were the acme of moderation.[100] By the middle of the decade, however, they had acquired a reputation for extremism. Many supported the North Vietnamese in their war with the United States and attended demonstrations organised by the Vietnam Solidarity Campaign (VSC). Tariq Ali, who led the VSC, asserted that the Vietnamese conflict would eventually provoke students to oppose the entire capitalist order.[101] Others argued that, owing to the role played by universities in the reproduction of capitalism, students were a strategic group, comparable to the working class in orthodox Marxist theory.[102] This perspective was apparently vindicated when Parisian students rioted in May 1968 and in July 3,000 VSC militants charged the US embassy in Grosvenor Square, which led to unprecedented violence, something celebrated by the Rolling Stones' song 'Street Fighting Man'.

Complementing these events were disturbances following from student demands for a greater voice in the running of their universities. Many higher-education administrators were unused to taking students' views seriously and their paranoia regarding the radical intentions of some provoked demonstrations and occupations on a number of campuses.[103] For the most part, students wanted modest reforms but when articulated in a quasi-Marxist language these could appear as the first step towards revolution. Matters were worst at the London School of Economics (LSE), where the newly appointed director was a former Rhodesian university official implicated in the apartheid regime. Even there, however, few students wanted a say in academic appointments and no more than two-fifths sought an influence over the content of their curriculum – although in excess of two-thirds demanded a role in running the library.[104]

Talk of student radicalism nevertheless disappeared as quickly as it had emerged: by the end of 1969 it was clear the French May events had led nowhere, the LSE disruptions had run their course and the VSC had fallen in on itself. Young militants had always been divided: the Trotskyists adhered to a 'vanguardist' view of change, and those associated with the 'New Left' wanted to build from the bottom up.[105] If this did not help, the basic problem for far-left radicals was most young people's profound lack of interest in political issues; and of those concerned with political change, few were ever revolutionary. With only 22,000 out of 350,000 students belonging to a political club, one National Union of Students official described the politically minded undergraduate as a 'freak'.[106] As James Jupp put it, the young were mostly 'conformist, conservative and respectable': the fact that by 1966 three-fifths of women in their early twenties were married possibly tells its own story.[107] Even those demonstrating behind VSC banners were not as militant as their leaders hoped: a survey of protestors at an October 1968 demonstration suggested that while half wanted an outright Vietnamese victory, two-fifths sought a compromise solution. More bizarrely, that protest ended with police and protestors linking arms to sing 'Auld Lang Syne'. As some suspected, that so many so-called street fighting men (and women) participated in such events said as much about fashion as it did about politics.[108]

Analysts thought this relative conservatism was due to the fact that, however affluent Britain was in the 1960s compared with the 1930s, the likes of France, Germany and the United States were even better off – and it was material well-being that lay at the root of the youth revolt. Thus, Inglehart suggested, in Britain the young were less committed to 'post-material values' than were their counterparts elsewhere.[109] Whatever the reason, despite the fears – and hopes – of some, the development of youth culture did not drag down the established order. Nevertheless, however modest was the actual threat, the 'generation gap' did briefly send shockwaves through many institutions – although that probably said more about the declining confidence of the latter than it did about the menace posed by the young.

Participation

One reason for the authorities' uncertainty was that, across the West, the 1960s saw demands for greater popular participation in decision-making reach unprecedented levels. The proliferation of strikes and violent demonstrations, as well as the emergence of single-issue pressure groups, suggested that an increasing number of individuals questioned the pre-eminence of representative institutions and wanted a more direct say in determining their fates. Inglehart saw this as evidence of how affluence encouraged the growth of 'post-material values', while some contemporaries considered it a natural reaction to the progressive concentration of power required by the post-war welfare state and economic efficiency.[110]

While most prominently embraced by the young, in particular student radicals, 'participation' denoted a disparate set of new and old concerns that together appeared to challenge the basis of the political order. Established academic opinion even suggested that too much participation, beyond simply voting in elections, threatened the stability of representative institutions and might open the way for totalitarianism.[111] Some also doubted how typical were those demanding to participate: even enthusiasts conceded greater political involvement interested only a minority, albeit, they claimed, a significant one.[112] Most manual workers, for example, appeared happy to vote for Labour candidates who promised to advance their material interests but were unwilling to assume a more direct role in achieving that outcome. Despite earlier hopes that the Second World War had prompted the development of an 'active democracy', a rise in the number of voters and members of the main political parties aside, the character of British democracy remained unchanged in the years following 1945.[113] The extent to which popular indifference was due to how the parties practised politics or the result of an ingrained antipathy to participation is open to doubt. While some commentators believed that affluence encouraged people to retreat into their private domains, others argued that the majority only appeared apathetic because they did not believe meaningful participation was possible. The events of 1968, the latter suggested, encouraged many to revise their sense of impotence.[114]

According to Des Wilson, director of the pressure group Shelter, despite 'participation' achieving the status of a radical cliché by the end of 1968, few of those demanding it had a clear idea of what it meant.[115] Yet, as those with practical experience of trying to promote popular political engagement conceded, participation was no trouble-free panacea. An increase in the numbers involved in decision-making would require a set of careful balancing acts. The most prominent of these was ensuring that elected representatives, while promoting participation, could maintain their legitimate leadership role. Just as importantly, it would also require opening up decisions to public scrutiny while preventing the process being monopolised by those dedicated to negative protest.[116] At least a few of those who blithely insisted on the people's right to participate refused to take such complications seriously, because they wanted not to reform Britain's established political order but to destroy it.

Although Britain's institutions were praised by many US observers, one did not have to be a revolutionary to find fault with them. The extension of the post-war welfare state and the nationalisation of one-fifth of industry had drained local government of much of its purpose and concentrated power in Westminster to an unprecedented extent. The accountability of the country's elected representatives, both local and national, was limited to say the least, as decision-making operated in a shroud of secrecy. Moreover, if rising incomes and educational levels meant that citizens were less inclined to defer to their leaders' wisdom, their sense of (at least relative) national decline by the early 1960s meant they also had more about which to be critical.

The most compelling expression of the people's apparent desire for a more immediate political voice was the demand for devolution or even full independence for Scotland and Wales. Since 1885 Scotland had enjoyed some administrative autonomy from London through the Scottish Office based in Edinburgh, headed by a Secretary of State with Cabinet rank. Wales was less favoured and was treated as if it were an adjunct of England. The demand for more self-government was not novel. In the case of Scotland, controversy stretched back to the 1707 Act of Union. It reached a particularly fevered pitch during the late nineteenth century, when radical Liberals embraced Home Rule for each of the three Celtic nations within the United Kingdom. Nonetheless, for much of the twentieth century the issue was less prominent and the decade or so that followed 1945 saw the issue sidelined by pressing economic matters.[117]

Ironically, given what was to come, when Labour debated its electoral problems after the 1959 general election, Scotland and Wales did not feature, because the party's hold on the electorate there looked secure. Labour's position even improved in the 1964 and 1966 elections, such that few considered it needed to take heed of the Scottish National Party (SNP) or Plaid Cymru, as their demand for independence was thought to appeal only to a cranky minority.[118] However, even when they voted Labour, many Scottish and Welsh people retained a strong sense of their own national identity and hankered for more freedom from Whitehall to give this expression.[119] That aspiration found political form after Wilson's re-election. In July 1966, Plaid took Carmarthen from Labour in a by-election while, a year later in the party's heartland of Rhondda West, and Caerphilly in 1968, they ran Labour a very close second. North of the border, the SNP trounced Labour in the Hamilton by-election of November 1967. Contests held in the Glasgow constituencies of Pollock and Gorbals either side of this triumph saw nationalists push Labour firmly on to the defensive. These unprecedented parliamentary performances were, moreover, reflected in innumerable local government contests. By the end of the decade, nationalists appeared to constitute a serious political force. Indeed, the SNP claimed to have tripled the size of its membership between 1966 and 1969, to 120,000, which meant it probably had more members than Labour north of the border.[120]

It is hard to be sure how far these developments marked a funda-mental shift in opinion or merely expressed passing discontent. While undoubtedly a mixture of both, the latter probably predominated, as only a minority of those voting nationalist in the late 1960s supported full independence. Yet, even if many voters abandoned Labour as a protest against rising unemployment, rather than anything else, their dalliance with nationalism still reflected something substantial. For, just like before 1966, voters wanted more national autonomy.[121] The tem-porary success of the SNP and Plaid subsequently made it more difficult for Westminster politicians to ignore this hitherto obscured desire.

Those who called for more participation undoubtedly identified a real and long-standing deficiency within Britain's political culture, although it was not one that lent itself to a simple answer. According to Samuel Beer, by bringing the issue to the fore, reformers actually helped destroy the country's traditional political culture by undermining the deference widely deemed so vital to it.[122] While some certainly wanted to devastate Britain's institutions, this was not true of all of those who talked of par-ticipation. Many simply sought to ensure that liberal democracy lived up to its full potential. It is, in any case, arguable that Beer's analysis was unnecessarily apocalyptical. For the most part, reforms inspired by the aspiration to increase participation were modest, locally focused initia-tives designed to bolster the ongoing reform of the political order.

Parties and change

Some imagine the Golden Age initiated the beginning of the end for party politics.[123] Yet, while both major parties' fortunes waxed and waned, Labour appeared at a distinct disadvantage compared with the Conservatives. Of the seven general elections held between 1950 and

Table 1.3 Labour and Conservative votes compared, 1950–70

	Number of votes		Percentage of vote	
	Labour	*Conservative*	*Labour*	*Conservative*
1950	13,266,592	12,502,567	46.1	43.5
1951	13,948,605	13,717,538	48.8	48.0
1955	12,404,970	13,311,936	46.4	49.7
1959	12,215,538	13,749,830	43.8	49.4
1964	12,205,814	12,001,396	44.1	43.4
1966	13,064,951	11,418,433	47.9	41.9
1970	12,178,295	13,145,123	43.0	46.4

Source: D. Butler, *British General Elections Since 1945* (Oxford, 1989), Appendix 1.

1970, Labour won three, only one of which – the 1966 landslide – gave it a working Commons majority. This was partly an effect of the first-past-the-post system, as Labour's average vote over the seven contests was 45.7 per cent, only 0.3 per cent less than that of the Conservatives. Even so, while Labour exceeded the Conservatives in terms of popular support on four occasions, this difference only twice amounted to more than 1 per cent of votes cast. In contrast, the Conservatives won four elections out of the seven, each of which gave the party a working majority, while at the three elections in which they gained a greater proportion of votes the difference was in excess of 3 per cent (see Table 1.3). The Conservatives also ended the 1960s on a better note. In 1970 Edward Heath led his party back from its worst defeat of the period with a hitherto unprecedented post-war switch of support from one party to another. In contrast, 1970 was Labour's worst result since 1935 – although nothing compared with what was to follow.

There was a time when Labour's relatively poor record would have been directly linked to the decline and transformation of the working class. Indeed, the decades following 1945 were once regarded as the culmination of long-term social trends of which the party system was a more or less accurate reflection.[124] To many it appeared that the two classes had spawned their own parties, within which arrangement Labour was, a few eccentric bourgeois voters aside, literally the party of those who laboured while the Conservatives, other than some aberrant proletarians, appealed to the middle and upper classes. This led Hobsbawm to suppose proletarians voted Labour as 'an automatic consequence of being workers'.[125]

Recent work by political historians questions whether political allegiances reflect social position in such a straightforward way. As Jon Lawrence and Miles Taylor suggest, interests and identities are not

'predetermined and self-evident, only requiring recognition and expression by the parties'. Instead, voters' interests are just 'signposts for
political behaviour in so far as language allows them to be described
and articulated'.[126] The political scientist Anthony Heath and his col-
laborators anticipated this emphasis when they outlined how far parties
can shape, rather than react to, voter attitudes.[127] Yet, if parties enjoyed
more freedom to influence electors than has been previously assumed,
this autonomy was only relative, as none could react to events in a purely
'pragmatic' manner. Thus, in his study of European social democracy,
Herbert Kitschelt noted how far a party's ideological tradition could
influence what members took to be 'acceptable arguments and ideas'
and so restrict how they might respond to change.[128]

Few argue that Labour was blessed with a tradition that fostered a
productive response.[129] The party was apparently in good company:
according to Donald Sassoon, owing to their more ideological nature,
all European social democrats failed to respond flexibly to cultural
change; only those on the right enjoyed the necessary pliability.[130] Yet,
like their left-wing counterparts, many British Conservatives also looked
on change with misgivings and often echoed a similar sense of despair.[131]

In any case, irrespective of particular party tradition, it was hard for
any contemporary politician to accurately identify a significant cultural
trend and virtually impossible to predict with precision what its political
impact might be. As the ex-Labour MP John Freeman observed in 1955,
politics is 'not a precise science which permits a diagnosis to be confirmed and presented with certainty'. Analysing Labour's decline was,
he believed, a subjective exercise, in which 'anybody's guess is as good
as the next man's'.[132] The greater use of opinion polling and the increasing number of academic politics specialists did not change matters much.
While the Labour leader Hugh Gaitskell and his revisionist followers
were confident their diagnosis of the party's late 1950s troubles was
endorsed by the 'facts', left critics believed the leadership cited surveys
deliberately constructed to serve its agenda.[133] More disarmingly, in 1964
the academic Richard Rose conceded that the power of socio-economic
trends, which in 1959 appeared to make ongoing Conservative victories
inevitable, should be reconsidered. He stated that the 'simple sociological or economic explanation' of politics – of which he had been an
advocate – was 'incomplete'.[134] In this uncertain context, it is little wonder
some believed 'pragmatism' no better a guide than ideology.

Labour and change

Perhaps Labour's most significant ideological characteristic was the extent to which members were unable to agree what their party ultimately

stood for. As the leading left-wing MP Michael Foot wrote in 1966, Labour encompassed a 'coalition of differing interests, ideas and aspirations', embracing a 'pale-Pink Right and a near-Red Left and all shades in between'. If 'Socialist by definition' thanks to a formal commitment to nationalisation, Labour was 'social reformist' 'by tradition and practice', although the balance between the two was 'constantly shifting'.[135] Labour's course in the late 1950s and early 1960s appeared to vindicate Foot's assessment. As the New Left writer Perry Anderson noted, by passing the policy document *Industry and Society* in 1957 the party conference legitimised capitalism, although it assumed an anti-capitalist stance when *Signposts for the Sixties* was embraced three years later.[136]

Despite this apparent indeterminacy, many authorities believe the key to Labour thinking was its association with the unions. This supposedly gave rise to 'Labourism', characterised as a preoccupation with the immediate interests of male, unionised, manual workers.[137] Yet, while the unions enjoyed a special place in the party, there were other members of the Labour coalition.[138] Many who originally established the party adhered to a moral vision, of which the improvement of working-class living standards was but one element; and by 1918 a number of 'New' Liberals had joined Labour's ranks. These contrasting concerns were drawn together by Ramsay MacDonald while he was leader and sometime Prime Minister during the 1920s to create what has been termed a 'Labour socialist ideology'.[139] MacDonald believed socialism could emerge only from the gradual development of the most progressive elements of the status quo: revolutionary overthrow would result in totalitarianism. This meant following the parliamentary road and using the opportunities presented by a largely unreformed constitution to their fullest extent. MacDonald's organic, incremental approach entailed promoting harmony rather than conflict and fostering community, not class, consciousness. Hence he couched Labour's programme in terms of universal principles rather than class interests, although, given inequality, improving workers' incomes was presented as a moral act. Labour socialism consequently sought to lift up all individuals, whatever their class, from selfish material concerns and, through education, endow them with an ennobling collective purpose. In spite of his defection to lead a 'National' government in 1931, MacDonald's outlook set the tone for much subsequent Labour thinking.[140] Thus, while the post-war membership continued to dispute the ends of party activity, invariably how far Labour should take the economy into state hands, MacDonald furnished them with an agreed means.

If the party encouraged members to think within certain parameters, Labour's was for the most part not an overly prescriptive creed. Just as there was scope for different interpretations of socialist ends, so members perceived cultural change in a variety of ways. Writing in 1962, the veteran Scottish MP Arthur Woodburn considered that, during the course of his life, he had 'seen a revolution in outlook and living conditions'. People were better off, healthier, better educated and expected to perform less arduous work; there were fewer class distinctions and even manners had improved. Prosperity had 'lifted the eyes and spirits of people, while the march of science gave hope for the future'.[141] This optimism was remarkable, given that Labour had just lost three elections in a row. If Woodburn was sanguine, the recently ennobled MP Reginald Sorenson, writing in 1968, was less happy, despite the fact that in 1966 Labour had seemingly been fully restored to electoral health. Sorenson believed that Britain was marked by 'the lure of easy leisure, nihilistic philosophies, the cult of the ephemeral and the irrational, the craze for bingo, casinos, football pools, gambling and betting, the sedatives of drugs and drink and a congealed indifference to choicer qualities of living'.[142]

There were also considerable differences over the extent to which Labour should accommodate change, however it was characterised. The 1966 national conference of Labour women was informed by Joan Liddle, who chaired the gathering, that in the 'kind of society we have in Britain today, we have to deal with a new generation, new habits, new interests and new reactions to the political problems of the time'. Labour, she believed, should 'adapt our political methods to the social and political realities of our time'.[143] The following year, Millie Miller addressed the same gathering as chair but outlined a contrary perspective. She declared that Labour should not bow down to each and every development, for members had 'a duty to assess what our society is to become and what we have to offer the nation' and to ask:

> Was it for their descendants to be slaves to the managerial age that the Tolpuddle Martyrs were sent into exile? Was it to have their mates chosen by computer that the Women's Labour League first sought to bring emancipation to women? Was it so that the people should spend their leisure time in gaming clubs that our early pioneers looked forward to universal free education? And what of the values for which they fought in the early days of our movement? Are the virtues of loyalty, brotherhood and international socialism just old hat?

With student discontent in mind, Miller concluded with a rhetorical flourish that would have made MacDonald proud. Hence, while it was 'very modern at the moment to attack established institutions', those present should be aware 'that to destroy a society and offer nothing to replace its organisations will lead only to anarchy and eventually to a darkness of the spirit such as has not been seen since the Dark Ages of history in Britain'.[144]

Approach

Writing in 1957, Raymond Williams believed a 'structure of feeling', once it has passed, is largely irrecoverable. Since then, an army of social historians have done their best to prove him wrong by exploring popular experience from any number of angles. For much of the post-war period, the Labour Party was mostly untouched by such research. It remained the preserve of traditional political historians, who viewed their subject in elitist terms, focused on 'high' politics and stressed the importance of party and trade union leaders. Some of their more radical colleagues did highlight the role of militant activists of whom they approved, but that merely substituted a concern with one kind of elite for another.[145] As a result, Labour history was preoccupied with the internal machinations of party activity or was measured against extraneous definitions of 'socialism'. It generally failed to study the wider context in which political activity occurred; nor did it explore the deeper dynamics that invested such activity with meaning. To some of those living in Margaret Thatcher's shadow, a Labour history couched purely in terms of class, socialism, party, union and great men looked increasingly distant from reality.

Since the early 1990s, an increasing number of historians have therefore situated Labour politics more firmly in its cultural setting, to recover what the party and its purpose meant to voters, members and leaders. This has transformed our picture of Labour's earliest years and helped challenge narratives based on the assumption that the party's 'rise', thanks to the development of a homogenous working-class culture, was unproblematic, not to say inevitable.[146] This has been complemented by similar work on the Conservatives, whose continued success led some finally to question exclusively class-based interpretations of politics. It is no accident that this new approach to Conservative history was largely the product of those who had also made a distinctive contribution to our understanding of Labour's past.[147]

Much of the present author's previous work was set in this post-Thatcher mould. On his own and in collaboration with Nick Tiratsoo and Peter Thompson in *'England Arise!'* (1995), he applied the methods and insights generated by social history to revise dominant perceptions of the post-war Labour Party, especially in relation to the critical decade of the 1940s.[148] At the heart of this enterprise was the desire to question the assumption, central to the work of Ralph Miliband and those following in his footsteps, that by not being a 'proper' socialist party Labour impeded the development of a radically class-conscious proletariat.[149] Despite the earlier optimism of the likes of Edward Thompson but in line with the more circumspect work of Ross McKibbin, it was believed British workers' socialist potential was much exaggerated.[150] *'England*

Arise!' even suggested that, instead of Labour inhibiting the development of the people's socialist potential, the party was often in advance of popular attitudes. Members of the Labour leadership, such as the usually reviled Herbert Morrison, were consequently forced to take Britons' widespread cultural conservatism into account when devising the party's strategy and policies. Needless to say, not everyone agreed with that viewpoint.[151]

The present work aims to develop this so-called revisionist approach chronologically, by moving into the 1960s, and conceptually, by looking more closely at how Labour understood and responded to its cultural setting. As already indicated, various authorities suggest that the relationship between any political party and the society in which it operates is more complicated than previously thought. The inversion of the Milibandian problematic, which underpinned *'England Arise!'*, is therefore itself in need of some revision, especially in light of work stressing the impact of what has been variously described as party 'discourse', 'language' or 'rhetoric' on popular political attitudes.[152]

Given this work's focus on cultural change, it is useful to establish how it relates to what James Vernon describes as a new post-modern 'cultural history of politics'.[153] In Vernon's articulation, this proceeds from the belief that the nineteenth-century 'rise of party' depended on politicians regulating popular sentiments. Through the law, physical constraint and above all language, the parties created and then imposed what they considered were suitable political identities on the populace.[154] In one of the few attempts to apply this approach to Labour, Jon Lawrence considers the party was also something of an imposition, for Labour's assertion of its vision of the people's 'interests' meant it denied the legitimacy of other voices, which might have more accurately expressed popular desires.[155] Ironically, then, while disparaging the Milibandian school for its assumption that politics is rooted in class, post-modernists agree that Labour stymied popular potential. Whereas the former imagine Labour stopped workers acquiring a socialist outlook, the latter are less certain what the party prevented the people achieving. Both are clear, however, that Labour impeded the development of something they appear to presume would have been superior to that actually achieved by the party.

As was *'England Arise!'*, this present work is sceptical of such a conclusion, resting as it does on a whole series of significant counterfactual assumptions. Most importantly, it exaggerates Labour's ability to stand outside the context which gave it birth – 'history' for want of a better word – and impose itself on the populace. As already suggested, parties have the ability to alter popular perceptions – something post-modernists are rightly keen to stress. There were, however, limits to this influence – and more compelling, entrenched competitors for the public's attention, including what Karl Marx once referred to as 'the dull compulsion of economic relations'.[156] Even so, the post-modern contribution should be welcomed insofar as it has problematised the direct nature of the relationship between party and people. Lawrence is surely right that Labour's claim to represent people was more rhetorical than real, for, as he points out, the world views of highly politically motivated, self-educated activists often found few echoes in those embraced by the majority of less committed voters – a point also made by the political scientist John May some time ago.[157]

Most pertinently for this work, Lawrence additionally notes that only 'constant processes of negotiation and renegotiation' can sustain the party's relationship with its supporters.[158] Labour's claim to represent people was certainly questioned during the 1960s, especially in relation to workers, women, black immigrants and the young. In addition, the institutional means through which Labour sought to act for its supporters – both as a party and as a government – were heavily criticised. How far the party's dilemma was exclusively played out in language – as those who have taken the 'linguistic turn' emphasise – is doubtful. While perception played a critical role in determining the party's responses, so did established institutional cultures, some of which had been appropriated by Labour's own activists, who succeeded in subverting their leaders' wishes. It is easy to forget that Labour was not a unitary political actor articulating one vision but, as Raphael Samuel and Gareth Stedman Jones put it, a 'perpetually shifting fulcrum' over which contesting discourses and interests constantly battled.[159]

Sources and structure

Consistent with the work's wider purpose, each chapter is underpinned by research that exploits sources rather different to those usually consulted by political historians of post-war Britain. Much energy has nonetheless been expended uncovering conventional material, notably recently released government files stored at the Public Record Office, national Labour records and the papers of prominent political figures. However, the work also benefits to an unprecedented degree from the insights provided by papers generated by seven regional, four borough and some forty constituency Labour parties. These ensure that the views of the party's most humble active members are given more than just passing mention and fully complement the opinions of the party elite to construct what aspires to be a 'total history' of Labour's dealings with cultural change during this period.

Like all historical work, the author's reach has inevitably exceeded his grasp, for even this array of records can tell us only so much. First,

because of their uneven survival rate, there was little hope of constructing a statistically representative sample of sources, although taken as
whole they cover much of Britain. Secondly, and more profoundly, these
records are not written from the perspective of 'ordinary' Labour members,
the vast majority of whom rarely attended or spoke at meetings. Thus,
historians can never completely recover Labour's 'structure of feeling':
no matter how far they look, only those who left paper trails – in this
case minutes, reports and letters – find themselves caught in the re-
searcher's gaze.

The chapters that follow build on the survey contained in this introduction. The first further sets the scene by outlining the nature of
Labour Party culture at the start of the 1960s. Chapter 3 then analyses
the contrasting ways in which members understood post-war affluence,
to establish the ideological and organisational state in which the party
entered office in 1964. The next looks at the key issue of class and how
Labour attempted to reconcile those differences said to have survived
into the 'affluent society'. Chapter 5 highlights Labour's attempts to
draw younger women into the party and how it handled the issue of
equal pay once in power. The following chapter takes up the issue of
black immigration and establishes the party's dilemma, given both its
commitment to integration and its need to retain the support of prejudiced white voters. Chapter 7 looks at the implications of the 'generation
gap' for Labour and how members tried to bridge it. Chapter 8 assesses
the party's response to calls for more direct political participation. The
conclusion establishes how the party approached the 1970 general
election and why members responded in the way they did to Labour's
decisive rejection by the electorate.

Notes

The place of publication is London unless otherwise specified.

1 This paragraph is based on R. Williams, *The Long Revolution* (Harmondsworth, 1965), pp. 57–88, and *idem*, *Keywords* (1976), pp. 76–82.
2 For an important and recent exception to this generalisation, see L. Black,
   The Political Culture of the Left in 'Affluent' Britain, 1951–64 (2003).
3 E. Hobsbawm, *Age of Extremes. The Short Twentieth Century 1914–1991*
   (1995), pp. 6 and 258.
4 A. Marwick, *The Sixties* (Oxford, 1998), p. 15.
5 R. Inglehart, *The Silent Revolution. Changing Values and Political Styles Among
   Western Publics* (Princeton, 1977).
6 R. McKibbin, *Classes and Cultures: England, 1918–51* (Oxford, 1998).
7 E. Shils and M. Young, 'The meaning of the Coronation', *Sociological
   Review*, 1 (1953); *Manchester Guardian*, 3 June 1953.
8 S. H. Beer, 'Why study British politics?', *British Politics Group Newsletter*, 100
   (2000), pp. 8–14.

9 G. A. Almond and S. Verba, *The Civic Culture. Political Attitudes and Democracy in Five Nations* (Princeton, 1963), pp. 5–6, 315.

10 G. A. Almond, 'The intellectual history of the civic culture concept', in G. A. Almond and S. Verba (eds), *The Civic Culture Revisited* (Boston, 1980), p. 29.

11 S. H. Beer, *Britain Against Itself* (1982), p. 5 and Part 3, *passim*.

12 B. Levin, *The Pendulum Years* (1970), p. 9; see also C. Booker, *The Neophiliacs* (1969).

13 K. O. Morgan, *The People's Peace. British History 1945–1990* (Oxford, 1992), pp. 297–8, 314–16; see also D. Kavanagh, 'Political culture in Great Britain: the decline of the civic culture', in Almond and Verba, *Revisited*.

14 R. Miliband, 'A state of de-subordination', *British Journal of Sociology*, 29:4 (1978); A. Sinfield, *Literature, Politics and Culture in Postwar Britain* (Oxford, 1989); S. Rowbotham, *Promise of a Dream. Remembering the Sixties* (Harmondsworth, 2000), pp. xi–xvii; J. Seed, 'Hegemony postponed: the unravelling of the culture of consensus in Britain in the 1960s', in B. Moore-Gilbert and J. Seed (eds), *Cultural Revolution? The Challenge of the Arts in the 1960s* (1992).

15 B. Conekin, F. Mort and C. Waters, 'Introduction', in B. Conekin, F. Mort and C. Waters (eds), *Moments of Modernity. Reconstructing Britain, 1945–1964* (1999), pp. 1–3.

16 H. Pelling, 'Then and now: popular attitudes since 1945', in his *Popular Politics and Society in Late Victorian Britain* (1968).

17 A. Giddens, *Beyond Left and Right* (Cambridge, 1994), pp. 5–7.

18 P. Thompson, 'Labour's "Gannex" conscience"? Politics and political attitudes to the "permissive society"', in R. Coopey, S. Fielding and N. Tiratsoo (eds), *The Wilson Governments, 1964–70* (1993).

19 Quoted in A. Sampson, *Macmillan. A Study in Ambiguity* (Harmondsworth, 1968), p. 159.

20 F. Zweig, *The Worker in an Affluent Society* (1961), p. ix.

21 S. Rowntree and G. R. Lavers, *Poverty and the Welfare State* (1951).

22 A. Capet, 'Rediscovering the "rediscovery of poverty" in the 1950s', paper presented to the conference 'Affluent Britain?', Bristol University, May 2002.

23 K. Coates and R. Silburn, *Poverty. The Forgotten Englishman* (Harmondsworth, 1970).

24 T. J. Hatton and R. E. Bailey, 'Seebohm Rowntree and the postwar poverty puzzle', *Economic History Review*, 53:2 (2000).

25 Quoted in R. Miliband, 'Politics and poverty', in D. Wedderburn (ed.), *Poverty, Inequality and Class Structure* (Cambridge, 1974), p. 186.

26 R. M. Titmus, *Income Distribution and Social Change* (1962).

27 J. H. Westergaard, 'Sociology: the myth of classlessness', in R. Blackburn (ed.), *Ideology in Social Science* (1972).

28 J. H. Goldthorpe, *Social Mobility and Class Structure in Modern Britain* (Oxford, 1980).

29 R. Hoggart, *Speaking to Each Other. Volume I* (Harmondsworth, 1970), pp. 48–9, 55–6.

30 E. Hobsbawm, 'The formation of British working class culture', in his *Worlds of Labour* (1984).

31 See, for example, A. Davies and S. Fielding (eds), *Workers' Worlds. Cultures and Communities in Manchester and Salford, 1880–1939* (Manchester, 1992).

32 E. J. Hobsbawm, 'The Labour aristocracy in nineteenth century Britain', in his *Labouring Men* (1964).

33 M. Clapson, *Invincible Green Suburbs, Brave New Towns* (Manchester, 1998), pp. 157–71, 185–6.

34 T. Harrisson, *Britain Revisited* (1961), pp. 28–45.

35 N. Dennis, F. Henriques and C. Slaughter, *Coal Is Our Life* (1969).
36 B. Lancaster, 'Who's a real Coventry kid? Migration into 20th century Coventry', in T. Mason and B. Lancaster (eds), *Life and Labour in a 20th Century City. The Experience of Coventry* (Coventry, 1986).
37 J. H. Goldthorpe, D. Lockwood, F. Bechhofer, and J. Platt, *The Affluent Worker in the Class Structure* (Cambridge, 1969).
38 G. S. Bain and R. Price, 'Union growth: dimensions, determinants and density', in G. S. Bain (ed.), *Industrial Relations in Britain* (Oxford, 1983), pp. 5–11.
39 See, for example, R. Blackburn and A. Cockburn (eds), *The Incompatibles: Trade Union Militancy and the Consensus* (Harmondsworth, 1967).
40 C. Wrigley, 'Trade unions, the government and the economy', in T. Gourvish and A. O'Day (eds), *Britain Since 1945* (1991), pp. 70–5; J. McIlroy and A. Campbell, 'The high tide of trade unionism: mapping industrial politics, 1964–79', in J. McIlroy, N. Fishman and A. Campbell (eds), *British Trade Unions and Industrial Politics. Volume II* (Aldershot, 1999).
41 *New Statesman*, 9 January 1970.
42 T. Nichols and P. Armstrong, *Workers Divided. A Study in Shopfloor Politics* (1976); and T. Lane and K. Roberts, *Strike at Pilkingtons* (1971).
43 N. Tiratsoo, 'Popular politics, affluence and the Labour party', in A. Gorst, L. Johnman and W. S. Lucas (eds), *Contemporary British History, 1931–61* (1991), pp. 55–6.
44 S. Rowbotham, 'The beginnings of women's liberation in Britain', in M. Wandor (ed.), *The Body Politic. Women's Liberation in Britain* (1972); D. Baucher, *The Feminist Challenge. The Movement for Women's Liberation in Britain and the USA* (1983), pp. 93–126; P. Byrne, 'The politics of the women's movement', *Parliamentary Affairs*, 49:1 (1996), pp. 58–9.
45 For an overview, see P. Thane, 'Towards equal opportunities? Women in Britain since 1945', in Gourvish and O'Day, *Britain*; J. Lewis, 'From equality to liberation: contextualising the emergence of the Women's Liberation Movement', in Moore-Gilbert and Seed, *Cultural Revolution*.
46 M. Pugh, 'Domesticity and the decline of feminism, 1930–1950', in H. L. Smith (ed.), *British Feminism in the Twentieth Century* (Aldershot, 1990), pp. 149–58.
47 J. Bourke, *Working-Class Cultures in Britain, 1890–1960* (1994), p. 128.
48 Lewis, 'Equality to liberation', pp. 107–8.
49 R. Ballaster, M. Beetham, E. Fraser and S. Hebra, *Women's Worlds. Ideology, Femininity and the Woman's Magazine* (1991), pp. 110–25; Baucher, *Feminist Challenge*, pp. 28–32.
50 J. Lewis, 'Myrdal, Klein, "Women's two roles" and postwar feminism, 1945–1960', in Smith, *Feminism*, pp. 167–8.
51 M. Young and P. Wilmott, *The Symmetrical Family* (Harmondsworth, 1975), p. 101; Thane, 'Equal opportunities', pp. 191–5.
52 Bain and Price, 'Union growth', p. 6.
53 Thane, 'Equal opportunities', pp. 202–4; Lewis, 'Equality to liberation', pp. 97–105.
54 Young and Wilmott, *Symmetrical*, pp. 102–9; Zweig, *Worker*, pp. 9, 44, 175.
55 Thane, 'Equal opportunities', pp. 198–204.
56 Rowbotham, 'Women's liberation', pp. 91–2.
57 McKibbin, *Classes*, pp. 164–76; Bourke, *Working-Class*, pp. 64–71.
58 Rowbotham, 'Women's liberation', p. 100.
59 McKibbin, *Classes*, pp. 165, 179.
60 P. Wilmott, *The Evolution of a Community* (1963), p. 109; M. Young and P.

Wilmott, *Family and Kinship in East London* (Harmondsworth, 1986), pp. 21, 25–7; Young and Wilmott, *Symmetrical*, pp. 114–15; Bourke, *Working-Class*, pp. 81–95.

61 M. P. M. Richards and B. J. Elliott, 'Sex and marriage in the 1960s and 1970s', in D. Clark (ed.), *Marriage, Domestic Life and Social Change* (1991), pp. 37–9.

62 Zweig, *Worker*, pp. 29–32.

63 J. Finch and P. Summerfield, 'Social reconstruction and the emergence of companionate marriage, 1945–59', in Clark, *Marriage*, pp. 15–23; E. Roberts, *Women and Families. An Oral History, 1940–1970* (Oxford, 1995), pp. 95–114.

64 Goldthorpe *et al.*, *Worker in Class Structure*, pp. 91–2, 98, 105–6.

65 For an overview, see C. Holmes, *John Bull's Island. Immigration and British Society, 1871–1971* (1988).

66 See, for example, S. Fielding, *Class and Ethnicity. Irish Catholics in England, 1880–1939* (Buckingham, 1993); D. Cesarani (ed.), *The Making of Modern Anglo-Jewry* (Oxford, 1990).

67 J. Cheetham, 'Immigration', in A. H. Halsey, *Trends in British Society Since 1900* (1972), p. 496, table 14.7; Holmes, *Bull's Island*, pp. 226–7.

68 Quoted in Holmes, *Bull's Island*, p. 210.

69 J. M. McKenzie, *Propaganda and Empire. The Manipulation of British Public Opinion 1880–1960* (Manchester, 1984).

70 I. Spencer, 'World War Two and the making of multiracial Britain', in P. Kirkham and D. Thoms (eds), *War Culture. Social Change and Changing Experience in World War Two* (1995); D. Reynolds, *Rich Relations. The American Occupation of Britain, 1942–1945* (1995), pp. 216–37.

71 R. Hansen, *Citizenship and Immigration in Post-war Britain* (Oxford, 2000), pp. 35–61; R. Weight, *Patriots. National Identity in Britain, 1940–2000* (2002), pp. 136–41.

72 Weight, *Patriots*, pp. 293–300.

73 For more on this see J. Davis, 'Rents and race in 1960s London: new light on Rachmanism', *Twentieth Century British History*, 12:1 (2001).

74 E. Pilkington, *Beyond the Mother Country. West Indians and the Notting Hill White Riots* (1988), pp. 106–24.

75 Hansen, *Citizenship*, pp. 100–24.

76 S. Brooke, 'The Conservative Party, immigration and national identity, 1948–1968', in M. Francis and I. Zweiniger-Bargielowska (eds), *The Conservatives and British Society, 1880–1990* (Cardiff, 1996), pp. 161–2; G. H. Gallup, *The Gallup International Public Opinion Polls. Great Britain, 1937–75. Volume I* (New York, 1976).

77 M. Banton, *White and Coloured. The Behaviour of British People Towards Coloured Immigrants* (New Brunswick, 1960), p. 184; see also R. Glass, *Newcomers. The West Indians in London* (1960), pp. 108–27.

78 E. J. B. Rose, *Colour and Citizenship* (1969), pp. 567–8.

79 *Sun*, 8 October 1964.

80 Rose, *Colour*, pp. 567–8.

81 See in particular the points raised in Weight, *Patriots*, p. 436.

82 C. S. Hill, *How Colour Prejudiced Is Britain?* (1965), pp. 26–45.

83 See, for example, Rose, *Colour*, pp. 1–9.

84 See, for example, P. Gilroy, *'There Ain't No Black in the Union Jack'. The Cultural Politics of Race and Nation* (1987).

85 D. T. Studlar, 'Policy voting in Britain: the coloured immigration issue in the 1964, 1966 and 1970 general elections', *American Political Science Review*, 72:1 (1978), pp. 53–4.

86 S. Heffer, *Like the Roman. The Life of Enoch Powell* (1999), 449–59.
87 D. T. Studlar, 'British public opinion, colour issues and Enoch Powell: a longitudinal analysis', *British Journal of Political Science*, 4:3 (1974); F. Lindrop, 'Racism and the working class: strikes in support of Enoch Powell in 1968', *Labour History Review*, 66:1 (2001).
88 Hobsbawm, *Extremes*, p. 324.
89 See, for example, F. Musgrove, *Ecstasy and Holiness. Counter Culture and the Open Society* (1974).
90 G. Pearson, *Hooligan. A History of Respectable Fears* (1983), pp. 94–6; D. Fowler, *The First Teenagers. The Lifestyle of Young Wage-Earners in Interwar Britain* (1995).
91 B. Osgerby, *Youth in Britain Since 1945* (Oxford, 1998), pp. 15–23; C. Rollett and J. Parker, 'Population and family', in Halsey, *Trends*, p. 33.
92 M. Abrams, *The Teenage Consumer* (1959); Osgerby, *Youth*, pp. 23–6.
93 P. Willmott, *Adolescent Boys of East London* (Harmondsworth, 1969), pp. 179–81.
94 S. Hall and T. Jefferson (eds), *Resistance Through Rituals* (1976).
95 See, in particular, T. R. Fyvel, *The Troublemakers. Rebellious Youth in an Affluent Society* (New York, 1964).
96 R. Hoggart, *The Uses of Literacy* (Harmondsworth, 1958), pp. 246–50.
97 J. Jupp, 'Children of affluence', *Socialist Commentary*, June 1969, p. 29.
98 F. Parkin, *Middle Class Radicalism* (Manchester, 1968), pp. 140–74.
99 H. Glennester, 'Education and inequality', in P. Townsend and N. Bosanquet (eds), *Labour and Inequality* (1972), pp. 88–92.
100 F. Zweig, *The Student in the Age of Anxiety* (1963), p. 199.
101 T. Ali, 'The extra-parliamentary opposition', in T. Ali (ed.), *New Revolutionaries. Left Opposition* (1969), pp. 70–4.
102 G. S. Jones, 'The meaning of the student revolt', in A. Cockburn and R. Blackburn, *Student Power* (Harmondsworth, 1969).
103 See, for example, E. P. Thompson (ed.), *Warwick University Ltd* (Harmondsworth, 1970).
104 T. Blackstone, K. Gales, R. Hadley and W. Lewis, *Students in Conflict. LSE in 1967* (1970).
105 N. Young, *An Infantile Disorder? The Crisis and Decline of the New Left* (1977), especially pp. 144–62.
106 *New Statesman*, 17 February 1967.
107 J. Jupp, 'The discontents of youth', *Political Quarterly*, 40 (1969); Rollett and Parker, 'Population', p. 41.
108 J. Callaghan, *Time and Chance* (1987), p. 260; Marwick, *Sixties*, pp. 639–40.
109 R. Inglehart, 'The Silent Revolution in Europe: intergenerational change in post-industrial societies', *American Political Science Review*, 65:4 (1971), pp. 998–1000.
110 A. Arblaster, 'Participation: context and conflict', in G. Parry (ed.), *Participation in Politics* (Manchester, 1972), pp. 41–6.
111 For a survey of these views, see C. Pateman, *Participation and Democratic Theory* (Cambridge, 1970), pp. 1–21; and, in particular, W. Kornhauser, *The Politics of Mass Society* (1960).
112 Arblaster, 'Participation', pp. 47–8.
113 S. Fielding, '"Don't know and don't care": popular political attitudes in Labour's Britain, 1945–51', in N. Tiratsoo (ed.), *The Attlee Years* (1991).
114 Arblaster, 'Participation', p. 50.
115 *Guardian*, 8 November 1968.
116 See, for example, D. M. Hill, *Participating in Local Affairs* (Harmondsworth, 1970).

117 For post-war Wales, see K. O. Morgan, *Rebirth of a Nation. Wales, 1880–1980* (Oxford, 1981), Part 3, *passim*.

118 J. Connell, 'Scotland's steady swing', *Socialist Commentary*, May 1966, p. 35.

119 For Scotland, see I. Budge and D. W. Urwin, *Scottish Political Behaviour* (1966), pp. 112–29.

120 National Library of Scotland, Scottish National Party papers, Acc 6038, Box 6, Reports of National Office Holders (May 1968) and Box 7, Reports of National Office-Bearers and Others (May 1969).

121 'The lost Labour voter', *Socialist Commentary*, February 1969, pp. 31–3.

122 Beer, *Britain*, pp. 111–14.

123 G. Mulgan, *Politics in an Antipolitical Age* (Cambridge, 1994), pp. 7–36.

124 See, for example, D. Butler and D. Stokes, *Political Change in Britain* (Harmondsworth, 1971).

125 E. Hobsbawm, 'The making of the working class, 1870–1914', in his *Worlds*, p. 211.

126 J. Lawrence and M. Taylor, 'Introduction', in J. Lawrence and M. Taylor (eds), *Party, State and Society* (Aldershot, 1997), p. 18.

127 A. Heath, R. Jowell, J. Curtice, G. Evans, J. Field and S. Witherspoon, *Understanding Political Change. The British Voter, 1964–87* (Oxford, 1991), p. 9.

128 H. Kitschelt, *The Transformation of European Social Democracy* (Cambridge, 1994), pp. 254–5, 271–2.

129 A. Heath, R. Jowell and J. Curtice, *How Britain Votes* (Oxford, 1985), p. 7.

130 D. Sassoon, *One Hundred Years of Socialism* (1997), pp. 197–200.

131 E. H. H. Green, 'The Conservative party, the state and the electorate', in Lawrence and Taylor, *Party*.

132 J. Freeman, 'Labour's decline', *Focus*, 2 (1955).

133 R. Samuel, 'Dr. Abrams and the end of politics', *New Left Review*, 5 (1960).

134 *New Society*, 5 March 1964.

135 *Tribune*, 14 January 1966.

136 P. Anderson, 'The left in the fifties', *New Left Review*, 29 (1965), pp. 5–9.

137 See, for example, G. Foote, *The Labour Party's Political Thought* (1997).

138 For a more developed critique of 'Labourism', see S. Fielding, '"Labourism" and the British Labour Party', in the Collection de l'Ecole Francaise de Rome – 267, *Les Familles Politiques en Europe Occidentale au XXe Siecle* (Rome, 2000).

139 S. Yeo, 'A new life: the religion of socialism in Britain, 1883–1896', *History Workshop Journal*, 4 (1977); P. Clarke, 'The social democratic theory of the class struggle', in J. Winter (ed.), *The Working Class in Modern British History* (Cambridge, 1983); S. MacIntyre, *A Proletarian Science. Marxism in Britain, 1917–1933* (Cambridge, 1980), pp. 47–65.

140 S. Fielding, P. Thompson and N. Tiratsoo, *'England Arise!' The Labour Party and Popular Politics in 1940s Britain* (Manchester, 1995), pp. 76–101.

141 *Edinburgh Evening News*, 13 September 1961 and 29 November 1962.

142 House of Lords Record Office, Reginald Sorenson papers, Hist. Coll. 102/230, A Backbencher's Pilgrimage, 1968, p. 397.

143 *Report of the Forty-Third National Conference of Labour Women* (1966), p. 17.

144 *Report of the Forty-Fourth National Conference of Labour Women* (1967), p. 15.

145 For more on this, see S. Fielding, '"New" Labour and the "new" labour history', *Mitteilungsblatt des Instituts fur soziale Bewegungen*, 28 (2002).

146 See, in particular, D. Tanner, *Political Change and the Labour Party, 1900–1918* (Cambridge, 1990); C. Waters, *British Socialists and the Politics of Popular Culture, 1884–1914* (Manchester, 1990); and A. Reid and E. Biagini (eds),

Currents of Radicalism. Popular Radicalism, Organized Labour and Party Politics in Britain, 1850–1914 (Cambridge, 1991).

147 See the chapters by Stephen Brooke, Martin Francis and Ina Zweiniger-Bargielowska in Francis and Zweiniger-Bargielowska, *The Conservatives*; and also E. H. H. Green, *The Crisis of Conservatism. The Politics, Economics and Ideology of the British Conservative Party, 1880–1914* (1995).

148 See Tiratsoo, *Attlee Years*; and Fielding *et al.*, '*England Arise!*'.

149 For a sympathetic evaluation of Miliband and his followers' work, see D. Coates and L. Panitch, 'The continuing relevance of the Milibandian perspective', in J. Callaghan, S. Fielding and S. Ludlam (eds), *Interpreting the Labour Party: Approaches to Labour Politics and History* (Manchester, 2004).

150 E. P. Thompson, *The Making of the English Working Class* (1963) and R. McKibbin, *The Ideologies of Class. Social Relations in Britain, 1880–1950* (Oxford, 1991).

151 For one especially resolute critic, see J. Hinton, '1945 and the Apathy School', *History Workshop Journal*, 43 (1997).

152 See, for example, D. Howarth, A. J. Norval and Y. Stavrakakis (eds), *Discourse Theory and Political Analysis* (Manchester, 2000); and B. Schwarz, 'Politics and rhetoric in the age of mass culture', *History Workshop Journal*, 46 (1998).

153 J. Vernon, 'Notes towards an introduction', in J. Vernon (ed.), *Re-reading the Constitution. New Narratives in the Political History of England's Long Nineteenth Century* (Cambridge, 1996).

154 J. Vernon, *Politics and the People. A Study in English Political Culture, c. 1815–1867* (Cambridge, 1993).

155 J. Lawrence, *Speaking for the People. Party, Language and Popular Politics in England, 1867–1914* (Cambridge, 1998), p. 4.

156 K. Marx, *Das Capital. Volume I* (Moscow, 1954), p. 689.

157 Lawrence, *Speaking for the People*, p. 66; J. D. May, 'Opinion structure of political parties: the special law of curvilinear disparity', *Political Studies*, 21 (1973).

158 Lawrence, *Speaking for the People*, p. 267.

159 R. Samuel and G. S. Jones, 'The Labour party and social democracy', in R. Samuel and G. S. Jones (eds), *Culture, Ideology and Politics* (1982), p. 327.

2

Labour's organisational culture

The purpose of this chapter is to establish the institutional context for Labour's response to cultural change.[1] It surveys the character of the party's organisation and the nature of its membership on the verge of the 1960s, and in particular highlights the activities and assumptions of those most responsible for the party's well-being. Before that can be done, however, it is necessary to outline Labour's organisational structure and identify some of the issues to which it gave rise.

The basic unit in all 618 constituency Labour parties (CLPs) was the ward or, in rural areas, local party. All members were entitled to attend their monthly gatherings, something that enabled them to elect a management committee and decide who should represent them on the CLP's general management committee (GMC). On the GMC also sat those appointed by affiliated organisations, usually local union branches, as well as by the women's or youth section if there was one. While a GMC might be guided by an executive committee (EC), the former determined who should attend Labour's annual conference as a delegate and how they could vote, and what resolution to submit (if any) for the consideration of conference. It also agreed whom to support in contests for the constituency section of the National Executive Committee (NEC). In addition, the GMC ratified the wards' preferred local government candidates and selected the constituency's parliamentary nominee. CLPs sometimes employed a professional agent to ensure its efficient administration but for the most part these matters were left in the hands of volunteer members.

In large urban areas where different constituencies were located within the same municipal boundary, borough or city parties coordinated activity relating to council elections. Above these entities existed a variety of bodies, such as county federations of CLPs and regional councils, whose purpose was often obscure even to experienced local members. Of more importance were the twelve Regional Offices, each staffed by one Regional Officer (RO) and two assistants. They answered to the National Agent operating from Transport House on Smith Square in

Westminster, Labour's headquarters. The Agent in turn was responsible to the NEC, and tried to ensure – not always with great success – that the party's rules were enforced.

Labour's structure was set in place by its 1918 constitution. At the time it was seen by some as a temporary settlement, particularly with regard to the influence it gave to the trade unions, but the constitution survived up to the 1960s without fundamental modification.[2] The constitution allowed for the development of two contrasting approaches to political mobilisation. On the one hand were those who considered that so long as Labour won Commons or council majorities, it did not much matter if the party had few members and engaged in little activity outside election time. On the other hand were those who thought Labour's principal purpose was to transform the outlook of individual voters: to them, a large and energetic membership engaged in a dynamic relationship with the electorate was as important as winning elections.[3] Despite their other differences, these instrumental and transformative approaches were both underpinned by what some may think a condescending view of the electorate: the former considered that the actions of a small number of bureaucrats could achieve more than the people; and although the latter ostensibly promoted mass participation, it did so only on terms acceptable to the party.

Labour's poor electoral performance during the 1950s and early 1960s encouraged some to believe neither approach held the key to success and led to numerous proposals to improve party organisation, culminating in two major NEC investigations, one conducted by Harold Wilson in 1955 and the other by Bill Simpson during 1967–8. Wilson famously concluded that Labour was 'still at the penny-farthing stage in a jet-propelled era' and its organisation 'rusty and deteriorating with age'.[4] While Simpson was less pessimistic, the party having recently won two elections, Labour's return to power did not convince everybody that all its problems had disappeared – especially as the 1966 victory was immediately followed by a collapse in membership.[5]

One of the most informed critics of Labour's organisational shortcomings was Jim Raisin, RO for the Northern Home Counties Region during the 1960s and before that a London organiser.[6] In 1966 he complained that the party 'functions to-day in almost exactly the same manner as it did 50 years ago', and asserted that it was 'probable that part of our relative failure as an instrument for change … is as much due to the unsuitability of some of our own devices as to external causes'. There was, Raisin suggested, a desperate need for a 'more sophisticated' structure. The GMC was, he claimed in 1955, deeply flawed, being both a 'very inefficient form of management' and unrepresentative of the wider membership. As he stated in 1968, while Labour claimed to be 'the Party of the People', 'the great bulk of those who belong to our Party simply will not come into our "market place", that is, the Ward or Local Party meeting'. Moreover, 'genuine contact', even between those few who attended meetings and their parliamentary leaders, was 'slight, occasional and accidental'. This meant the NEC's 'intentions and even ... decisions' in relation to party affairs were 'little understood and hardly ever put into effect'. If matters reached crisis proportions at the end of the 1960s, Raisin believed that was merely the continuation of long-running trends, showing 'comparatively little variation with the changes in our political fortunes'.

Despite this, Labour's basic organisational character remained the same: the reasons for this inertia, which were cultural rather than overtly political, provide further insight into members' response to post-war change.

The union link

The defining characteristic of Labour organisation during the 1960s is widely supposed to have been its close connection with the trade unions. They were certainly of critical financial importance: in 1960, 86 national unions affiliated 5,512,688 of their members, thereby contributing £204,711 or 83 per cent of Labour's annual income; ten years later they donated £401,792 or 78 per cent of party revenue. In return for their invaluable assistance, those drafting the 1918 constitution had granted the unions' formal dominance within the party, at least as measured by numbers of annual conference votes and NEC seats. Locally the unions were linked to the party in three ways. First, about two-thirds of Labour members were trade unionists and among activists the proportion was even higher.[7] Secondly, union branches could affiliate to their local CLP and so send delegates to GMC meetings; in areas dominated by one particular industry this arrangement often gave a single union effective control. Finally, unions commonly made a variety of financial contributions to offset the habitual poverty of most CLPs, which could include underwriting an agent's salary, sponsoring a parliamentary candidate or granting free use of office space.

While, for the most part, they made little use of their formal authority, it was common for trade unionists – such as Tom Jones, a leading Welsh Transport and General Workers' Union official – to look on Labour and the unions as forming a single entity which they rightly dominated.[8] Some even believed Labour's essential purpose was limited to improving the material existence of the 'man on the shop floor'.[9] Indeed, more than a few of Labour's middle-class activists adhered to that view: it was a retired schoolteacher who promised to support the unions' attempts to increase wages 'to the utmost of my strength and sensitivity'.[10]

Despite these formal and rhetorical links, local union–party relations were rarely intimate. Most affiliated unions paid little heed to CLPs except in relation to candidate selection – and only then when one of their favourites stood some chance of preferment. Apart from such moments, union GMC delegates were conspicuous by their absence: when only two attended Coventry North's 1958 annual general meeting, those present urged the unions to 'play their part in the Political life of our Movement'.[11] This was an often-made plea, one echoed by the Wilson report, which noted that even in industrial areas unions usually played a minor role in CLPs.[12] Indeed, Raisin reported that for many agents in London contact with the unions was so slight that a discussion of how to improve relations 'had, for them, a somewhat academic quality'.[13]

To address this problem, in 1957 the NEC created the temporary post of Industrial Organiser, whose purpose was to bring together CLPs and local union branches in urban Essex. This initiative merely underlined the intractable nature of the problem, for after five months the Organiser had affiliated only three branches to the appropriate CLP and ensured a mere four already affiliated branches sent delegates to GMC meetings. This meagre return was blamed on a profound lack of interest shown by union officials and the post was not made permanent.[14] Leading members in the Eastern Region believed the NEC had not given the Organiser enough time, but his failure was reflected elsewhere: Coventry Borough's union liaison committee had also withered in the face of union indifference.[15] Moreover, even if branch officials had been willing to help improve relations, it is unlikely that Labour would have benefited by much: as one trade unionist later conceded, branches were often the 'semi-private empires of political cliques'.[16] Thus, while it was possible for a CLP to establish contact with a branch official, as Raisin pointed out, given that so few unionists attended their own meetings, there was little chance the party would make an impression on the rank and file.[17]

The desire to strengthen party–union links was revived before the 1964 election.[18] While some on the NEC wanted a national Industrial Organiser to help establish relationships that would survive the campaign, ambitions were soon focused on immediate electoral activities, such as encouraging branches to disseminate propaganda at the workplace and recruiting members to help in marginal seats.[19] The model for these kinds of efforts was the Birmingham Borough Party's impressive mobilisation of union support, which in 1964 involved contacting over 4,000 shop stewards.[20] Even so, in the aftermath of the 1966 electoral landslide, some activists persisted in trying to establish more organic links. Believing unions should play a greater role in the party, Labour's Scottish Council asked every CLP to establish a union liaison committee and organise workplace meetings. Like all such earlier schemes, however, these efforts bore little fruit.[21]

Membership: ideal and reality

It is hard to escape the conclusion that most CLPs had a distant and instrumental relationship with local unions because that is how the latter were content for it to be. In practice this meant that Labour's grass-roots organisation hinged on the exertions of its individual members. In fact, a study of political activity in Greenwich, south London, conducted during 1950 noted that, compared with the Conservatives, Labour membership was the more onerous. Investigators believed the party's relative poverty explained why members contributed more of their time: CLPs could not afford the kind of professional help Conservatives took for granted.[22]

Poverty was undoubtedly a factor but so was the belief that, as Herbert Morrison declared in 1951, Labour was 'not only a vote winning machine' but also 'something great and glorious that stands for a new way of life'.[23] Members had long been told that, working together, they would transform society and themselves, for they would acquire 'fellowship' and develop a 'more vital kind of citizenship'. Such 'selfless service' was considered 'the reality of Socialism and the guarantee that it would "work"'.[24] Hence, if members constantly reminded each other that belonging to Labour entailed numerous 'duties' and 'obligations', they were at least comforted by the belief these tasks were vital.[25] Thus, after Clement Attlee failed to retain office in 1951, members in Stockport were solemnly informed that the 'destiny of this great Movement' now resided 'in the hands of each one of us'.[26] In deference to this belief in the virtues of voluntarism, and despite its many criticisms, the Wilson report warned against turning Labour into a 'streamlined professional machine'.[27]

As part of their mission to build socialism, members were exhorted not only to be active in the party but to do the same outside and embrace a diverse range of 'socially useful tasks', such as donating blood and becoming a special constable, for the good of the party, society and themselves.[28] Activity – of the appropriate sort – was presented to Warrington members as a good in itself:

> [for even leisure] gives wisdom IF USED RIGHTLY; not in idleness, doing NOTHING ... 'Nothing to do' should be just the opportunity to do something which we have been wishing to do for a long time. To read some particular book, to see someone who somehow or other has not been available; to tackle a job for which there has never been time. And if the reason of our idleness be summer, well, it is a poor soul who then says, 'There is NOTHING TO DO.'[29]

Given this outlook, the extension of television ownership was looked on as a largely negative development. As one Bristol activist – also a member of a parent–teacher association and amateur dramatic group – believed 'our most precious gift' was time, he condemned the millions who sat apparently stupefied for hours on end in front of their newly acquired sets.[30]

Despite this stress on participation, only a small minority of those counted as members actually helped build Labour's 'new way of life'. Most did no more than attend the occasional meeting or help during an election campaign; the majority probably responded only to a collector's infrequent request for their modest monthly membership fee; and more than a few did not even do that. A study conducted in marginal Stretford during the early 1950s discovered that only 19 per cent of members had attended a meeting during the previous six months.[31] In safer Labour territory such a proportion would have been thought high. At the start of the 1960s only 11 per cent of Glasgow members were described as 'active' – which meant that little more than 500 individuals maintained the party's vital functions in a city with fifteen CLPs (see Table 2.5, p. 49). The extent to which only the dedicated few did what was expected was indicated by attendances in Salford East's Trinity ward. There, during 1958–66, fifty-two people were recorded as being at one time or another present at meetings – but only six went to more than half.[32] This situation was, moreover, not unique to parties in Labour's heartlands. In Ongar, Essex, where the Conservatives enjoyed predominance, between 1958 and 1962 twenty-three members attended twenty-one meetings held in Loughton ward; of those, only five went to more than half.[33]

The members

As academic surveys conducted across the country reiterated, Labour's members were largely, but not disproportionately, drawn from the manual working class.[34] In some CLPs, such was the dominance of working-class members that those from the middle class were viewed as intruders, although officials did their best to discourage 'petty class distinctions'.[35] In the main, however, only a particular kind of proletarian became active in the party. As Labour's agent in Hulme, Manchester, stated in 1947, it was 'the better types', the sort that even then were moving from the inner city to the suburbs, who formed the backbone of CLPs in working-class districts.[36] Across Manchester as a whole, over two-fifths of ward secretaries in the late 1950s had taken a National Council of Labour Colleges course and nearly a third had attended Workers' Education Association classes.[37] Labour's active working-class members therefore often constituted what the cultural observer Richard Hoggart described as an 'earnest minority' of autodidacts, those who considered themselves 'thinking men'.[38] As a result, and despite their commitment to egalitarianism, many activists looked on fellow workers from an elevated position, a phenomenon exemplified by the case of a 29-year-old organiser and councillor from East Anglia interviewed during the late 1960s. Describing himself as an 'ordinary country boy', he nonetheless appreciated that he was more intelligent than those among whom he lived – albeit in a superior newly built house. His higher status was also reflected by the fact that neighbours referred to him as 'Mr' – just as they would an employer – although he claimed to apply his talents not for selfish ends but to 'serve' the people.[39] In any case, while constituting a majority of members, manual workers were less prominent among activists: one national survey confirmed that 49 per cent of Labour 'leaders' came from outside the proletariat. Even in predominantly working-class areas, professional, self-employed or white-collar members might hold the majority of party posts, although many such activists originated in proletarian homes. Even so, such could be their prominence some believed active middle-class members deterred manual workers participating in CLP affairs.[40]

Well before 1960, the vast majority of members were middle aged at best. In fact, one Salford ward was described in 1955 as 'largely made up of old age pensioners'.[41] As the party's official membership increased fivefold to one million between 1942 and 1952, this meant many 1960s activists had experienced a very specific politicisation, one that combined keen memories of inter-war unemployment with the hope of a new society created through wartime collectivism. This perspective appeared increasingly anachronistic to those outside the party but stalwarts measured the present against what, as the years passed, appeared a golden age. Indeed, as early as 1952 one portrayed the 1930s as a much happier time because, he claimed, Labour members then were more enthusiastic and attended meetings in greater numbers.[42]

Although official figures indicated that just over 40 per cent of party members were female, women were less well represented among Labour's keenest volunteers.[43] There was considerable variation across the country: in Salford's Trinity ward just over one in twenty of those attending meetings held during the late 1950s and early 1960s were women but in Southall's Hambrough ward they accounted for more than a third.[44] Elsewhere, women might even dominate gatherings: during the 1950s in one of marginal Halifax's wards they formed nearly two-thirds of attendees and held most posts.[45] It would therefore be wrong to describe all CLPs as 'male clubs', even though female activists usually performed tasks that revealed how far most in the party were wedded to conventional gender roles.[46]

Such was the association between membership and family, participation in Greenwich was said to be 'a family rather than individual commitment'.[47] At one 1951 Halifax ward gathering, among the eight present there were two married couples, one of whom had also brought a relative, and two sisters; of the 16 who turned out for a meeting in a Southall ward ten years later, half came as part of a married couple.[48] It is probable, however, that Pontefract's Tanshelf ward, in which five of seven members came from the same family, was an extreme case.[49] This did not always reflect a genuine political commitment: in more than a few instances relatives attended meetings just to maintain a family member's hold on power. In one Bristol ward, for example, a councillor was said to control the selection of municipal candidates by dragooning otherwise inactive relatives to relevant meetings.[50]

Fellowship

If not all were related, Manchester activists apparently attended meetings 'rather as they would go to a club', that is 'to meet friends': friendship helped sustain many in their party work.[51] This aspect was also noted in Huddersfield, where wards were seen as promoting social bonds, just like bowls clubs or brass bands.[52] The regular round of party events undoubtedly encouraged 'fellowship'. During 1954, one local party in Birmingham not untypically held monthly social evenings; organised a coach trip and a 'mystery' evening; put on a jumble sale; and at Christmas arranged children's and pensioners' parties, as well as a festive bazaar.[53] As a result, activists could exhibit a familial concern for their associates. Meetings stood in silence in respect for the deceased; wards organised visits, dispatched flowers or at least a sympathetic letter to members or their families during periods of illness; and sent gifts to mark the birth of children.[54] Indeed, one hospitalised member was so hurt after *not* receiving any solicitous communication from his party that he wrote to Labour's *London News* to complain. 'I expected', he stated, in a party 'with the traditions of humanitarians like William Morris, Keir Hardie and George Lansbury, at least a short letter, hoping for my speedy recovery, but I was disappointed'.[55]

However strong was the fellowship within particular wards or constituencies, it was rarely extended to those in adjacent parties. Wilson noted the 'lamentable' assistance granted by CLPs with guaranteed majorities to more marginal neighbours.[56] Personal loyalty could impede Labour's general interest in other ways, especially when the redrawing of electoral boundaries forced unfamiliar members together and pushed apart old friends. After some Bermondsey wards were abolished or amalgamated, a few activists became so alienated they refused to collect subscriptions for their new comrades.[57]

Familiarity could also breed the very opposite of fellowship. In Burnley, such was the antipathy between two prominent figures they ended up in a street brawl.[58] Some conflicts derived from political differences, but NEC investigators were aware that claims of far-left take-overs sometimes resulted purely from personal conflicts.[59] As a consequence, gatherings could be anything but pleasant. One retiring Halifax ward secretary claimed he had never 'encountered in any Organisation with which I have been connected so much apathy, bigotedness and petty jealousy such as I have discovered in the Labour Party'.[60] After one too many GMC meetings, an East Hertfordshire delegate stated that, after every gathering for the past three years, 'my wife has asked me "how did it go" and I have said "terrible"'. 'I have said', he confessed, 'more than once that I wouldn't come to any more of them'.[61]

Counting the members

The need to raise the number of members and increase their level of participation was one of the most insistent imperatives conveyed by Transport House to the constituencies. Even when Labour was officially a million strong, Raisin thought it could do better; and in the wake of Wilson's 1966 re-election, the NEC launched an ambitious recruitment campaign.[62] If the message got through, it made no discernable impact:

Table 2.1 Labour's official membership, 1955–70

Year	Number of members
1955	843,356
1956	845,129
1957	912,987
1958	888,955
1959	847,526
1960	790,192
1961	750,565
1962	767,459
1963	830,346
1964	830,116
1965	816,765
1966	775,693
1967	733,932
1968	700,856
1969	680,656
1970	690,191

Source: *Report of the Sixty-Ninth Annual Conference of the Labour Party* (1970).

Table 2.2 Proportion of constituency Labour parties (CLPs) affiliating the minimum number of members, revised membership and average CLP membership, by region, 1965

Region (in order of average CLP size)	Number of of CLPs	Percentage affiliating minimum	Revised membership[a]	Average per CLP
Eastern	43	21	70,401	1,637
London	42	26	66,531	1,584
Northern Home Counties	54	26	67,318	1,247
Southern	66	52	81,275	1,231
North West	80	49	81,985	1,025
Wales	36	61	24,951	693
South West	43	71	27,213	634
East Midlands	41	71	25,208	615
Northern	37	68	21,631	585
Scotland	71	86	33,304	469
West Midlands	54	83	24,003	445
North East	51	82	22,195	435
Total	618	58	546,015	884

[a]Calculated on the assumption that CLPs claiming the minimum (1,000) members actually had a membership of 250, whereas those returning over that figure were accurate.
Source: National Executive Committee minutes, 19 July 1966, Individual membership, NAD/43/5/66.

official membership went into steady decline after 1952 and suffered a collapse during 1966–8 (see Table 2.1).

If nothing else, members were a key resource: as Wilson stated, no other single development would improve Labour's weak financial position more than an increase in their number.[63] Some officials also hoped the introduction of new blood would reduce the influence of older activists, whom they thought ineffective or troublesome.[64] Raisin, for example, wanted not just more but also different members, in particular young married couples living on private housing estates. Too many working-class activists, he complained, 'heavily handicapped' the party, as they were incapable of managing their affairs without constant guidance. In contrast, Raisin believed administrators, teachers, skilled mechanics and the like 'soon grasp the value of really good electoral schemes'.[65]

Membership was certainly cheap. Between 1944 and 1966 it cost only 6s (30p) per annum, although it was subsequently raised to 12s. Formally, at least, it was also easy to join. While some wanted procedures tightening up, National Agent Len Williams stated that a 'loose kind of

Table 2.3 Proportion of constituency Labour parties (CLPs) affiliating the minimum number of members, revised membership and average CLP membership, by region, 1968

Region (in order of average CLP size)	Number of of CLPs	Percentage affiliating minimum	Revised membership[a]	Average per CLP
Eastern	43	45	43,118	1,003
Greater London	100	58	85,911	859
Southern	64	73	43,970	687
North West	79	78	44,378	562
Wales	36	78	18,270	508
Northern	38	87	14,416	379
Scotland	71	90	26,446	372
West Midlands	54	91	18,464	342
South West	43	91	14,485	337
East Midlands	40	93	12,887	322
North East	51	94	15,511	304
Total	618	78	337,856	547

[a]Calculated on the same basis as in Table 2.2.
Source: National Executive Committee Organisation Sub-committee minutes, 21 May 1969, Individual membership 1968, NAD/58/5/69.

organisation recruiting as many supporters as it can' was 'more in accord with the purpose of a democratic party' wanting to win elections.[66] An interested individual was supposed to apply to the secretary of the local CLP, who would then put the matter before the EC; taking its advice into consideration, the GMC decided whether the person concerned could be issued with a membership card. So long as an applicant did not belong to a rival political organisation, this should have been a straightforward and quick process.

In fact, to the chagrin of Transport House, many parties gave away membership cards indiscriminately during recruitment campaigns to those prepared to give a canvasser their initial monthly subscription of 6*d* (2.5p). Oftentimes this was the last the CLP saw of their new 'member'.[67] One consequence of this lax approach was that nobody knew how many individuals truly belonged to the party – although that was not the only reason. For official figures were compiled on the basis of how many members CLPs affiliated to the national party. To help secure some non-union income, Transport House stipulated that CLPs had to affiliate a minimum number of members, which was increased from 240 to 800 in 1957 and then set at 1,000 in 1963. If it failed to do this, a CLP was not

Table 2.4 Official and 'actual' memberships compared in the South
West Region, 1965

Constituency party	Official membership	'Actual' membership
Bath	1,344	880
Bodmin	1,000	100
Bridgwater	1,382	1,127
Bristol Central	1,000	625
Bristol North East	1,000	400
Bristol North West	1,608	1,352
Bristol South	1,000	684
Bristol South East	1,000	400
Bristol West	1,000	342
Cheltenham	1,129	1,000
Chippenham	1,000	508
Cirencester	1,000	493
Devizes	1,503	1,274
Exeter	1,000	638
Falmouth and Cambourne	1,000	300
Gloucester	1,000	370
Honiton	1,000	241
North Cornwall	1,000	150
North Devon	1,000	150
North Dorset	1,000	700
North Somerset	1,247	1,250
Plymouth Devonport	1,569	Not given
Plymouth Sutton	1,656	1,263
Poole	1,000	232
St Ives	1,000	180
Salisbury	1,000	450
South Dorset	1,905	1,200
South Gloucestershire	1,743	1,100
Stroud	1,398	1,000
Swindon	1,000	373
Taunton	1,916	1,100
Tavistock	1,000	500
Tiverton	1,000	350
Torquay	1,000	353
Torrington	1,000	530
Totnes	1,000	350
Truro	1,000	200
Wells	1,024	960
West Dorset	1,000	500
West Gloucestershire	1,000	800
Westbury	1,079	800
Weston	1,000	300
Yeovil	3,500	3,000
Total	52,003	28,525

Source: Bristol Record Office, Labour Party South West Region papers, 38423/14.

allowed to send a delegate or submit a resolution to conference. As a consequence, during the 1960s an increasing number of CLPs affiliated exactly 1,000 members: between 1965 and 1968 the proportion rose from 58 to 78 per cent. Nobody believed this reflected reality: Sara Barker, when National Agent, guessed parties claiming the minimum were between 200 and 300 strong.[68] On that basis, Labour's actual membership in 1965 was two-thirds of the official total of 816,765 and just under half the 700,856 claimed for 1968 (see Tables 2.2 and 2.3). Data for the South West Region suggest Barker's calculations were possibly slightly pessimistic. Insofar as they knew what their number of members was, CLPs in the region claiming 1,000 admitted to their RO an 'actual' membership of, on average, 400, with one as low as 100. Offsetting this, however, was the fact that those officially claiming more members than the minimum also often exaggerated their position (see Table 2.4). As a rough guide, then, Barker's estimates appear as good as any, as it is impossible to determine the truth of the matter precisely.

Even had they not been obliged to return mostly fictional figures, few CLPs could have given Transport House an accurate total, owing to the means by which subscriptions were gathered. Members largely paid their fee in monthly instalments to a collector visiting them at home: as so few attended meetings, the collector was often their only link with the party. Despite this, and the financial importance of the post, many collectors performed the task erratically: some were overburdened with party duties, while others were simply incapable of performing the job properly. Given the high turnover of those willing to perform this un-popular task, membership lists were often lost.[69] Such was the inefficiency of collecting, it led to an 'unofficial understanding' that those paying half their annual subscription would still be counted members.[70] A fully paid-up member was almost as rare as the dodo: in 1960 only 10 per cent of the supposedly 230-strong Stockwell ward in Brixton were in this happy state, while 77 per cent had made no recorded contribution for more than four of the previous twelve months.[71] When the East Midlands RO estimated that, on average, CLPs in his region collected two-thirds of their membership income, this was considered laudable.[72] It took the Simpson report to suggest that members should be encouraged to pay annually direct from their bank accounts – although, as many workers were still paid in cash, little progress had been made by 1970.

Recruitment

It had long been apparent that CLPs whose MPs enjoyed the largest majorities often had the lowest memberships. This concerned the authors of the Wilson report, if only because it meant such local parties were not making their proper financial contribution to Transport House. Wilson therefore proposed setting the affiliation fee that CLPs were to pass on to the national organisation at 6*d* per member or £2 per 1,000 votes, whichever was the greater. While increasing income for the centre, this would also have encouraged local parties to increase their membership. While endorsed by numerous ROs and agents, this proved too controversial a step.[73] Thus, the situation became progressively worse, such that by the late 1960s CLPs in heartland regions such as North East England and Scotland probably had as few as one-third the members of regions in the south of England, where the Conservatives dominated (see Tables 2.2 and 2.3).

Despite officials' frequent promptings, many of those running CLPs with secure (albeit small) incomes in safe Labour areas saw little reason to recruit more members or indulge in electoral work. Parties in mining districts were among the most reluctant, enjoying as they did the generous financial support of the National Union of Mineworkers and the loyal votes of its members and their families.[74] Yet, whatever the source of financial security – be it a successful bingo competition, tote scheme or a large Labour club – CLPs were inclined to neglect recruitment, despite officials arguing that a healthy bank balance without a large membership would ultimately prove an electoral handicap.[75]

The position in the big cities was particularly bad: in 1966 the National Agent described the situation as 'deplorable'.[76] The NEC suspected that borough and city parties diverted the energies of too many activists from ensuring the healthy running of their own CLPs.[77] This would have been a credible explanation if borough parties were not themselves in a dire state. Glasgow was by far the most horrible example of a city party gone from bad in the 1950s to worse in the 1960s.[78] In 1961 the NEC described membership in Glasgow's fifteen CLPs as 'deplorably low': on average they had 320 members and 35 activists, figures that had slipped to 119 and 29, respectively, seven years later (see Table 2.5). Slum clearance played its part, as did administrative incompetence, but so did the fact that low memberships served the interests of those cliques that ran the party in Glasgow. Allowing CLPs to atrophy, such that EC and GMC meetings became rare events, meant they were more easily managed. Moreover, reformers who challenged the situation were confronted by an array of unconstitutional practices. Yet Glasgow was but the most extreme example of what Raisin feared was a widespread 'unspoken reluctance' to take membership recruitment seriously. He and other organisers believed that at the heart of this indolence was the fear of local party notables that new members would threaten their position.[79]

There was one further cause of low recruitment, especially relevant to parties in working-class districts. It is very likely that had more activists been willing and able to recruit, many CLPs would have significantly

Table 2.5 Numbers of members and activists in Glasgow, 1961 and 1968

Constituency party	1961		1968	
	Members	*Activists*	*Members*	*Activists*
Bridgeton	250	20	45	32
Cathcart	–	30	95	46
Central	130	8–10	44	27
Craigton	370	24	175	36
Gorbals	350	20	39	27
Govan	400	60	38	26
Hillhead	30	5	57	14
Kelvingrove	80	60	24	12
Maryhill	983	50–60	212	30–40
Pollock	–	23	320	43
Provan	354	70	242	25
Scotstoun	1,000	50	185	50
Shettleston	200	20	30	11
Springburn	200	40	200	32
Woodside	450	40	80	26
Totals	4,797	526	1,786	442

Source: National Executive Committee Organisation Sub-committee minutes, 14 February 1961, Enquiry into party organisation in Glasgow, NAD/21/2/61, and 18 February 1969, Enquiry into party organisation in Glasgow, NAD/14/2/69.

increased in size, as there were numerous instances of a few nights' canvassing producing spectacular results. For example, in Salford's Trinity ward during one September evening in 1962, three councillors claimed to have recruited thirty-nine new members inside thirty minutes.[80] Yet such new members required someone to collect their subscriptions and, as it was anticipated that few recruits would help out, this meant more work for already stretched activists. Therefore many stalwarts looked on new members as more trouble than they were – literally – worth. To the frustration of one constituency agent, after two keen Ebbw Vale activists had enrolled 160 recruits, ward officers simply refused to issue them with membership cards.[81]

A professional solution?

By the 1960s, some feared the party's attachment to voluntarism was electorally debilitating. As *Socialist Commentary* noted in 1965, Labour suffered from a 'distrust of the professional … [and] in a mistaken interpretation of what "democracy" means, the Party clings to the belief that almost anything can be done by almost anyone'.[82] There were plenty of instances in which elemental electoral work appeared to be beyond the abilities of long-standing activists. As was said of one struggling Welsh branch secretary, 'I have no doubt that he is giving of his best, but like so many of us, his best is not good enough'.[83] Hence, while Wilson disavowed transforming Labour into a professional body, the report still criticised the extent to which CLPs adhered to 'time-honoured rituals' and 'ancient techniques'.[84]

One device to increase membership especially favoured by organisers was to give collectors a commission on subscriptions successfully gathered in. They hoped this would increase the number of those willing to undertake such work and give them an extra incentive to be efficient: as a result, more members could be recruited and organisers would be safe in the knowledge they would not be misplaced. Despite its theoretical advantages, even CLPs in decline, like Bethnal Green, sometimes rejected the measure: wanting to maintain the 'spirit of voluntary service', commissions were, that GMC believed, 'opposed to Socialist principle'.[85] Even CLPs that gave collectors a commission undermined its effect by asking elderly, disabled or unemployed people to do the work, that is, those whose need was often greater than their ability.[86] This charitable practice subverted officials' covert reason for introducing a financial element to recruitment: they hoped it would sidestep the influence of local worthies, who 'insisted they had a right to determine the rate at which the Party should advance'.[87]

Reformers also expected that the employment of full-time constituency agents would improve Labour's organisation, as they could devote all their time to increasing income, membership and ensuring affairs were conducted along approved lines.[88] The spread of agents was probably the only means of promoting a 'professional' ethos. Yet, while Wilson and Simpson both called for a National Agency Service, Transport House claimed it could not afford one, although subsidies were increased to marginal constituencies to encourage their employment. As most CLPs were expected to underwrite all an agent's salary, officials were in no position to compel them to employ one. As a result, only a minority ever used a professional agent for any length of time: most made do with part-time volunteers. In fact, as membership declined, so did the financial ability of local parties to employ an agent: from 296 in 1951, the number of CLPs with full-time agents fell to 144 by 1970. Cost, however, was not the only reason: some activists were said to be 'anti-Agent in principle', because they feared a professional would reduce the need for voluntary effort.[89] Some established cliques also feared that, as in Stockton-on-Tees and Burnley, a keen agent would challenge the dubious methods that helped sustain them in power.[90]

Education

It was a common complaint that activists devoted most of their time to managing the party but hardly any to talking about political issues: as various surveys confirmed, less than half of GMC or ward meetings featured invited speakers or policy debates.[91] Yet, during the 1950s, ROs supported attempts to incorporate policy discussion into meetings, and they held regular weekend and day schools on a variety of topics. Even so, Wilson urged the NEC to look into education 'as a matter of urgency' and members of the NEC's Organisation Sub-committee agreed it was 'desirable to bring political education more easily within the reach of the active Party member in circumstances which will enable him [*sic*] really to understand the problems of policy and organisation and to discuss their implications in a detailed and practical way'.[92] Over a decade later, Simpson reported matters had not improved, as too much of the party's educational work was 'haphazardly and unsystematically' applied, while 'far too much of it stays at an elementary level'.[93] By the end of the 1960s, Transport House feared it was failing to give members a clear idea of the party's principles or the background to government policy, thereby limiting their ability to contribute to debate.[94]

Nonetheless, as local studies also discovered, there was a 'very genuine interest' in preventing routine business dominating every meeting, and when political issues were discussed a lively debate often ensued.[95] Many CLPs appointed a Political Education Officer (PEO); formed education sub-committees to encourage discussions at meetings; published news-letters; and established libraries. To some activists, member education was a critical part of their work. Thus, in 1967, Birmingham Yardley's PEO wrote in the first issue of his constituency newsletter that 'Making Socialists is an educational process and there is a pressing need for people to gain an understanding of the socialist solutions to the grave social problems of the day'. Therefore, he proposed using the newsletter 'to stimulate discussion and understanding among you ... the members ... and through you ... the general public'.[96] Southall's PEO also believed that, through education, Labour would create an 'enlightened and educated democracy', defining his ambition as:

> to educate every Party Member up to a certain standard. When each member is able to judge political programmes in their proper light and choose the one which will benefit mankind the most then they have reached that standard. From this the Party should be able to surge ahead and spread this learning to the general public, the voters.[97]

It might be expected that middle-class members would see merit in education and debate, so it is no revelation that during the mid-1950s

Warwick and Leamington Spa CLP regularly held discussions at meetings; organised a constituency-wide speaking contest; published a
newsletter addressing contentious issues; and that its PEO established a
Sunday discussion group.[98] Yet Poplar in London's East End also promoted discussion and in 1952 responded to national officials' request
that constituencies debate *Problems of Foreign Policy*.[99] The GMC urged
wards to study the pamphlet and report their conclusions. Most did;
some even held two meetings to discuss it and as a result attendances
were said to have improved. This was no isolated episode: wards would
also use pamphlets specially designed by Transport House to aid argument. Furthermore, the 1952 exercise was repeated a year later when
copies of *Challenge to Britain* were distributed to wards. If less extensive
than the previous initiative, the process concluded with a special GMC
meeting that saw an unusually large number of delegates contribute to
discussion.

Poplar's initiative was not sustained and in this respect it was typical.
Numerous CLPs periodically promoted education, only to fall foul of
members' lack of enthusiasm. Thus, in Brixton during 1950–1, delegates failed to attend the GMC's propaganda committee meetings;
there was little support for its weekly discussions; a quiz night failed to
attract many; and open-air gatherings were abandoned because of
insufficient support. Despite this, two years later the GMC resolved to
re-establish its political education committee, although some opposed
this move. In 1953 a resolution submitted to the GMC suggested that
policy discussion be placed higher up the agenda – although, ironically,
it was debated only one full year after having first been tabled. Having
been passed, it made no difference and in 1956 a frustrated CLP chair
complained that meetings contained no real discussion of politics, and
exhorted members to 'take more interest in Socialism and not the
"Social Committee"'.[100]

Not all activists, many of whom possessed only a basic education,
were comfortable debating ideas and complicated issues.[101] There were
undoubtedly many like the Brixton stalwart who was described after his
death as 'a good member not an outstanding one as regards getting up
and making speeches or voicing his thoughts at meetings but he was
one that helped to keep the Party going by his background work'.[102] If
such reticence resulted from a lack of confidence, others aggressively
dismissed debate as an unnecessary luxury. As one councillor stated in
opposing political discussions becoming an integral part of his GMC
meetings, it would be a 'waste of time', as those present 'all know what
we mean by the Labour Party'.[103] To such activists, the job of Labour
members was to knock on doors and tell people the good news, not
debate the nature of the message.

A hegemonic party?

Some believe that the party was uninterested in establishing a relation-ship with the voters that went beyond the electoral – that Labour saw no point in becoming a hegemonic cultural institution promoting a distinctively socialist vision of society.[104] A number of CLPs certainly adhered to an instrumental view and there were sound practical (usually financial) reasons for avoiding activities that did not directly relate to electing Labour representatives. Yet some CLPs in safe Labour areas did try to establish a more lively relationship with voters. Bethnal Green was, however, unusual in having a sports section, which organised a darts league, table tennis competitions and a cricket team – and by the early 1950s even that was ailing.[105] At the start of the 1960s, members in Gateshead hoped to make their party more attractive to locals by establishing a club for pensioners, a coffee bar for adolescents and a 'space-age' club for children.[106] If North Kensington lacked a social wing, it attempted to mobilise voters through more directly political activities, such as an annual autumn propaganda campaign, which in 1954 con-sisted of four open-air and three indoor meetings and the distribution of 10,000 leaflets.[107] One reason why few other parties experimented with similar kinds of initiative was that they invariably failed to generate a popular response. Leith CLP was another party whose MP sat on a large Commons majority but, unhappy with the apparently apathetic nature of the 1955 general election campaign, the GMC decided to go out and preach 'basic Socialism'. To that end they formed a propaganda committee that ran a 'Brains Trust' and printed 2,000 tickets for a proposed public meeting, whose main speaker was to be Tony Benn. Unfortunately, the former did not generate much support and was dis-continued, while advance sales for the latter event were so bad it was cancelled.[108]

More salutary still was the experience of Shoreditch and Finsbury CLP. In 1952, London's Assistant RO considered membership in this safe Labour constituency 'lamentably small', so the newly elected MP, Victor Collins, decided to reinvigorate the party.[109] 'Let people see', he declared, that 'the Labour Party is alive and caring for their welfare and happiness, not only in Whitehall, but here in Shoreditch'. 'We need', he announced, 'new blood, new ideas', and active members in every block of flats and on every street. Specifically, Collins wanted to double membership to 3,000, employ an agent and acquire a constitu-ency headquarters. By the end of 1955, he had achieved this and more, including launching a paper, *The Citizen*. Success, however, brought its own problems. First, the agent and party premises imposed a painful financial burden. Secondly, the collection of new members' subscrip-tions proved too much for what remained a small band of activists, who were also now expected to deliver 10,000 copies of *The Citizen*. The result was that most new recruits were quickly lost, while *The Citizen* failed to reach many homes. By 1961 the party was heavily in debt and membership had fallen to 1,611, little more than before Collins' adventure.

One of the more popular means by which local parties tried to establish a presence in wider society was through their May Day celebrations.[110] In London and across the country, tradition stipulated that a march should be held, followed by speeches, the purpose of which was to demonstrate the strength of the forces supporting Labour, to impress onlookers and encourage participants. Yet, by the later 1950s, some wanted May Day rethought, especially in London, where it was customary for members to gather at Victoria Embankment on the first Sunday after 1 May and process with bands and banners to Hyde Park. At the 1958 London Labour conference, both Acton and Woolwich CLPs proposed reform, and reported that their members considered the event a shambles and participated only out of a sense of duty. As such, it neither enthused participants nor created valuable publicity; its small size, moreover, was judged a 'disgrace'. The form taken by the celebration, Acton's secretary suggested, was out of tune with changes in popular leisure. 'If the present method continues', he warned, 'May Day, like the Street Corner meetings, will shortly be a thing of the past', a view echoed by Deptford's agent, who thought marching behind brass bands belonged 'to the times of mass unemployment and empty bellies'.

Discontent was not confined to the capital. As early as 1955, May Day in Glasgow was described as 'a mere shadow of its former self' and questions were asked about its purpose.[111] In Coventry, leading figures also considered the march tended 'to demonstrate our weaknesses rather than our strength'.[112] In Bristol, by the early 1960s, even left-inclined activists feared their march had just become the occasion for 'undesirable elements' to win publicity for themselves.[113] This echoed the opinion of Wilson's first Chief Whip, Edward Short, who complained that Newcastle upon Tyne's May Day celebrations were ruined by a 'ragtag and bobtail' of Communists, Trotskyists and anarchists, who made it their business to heckle speakers.[114]

Asked by *Tribune* in 1966 what May Day meant to them, two trade unionists summed up both sides of the argument. One from South Wales stated that, for him, it recalled workers' conditions before the war, and he thought the 'memory of those conditions is needed because so many workers, having achieved a reasonable standard of living, believe that the objects of trade unionism have been accomplished'. In contrast, a West Indian-born councillor from Camberwell confessed it meant little to him, as he had not participated in any of the struggles it honoured. He called for the celebrations to be made more relevant, not just for the sake of immigrants but also for native-born youngsters.[115]

As a result of criticisms made in 1958, the committee charged with arranging the London event was instructed to give the celebrations a 'more varied and colourful nature', while it should still retain its essential character. Consequently, May Day was marked in much the same way as before, until a decision was taken to 'present the traditional celebration in a modern setting'. Thus, in 1969, the party marked May Day at the Royal Festival Hall, the first half of the evening consisting of a performance by the Royal Shakespeare Company and the second being taken up by political speeches. While committee members considered this a success, after the third Festival Hall event, in 1971, at which the audience was entertained by classical music, they were forced to take account of other points of view. Constituencies and union branches were asked whether they approved of this innovation or wanted to revert to the former format: an overwhelming number wanted the latter and, despite the committee's misgivings, that is what they got.

Conclusion

The debate provoked by how the London Party marked May Day neatly encapsulates the dilemma faced by Labour across the country. A few activists and officials recognised that the form adopted to observe 1 May was considered antediluvian outside the party and so called for change, although in truth their proposals were not guaranteed to be any more popular. In any case, those for whom the shape assumed by this ritual was inextricably associated with the message they hoped to convey ultimately prevailed. So far as opponents of change were concerned, there was nothing wrong with marching behind brass bands – if that evoked the 1930s, so much the better. The party actually needed more brass bands playing their tunes with greater enthusiasm.

That Labour's active membership formed a contracting and ageing group, who by the mid-1960s possibly numbered only 50,000, helped sustain hostility to change. The commitment required to work within the party, compounded by a remoteness from popular concerns, imbued many – whether they formed self-interested cliques or embraced the transforming power of education and voluntary service – with an implacable (if often unconscious) sense of superiority. Their inability to appeal to the majority of Labour members, let alone those who merely voted for the party, only further underpinned this conservatism. For, so far as many activists were concerned, the refusal of most of the population to follow their lead reflected badly on the people rather than on themselves. Within this frame of reference, cultural change was something that might – or might not – be accommodated, but only on their own terms, which, so far as most were concerned, were beyond reproach.

Not everybody assumed this stark attitude to change. As the debate on 'affluence' (to be analysed in the following chapter) indicates, those in the parliamentary leadership, who were preoccupied with winning elections, could be more flexible. Even revisionists such as Hugh Gaitskell were, however, less pragmatic than they liked to imagine.

Notes

The place of publication is London unless otherwise specified.

1 Some of the material contained in this chapter has appeared in 'The "penny farthing machine" revisited: Labour party members and participation in the 1950s and 1960s', in C. Pierson and S. Tormey (eds), *Politics at the Edge* (2000), and 'Activists against "affluence": Labour party culture during the "Golden Age", c. 1950–1970', *Journal of British Studies* 40:2 (2001).

2 D. McHugh, 'A "mass" party frustrated? The development of the Labour party in Manchester, 1918–31', PhD thesis, University of Salford (2001), pp. 47–76.

3 This is an adaptation of the mechanical/moral distinction outlined by P. F. Clarke, *Liberals and Social Democrats* (Cambridge, 1978), pp. 1–8.

4 *Report of the Fifty-Fourth Annual Conference of the Labour Party* (1955), pp. 63–91.

5 For the debate provoked by Simpson, see *Report of the Sixty-Sixth Annual Conference of the Labour Party* (1967), pp. 237–53, 333–52; *Report of the Sixty-Seventh Annual Conference of the Labour Party* (1968), pp. 219–30; and *Report of the Sixty-Eighth Annual Conference of the Labour Party* (1969), p. 9.

6 This account is based on: London Metropolitan Archive (LMA), J. W. Raisin papers, Acc 2783/JWR/AG/2, The modernisation of party structures, paper for agents' conference, 7–9 November 1966, and The political situation, 1967, paper for agents' conference, 30 October–1 November 1967; Modern Records Centre (MRC), Labour Party East Midlands Region papers, MSS 9/3/1/17, The structure of the Labour Party, paper for agents' conference, 21–23 September 1955; and MSS 9/3/8/4, The activists and 'participation', paper for Northern Home Counties Regional Conference 1968; and LMA, *London News*, October 1952.

7 D. V. Donnison and D. E. G. Plowman, 'The functions of local Labour parties', *Political Studies*, 2:3 (1954), p. 162; W. Fienburgh and the Manchester Fabian Society, 'Put policy on the agenda', *Fabian Journal*, February 1952, p. 29; F. Bealey, J. Blondel and W. P. McCann, *Constituency Politics* (1965), p. 252.

8 See the argument in L. Minkin, *The Contentious Alliance* (Edinburgh, 1992); *Report of the Forty-Fifth National Conference of Labour Women* (1968), p. 10.

9 Labour Party Archive (LPA), *Huddersfield Citizen*, May 1964.

10 *Report of the Sixty-Ninth Annual Conference of the Labour Party* (1970), p. 120.

11 MRC, Coventry North CLP papers, MSS7/3/4, circular to trade union secretaries from CLP secretary, 28 October 1958.

12 *Fifty-Fourth Annual Conference of Labour*, pp. 74–5.

13 Raisin papers, Acc 2783/JWR/ORG/55/125, organiser's report.

14 LPA, NEC minutes, 10 October 1957, Report of the Industrial Organiser, NAD/68/9/57.

15 Essex County Record Office (ECRO), Labour Party Eastern Region papers,

D/Z 215/2, EC minutes, 14 December 1957; MRC, Coventry Borough Labour Party papers, MSS 11/3/78/59, minutes of a meeting of full-time trade union officials and representatives of Coventry Borough Labour Party, 19 July 1961.

16 J. Edmonds, 'The worker', in B. Lapping and G. Radice (eds), *More Power to the People* (1968), pp. 48–9.

17 Raisin papers, Acc 2783/JWR/ORG/62/17, organiser's report.

18 LPA, NEC Organisation Sub-committee (OSC) minutes, 12 December 1962.

19 OSC minutes, 20 February 1963, Labour's influence in the industrial field, NAD/14/2/63, and 15 May 1963, Trade union liaison, NAD/44/5/63.

20 Birmingham Public Library (BPL), Birmingham Borough Labour Party papers, Subject Collection: General Election 1959, vol. 1, minutes of meeting of Joint Trade Union Liaison Committee and the General Election Committees, 3 July 1959; General Election 1964, vol. 1, circular from the Joint Trade Union and Labour Party Liaison Committee, 27 August 1964; OSC minutes, 15 January 1964, Trade union liaison, NAD/64/7/63.

21 Mitchell Library, Scottish Labour Party papers, TD 1384/1/5, Scottish Council Executive Council minutes, 20 August and 19 October 1966.

22 M. Benney, A. P. Gray and R. H. Pear, *How People Vote. A Study of Electoral Behaviour in Greenwich* (1956), pp. 41–6.

23 NEC minutes, 12 December 1951, H. Morrison, Considerations arising out of the General Election of 1951.

24 S. Fielding, P. Thompson and N. Tiratsoo, *'England Arise!' The Labour Party and Popular Politics in 1940s Britain* (Manchester, 1995), pp. 93–5; M. A. Hamilton, *The Labour Party Today* (1939), p. 94.

25 West Yorkshire Archive (WYA), City of Bradford Labour Party papers, 49D84/3, Bradford East CLP minutes, 22 May 1951; LMA, Norwood CLP papers, Acc 2417/E/6/22, annual general meeting 1959 papers.

26 Stockport Local Heritage Library, Stockport CLP papers, B/MM/3/5, annual report 1951, p. 51.

27 *Fifty-Fourth Annual Conference of Labour,* p. 65.

28 British Library of Political and Economic Science, North Kensington CLP papers, *North Kensington Labour Questionmaster*, December 1951, Circulars to members, agenda of borough electoral committee, agenda of general council; City of Bradford papers 49D84/3, Bradford East minutes, 16 January 1951; J. Gould, '"Riverside": a Labour constituency', *Fabian Journal*, November 1954, p. 18.

29 Warrington Local Studies Library, *Warrington and District Labour News*, 17 January 1953.

30 Bristol Record Office (BRO), Labour Party South West Region papers, 38423/46, J. Baldwin, 'More leisure time – to watch television – or?', *Labour Voice*, February 1967.

31 Donnison and Plowman, 'Functions', pp. 157, 160.

32 Working Class Movement Library, Salford East CLP papers, Trinity ward minutes, 1958–66, *passim*.

33 ECRO, Chigwell and Ongar CLP papers, D/Z 84/4, Loughton ward minutes, *passim*.

34 Bealey *et al.*, *Constituency Politics*, p. 250; A. H. Birch, *Small Town Politics* (Oxford, 1959), pp. 66–7, 80–1; Gould, 'Riverside', p. 13.

35 *London News*, July 1951.

36 LPA, Morgan Phillips papers, constituency correspondence: Manchester/Hulme, Secretary/Agent, Hulme Divisional Labour Party to Phillips, 12 June 1947.

37 J. M. Bochel, 'Activists in the Conservative and Labour parties. A study of

ward secretaries in Manchester', MA thesis, University of Manchester (1965), p. 80.

38 R. Hoggart, *The Uses of Literacy* (Harmondsworth, 1958), p. 318; Birch, *Small Town*, pp. 68–9.

39 R. Blythe, *Akenfield* (Harmondsworth, 1969), pp. 90–7.

40 Benney *et al.*, *People Vote*, pp. 47, 51; Birch, *Small Town*, pp. 66–7, 80–1; Bochel, 'Activists', pp. 34–5; Fienburgh, 'Policy', p. 28–9; Gould, 'Riverside', p. 13; E. G. Janosik, *Constituency Labour Parties in Britain* (1968), pp. 11, 17; MRC, Socialist Vanguard Group papers, MSS 173, Box 11, Democracy in the Labour Party group minutes, 6 December 1955.

41 OSC minutes, 16 February 1955, Report of an enquiry …, NAD 12/2/55.

42 *London News*, April 1952. More generally, see R. Miliband, 'Socialism and the myth of the golden past', in R. Miliband and J. Saville (eds), *Socialist Register 1964* (1964).

43 Fienburgh, 'Policy', p. 29.

44 Salford East CLP papers, Trinity ward minutes, 1958–66, *passim*; LMA, Southall CLP papers, Acc 1267/15, Hambrough ward minutes, 1959–63, *passim*.

45 Calderdale Archives, Halifax CLP papers, TU:28/14, Warley ward group minutes, 1953–6, *passim*.

46 P. Graves, *Labour Women: Women in British Working-Class Politics, 1918–1939* (Cambridge, 1994), p. 3.

47 Benney *et al.*, *How People Vote*, p. 52; Gould, 'Riverside', p. 15.

48 Halifax CLP papers, TU:28/14, Warley ward group minutes, 26 September 1951; Southall papers, Hambrough ward minutes,14 June 1961.

49 OSC minutes, 16 September 1969, Report of an enquiry …, NAD/91/9/69.

50 South West Region papers, 38423/27, Stephen to Lobb, 10 February 1971.

51 Fienburgh, 'Policy', p. 32; Bochel, 'Activists', p. 187.

52 B. Jackson, *Working Class Community* (Harmondsworth, 1972), p. 168. See also E. Shaw, *Discipline and Discord in the Labour Party* (Manchester, 1988), pp. 141–53.

53 BPL, Birmingham Northfield CLP papers, Weoley Castle section minutes, 1954, *passim*.

54 Lambeth Archives, Brixton CLP papers, IV/156/1/8, Town hall minutes, 11 November 1959; Tameside Local Studies Library, Ashton-under-Lyne CLP papers, DD88/3/1, EC minutes, 10 February 1959.

55 *London News*, February 1954.

56 *Fifty-Fourth Annual Conference of Labour*, pp. 81–3.

57 Southwark Local Studies Library (SLSL), Bermondsey CLP papers, Annual report 1953; Raisin papers, Acc 2783/JWR/ORG/55/37 and 117, organiser's reports.

58 OSC minutes, 14 September 1965, Report of an enquiry …, NAD/118/9/65.

59 OSC minutes, 20 November 1962, Report of an enquiry …, NAD/114/11/62.

60 Halifax CLP papers, TU:28/16, Atkinson to Secretary/Agent, 4 January 1959.

61 Raisin papers, Acc 2783/JWR/ORG/59/131, organiser's report.

62 *London News*, October 1952; OSC minutes, 17 May 1966, Individual membership, NAD/43/5/66; NEC minutes, 26 October 1966, Party organisation, NEC/22/7/66.

63 *Fifty-Fourth Annual Conference of Labour*, p. 84.

64 South West Region papers, 38423/21/4, Cox to Marston, 13 April 1970.

65 MRC, Labour Party West Midlands Region papers, MSS 6/3/2/12, organiser's

report; Raisin papers, Acc 2783/JWR/ORG/66/104 and Acc 2783/JWR/ORG/67/63 and 68, organiser's reports.

66 OSC minutes, 17 July 1962, L. Williams, The meaning of individual membership, part 2.

67 OSC minutes, 15 May 1962, L. Williams, The meaning of individual membership.

68 NEC minutes, 19 July 1966, S. Barker, Individual membership, NAD/43/5/66.

69 Raisin papers, Acc 2783/JWR/OA/2, Mrs M. Raisin, Individual membership – collection of subscriptions, paper for conference of London Labour Party agents, 27–29 November 1956.

70 T. E. M. McKitterick, 'The membership of the party', *Political Quarterly*, 31 (1960), p. 312.

71 Brixton CLP papers, IV/156/1/9, Stockwell ward minutes, 4 May 1960.

72 OSC minutes, 18 July 1956, The case against a smaller individual membership contribution and an associate membership, NAD/56/7/56.

73 *Fifty-Fourth Annual Conference of Labour*, pp. 84–5.

74 East Midlands Region papers, MSS 9/3/14/153, MSS 9/3/15/7 and 59, organiser's reports; West Midlands Region papers, MSS 6/3/3/191, organiser's reports.

75 East Midlands Region papers, MSS 9/3/17/214, organiser's report; OSC minutes, 16 May 1956, Affiliation of National Union of Labour and Socialist Clubs, NAD/42/5/56.

76 OSC minutes, 17 May 1966, Individual membership, NAD/43/5/66.

77 OSC minutes, 8 December 1955, City and borough parties, NAD 63/11/55.

78 This account is based on OSC minutes, 14 February 1961, Enquiry into party organization in Glasgow, NAD/21/2/61; 20 March 1962, Report of an enquiry into ..., NAD/28/3/62; 18 September and 20 November 1963, and 18 February 1969, Enquiry into party organization in Glasgow, NAD/14/2/69; Scottish Labour papers, TD 1384/1/5, Scottish Council EC minutes, 14 December 1968.

79 LMA, Labour Party London Region papers, Acc 2417/A/70/1, organiser's report; East Midlands Region papers, MSS 9/3/14/104, organiser's report; Raisin papers, Acc 2783/JWR/ORG/66/86, organiser's reports.

80 Salford East CLP papers, Trinity ward minutes, 4 October 1962.

81 East Midlands Region papers, MSS 9/3/11/12, L. R. Chamberlain, A fresh approach to membership!, n.d. (but 1969); National Library of Wales (NLW), Ron Evans papers, 16/, Carter to Evans, 28 May 1964, and Evans to Carter, 1 June 1964.

82 'Our penny farthing machine', *Socialist Commentary*, October 1965, p. xxx.

83 NLW, Brecon and Radnor CLP papers, 63/, L. Conway, Report of Llandrindod Wells Labour Party, 10 April 1956.

84 *Fifty-Fourth Annual Conference of Labour*, p. 73.

85 *London News*, October 1952; Bancroft Library, Bethnal Green CLP papers, TH/8488, GMC minutes, 22 April 1954.

86 *Fifty-Fourth Annual Conference of Labour*, p. 84.

87 Raisin papers, Acc 2783/JWR/0A/2, minutes of a meeting with organisers, 16 October 1956.

88 'Penny farthing', pp. xi–xii.

89 Raisin papers, Acc 2783/JWR/ORG/59/9, organiser's report and Acc 2783/JWR/ORG/66/28, organiser's report.

90 OSC minutes, 7 May 1957, Regional schemes. Regional organisers' reports, NAD/35/4/57, and 14 September 1965, Report of an enquiry ..., NAD/118/9/65.

91 Socialist Vanguard Group papers, MSS 173, Box 11, Democracy in the Labour Party Group file, W. Guttsman circular to members, 3 February 1956; Bealey *et al.*, *Constituency Politics*, p. 102; Donnison and Plowman, 'Functions', pp. 157, 160.

92 *Fifty-Fourth Annual Conference of Labour*, p. 63; OSC minutes, 20 July 1955, A party education campaign, NAD 47/7/55.

93 *Sixty-Sixth Annual Conference of Labour*, pp. 241, 343–4.

94 NEC minutes, 13 September 1967, Working party on political education. Report.

95 Donnison and Plowman, 'Functions', pp. 157–8; Fienburgh, 'Policy', p. 28; Gould, 'Riverside', p. 15.

96 West Midlands Region papers, MSS 6/5/4, *Labour News. Journal of Yardley Constituency Labour Party* (1967).

97 Southall CLP papers, Acc 1267/58, annual reports, 1959 and 1960.

98 MRC, Warwick and Leamington Spa CLP papers, MSS 133, EC minutes, 20 December 1956.

99 This account is based on Bancroft Library, Poplar CLP papers, TH/8488, constituency agent's reports for 1952 and 1953; West ward minute book, 23 April and 28 May 1952 and 24 June 1953.

100 Brixton CLP papers, IV/156/2, GMC minutes, 1950–6 *passim*.

101 Raisin papers, Acc 2783/JWR/AG/2, The political situation, 1967, paper for Northern Home Counties' agents' conference, 30 October–1 November 1967.

102 Brixton CLP papers, IV/156/1/9, Stockwell ward minutes, 22 September 1960.

103 Anonymous, 'Down to the grass roots', *Socialist Commentary*, 18, January 1954, p. 23; Gould, 'Riverside', pp. 16–18.

104 See, for example, D. Coates, 'Labour governments: old constraints and new parameters', *New Left Review*, 291 (1996), pp. 63–4.

105 Bethnal Green CLP papers, TH/8488, GMC minutes, 6 and 24 January 1951.

106 *Labour Organiser*, 40:464 (1961), pp. 25–6.

107 North Kensington CLP papers, circulars to members, Agenda of Borough Electoral Committee, Agenda of General Council, 1949–57, annual reports 1954, 1955.

108 National Library of Scotland, Leith CLP papers, Acc 4977/18, minutes 1955–6, *passim*.

109 This account is based on: East Midlands Region papers, MSS 9/3/14/36, organiser's report; Hackney Archives, Shoreditch and Finsbury CLP papers, D/S/25/3–8, GMC minutes, 1954–61, *passim*; *Hackney Gazette*, 21 October 1953.

110 This account is based on: London Region papers, Acc 2417/A/39, J. S. Keys, Supplement to secretary's report, May Day celebrations, 5 March 1958; Acc 2417/A/59, minutes of the joint May Day committee, 1 July 1958, 16 May 1961; Acc 2417/A/40, P. Robshaw, Secretary's report, 29 October 1959; LMA, Greater London Labour Party papers (unsorted), joint May Day committee minutes, 24 April and 19 May 1969; *May Day Festival of Labour Programme*, 1969; circulars from the joint May Day committee to all affiliated organisations, March and August 1971; *London News*, June and July 1958.

111 Mitchell Library, Glasgow Maryhill CLP papers, Secretary's report for constituency annual general meeting, 5 February 1956.

112 Coventry Borough papers, MSS 11/3/19, Ritchie to Edelman, 6 April 1959.

113 BRO, Bristol West CLP papers, 38598/1/b, GMC minutes, 13 June 1963.

114 E. Short, *Whip to Wilson* (1989), p. 148.

115 *Tribune*, 29 April 1966.

3

Responding to affluence

Many commentators viewed Labour's failure to win the 1959 general election as evidence that, without fundamental change, the party could not prosper in what they described as the 'affluent society'.[1] By 1966, many of the same people believed Labour had been transformed and was largely in tune with contemporary developments. In accounting for this turn-about, most pointed to the impact of Harold Wilson, who became leader in February 1963. At Labour's annual conference in October that year, he tied his party's fortunes to the development of the 'scientific and technological revolution' and the promotion of 'the white heat of technological change'. Members drawn from across the party believed Wilson had given Labour a new vision for a new era.[2]

This chapter examines the development of Labour strategy between 1959 and 1966 and highlights the debate it provoked, as this revealed how members thought their party should best respond to change. Hugh Gaitskell and his successor assumed – just like many other contemporaries – that rising incomes had restructured society and that popular political attitudes had changed in step. As a consequence, they believed Labour had to reform itself, in particular how it communicated with key parts of the electorate: less stress was placed on the need to alter the party's organisation and policies. How far this approach contributed to Labour's 1964 and 1966 victories is moot. While it would be unwise to think the party played the most significant role in its electoral revival, it would be obtuse to imagine Labour contributed nothing at all.

The 1959 campaign

As with all such contests, it was only *after* the Conservatives won the 1959 general election that the result appeared inevitable. Armed with the belief that rising incomes were blurring class differences, such that better-off manual workers adhered to 'middle-class' values, many observers argued that the basic cause of Gaitskell's defeat was Labour's failure to come to terms with 'affluence'. Harold Macmillan's party won, in contrast, because it had responded with greater understanding. Authoritative sources predicted that if Labour did not react in like manner, it would probably never return to office.[3] Having shared many of the assumptions of such analysts for a number of years, Gaitskell and his cohorts readily accepted their interpretation.

The result of the election had greatly disappointed Labour members, as it was the fourth time in a row the Conservatives had increased their share of the vote and the third in which their party's had declined.[4] However, the extent to which Labour's defeat was the product of intractable and progressive social processes is, despite what was said afterwards, open to doubt. Certainly, before the election Gaitskell and many others in the leadership believed their party had more than a fair chance of winning. During the campaign, opinion polls indicated it was a close contest, so close in fact that the Conservatives feared the possibility of defeat. Even so, Macmillan was an assiduous operator, who invariably bested Gaitskell over tactics, and opinion polls showed that voters regarded him as the more effective of the two. Moreover, in the immediate run-up to the election the Conservative-inclined press had done its best to present Labour as divided over nuclear disarmament and nationalisation. Despite that, Labour's campaign was judged superior to the ruling party's, up to the point at which Gaitskell made what even sympathisers viewed as a serious blunder. He promised that taxes would not rise under a Labour government, as any extra spending would be financed through growth. This the Conservatives successfully presented as an irresponsible electoral bribe and Labour never recovered its momentum.

How important such matters were to the final outcome is questionable, as the contest was held during a period of general, sustained and unprecedented prosperity, which inevitably favoured the government. This was underlined by what was an exceptional two-year £500,000 Conservative advertising campaign, the basic message of which was, as one poster put it, 'Life's better under the Conservatives. Don't let Labour ruin it.' Instead of fighting on other ground, Labour compounded its disadvantage by concentrating its campaign on the economy, thereby encouraging voters to focus on an issue from which the government could only gain.

Insofar as Gallup's polling was accurate, some clear patterns emerge from the 1959 poll compared with that of 1955 and it is worth bearing these in mind (see Table 3.1). Labour lost support among upper-middle-class, middle-class and even working-class voters but enjoyed considerably more backing from those categorised as 'very poor'. Among the youngest cohort of voters the party's position deteriorated, although it held on to most support among the middle-aged and actually improved

Table 3.1 Labour's vote by social category, 1955–66

	1955	1959	1964	1966
Upper middle class	9	6	9	8
Middle class	21	16	22	24
Working class	57	54	53	61
Very poor	54	68	59	72
Men	51	48	49	56
Women	42	43	39	48
21–29 years	54	47	47	56
30–49 years	48	47	45	53
50–64 years	42	40	40	53
65 and above	45	51	44	48

Source: Gallup Poll, 'Voting behaviour in Britain, 1945–1974', in R. Rose (ed.), *Studies in British Politics* (1976), p. 206.

its popularity with the oldest voters. Labour also lost ground among men, while women electors showed a marginally greater inclination to support the party than previously – although far fewer still voted Labour compared with men.

The numerous post-mortems written by Labour's constituency agents, candidates and regional officials broadly agreed that their party had failed to appeal to enough younger, well-off workers. Husbands and working wives in their twenties – that is, the most affluent members of the working class – appeared especially resistant.[5] It was, however, unclear how far the party's promise to increase nationalisation had created this situation, as Gaitskell was soon to claim. Reports from marginal seats in the East Midlands, for example, concurred that voters' prosperity went against the party.[6] The agent in Bristol South East also painted a picture of Labour failing to win over young working-class couples enjoying a purchasing power beyond their parents' dreams. Ominously, he predicted that, 'short of an economic calamity', Labour was unlikely to increase support among such voters.[7] In accounting for their party's victory, Conservative officials privately believed nationalisation was much less important than Gaitskell's tax pledge.[8] Moreover, while Macmillan claimed the 'class war is over and we have won it', his party's officials were more cautious, appreciating that younger workers were unsteady Conservatives and so could not yet be counted firm supporters.[9]

Although it appeared to leave certain affluent voters unimpressed, Labour's campaign was hardly antediluvian. Through lack of money and inclination, the party did not use advertising to anything like the extent employed by the Conservatives. Still, it did try to reach voters in innovative ways, most especially with its pre-election statement *The*

Future Labour Offers You (1958), which summarised Labour policy in an accessible and attractively illustrated manner. Commentators and voters alike thought the party's television broadcasts impressive – although some activists thought them 'a little too "clever"'.[10] The national campaign directed from Transport House was, additionally, generally regarded as supremely professional.

The party's overall message was that its leaders were economically responsible, better able than the Conservatives to increase growth, and reflected the interests of the whole of society, while their opponents were concerned only for the rich. Promising to promote individual freedom, Labour believed this should not occur at the expense of wider social justice. *Britain Belongs to You*, its manifesto, stressed that Labour's socialist ethic meant 'none of us, however lucky or well-off we may happen to be, ought to feel comfortable in a society in which the old and sick are not decently cared for'. It pointed to the 'many millions' of 'have-nots', and promised to raise pensions and improve provision for widows. Yet the manifesto also addressed the 'haves', and promised to extend personal liberty by setting up enquiries into betting restrictions, Sunday observance statutes and licensing laws. Labour's desire to enable people to take advantage of the opportunities created by full employment was more completely articulated in *Leisure for Living* (1959), issued some months before the campaign. This constituted an attempt to promote what Roy Jenkins described as 'gaiety, tolerance and beauty' and thereby extend party competition to areas beyond the economic.[11]

Labour tried to appeal specifically to the young as well, by promising to enhance their opportunities through creating a maintenance grant for sixth-formers and increasing it for university students, while improving access to education and training for those leaving school at fifteen years of age. It also pledged to improve leisure facilities for young people and promised that a Labour government would at least consider lowering the voting age from twenty-one.

Similarly, the party made numerous discrete appeals to women, largely – but not exclusively – on the basis of their domestic responsibilities. Thus, in a list of housewives' supposed 'Top Ten points of interest', one leaflet had, at number one, the 'house you live in', declaring it should be 'easy to run with modern amenities'. Number three was 'good health', and here the leaflet focused on pre- and post-natal care; numbers four and five also related to children, being 'education' and 'careers'. Six and seven referred to prices and consumer protection. Perhaps less conventionally, number eight – 'leisure' – asserted that the welfare state should give wives and mothers time to find paid employment or develop a hobby. Point nine stated that the party's pension plan would give housewives equality with wage earners.[12] Labour's main emphasis nonetheless fell on consumer issues. It promised to guarantee 'value for money' by preventing monopolistic prices, ensuring the accurate labelling of goods and encouraging the activities of the Consumers' Association.[13] This message was reflected in the party's television broadcasts. In one, the front-bench MP Eirene White claimed Labour's women MPs were especially concerned to keep down the cost of living, while, in contrast, the 'housewife's voice' was not heard on the Conservative side. Moreover, shown returning home with some shopping, White described herself as a 'working housewife' and sympathised with women trying to reconcile jobs with domestic duties, a message strikingly underlined by film of the redoubtable MP Bessie Braddock dressed in a pinafore wielding a Ewbank cleaner.

Labour's message was therefore a mix of appeals designed to maximise its vote among a variety of groups. It contained measures to maintain support among the 'traditional' working class while gesturing towards voters who had become more affluent. There were undoubtedly some at the top of the party, such as Morgan Phillips, the General Secretary, who believed unemployment 'marked the real difference' between the parties.[14] Yet Labour's programme also addressed the concerns of those who took a well paid job for granted, rather than thinking it something for which they should be permanently grateful. Nonetheless, leading academic commentators believed that if the party was to stand any chance of ever again winning power, it had to abandon what they termed its 'schizophrenic image'. If Labour's manifesto had been a mixture of appeals, it was thought the party had to alter the balance and more explicitly win over the young and well-off. For, they believed, so far as Labour was concerned, the electoral consequences of social change meant things could only get worse.[15] Thus, while Labour's national campaign had largely reflected their outlook, to Gaitskell and his closest lieutenants defeat meant the party should adhere ever more closely to their 'revisionism'.

Accommodating affluence

Although associated with Anthony Crosland's *The Future of Socialism*, first published in 1956, revisionism traced its immediate origins back to Evan Durbin's *The Politics of Democratic Socialism* (1940), which was written in the late 1930s, when Britain still experienced mass unemployment. Crosland gave this perspective a more contemporary gloss – although even his thinking was clarified during post-war austerity. In 1950 he had claimed that capitalism was evolving into a new economic configuration, one that mitigated the worst excesses of the unbridled free market.[16] While not socialism, this new order produced ineluctable growth and attenuated class conflict by improving incomes and increasing the size of those 'intermediate classes' who were neither manual workers nor employers. This new system resolved what Karl Marx supposed were capitalism's inherent contradictions and was capable of delivering continued rising living standards to the working class. As a result, the worst injustices and miseries associated with capitalism were on the verge of abolition. Yet, while making life better, what Crosland termed 'Progressive Capitalism' could never eliminate class distinctions and would not evolve into socialism without further political pressure. Socialism was therefore still necessary but might take several generations to come about – and in order to win power Labour had to make a special appeal to the 'intermediate classes', as they would in future determine the outcome of elections.

In 1951 a *Socialist Commentary* editorial elaborated on Crosland's view and outlined what would become party strategy under Gaitskell and Wilson. This stipulated that if Labour was to regain power, it had to win over the 'floating vote', which meant standing on the centre ground. The 'glaring grievances of the past' had been 'eliminated' and while 'no one pretends that the whole job has been done', poverty was much diminished and a substantial redistribution of income had taken place: Britain was experiencing 'at least the beginnings of an egalitarian society'. This meant Labour had to 'look beyond the old gospel of more and more nationalisation, "workers' control" or class appeals to "soak the rich"'.[17] Gaitskell's response to the party's 1955 defeat reflected this perspective and anticipated his attitude to the 1959 loss. Hence he believed unprecedented access to 'TV, new gadgets like refrigerators and washing machines, the glossy magazines with their special appeal to women and even the flood of new cars on the home markets' meant 'more and more people are beginning to turn to their own personal affairs and to concentrate on their own material advance'. It was, he advised members, 'no good moaning about it'; policy should be made to fit in with this new individualism and presented in terms sympathetic to it.[18] After becoming leader in 1955, Gaitskell consequently did his best to dilute Labour's close connection with state ownership and ensured it went into the 1959 campaign committed only to renationalising steel and long-distance road haulage companies.

The revisionists were determined, as Jenkins put it, to 'use this shock' generated by defeat to promote Labour's further transformation.[19] Thus, Gaitskell or those closest to him: demanded that the party recast its links with the unions; called for a rethink about its relationship with the Liberals; and suggested Labour should change its name. Gaitskell's own preoccupation, however, was with nationalisation, specifically clause four of the party's constitution, which associated Labour with a seemingly unqualified aspiration to increase public ownership. Although he considered it irrelevant to policy-making, Gaitskell believed the clause distorted affluent voters' perception of his party because it allowed the Conservatives to claim Labour wanted to nationalise everything. Revising the clause would, he thought, more accurately reflect Labour's purpose and thereby make the party seem more relevant to modern Britain.

This analysis underscored Gaitskell's contribution to the debate on the election held at Labour's 1959 conference.[20] The fundamental cause of defeat, he argued, was the transformation of capitalism, to which Labour had to fully adapt. This meant members needed to accept that most workers were well off and free of the fear of unemployment. They also had to appreciate that the party could no longer rely on manual workers' 'instinctive loyalty' to secure power. White-collar employees would, he predicted, eventually outnumber the proletariat, who, in turn, would be transformed, such that the 'typical worker of the future' would be a 'skilled man in a white overall, watching dials in a bright new modern factory [rather] than a badly paid cotton operative working in a dark and obsolete 19th-century mill'. Owing to the 'particularly notable increase in comforts, pleasures and conveniences' in the home, women's lives were, Gaitskell stated, now 'a good deal easier'. Yet, owning washing machines, refrigerators and the like made them even less likely to vote Labour than in the past. It was, he warned, no use 'dismissing the problem, as some do, by saying that women are too snobbish or too politically apathetic': they were, Gaitskell declared, 'voters and count just as much as men'. In order for Labour to improve its appeal, he told delegates, the party should revise its aims.

While not dissenting from his analysis, members of Gaitskell's shadow Cabinet, along with those at the top of the Transport House bureaucracy, thought it foolish to try to change clause four.[21] Most believed it less electorally significant than their leader and feared the process of revision would expose divisions in the party, for activist members thought the promotion of public ownership inherent to the party's basic purpose and looked on clause four as a guarantor of its commitment to socialism.[22] The year 1959 was in fact the first to see the clause printed on the back of membership cards, which was the result of a campaign by activists in Newcastle upon Tyne who were concerned by the leader's lack of enthusiasm for nationalisation.[23] This sentiment was, in contrast, less obvious among the party's wider membership: indeed, at the height of the controversy, 54 per cent of those in the Newcastle-under-Lyme party claimed never to have heard of clause four.[24]

Gaitskell lacked sufficient support among trade union representatives on the National Executive Committee (NEC) for revision, although he was allowed to add a statement of aims that could sit side by side with the clause. This additional statement claimed Labour's 'central ideal' was 'the brotherhood of man', which meant it rejected 'discrimination on grounds of race, colour or creed' and held 'men should accord to one another equal consideration and status in recognition of the fundamental dignity of man'. As it stood for 'social justice', Labour also sought a 'classless society', in which the 'wealth produced by all is fairly shared among all', where 'differences in rewards depend not upon birth or inheritance but on the effort, skill and creative energy contributed to the common good' and where 'equal opportunities exist for all to live a full and varied life'. The party also embraced 'democracy in industry, and ... the right of the workers both in the public and private sectors to full consultation in all the vital decisions of management, especially those affecting conditions of work'. It, moreover, remained convinced that these objectives could be achieved only through 'an expansion of common ownership substantial enough to give the community power over the commanding heights of the economy' – although private enterprise had a legitimate place in the economy and nationalisation would be applied only 'according to circumstances'. Finally, Labour stood for 'the happiness and freedom of the individual against the glorification of the state' and 'any exercise of arbitrary power'.[25] Few in the party were impressed with these additional aims: Bradford East's general management committee (GMC) considered them an 'unnecessary and meaningless conglomeration of words', while Frank Cousins, left-wing leader of the Transport and General Workers' Union, believed they meant 'all things to all people'.[26]

Criticising affluence

After his leader's rebuff over clause four, Crosland wanted to reduce the influence of the left by expelling about twenty MPs from the Parliamentary Labour Party, including those, such as Michael Foot, he termed '*Tribune* extremists'. The left needed to be reined in, Crosland figured, because they prevented Gaitskell taking full account of the electorate's new mood by forcing him into compromises that blurred the necessary message.[27] Unfortunately for Crosland, more than a few rebellious MPs stood between Labour and what he considered the correct reaction to defeat. Many of the left's misgivings about 'affluence' were widely shared, even by some normally defined as revisionists.

For most party members, 'affluence' was neither expected nor welcome. Labour entered opposition in 1951 believing it had won a moral victory because Clement Attlee had gained more votes – if fewer seats – than Winston Churchill. Members generally believed the outgoing government had applied policies that were both correct, in terms of moving the country closer to socialism, and popular. To them, it was self-evident that the state was superior to the market and that collective provision was more effective than any system dependent on individual resources.[28]

Few considered there was any need to adapt the programme first out-lined in 1945. As one Labour journal published in Essex put it, after a brief hiatus, the people would:

> return to the Socialist planning now interrupted, which has saved and revived this country, and will turn again with relief to the policy of social justice which is implicit in Labour's principles, and of which Toryism knows nothing.... This Tory night can only be brief ... they cannot reverse the march of social progress. With the first light of dawn, they and their misdeeds will vanish.[29]

Activists expected the Conservatives, in attempting to reverse 'pro-gress', would attack living standards and raise unemployment. In the face of much contrary evidence, that is what many claimed to see. In 1953, for example, members across the country were informed that the return of the 'hungry' thirties was imminent.[30] At the 1955 election, some candidates claimed the Conservatives had caused real wages to fall and inequality to increase.[31] In 1957, Judith Hart similarly drew the attention of her selection meeting in Lanark to the apparent fact that poverty was 'striking again at the underprivileged' owing to the impact of conscious Conservative strategy.[32] At the time of the 1959 contest, a number claimed inter-war conditions were returning to some parts of the country.[33]

Even members who accepted the reality of 'affluence' and believed the party needed to adapt were often critical of its wider impact. One of Gaitskell's own additional aims asserted that, as the 'pursuit of material wealth by and for itself' was 'empty and barren', the party rejected the 'selfish, acquisitive doctrines of capitalism' and strove to create a 'socialist community based on fellowship, co-operation and service'. As one of Labour's few teenage activists had it, affluence caused the people to lose their sense of purpose: they were 'working all day for money and then making their main hobby gambling for more' because they were wallowing in an ignorance induced by bingo, fashion and pop music.[34] It was this crude materialism that offended those like the MP Reginald Sorenson, who feared the 'feverish obsession with com-petition for private gain' threatened to submerge those 'deeper values', based on 'communal service and co-operation', that Labour cherished.[35] It was for this reason the revisionist Douglas Jay led the campaign to prevent the introduction of independent television during the early 1950s; after its authorisation by Act of parliament in 1954, the loyalist MP George Rogers deprecated it as further strengthening the 'cor-rupting influence of commercialism'.[36] Later in the decade, many opposed the introduction of Premium Bonds on the same basis.[37]

Some held those who rose up the social ladder during this period in withering contempt. A Labour veteran from Wapping noted that affluence enabled former residents to move to the suburbs and buy cars, television and radios. This new-found individual security had, however, caused them to abandon the pursuit of 'disinterested public service'.[38] Writing in the late 1960s, the left-wing MP Leah Manning recalled canvassing in Chingford during the 1950 campaign, where she noted early signs of 'a phenomenon which is part of our changing society': having moved to a more middle-class district, voters born into the working class had apparently changed their party affiliation. 'One can only admire', she conceded, 'their anxiety to do better for their children and obtain the amenities which make their homes and lives more comfortable'. Manning, nonetheless, doubted they had changed party through conviction and believed it was merely 'an outward and visible sign of that inward grace which had transferred them into "middle class" respectability'.[39] Others were less patronising but equally disappointed by evidence of such aspirations: when a meeting of Bedford's GMC was informed that a majority of council tenants wanted to own their home, those present let out audible sighs of dismay.[40]

Like their revisionist counterparts, the left had a ready-made explanation for defeat in 1959, one prefigured in debates conducted at least as far back as the late 1940s. Indeed, many believed matters had gone awry when the Attlee government refused to nationalise even more of the private sector than was promised in 1945.[41] The MP Geoffrey Bing accepted that the Conservatives returned to office in 1951 on the back of support from a significant minority of the working class. His solution was, however, the reverse of that proposed by *Socialist Commentary*: Bing thought Labour would win back proletarian Tories if Labour advocated a 'clear, simple Socialist policy' of drastically extending public ownership.[42] The ex-MP John Freeman later argued that, if Labour chased middle-class voters by watering down its commitment to state control, it would not only fail but would also alienate working-class supporters.[43] Thus, Cousins was not alone in believing that what one activist described as the leadership's 'wishy-washy thinking' had prevented up to six million 'Socialists in embryo' from supporting the party in 1959.[44] As Aneurin Bevan's Ebbw Vale constituency Labour party (CLP) advised the ailing *Daily Herald*, the paper – just like Labour – would revive its popularity if it decided to 'rededicate itself to a socialist policy, divesting itself of the idea that we can make capitalism work better than the establishment'.[45]

What Crosland thought a permanently reformed capitalism, the left took to be a 'halfway house that cannot endure', which would inevitably usher back mass unemployment.[46] Revisionists tended to look to the United States for clues to Britain's future and saw merit in emulating at least some aspects of American society.[47] On the left, only economies dominated by state ownership were thought worthy of study, for they alone had permanently freed themselves of the threat of unemployment. As Labour's candidate in Folkestone told activists in 1959, collective ownership was the reason why the Soviet Union had achieved unknown levels of prosperity and equality and had outstripped the United States in economic performance.[48] Edinburgh Fabians were informed by one of their number that too much was made of the drabness of life in the Soviet Union. The people now dressed in colourful fashions and, while their styles were not too modern, the material was more than adequate. Moreover, consumer goods were in ample supply and generally of the same quality evident in Britain. Furthermore, and possibly for a Fabian audience more importantly, workers were tidier and more civil than their British counterparts.[49] Thus, as affluence would inevitably give way to depression, Labour should remain what the MP Richard Crossman described as a 'Fighting Socialist Opposition', unsullied by compromise.[50]

If accommodating the needs of a transient affluence was thought unwise, many also considered it unscrupulous. The Conservatives won in 1959 because they had appealed to what one Basingstoke activist said was 'Snobbery, Selfishness and Fear'. If Labour emulated its rival, the party would betray socialism.[51] As Foot had it, 'we have to change the mood of the people of this country, to open their eyes to what an evil and disgraceful and rotten society it is'.[52] One self-consciously 'old-fashioned Socialist' active in Falmouth argued that Labour's purpose was to 'liberate the people from this TV–Bingo pseudo-culture, and in its place make the people of this country feel that life can be a grand adventure, and give them a horizon that they never thought possible'.[53] The secretary of Warwick and Leamington Spa CLP also argued that Labour should persuade voters that socialism was a 'way of life that can lead to a better understanding between man and man, nation and nation; that it is an alternative to the way that glorifies the money lender and the gambler, that it can lead to a better life for all'.[54] Thus, Mary Sutherland, Labour's Chief Woman Officer, considered that rather than change policy, the party should 'think hard about how to improve our methods of educating the electors'.[55] In particular, Labour's task was, the agent in Bristol Central believed, to alert affluent voters unconcerned about the plight of 'those less well off, either the older folk in their own country or the underprivileged overseas', to their 'responsibilities'.[56]

It was not, therefore, Labour's job to change itself, but to reform society in its own image. As it was believed workers voted Conservative owing to the deliberate manipulation of their most irrational impulses, just because the party lost votes did not mean it was wrong.[57] A delegate at the 1959 Labour Party annual conference forcefully advanced this perspective by declaring how appalled he was that so many speakers proposed 'appeasing public opinion'. Instead, he suggested:

Let us show we are basically a moral Party, who believe in truth and
believe in socialism! If we do that, it does not matter whether we
become a Government in 1964, 1974 or 1984. When we do form a
government, I know that we have something to offer the country. We
have a new world to offer them, and a new society, not a botched-up
old system. Let us go forward from this Conference! Let us go
forward and not turn back![58]

Many believed this approach would work. MPs like Coventry's Maurice
Edelman, a long-time left-winger, believed their own constituency victories derived from 'our advocacy of an uncompromising Socialism with
nationalisation'.[59] If Gaitskell wanted to win national office, he should
adopt a similar strategy.

Focus on image

Crosland opposed his leader's attempt to alter clause four because he
thought Labour could transform its fortunes without substantially changing principles or policies. Instead, he thought the main task should be
to reshape its 'image'.[60] As the West Leeds MP and Gaitskell loyalist
Charles Pannell suggested, Labour lost in 1959 mainly because it had
not resonated with affluent voters 'kidded' by the Conservatives' posters.[61]
This interpretation was also favoured at Transport House, where Phillips
was keen to avoid a divisive debate about policy and ideology.[62]

Crosland had long considered that 'intermediate' groups, such as
white-collar workers, were politically unstable because of the tension he
detected between their incomes, often no more than those of skilled
manual workers, and their conviction that they belonged to a superior
class. This contradiction between objective and subjective position
meant non-manual workers were, Crosland thought, fated to 'float'
between the two essentially class-based parties. Moreover, as he believed
rising incomes had reduced class differences, Crosland thought voters
as a whole were less inclined to make 'automatic' assessments of their
interests than hitherto. Instead, they were more 'pragmatic' in their
judgements and so amenable to 'rational persuasion'. This meant
Labour should concentrate on how it presented 'itself and its policies
to the public, to the tone and content of its propaganda, and generally
to the impression which it makes on the voters'. Labour also needed to
abandon the 'sectional, traditional class appeal', which Crosland considered still dominated the 1959 campaign, and to portray itself as 'a
progressive, national, social-democratic party'. As others suggested,
Labour should develop an all-embracing image, one that appealed to
the interests of both 'haves' and 'have-nots'.[63]

After failing to revise clause four, Gaitskell and his advisers fully endorsed this perspective, considering the best way to project Labour's image was through an advertising campaign based on research into voter attitudes similar to the one undertaken by the Conservatives. They believed there was no other way of reaching affluent voters, as they were unlikely to attend public meetings, preferring as they apparently did to stay at home watching television. As they were also deemed to have no interest in the minutiae of political debate, these electors were thought likely to be swayed by comparatively unimportant, non-intellectual influences. Hence the right image was critical to advancing Labour's fortunes.

Employing techniques associated with advertising proved not much less controversial than trying to revise clause four. Some Labour members viewed them as immoral, owing to their association with the Conservative enemy. Given that one of the least savoury aspects of affluence was considered to be the burgeoning of advertising, others were queasy about using the same methods to promote their party.[64] As one agent declaimed: 'Ad men are no more interested in the Labour Party than they are in my Aunt Fanny ... all they know about is appealing to people's greed, whereas we are trying to appeal to their ideals'.[65] Others, including the National Agent, thought Labour could recover its position through better organisation; to his mind, advertising would just waste precious funds.[66]

Opening up the organisation

Given the leadership's emphasis on advertising, one constituency agent claimed a growing number of activists were 'beginning to wonder if some of our more traditional activities are not just a sheer waste of time and energy'.[67] Yet even the most enthusiastic advocates of advertising, such as the pollster Mark Abrams, believed members could still help by opening up their parties to uncommitted groups of voters.[68] As subsequent chapters focus on attempts to attract women, black immigrants and the young, this section concentrates on initiatives to increase the participation of 'intermediate' voters. In his analysis of Labour's problems, Phillips laid great stress on the fact that Labour was ceasing to be a 'mirror of the nation at work', owing to the relative lack of non-manual workers in its ranks.[69] This imperative dominated after 1959 and was underlined by the spectacular Liberal 1962 by-election victory in the Conservative stronghold of Orpington, which suggested that even suburban voters disenchanted with Macmillan's government were resistant to Labour's charms.[70]

To encourage activists to help change Labour's image, and make local parties more attractive to non-manual workers, a national competition was established in 1961 to improve the appearance of constituency offices. Members were asked whether passers-by would, 'from looking at YOUR premises, get the idea that Labour is finished, down at heel, out of date, or do they get an impression of a modern forward looking Party, clean, efficient and belonging to the space age?'[71] Officials urged activists to hold special meetings for doctors, teachers and managers in what they supposed would be amenable surroundings, like hotels, where cocktails might be served.[72] Opposition to these proposals was not necessarily due to politics: left-wingers were not averse to attracting middle-class supporters so long as this was not accompanied by any watering down of policy.[73] Some hostility, though, was due to cultural prejudice, so that in the eyes of one agent, 'petty bourgeois wine bibbing' appeared 'a load of gimmick-dressed tripe'.[74]

Officials initially hoped the unions would help them attract more white-collar members. Yet discussions held in Transport House during 1961 with eleven non-manual workers' unions affiliated to the party were inconclusive: few were prepared to make a special effort.[75] In light of that, Labour would have to approach such workers not as trade unionists but as individual voters.[76] One possible means was revealed during Tony Benn's campaign to remain an MP after being forcibly elevated to the Lords after the death in 1960 of his father, who happened to be a hereditary peer. This saw Labour in his Bristol South East constituency tap into support normally beyond its reach and raised questions in Benn's mind about how Labour nationally could attract 'progressive' members of the middle class.[77] Benn and others believed the Bristol experience – as well as that of the Democrats in the United States – showed the advantages of establishing a more flexible organis-ation he called 'Citizens for Labour'. He hoped to create the category of 'associate member', which would allow individuals to avoid being a full party member but would encourage them to donate their cash and help at election time.

Considering his own CLP 'effectively dead', Benn believed his scheme would help create 'a more or less new Party which can somehow be latched on to the old one'.[78] While a party on the left – which in 1960 called for Gaitskell's resignation – Bristol South East was run by a small aged coterie of about fifteen activists whose secretary had been in the party since 1918. GMC meetings rarely involved policy debates – unless Benn was present, which, as a busy MP with wider responsibilities within the national Labour Party, he rarely was. When it was suggested they should have speakers to promote discussions the proposal was rejected ostensibly because, as so few attended GMC meetings, it was not worth the effort.[79]

Benn's scheme required the permission of the NEC. Despite the fact that in 1929 the NEC had proposed a similar scheme, members of the

Organisation Sub-committee (OSC) thought it dangerously novel and, after what Benn described as an 'appalling row', refused to endorse it.[80] The majority felt associate membership would leave Labour's basic problems untouched, as it would not challenge the control of 'small cliques of full members', who dominated too many local parties. Instead, Labour needed to bring new groups into full membership so they could change the organisation from within. In fact, the OSC mainly reproduced objections to a not dissimilar proposal aired in the wake of Labour's 1955 defeat.[81] Undeterred, Benn put his case to the Sub-committee again. Despite the shadow Cabinet minister Ray Gunter warning of its 'subversive' potential, this time the NEC allowed Benn to launch Citizens for Labour, although only on an experimental basis in Bristol South East.[82] Transport House officials remained doubtful. Sara Barker, the National Agent, thought there were too few activists to develop such informal arrangements: above all else, Labour needed more active members.[83]

Few in Benn's local party believed in the scheme. While endorsing Citizens for Labour in the MP's presence, the GMC was unwilling to take it seriously in his absence. From the start some believed they should oppose 'anything out-of-line with general thinking'. Unfortunately for Benn, the NEC stipulated the CLP had to form a sub-committee drawn from GMC members to supervise the initiative, so it remained firmly under activists' control.[84] It was therefore no surprise that it made little impression. Local activists also opposed Benn's other initiative of this period, the New Bristol Group, which was again founded in the wake of his campaign to stay in the Commons. The aim of this body was to bring together those the MP termed 'thoughtful people' to stimulate debate about the city's problems. The extent to which his GMC looked with disfavour on the Group was reflected in its endorsement of the city council's decision to prevent libraries stocking its publications.[85]

'Let's Go!'

Attempts to make CLPs more attractive to non-manual workers largely foundered, but more headway was made centrally in improving the party's image. In 1961 the NEC established the Campaign Sub-committee to take command of the party's election preparations.[86] This took note of surveys conducted by Abrams, all of which underlined the importance of projecting Labour as a 'classless' organisation that was representative of the interests of the entire working population. The main result of this work was a £100,000 advertising campaign, which ran during the second half of 1963, the main purpose of which was to convince affluent voters that Labour could improve their standards of living. Its basic message was summed up in the first press advertisement, which comprised a large picture of the Labour leader and a brief explanation of the party's case, under the legend, 'Harold Wilson explains Labour's New Plans for making Britain Dynamic and Prosperous Again'.[87]

As affluent voters were supposed to decide how to vote on the basis of 'impressions and instincts', it was 'their idea of what kind of party' Labour was that mattered. Thus, the campaign was thought to require a phrase and symbol to encapsulate what Labour stood for. After some debate, a supposedly cheerful thumbs-up sign accompanied by the slogan 'Let's Go with Labour and we'll get things done' became the favoured devices. Some found them distasteful. When the 'Let's Go' campaign was launched, Pannell confided to his Leeds members, 'I am afraid we will have to do it that way' to win over the 'soft south', that is, inhabitants of 'rootless constituencies – those places without collective memory which have sprung up over night with no long civic tradition'.[88] Even worse, from Pannell's perspective, Transport House encouraged Labour mothers to put 'Let's Go' badges on their children; there was also 'Let's Go' window posters, envelope and car stickers – in Doncaster activists even held a 'Let's Go' balloon race.[89]

Wilson's reference to 'white heat' during his 1963 conference speech was designed to complement this work. Although his emphasis on the 'scientific revolution' appeared to distinguish the Labour leader from his late predecessor, others had called for the party to associate itself with science some years before.[90] If any one person was responsible for Labour's invocation of science, it was Morgan Phillips – although he owed much to the unacknowledged help of Richard Crossman and Peter Shore.[91] Phillips initially hoped science would draw members away from their disagreements over clause four – only later on did it appear an important means of signifying the party's modernity.[92] With these objects in mind, in July 1960 Phillips presented to the NEC a document entitled 'The state of the party', which: was subsequently expanded and given the more optimistic title of 'The future of the party'; eventually became *Labour in the Sixties*; was elaborated into the pamphlet series *Signposts for the Sixties*; and finally formed the basis for Labour's 1964 manifesto.

The NEC commended *Labour in the Sixties* to the 1960 conference, although it did not, as was customary with such documents, endorse it. Instead, it was designated as 'the work of the General Secretary', an unusual formula, the result of Gaitskellites and their left-wing opponents being initially unable to agree on its merits.[93] Introducing it, on behalf of an ill Phillips, Ray Gunter told delegates that its intention was to 'project our thoughts away' from internal disputes. In anticipation of Wilson's speech three years later, he affirmed that 'never in history have Socialist principles been more relevant than they are in the 60s', owing to the need for the state to direct scientific developments. Wilson in fact closed the debate by hoping the document marked the end of 'sterile' arguments over nationalisation and would help Labour face the future rather than dwell on the past.[94] If most on the left saw it as marking a welcome move from revisionism, at least one conference delegate, from Toxteth, considered the document so 'obviously intended to attract middle-class votes' that it should be renamed *Signposts for the Right*.[95]

What the leadership hoped would be a reforging of Labour's image went hand in hand with the projection of Wilson, for the successful dramatisation of Macmillan's supposed traits was thought to have been one of the reasons for the Conservative 1959 victory. So far as affluent voters went, Labour's image needed personification and this was obviously to be achieved through the leader.[96] In this process even Michael Foot played a part, penning a hagiography of Wilson during the run-up to the 1964 campaign. These efforts were undoubtedly helped by the fact that, by 1963, Macmillan was widely regarded as 'old, effete, worn out'. Labour strategists could not believe their luck when he was replaced in 1963 by the epitome of upper-class languor, Sir Alec Douglas-Home.[97]

While Labour's approach was established before Wilson's election as leader, he made it his own in a series of speeches delivered between January and April 1964.[98] These took as their theme the hope for a 'New Britain', which deliberately echoed the late President Kennedy's 'New Frontier' rhetoric. Wilson linked the economy's by now obvious decline (relative to the faster-growing French, German and Japanese economies) to the failure of the aristocratic Conservatives fully to utilise the talents of skilled manual and non-manual workers. As he suggested in 1963:

> We need a shake-up in industry. There's still too much dead-wood – too many directors sitting in boardrooms not because they can produce or sell, but because of their family background. To make industry dynamic we need vigorous young executives, scientists and sales experts chosen for their abilities – not their connections.[99]

Wilson's contention was that the Conservatives, by their very nature, were unable and unwilling to accomplish this task because theirs was a sectional party that identified with those who made money by speculation, not with those who earned it through work. A Labour government would use state planning to encourage industrial modernisation and thereby represent the 'thrusting ability, even iconoclasm' of grammar and comprehensive school pupils. It would also remove impediments to initiative endured by scientists, technicians, artisans and skilled workers. While the Conservatives allowed 'the spiv, the speculator, the take-over bidder, the tax evader, the land grabber' to prosper, Wilson promised Labour would promote 'the useful people', 'who earn money by useful service to the community'.

Only Labour, Wilson claimed, could liberate the energies of 'the useful people' and grant them the status they deserved. In so doing, Wilson was, as he admitted, 'making myself acceptable to the suburbs'.[100] Indeed, such was the fear of being exclusively linked with 'traditional' working-class concerns that, during the 1964 campaign, a Labour official bemoaned a *Daily Mirror* 'shock issue' on housing because it associated the party with slums.[101] This national emphasis was echoed in numerous local campaigns. In marginal Rugby, for example, Labour tried to appeal to young professionals by ensuring its candidate, a university lecturer, was 'pushed as a young technocrat and the word DOCTOR was pushed on every occasion'.[102] In marginal Berwick the candidate, John Mackintosh – coincidentally another university lecturer – also echoed Wilson's rhetoric by suggesting that the Conservatives could not appreciate ordinary people's problems because they 'live in country houses or Mayfair'.[103]

Complementing this focus, strategists tried to address what they took to be women's concerns by underlining domestic issues. In particular, one internal discussion paper asserted that prosperity was 'nowhere more deeply felt than in the home'. Moreover, it went on, 'home to the housewife, irrespective of whether she goes out to work or merely remains at home, is the focal point of her life'. In such women's lives a 'new house (Council or private), a family car, a television, an electric washer, cooker, and perhaps even a "frig", predominate'. Moreover, if a young housewife did not possess such things, she 'aspires to do so as quickly as possible, and the "telly" is a daily reminder that life is not complete without them'.[104] With that in mind, the party largely talked to women as consumers, which entailed a particular emphasis on the cost of living. As one delegate to the 1967 national conference of Labour women stated, 'all women were aggressive on the question of prices', in comparison with which other issues 'faded into insignificance'.[105] Women's dependence on a male breadwinner was taken for granted: even one Labour woman defined the female electorate as consisting of 'the wives, the mothers, the widows, the sweethearts'.[106] The party also assiduously appealed to them as mothers; one leaflet issued before the 1964 election, on which appeared a photograph of two children, simply urged women to 'Vote for Them'. Echoing the themes of 1959, they were exhorted to support Labour because it offered a 'new deal for the family' that focused on housing, education for children, improving pensions and provision for widows. By this time, however, there was a greater emphasis on the workplace: the promises to introduce equal pay and to improve nursery facilities for working mothers were both highlighted.[107]

Despite this frenetic activity, the substance of Labour's 1964 programme was strikingly similar to that of 1959. Only a few industries were to be nationalised; and the party's main aim was to promote expansion to the benefit of all, but most especially those in greatest need, who would gain from more welfare spending. Labour was asserted to be the party of all the people – as opposed to the sectional Conservatives. While suffused with a self-conscious modernity, Wilson's rhetoric betrayed a more fundamental continuity of approach. His reference to the 'useful people' could have been taken from speeches delivered by Herbert Morrison during the 1940s; indeed, the juxtaposition of 'unproductive' with 'productive' labour would have been familiar to any eighteenth-century radical. Wilson's emphasis on the need for hard work to increase productivity also had a 1940s tinge to it: implicitly at least it stood as a criticism of what many Labour members took to be a morally dubious affluent society in which easy money took precedence.

Impact

On 16 October 1964, Harold Wilson entered Downing Street as Prime Minister. While cause for celebration, Labour's victory was slender in terms of seats – it won a Commons majority of but four – and based on the share of votes cast, only 0.3 per cent higher and 10,000 votes fewer than in 1959.

The 1964 result was due more to the collapse of Conservative strength rather than any Labour recovery, the main beneficiary being the Liberal Party. The government had been unable to restore its authority after the Profumo scandal and Macmillan's failure to take Britain into the Common Market. Moreover, it was increasingly apparent that the relative performance of the British economy was unimpressive, as other countries were beginning to catch up. As a result, some suggest, there was a change in the national mood, from the optimism of the late 1950s to a pervasive cynicism, which undermined support for the governing party.[108] Yet the Conservatives still presided over rising standards of living after 1959, even if the rate of increase had slackened. On the eve of the campaign, 47 per cent of those asked by Gallup still considered the Conservatives the better able to maintain prosperity, as opposed to only 34 per cent who thought the task better entrusted to Labour.[109] It appears that while Labour was seen to be more sympathetic to the needs of voters, it was still thought less economically competent than the Conservatives.[110]

Detailed evidence for the effectiveness of Labour's post-1959 strategy is limited but suggests strategists were not entirely successful in their efforts (see Table 3.1, p. 63). Labour increased its support among the middle classes but lost substantially among the 'very poor' and marginally so among the working class. Given that Labour's campaign concentrated on affluent voters, this was perhaps to be expected. More surprisingly, in terms of age, the party made no measurable gains in any category – even among those in their twenties – while significant losses were registered among those over sixty-five years old, possibly because Labour did not stress pensions to the same degree as 1959. Similarly, with male voters the gains were marginal, while, despite its greater emphasis on women voters, the party had lost female support.

Even though it showed little immediate return for Labour's attempt to alter voters' perceptions, Conservative research discovered that by 1964 Labour was at least considered the more 'modern' of the two parties.[111] More impressionistic still, during the campaign the *Sun* newspaper asked first-time voters to explain why they favoured a particular party. By no means all chose Labour, but a clear majority of letters published did: given the *Sun*'s pro-Wilson inclination, this was no revelation. Even so, the reasons proffered revealed the extent to which Wilson's rhetoric made an impact on younger electors. One correspondent, for example, stated he would vote Labour as 'I believe a vast amount of talent and energy, especially among the young, will be released if we give Labour a chance to make a new Britain'. Another suggested that, under Wilson, 'the Britain of the future shall be a classless one, where all petty snobbisms of accent, dress, education will be defunct … [it will be] a society which seeks to harness the talents of all in the best possible manner'. A third reader stated, 'I shall vote for the party of teachers and trained economists, the Labour Party; not the party of company directors and blimps'.[112] At least in relation to that minority of young voters in the habit of writing letters to national newspapers, Labour left some sort of mark.

While Prime Minister, Wilson tried to build on the party's efforts after 1959 by showing that Labour was both economically responsible and able to live up to its spending promises.[113] The result was what many considered Labour's landslide victory of 1966, a performance the junior minister Tony Benn thought indicated it was on the verge of becoming 'a truly national party'.[114] Gallup's findings suggest there was some merit to this claim, for Labour's 1964 gains among the better-off classes were sustained, while support from the working class and poor rose markedly – as it did among both genders and all age groups (see Table 3.1, p. 63). Academic analysts now speculated that Labour was set to enjoy a prolonged period in office; in fact, because of the weight they gave parental influence over voter allegiance, some suggested that the Conservatives – lauded in 1959 as the 'normal' majority party – were in danger of remaining out of office in perpetuity.[115]

Labour's re-election was, in contrast, taken very calmly at Transport House. The official report on the campaign was remarkably pessimistic

but, as it turned out, prescient. The report identified the 'most significant feature' of the 1966 contest as the drop in turnout, from 77.1
per cent in 1964 to 75.8 per cent. Moreover, the report also found it
worrying that the loss of two million Conservative voters since 1959
had been accompanied by only an 800,000 rise in Labour's poll. Given
the party's failure to pick up a majority of Conservative losses, that
many of the votes given to Liberals in 1964 went to Labour only because
fewer Liberal candidates stood in 1966, and that twenty-five seats were
won on a minority of the poll, the report firmly denied 1966 was anything like an 'overwhelming landslide'.[116] Victory certainly did not mean
Labour's organisational foundations were any less fragile than in 1959,
for it was still unable to attract the participation of many women, the
young or non-manual workers; existing activists remained too few in
number, too ignorant of policy and procedure, and in need of more
professional help.[117] Despite appearances, Labour's 'landslide' victory
did not mean anything had changed since 1959.

Notes

The place of publication is London unless otherwise specified.

1 Some of the material contained in this chapter has appeared in '"White
   heat" and white collars: the evolution of "Wilsonism"', in R. Coopey, S.
   Fielding and N. Tiratsoo (eds), *The Wilson Governments, 1964–70* (1993).
2 *Socialist Commentary*, November 1963, pp. 3, 12; and *Tribune*, 4 October
   1963.
3 D. E. Butler and R. Rose, *The British General Election of 1959* (1960), pp.
   196–201.
4 This account is based on P. M. Williams, *Hugh Gaitskell* (Oxford, 1982),
   pp. 299–313; B. Brivati, *Hugh Gaitskell* (1996), pp. 306–29; and Butler and
   Rose, *1959*.
5 Labour Party Archive (LPA), NEC minutes, 28 October 1959; National
   Labour Women's Advisory Committee minutes, 5 November 1959 and 4
   February 1960, Women's organisation and activities, p. 1; *Labour Organiser*,
   38:499 (1959), pp. 211–12; London Metropolitan Archive (LMA), J. W.
   Raisin papers, Acc 2783/JWR/OA/2, R. Butterworth, Employment in the
   Northern Home Counties Region, conference for full-time agents, 26–28
   April 1960.
6 Modern Records Centre (MRC), Labour Party East Midlands Region
   papers, MSS 9/3/79, reports on the 1959 campaign.
7 Bristol Record Office (BRO), Bristol South East CLP papers, 38423/48,
   H. Rogers, Parliamentary election, 8 October 1959 and 5 November 1959.
8 Bodleian Library, Conservative Party Archive (CPA), CCO 4/8/107, Northern
   Area, Review of the general election campaign, 1959, and South Eastern
   Area, Report on the general election, 1959.
9 CPA, CCO 500/9/9/1/2, General election 1959, The organisation and the
   future – notes for discussion, 12 December 1959.
10 East Midlands Region papers, MSS 9/3/79, East Midlands Regional Council

Executive Committee minutes, 17 October 1959; CPA, CCO 4/8/107; J. Trenaman and D. McQuail, *Television and the Political Image* (1961).

11 R. Jenkins, *The Labour Case* (Harmondsworth, 1959), p. 135.

12 Labour Party, *Housewives' Choice* (1959).

13 Labour Party, *The Britain We Want* (1959), pp. 8–9.

14 *Report of the Thirty-Sixth National Conference of Labour Women* (1959), p. 20.

15 Butler and Rose, *1959*, pp. 199–201; M. Abrams, R. Rose and R. Hinden, *Must Labour Lose?* (Harmondsworth, 1960).

16 British Library of Political and Economic Science (BLPES), Anthony Crosland papers, 13/23, paper for the 'Problems Ahead' conference, 14–15 October 1950. This was subsequently published as 'The transition from capitalism', in R. Crossman (ed.), *New Fabian Essays* (1952).

17 *Socialist Commentary*, November 1951, pp. 246–7.

18 LMA, *London News*, January 1956.

19 This account is based on T. Benn, *Years of Hope. Diaries, Papers and Letters 1940–1962* (1994), pp. 317–19; T. Jones, *Remaking the Labour Party* (1996); Brivati, *Gaitskell*, pp. 330–48; Williams, *Gaitskell*, pp. 314–34.

20 *Report of the Fifty-Eighth Annual Conference of the Labour Party* (1959), pp. 105–14.

21 LPA, NEC Home Policy Sub-committee (HPSC) minutes, 11 January 1960; and Williams, *Gaitskell*, pp. 329–30.

22 J. M. Bochel, 'Activists in the Conservative and Labour parties. A study of ward secretaries in Manchester', MA thesis, University of Manchester (1965), pp. 140–2. More generally see Jones, *Remaking*, pp. 1–24.

23 *Report of the Fifty-Fifth Annual Conference of the Labour Party* (1956), p. 171; LPA, Morgan Phillips papers, GS/CMR/95, Secretary's Department to Eagles, 8 November 1957.

24 F. Bealey, J. Blondel and W. P. McCann, *Constituency Politics* (1965), pp. 271–2, 283.

25 *Report of the Fifty-Ninth Annual Conference of the Labour Party* (1960), p. 12.

26 West Yorkshire Archive, City of Bradford Labour Party, Bradford East CLP minutes, 12 April 1960; MRC, Frank Cousins papers, MSS 282/TBN 13, notebook, 26 March 1960.

27 Crosland papers, 6/1, Crosland to Gaitskell, November 1960.

28 S. Fielding, 'Labourism in the 1940s', *Twentieth Century British History*, 3:2 (1992).

29 LPA, *Romford, Hornchurch and Brentwood Labour Voice*, mid-November 1951.

30 BLPES, Bedford CLP papers, 1/5A, GMC minutes, 12 February 1953; Warrington Local Studies Library, *Warrington and District Labour News*, 3 January 1953.

31 LPA, Bob Edwards papers, BE/EL/1955, Box 4, Personal files, General election 1955.

32 LPA, Judith Hart papers, Section 1, File 1 (ii), speech to selection meeting, Lanark, 1957.

33 LPA, *Barons Court Citizen*, July 1959; *Report of the Thirty-Sixth National Conference of Labour Women* (1959), pp. 8, 10–11, 19.

34 BRO, Labour Party South West Region papers, 10/3, G. Care, application for a Laski Memorial Scholarship, April 1963.

35 House of Lords Record Office (HLRO), Reginald Sorenson papers, Hist. Coll. 102/230, A backbencher's pilgrimage, 1968, pp. 245, 403.

36 BLPES, North Kensington CLP papers, *North Kensington Labour Questionmaster*, April 1955.

37 G. McClymont, '"A squalid raffle"? Labour, affluence and the introduction

of Premium Bonds, 1956', paper presented to the conference 'Affluent Britain?', Bristol University, May 2002.
38 *London News*, June 1958.
39 L. Manning, *A Life for Education* (1970), pp. 193, 195.
40 Bedford CLP papers, 1/12, GMC minutes, 8 June 1967.
41 *Focus*, 2 (1955), pp. 9–10.
42 *Tribune*, 28 December 1951.
43 J. Freeman, 'Labour's decline', *Focus*, 2 (1955), pp. 12–13.
44 *Fifty-Eighth Annual Conference of Labour*, p. 127; *Baron's Court Citizen*, November–December 1959.
45 National Library of Wales (NLW), Ron Evans papers, 5, Evans to Machray, 22 November 1959.
46 H. Jenkins, R. Lewis. G. Southgate and W. Wolfgang, 'The red sixties', *Victory for Socialism Pamphlet* (1957), pp. 7, 12.
47 S. Fielding, '"But westward, look, the land is bright!" Labour's revisionists and the imagining of America, c. 1945–64', in J. Hollowell (ed.), *Twentieth-Century Anglo-American Relations* (2001).
48 BLPES, Edgar Simpkins papers, MISC 0502, Folkestone 1959 general election scrapbook.
49 *Forward*, 28 October 1955.
50 R. H. S. Crossman, *Planning for Freedom* (1965), pp. 86–112.
51 *Labour Woman*, 48:5 (1960), p. 59; *Tribune*, 16 October 1959.
52 *Fifty-Eighth Annual Conference of Labour*, p. 122.
53 South West Region papers, 10/3, Cormack application.
54 MRC, Warwick and Leamington Spa CLP papers, MSS 133, Box 1, Annual report 1959.
55 *Labour Woman*, 47:9 (1959), p. 122.
56 South West Region papers, 38423/43, J. H. Knight, General election, 1959 report.
57 P. Shore, *The Real Nature of Conservatism* (1952), pp. 26–9.
58 *Fifty-Eighth Annual Conference of Labour*, pp. 126–7.
59 MRC, Maurice Edelman papers, MSS 125/3/Temp 5, Report by Maurice Edelman MP for the year ended 31 August 1960.
60 This account is based on C. A. R. Crosland, *The Conservative Enemy* (1962), pp. 116, 144–6, 149–50, 152, 157, 161–2. See also J. Pearson and G. Turner, *The Persuasion Industry* (1965) and R. Rose, *Influencing Voters* (1967).
61 HLRO, Charles Pannell papers, Hist. Coll. 124/ D1, *Leeds Weekly Citizen*, 20 November and 11 December 1959.
62 NEC minutes, 28 October 1959; HPSC minutes, 11 January 1960.
63 P. Crane, 'What's in a party image?', *Political Quarterly*, 30:3 (1959), pp. 233–5.
64 C. Rowland, 'Labour publicity', *Political Quarterly*, 31:3 (1960), pp. 349–50; and *Labour Organiser*, 39:458 (1960), pp. 147–8.
65 *Labour Organiser*, 42:488 (1963), p. 32.
66 *Labour Organiser*, 39:459 (1960), pp. 174–6; 39:462 (1960), pp. 225–6; and 41:486 (1962), pp. 225–6.
67 *Labour Organiser*, 42:489 (1963), p. 57.
68 M. Abrams, 'Opinion polls and party propaganda', *Public Opinion Quarterly*, 28:1 (1964), p. 16.
69 NEC minutes, 13 July 1960, The state of the party, Sec. No. 104, pp. 11–14.
70 K. Young, 'Orpington and the "Liberal revival"', in C. Cook and J. Ramsden (eds), *By-elections in British Politics* (1973).
71 *Labour Organiser*, 40:467 (1961), p. 95.

72 *Labour Organiser*, 40:463 (1961), p. 5; and 40:468 (1961), p. 109.
73 BLPES, Hugh Jenkins papers, 6/46, Trade unions and the middle classes, *c.* 1950.
74 *Labour Organiser*, 40:465 (1961), pp. 54.
75 NEC, Organisation Sub-committee (OSC) minutes, 14 February 1961, Meeting of representatives of non-manual workers' unions, NAD/21/2/61, and L. Williams, Preliminary meeting of non-manual workers' unions to be held on Thursday 9 February 1961; and 19 September 1961, Non-manual workers' unions and the Labour party, NAD/76/8/61; *Labour Organiser*, 40:467 (1961), pp. 83–5; *Tribune*, 23 October 1959; *Labour Woman*, 50:7 (1962), pp. 4–5.
76 HPSC minutes, 9 July 1962, Non-manual workers and the Labour party, RD 300.
77 Bristol South East CLP papers, 39035/133, H. E. Rogers, Parliamentary by-election, 4 May 1961, 29 May 1961.
78 T. Benn, *Out of the Wilderness. Diaries, 1963–67* (1987), pp. 136, 213.
79 Bristol South East CLP papers, 39035/47, GMC minutes, *passim* and 4 November 1965; 39035/21, Young Socialist minutes, 1 November 1960.
80 MRC, Socialist Vanguard Group papers, MSS 173, Box 5, Penny Farthing file, Benn to Hinden, 7 January 1965.
81 OSC minutes, 17 July 1962, The case against a smaller individual membership contribution and an associate membership, NAD/72/7/62.
82 OSC minutes, 18 September 1963; Benn, *Wilderness*, p. 65; South West Region papers, 38423/48, Benn to Rees, 9 December 1963.
83 OSC minutes, 18 November 1964, Support for the Labour Party, NAD/70/11/64.
84 Bristol South East CLP papers, 39035/21, GMC minutes, 12 December 1963 and 6 February 1964.
85 Bristol South East CLP papers, 39035/146, GMC minutes, 3 December 1964; New Bristol Group, *Output 1962/3* (1963), p. 2.
86 This account is based on LPA, Campaign Sub-committee (CSC) minutes, 22 January, 19 July and 19 December 1962, and 11 March and 13 May 1963; Labour Party, *'Let's Go' Campaign Guide* (1963); *Socialist Commentary*, July 1963, pp. 10–12; *Labour Organiser*, 42:493 (1963), pp. 130–2; and *New Society*, 6 June 1963.
87 *Daily Mirror*, 21 May 1963.
88 Pannell papers, Hist. Coll. 124/ D3, *Leeds Weekly Citizen*, 27 April 1962 and 31 May 1963.
89 *Labour Organiser*, 42:491 (1963), p. 90; 42:492 (1963), pp. 107–8; 42:496 (1963), pp. 186–8 and 195–6; 43:499 (1964), p. 9; and *Labour Woman*, 51:6 (1963), p. 7.
90 *Forward*, 22 January 1960; Labour Party, *Science and the Future of Britain* (1961); A. Howard, *Crossman. The Pursuit of Power* (1990), p. 248.
91 J. Morgan (ed.), *The Backbench Diaries of Richard Crossman* (1981), pp. 860–1.
92 LPA, Publicity and Political Education Sub-committee minutes, 20 June 1960.
93 NEC minutes, 27 July 1960.
94 *Report of the Fifty-Ninth Annual Conference of the Labour Party* (1960), pp. 133–4, 149.
95 *Report of the Sixtieth Annual Conference of the Labour Party* (1961), pp. 129–30.
96 Abrams, 'Opinion polls', p. 17.
97 Benn, *Wilderness*, p. 70.
98 Unless otherwise stated, references for the next three paragraphs are taken from H. Wilson, *The New Britain* (Harmondsworth, 1964).

99 *National Union of Sheet Metal Workers and Coppersmiths Quarterly Journal*, July 1963, pp. 25–6.

100 A. Watkins, 'Labour in power', in G. Kaufman (ed.), *The Left* (1966), p. 176.

101 R. West, 'Campaign journal', *Encounter*, December 1964, p. 19.

102 MRC, Rugby CLP papers, MSS 10/3/7/39/1, R. Page, General election 1964.

103 National Library of Scotland, John P. Mackintosh papers, Dep 323/70, Notes for Dunbar meeting, 30 January 1964.

104 Calderdale Archives, Halifax CLP papers, TU: 28/16, Miscellaneous correspondence, 1959–60, Yorkshire Regional Office of the Labour Party, Report on Women's Organisation for consideration at special meetings of Women's Advisory Councils with the Chief Woman Officer on 13, 14 and 15 January 1960, January 1960.

105 *Report of the Forty-Fourth National Conference of Labour Women* (1967), p. 43.

106 *Report of the Forty-First National Conference of Labour Women* (1964), pp. 11, 14.

107 Labour Party, *Let's Have a Party That Will Get Things Done* (1963), and *Vote for Them* (1964).

108 D. Butler and A. King, *The British General Election of 1964* (1965), pp. 30–4, 97 and 145.

109 G. H. Gallup, *The Gallup International Public Opinion Polls. Great Britain, 1937–75. Volume I* (New York, 1976), p. 768.

110 CSC minutes, 13 May 1963.

111 CPA, 180/11/2/1, Thomson Organisation, 'Voters and the 1964 general election', March 1964.

112 *Sun*, 30 September, 2 and 6 October 1964.

113 For this period, see in particular E. Short, *Whip to Wilson* (1989).

114 Benn, *Wilderness*, p. 399.

115 Butler and Rose, *1959*, p. 197; D. Butler and A. King, *The British General Election of 1966* (1966), pp. ix and 267–9.

116 HPSC minutes, 11 July 1966, The 1966 general election, re 20 July 1966.

117 NEC minutes, SEC/22/7/66, 26 October 1966, Party organisation.

4

Reconciling the classes

Many contemporaries were convinced that by the 1960s class barriers
had been at least attenuated compared with the 1930s. The children of
manual workers were believed to be better able to enter the middle
class; and it was thought that many of those remaining on the factory
floor were adopting bourgeois ways. Labour members appeared more
divided over this issue than they actually were. While the left considered
'affluence' made only a modest impact on the social structure and
revisionists thought its influence profound, few denied Britain remained
a society tainted by class. In 1956, Labour's conference approved *Towards
Equality*, a document broadly in tune with revisionist thinking and which
confirmed the existence of 'a strong, persistent trend towards economic
and social inequality'.[1] Even Anthony Crosland, who in the same year
predicted that 'primary poverty' (i.e. insufficient incomes) would disappear by the mid-1960s, still considered inequality a serious problem
that only government action could finally eradicate.[2] A key element in
Labour's solution to the persistence of class differences was the fostering
of a common culture based on co-operation rather than conflict. This
chapter looks at secondary education and industrial democracy to assess
how Harold Wilson's governments tried to promote this culture – and
why they failed.

If Labour derived most of its electoral support from manual workers
and was dependent on trade union money, it was not a class party in
the Marxist sense. The desirability of promoting an identity other than
one based on class had inspired much Labour thinking since at least
Ramsay MacDonald's day. Accordingly, Reginald Sorenson, MP for
Leyton until elevated to the Lords in 1965, believed that, whatever a
person's class, all were 'members of a common humanity' and needed
to nourish what the poet William Blake referred to as 'Mercy, Pity, Peace
and Love' or succumb to 'lethal enmities'.[3] Similarly, Norman Willis, a
young activist in Surrey – and incidentally a future General Secretary of
the Trades Union Congress (TUC) – conceived of socialism as a society
in which 'people really feel a sense of identity between themselves and

their neighbours'.[4] More pertinently, Wilson's appeal to the 'useful people' (see Chapter 3) proceeded from the assumption that the working and middle classes shared a common economic interest, against which their other differences paled.

Towards Equality confirmed Labour's commitment to reduce inequality through 'deliberate and continuous State intervention'.[5] For many on the left, this meant ensuring the economy was dominated by the state. So far as the leadership was concerned, however, nationalisation was less important than maintaining full employment, increasing taxes on unearned wealth, creating a more generous welfare system and, most crucially, accelerating economic growth. While this did not imply totally abolishing income inequality, it nonetheless required establishing a 'decent' minimum income and ensuring differentials reflected the nature of the work undertaken.[6] If confident their policies would promote a greater equality of outcome, revisionists still believed the party needed to take further steps to increase equality of opportunity, for, despite rising incomes, only the fortunate few were exploiting their full potential. Hugh Gaitskell, for one, considered a society where class origin determined opportunity and in which there were 'feelings or attitudes of superiority or inferiority between groups' could not be considered egalitarian.[7] So far as revisionists – and others in the party for that matter – were concerned, this meant focusing on culture as much as on the economy, in particular ending segregated secondary education.

If most Labour members agreed that education needed reform, a similar consensus was lacking over how to establish workplace harmony.[8] Despite rising incomes, Britain's industrial relations record suggested the point of production remained the main venue for class conflict. Indeed, soon after Wilson entered Downing Street, class feeling – as measured in terms of number of strikes – increased. Industrial democracy appeared a possible solution, as it was hoped it would improve workers' status, help them develop their own potential and promote co-operation. However, while it appeared to some to be a panacea, it raised awkward and fundamental questions that Labour was unable to resolve. While all in the party aspired to create a more peaceful industrial scene, members were seriously at odds regarding on whose basis – the employers' or the unions' – co-operation should proceed.

Stopping snobbery

As the junior education minister Alice Bacon declared in 1969, Labour believed education was 'not only the means of individual development, but an instrument for the creation of a better society'.[9] The 1964 manifesto promised a 'revolution in our educational system' that would:

reduce class sizes; raise the school-leaving age from fifteen to sixteen years; improve technical training; and increase the number of places in higher education. The main emphasis was, however, on reforming second-ary education, in particular abolishing segregated schooling. Labour's overall aim was to equalise opportunities, to improve individual attain-ment and to increase economic output, as it was asserted that a fairer society would be more productive.[10]

The 1945–51 Labour governments had applied the 1944 Education Act (passed by the wartime coalition) because it enshrined the principle of universal free secondary education.[11] Hitherto, those who had won entry to grammar school by taking a competitive examination at the age of ten were expected to pay a variety of costs: this impeded the progress of working-class children. So long as all children of talent could win free places in grammar schools, most members were little troubled by the fact that they continued to be separated by examination, with at most 20 per cent going to grammar schools and the rest entering secondary modern schools. Even so, Labour was formally committed to experimenting with 'common' or comprehensive schools that transcended the grammar–secondary-modern divide. If ministers were uninterested in innovation, Labour-controlled local authorities in places such as London and Coventry built comprehensives. Subsequent investigations also revealed the system established after 1945 was not as fair as some thought, because middle-class offspring dominated grammar schools owing to advantages imbued by family background rather than innate intelligence.[12]

After 1951, support grew for a change to party policy and by 1955 Labour was committed to actively promoting comprehensive educa-tion.[13] The extent to which this shift was based, as Labour's then deputy leader James Griffiths claimed, on an empirical assessment of the edu-cational system's defects is moot.[14] Michael Stewart and Margaret Cole – leading party thinkers on this subject – certainly believed most members did not object to ten-year-olds being examined but strongly opposed their segregation.[15] *Towards Equality* had also stressed the social harm done to children educated in separate institutions, and concluded that it was incompatible with a classless society.[16] It was not until 1970 that conference delegates expressed interest in how children were taught in the new schools. Even then, their concern was mostly limited to the fact that they often streamed pupils along academic lines, meaning children were still taught in groups differentiated by background.[17]

Most of the arguments members used to convince each other of the merits of comprehensive schooling therefore relied on social criteria: a 1953 headline in *London News* even dubbed them 'Schools to Stop Snobbery'.[18] As one Abingdon alderman put it, in a comprehensive school, children of '[a]ll levels of intelligence play games together, join the same school clubs and eat together' and were subject to the 'same standards of behaviour, manners and social responses'.[19] Members in North Kensington were urged to support comprehensives because 'if everybody, whatever job they were to perform later in life' were educated together, they would enjoy a 'common social and cultural background' and create 'a happier, more united and less class conscious nation'.[20] A comprehensive, members of a 1957 National Executive Committee (NEC) Study Group on Education believed, could 'benefit both bright and less bright children' by acting as a 'useful focus' for the growth of 'community spirit'.[21]

While some local Labour authorities promoted comprehensives, most remained loyal to grammars, which still retained popular support. In the late 1950s, a Transport House survey revealed that only a small minority of parents questioned the educational status quo; however, while no more than 10 per cent believed selection undesirable, once the case for comprehensives was put, over half wanted reform.[22] The party's argument in favour of comprehensives was consequently tailored to win over doubters by stressing the unfairness of selection while guaranteeing that the standards established by grammar schools would be maintained. Writing in 1964, one Bristol activist acknowledged that grammar schools had a fine tradition but argued that comprehensive schools would provide 'an education in tune with the democratic 1960's which allows every child to fully develop his talents'.[23] The impression that class division was already weakening possibly helped the party make its case, for it was argued at its 1967 annual conference that segregation maintained 'rigid and unjust divisions' at a time when 'social barriers should be crumbling'.[24]

Even so, members remained at odds over the issue, with some activists complaining that it was not just Conservatives who opposed comprehensives: their own local representatives could be equally 'backward'.[25] The nature of the division was highlighted during 1966 in the columns of Warwick and Leamington Spa's constituency magazine. This contained an article praising comprehensives for encouraging the spirit of co-operation and mutual respect and so showing society a way of escaping the 'jungle of capitalism'. That view was criticised by a lifelong member who believed comprehensives denied the hereditary basis to education, for if middle-class children won grammar places it was because they were 'innately more clever' than the rest. While 'it would be very nice if the mental inferiority of working-class children could all be explained away', this member believed it could not.[26]

The Wilson governments' move towards a national comprehensive system was slower than enthusiasts demanded.[27] Crosland's personal dedication to reform while he was at the Department for Education, however, should not be doubted: as he announced to his wife, even if it was 'the last thing I do, I'm going to destroy every fucking grammar school in England. And Wales. And Northern Ireland'.[28] Crosland was mistaken about Northern Ireland, as his remit did not run there; and nor did it extend to Scotland. Moreover, while mostly funded by central government, education in England and Wales was the responsibility of 163 local education authorities. Without altering that relationship, Crosland could not impose his will directly. Thus, in July 1965 he only requested authorities submit plans for the reorganisation of education along comprehensive lines. Much was done to encourage reluctant authorities to toe the line. A year later he announced that only those authorities committed to comprehensive education would be granted funds to build new schools. This, at least, accorded with party policy as articulated by the earlier NEC Study Group on Education, which determined that comprehensives should develop according to 'local wishes and circumstances'. On that basis the Group calculated it would take at least fifteen years for the comprehensive system to become universal.[29]

Only a few authorities refused to adhere to Crosland's request, but he nonetheless sought compulsory powers.[30] This was partly for political reasons. Such had been the transformation in attitudes to comprehensive schools that Labour strategists thought there were electoral advantages in forcing authorities to abide by government policy. They believed this would appeal particularly to middle-class parents living under rebel Conservative authorities, as they could ill-afford to send children who had flunked the grammar entrance examination to fee-paying schools (on which, see below).[31] Thus, when Wilson announced the date of the 1970 general election, legislation was in process to force authorities to adhere to the comprehensive principle. Even without that power, government had accelerated the move from selection, so that if 10 per cent of children were educated in comprehensives in 1964 by 1970 nearer one-third were. This proportion was guaranteed to rise, as most authorities had established a comprehensive system or had imminent plans to do so.

Playgrounds for plutocrats

The private sector comprised two different kinds of educational establishment: those termed 'public', whose intake was determined by the ability to pay; and what were described as 'grant maintained', which, in return for setting aside one-quarter of places to non-fee-payers, received a government subsidy. By June 1970, Labour had done nothing of substance to reduce their influence, despite Crosland considering it was the 'greatest single cause of stratification and class-consciousness in Britain'.[32]

Although private schools had long been thought inimical to socialism, Clement Attlee's ministers left them alone, with a few openly expressing their admiration for the education they provided. Even most reformers called only for a minority of public school places to be made available to non-fee-payers.[33] As with comprehensives, after 1951 the leadership showed a greater determination to challenge the status quo, with revisionists taking a lead. In 1953 Gaitskell went so far as to urge the next Labour government to ensure that a majority of public school places were immediately made free and to abolish all fee-paying soon thereafter.[34] Revisionists did not want to destroy private schools but sought to integrate them within the state sector. This meant they favoured change through agreement – which Crosland thought possible, if only because many private teachers felt guilty about perpetuating privilege.[35] In contrast, while agreeing with their leaders' ends, most who spoke on the subject at Labour conferences demanded instant abolition.

Despite the consensus over aims, and the fact that the NEC Study Group on Education confirmed that private education was 'repugnant' to party principles, Labour members could not agree how to approach reform in time for the 1959 general election.[36] With only a small minority favouring immediate abolition, the Group was initially inclined to stop grant maintained schools receiving state funds and to ensure that up to 75 per cent of public school places were opened to non-fee-payers. However, the former two proposals were thought politically dangerous and the latter raised an intractable issue, as it was unclear how non-fee-payers should be selected. Gaitskell supported the use of intelligence tests for selection, although others contended this would not prevent public schools remaining socially exclusive. Whatever the criteria, selection was incompatible with Labour's support for comprehensives and it was to avoid this contradiction that friendly experts advised the Group either to recommend immediate radical change or to leave private education alone. Crosland agreed, as he thought limited change would merely endow private education with greater legitimacy.[37] In any case, survey evidence indicated that voters broadly supported private schooling: 80 per cent – including a majority of the working class – claimed they would pay for their child's education if they could.[38] Thus, having toyed with reform, the Group recommended that no action be taken, and it asserted Labour should instead concentrate on increasing investment in state schools and transforming them into comprehensives. The professed aim was to raise the standard of state education so that it would equal that provided by the private sector.[39] Few thought this credible: Stewart and Cole calculated the former would need at least four decades to catch up with the latter.[40]

As part of the attempt to foster reconciliation within the party, *Signposts for the Sixties* embraced a radical approach to private education: it

committed Labour to establishing an educational trust that would determine how to integrate private schools into the state system.[41] As Bacon
characterised it, Labour entered the 1964 campaign aiming to turn
public schools from 'playgrounds for plutocrats into training grounds
for democrats'.[42] Labour's initially small majority encouraged Wilson
and Michael Stewart, his first Education Secretary, to tread with
caution.[43] When Crosland replaced Stewart, however, he won Cabinet
approval in November 1965 to establish a commission to make good
the promise made in *Signposts*. This body was instructed to see how
private schools could best be used 'to meet the needs of the nation'
while eliminating their 'divisive influence'. If some feared ministers were
wary of fundamental change, Crosland remained committed to making
at least 75 per cent of public school places open to non-fee-payers.[44]
Even that would have disappointed contributors to conference debates:
in 1967 the only speaker from the floor to advocate something other
than immediate abolition was the MP Robert Maxwell, who was severely
heckled for his trouble.[45]

After being turned down by his first five choices, Crosland secured
the services of Sir John Newsom to chair the commission. Newsom proved
ineffective and after much prevarication delivered but the first volume
of his report in the summer of 1968. This agreed that private schools
were divisive and that society would benefit if their pupils came from
more diverse backgrounds. However, while proposing that public schools
be deprived of their lucrative charitable status, the report did not pro-
pose bringing them within the state system. Moreover, much of the
report focused on altering the intake of pupil boarders, with the suggestion that up to half of boarding places should go to non-fee-payers.[46]
This eccentric emphasis failed to impress. Edward Short, Crosland's
successor, was disappointed, while Tony Benn described the report as
'ghastly': consequently the Cabinet agreed it should be published without comment, believing it best to await the final volume before drafting
legislation.[47]

Even had Newsom made a better fist of his commission, 1968 was an
inauspicious time for the government to take action: he called for spending on a few thousand children, while ministers had just delayed raising
the school-leaving age for state pupils, in order to accommodate post-
devaluation spending cuts. Endorsing the report would have further
alienated already disenchanted activists, while taking a more radical
line could have only reduced support among the middle class and made
little impact on working-class voters, at a moment when Labour was
losing elections at a record rate. Therefore, with NEC blessing, the 1968
conference rejected Newsom, with one delegate describing his proposal
for more government support but not control as 'a travesty of Socialist
principles'.[48]

The more radical David Donnison took responsibility for the second part of the commission's work and recommended the integration of grant maintained schools into a comprehensive state system. Unfortunately, his report was published in the run-up to the 1970 election and, as one member of the commission admitted, it threatened to antagonise middle-class parents, whose children were the main beneficiaries of free places.[49] Once again, this was not the best of times to discuss a matter that could only lose Labour support; despite this, ministers were prepared to stop funding grant maintained schools by 1974.[50]

It is not true, therefore, that Labour in power did nothing about private education: fee paying in grant maintained schools was abolished in Scotland, while a loophole was closed that allowed parents who borrowed money to pay fees to avoid tax. These were, however, modest measures, given the kind of impediment to an egalitarian society private education was believed to be. Perhaps Crosland had spoken more truly than he realised when laconically confiding to Cabinet in 1965 that private education posed a 'strictly insoluble problem'.[51]

Ministers and militancy

If for none other than pressing economic reasons, Wilson's ministers wanted to promote a greater understanding between the classes at the workplace. While contemporaries influenced by Marxism believed that impossible, even leading left-wing Labour MPs, such as Ian Mikardo, thought conflict need not be endemic to industrial relations. In the early 1950s Mikardo had echoed arguments normally associated with revisionism when he suggested that the emergence of salaried, professional managers lacking the 'same urge to take unfair advantage of workers' as their inter-war predecessors meant both sides of industry could co-operate to mutual advantage.[52] As the more mainstream veteran Scottish MP Arthur Woodburn stated in 1962, antagonism between worker and employer was '[o]ne of the greatest tragedies' of the contemporary scene and an entirely avoidable one at that. If irrational mistrust were overcome, he predicted, productivity would increase, 'scientific advance would leap ahead and poverty and a thousand ills would disappear'.[53] That workers' rising living standards could be sustained only if they were based on improving productivity was a point reiterated with monotonous regularity by Wilson and his colleagues.[54]

From such a perspective, only politically malign or unaccountably obtuse groups would promote unrest. Thus, Wilson erroneously believed a dispute at the components firm Harvey Spicer, which broke out during the 1964 election campaign, was provoked by Conservative sympathisers to discredit Labour.[55] Once in office, however, Wilson – as well as his Minister of Labour Ray Gunter and later Barbara Castle at the Department for Employment and Productivity (DEP) – was inclined to think disharmony the work of enemies to Labour's left, in particular the Communist Party (CP). The Cold War gave some credibility to these suspicions, as did the prominence of individual Communists in a number of unions. Wilson had, moreover, been warned by the security services that the CP saw strikes as one way of destroying his incomes policy (which it saw as exploiting workers), on the success of which so much hinged.[56]

Most on the left believed the leadership was biased against the unions. The government's response to industrial disputes was, however, often more conciliatory than confrontational, something illustrated by the 1967 rail strike. This was provoked by an inter-union dispute, between ASLEF, the rail drivers' union, and the National Union of Railwaymen, whose members were encroaching on traditional ASLEF territory. In the shadow of sterling's devaluation, Wilson feared the economic implications of a strike: if it upset overseas speculators, confidence in the currency might collapse.[57] Taking this into account, Gunter's television broadcast explaining the context of the dispute was remarkably sympathetic to ASLEF's plight. He described the union as representing the 'aristocrats of railwaymen' and noted officials' 'understandable pride'. Gunter then gave a sensitive outline of the unions' position, even though he concluded that any action would be unjustified.[58]

This is not to say Wilson was unaware of the political advantages of defeating a union, given the right circumstances. As the Prime Minister's Private Secretary stated in 1965, he 'would be glad to find a case of a strike of unskilled men for which there was no legitimate grounds and in which a direct attack on the public was involved' so he might send in the troops. Wilson initially thought a dispute concerning milk delivery at United Dairies in London was such an occasion, but he was persuaded that, before soldiers could commandeer the milk floats, a state of emergency would have to be called. As a result he lost enthusiasm for the scheme.[59]

Leftist critics thought Wilson's conduct during the prolonged 1966 seamen's strike vindicated their suspicion that the government would support employers against workers whatever the legitimacy of the latter's case.[60] In fact, from the outset Wilson put numerous compromise formulae to the National Union of Seamen (NUS) to avoid a strike he knew would have a severe economic impact.[61] In particular, he proposed establishing an inquiry to consider reforming the draconian legislation that governed seafarers' conditions. The Prime Minister was, however, unwilling to allow the NUS to gain what it wanted, in effect a pay rise of 20 per cent, as that would have blasted a hole in his attempt to keep

wage costs down. Nor was Wilson alone in becoming frustrated with the
union's rejection of attempts to find common ground: so irritated did
the TUC become, it withdrew support for the NUS.[62] Thus, when the
Prime Minister asserted that the dispute was due to the influence of a
'tightly knit group of politically motivated men', he did so with what he
imagined was just cause.[63] Not all of Wilson's colleagues were convinced,
and looked on his claims as evidence of Prime Ministerial paranoia:
Peter Shore even thought his boss had gone 'completely bonkers'.[64]

Whatever the merits of Wilson's case, Communist influence was a
deus ex machina that appeared to explain why the strike continued for so
long. The Prime Minister believed the intervention of CP members was
the only plausible explanation why an 'otherwise sturdy union', composed of 'realistic and reasonable men', allowed the strike to drag on.
That some of the union's executive were, as he put it, 'very close' to
Communists was undoubtedly true and it was known that these figures
exerted a disproportionate, if legitimate, influence within the union's
upper echelons. Such was their sway that they discouraged moderate
but feeble executive members from openly calling for a return to work.
Indeed, Wilson's rhetoric was partly aimed at shaming into action those
he thought lacked backbone.[65]

For the most part, the Prime Minister – and even the security services
– saw Communist influence as an irritant but not the basic cause of
most disputes.[66] Ministers were much more concerned with their lack
of a proper administrative device to prevent disputes reaching the point
at which production would be disrupted. As Lord Brown, an indust-
rialist Wilson made a junior minister at the Board of Trade, suggested,
much of the hostility marking employer–employee relations was due to
'sheer confusion'.[67] That so many strikes in key industries were 'unofficial', that is, called without formal union sanction, added weight to
the view that if only agreements were adhered to, and appropriate conciliation machinery were put in place, harmony could be maintained.
To that end, ministers promoted a variety of joint management–union
remedies, most especially in the strike-prone motor industry. They also
supported giving union leaderships more power. In 1965 Gunter proposed that the motor unions should revoke the membership of workers
who took unofficial action. In return, he wanted employers to require
all employees to join a union. If this arrangement would increase union
influence at the workplace, it also meant dissidents would be barred
from working in the industry.[68] Unfortunately for Gunter, union leaders
such as Hugh Scanlon of the Amalgamated Engineering Union (AEU)
and Jack Jones of the Transport and General Workers' Union (TGWU)
were inclined to reflect the demands of workers ministers viewed as
trouble-makers.[69]

Defending the unions?

The Wilson governments are generally assumed to have antagonised
Labour activists, largely because of the extent to which their policies
were thought to harm the unions. After 1966 the leadership certainly
suffered numerous reverses at conference over policies delegates felt
hurt workers' interests. It is, however, impossible to be sure how far
these conference decisions represented the views of union leaders, who
were able to cast their block votes, rather than those of constituency
delegates, although one authoritative assessment suggests most of the
latter supported ministers' attempts to control wages.[70]

It would be wrong, therefore, to imagine that all activists thought
their first duty was to defend the unions: given that only one-quarter of
manual workers routinely sympathised with strikers during an industrial
dispute, this should not be surprising.[71] One member of Clapham's
women's section asked, as early as 1957, 'if workers were pulling their
weight' in the economy and suggested, on the basis that 'in order to
take out we must also put in', the answer was in the negative.[72] A leading
Labour woman went even further in 1966, declaring that 'in return for
a fair wage all workers must work to their utmost so their products could
be sold'. Indeed, anyone 'who did not do that, or incited or joined in
unofficial action did disservice to the Government and the Nation, and
in wartime would have been referred to as Quislings'.[73] Possibly with
such comments in mind, one delegate to the 1963 national conference
of Labour women stated that too many in the party were 'only too willing to condemn the trade unions and the industrial action they took'.[74]

The left nonetheless believed that Labour should follow policies
favourable to the unions, if only because they formed 'an enormous,
and largely untapped potential of active support'.[75] While Tribune MPs
feared Wilson was alienating union leaders, that at least had the welcome consequence of encouraging unions to make common cause with
the left.[76] Michael Foot believed the shift leftwards of numerous union
bureaucracies was 'one of the most significant events in modern British
politics', because it meant the final transformation of Labour into a
party fully committed to socialism was at hand.[77] While the left therefore
increasingly identified with the unions, Castle went a little far when
noting *Tribune*'s 'constant propaganda to the effect that every wage claim
is sacrosanct and every industrial dispute noble'.[78] If those on the left
did not endorse every unofficial strike, they usually suggested such disputes arose from 'fundamental inequalities' and would stop only when
the economy was transformed through more public ownership.[79]

Support for union demands was, however, less certain at the party's
grass roots, and was contested even in CLPs that generally endorsed
the Tribunite perspective, such as Chigwell and Ongar.[80] There, in 1966,

the executive committee (EC) placed before its general management committee (GMC) a motion endorsing the government's incomes policy, only to see it rejected by delegates, who condemned it as 'detrimental to the achievements of a Socialist Society'. Later in the year, the GMC was faced with two resolutions, one of which regretted the NUS strike while the other supported it: the former was defeated and the latter supported by the same six-to-four margin. Similarly, a later motion critical of an unofficial strike on the London docks took a Gunter-like line by calling on the TGWU to withdraw membership from participants; this also was lost. The balance of opinion, however, shifted in the wake of Castle's attempt to regulate industrial relations and to reduce unofficial strikes through her proposals set out in *In Place of Strife*. The GMC sent for the consideration of the 1969 conference a resolution expressing distress that some were:

> completely deserting adherence to the cause of Socialism. This is most marked in the vocal sections misnamed 'the militants' who have succeeded in persuading the trade unionists in special key industries that they have no concern with the rest of the movement. They can, by a process of blackmail, obtain their demands even though, under Capitalism, these tend to be at the expense of the rest of the workers.

In other left-inclined local parties, support for the unions was conspicuous by its absence. In 1968 the Warwick and Leamington Spa GMC mandated its conference delegate: to protest against the imposition of prescription charges; to call for the North Atlantic Treaty Organisation to be disbanded; to dissociate the party from US policy in Vietnam; but to support the government's incomes policy.[81] A similar contrast in attitudes was evident in Edinburgh South, whose GMC sided with the left over Vietnam, Rhodesia and South Africa but which refused to criticise the government's wages policy.[82]

Industrial democracy

'Industrial democracy' was described in 1967 as 'one of those splendid catch-phrases with which the Labour Movement is so richly endowed … a safe subject to wax platitudinous about'.[83] If a harsh assessment, it was true that, although it was discussed with increasing fervour during the 1960s, industrial democracy remained a topic in need of clarification. Most Labour members supposed that increasing employees' involvement in management would help to improve industrial relations, but they remained at odds over the form such involvement should take, and even disputed its ultimate purpose. Precision was not helped by it being seen as but one aspect of the wider demand for individuals to 'participate' directly in decision-making, something discussed in Chapter 8.

While some enthusiasts believed in the existence of a 'huge powder-keg' of interest in industrial democracy, others conceded that most workers were unaware of its importance and would need to be 'stimulated' to demand it.[84] Survey evidence confirmed that workers were, at best, lukewarm. Fairly typical was a 1970 Ministry of Transport investigation into the attitudes of British Rail employees. This concluded that a majority were vaguely interested in contributing to decision-making but only if it was limited to being consulted by management rather than assuming responsibility themselves. Most were also concerned only with issues of immediate relevance to their own work.[85] This reluctance to challenge managerial prerogatives confirmed Goldthorpe and Lockwood's suggestion that most workers adhered to an instrumental attitude to work.[86] Given that they saw their job as an unpleasant means to an end, it was understandable why few employees wanted to spend time think-ing about it any more than they had to. Most employers also angrily opposed any proposals that threatened their freedom to manage: John Davies, Director General of the Confederation of British Industry (CBI), considered that while managers 'should be susceptible to a great deal of advice and help … that is as far as it should go'.[87] Leading civil servants in the Ministry of Labour were also sceptical and, only months before Wilson took office, had decided that most employees were in-capable of assuming the necessary interest in their workplace to make it practical.[88]

Increasing workers' influence had been the ambition of Labour members earlier in the century: co-operators, syndicalists and guild socialists aimed to give employees varying levels of managerial authority. Most unions, however, refused to countenance such schemes, and con-sidered it best to pursue their interests unhindered. Therefore when Labour extended the public sector after 1945, the unions sought only participation in joint consultative committees, while a few retired general secretaries sat on nationalised boards, usually for industries of which they had no experience.[89] Writing in 1949, the MP Eirene White ex-pressed the general view when she asserted that these boards ran the nationalised sector on behalf of the whole community. Workers should not have representatives on these bodies, as that would compromise their ability to act for the nation, by tilting them too much in the direc-tion of the employees' interest. It would also inhibit efficiency: managers still required the ability to take decisions workers might oppose. In any case, the fact of nationalisation, White believed, had eliminated a major disincentive to co-operation and so greater productivity: for miners and the like now laboured on behalf of the people rather than for the profit of a few capitalists.[90]

Despite such hopes, as the Attlee government drew to a close, the nationalised sector did not produce a marked increase in output: Mikardo, for one, believed this was partly because, consultation notwithstanding, publicly owned industries were still run in the traditional manner. Others held that the consultation machinery was adequate but believed neither managers nor unions took it seriously, because they remained obsessed with the notion of conflict.[91] As the MP Austen Albu stated at this time, '[t]he creation of a feeling of common purpose in the activities of industry remains ... one of the outstanding unattained objectives of socialist industrial policy'.[92]

An important issue?

During Labour's years of opposition, how the party might promote this 'common purpose' did not exactly dominate members' horizons. Most remained preoccupied with maintaining full employment, improving incomes and debating how far the public sector should be extended. Yet, as *Towards Equality* put it, while full employment improved the 'traditional manager–worker relationship', an extension of industrial democracy was still required if it was to transform into a 'genuine partnership'.[93]

The failure of the Labour left to take up this issue was surprising given their critique of consultation. Left-wingers like Judith Hart, when seeking adoption as a parliamentary candidate, certainly felt it advantageous to refer to the need to give workers 'greater satisfaction and a greater sense of participation'.[94] Indeed, Aneurin Bevan's *In Place of Fear* (1952) stressed how important it was that state employees experienced a more co-operative relationship, for, he argued, 'the individual citizen will still feel that society is on top of him until he is enfranchised in the workshop as well as at the ballot box'.[95] As others argued later in the decade, industrial democracy was a matter of political rights.[96] Yet, despite such fervour, thinking on the subject rarely became specific: to many, simply expressing their aspiration that workers should achieve a managerial role appeared sufficient.[97]

In contrast, two of the party's leading revisionists, Crosland and Douglas Jay, advanced clear proposals, although, like White, both questioned the wisdom of giving workers a direct say in management.[98] As had White, both men believed there would always be two sides to industry, with management taking the decisions while the unions assumed the mantle of permanent opposition. Given the nature of the workplace it was, they asserted, unrealistic to impose notions of democracy applicable outside the factory gate. In any case, Crosland argued, workers did not need special measures to give them influence. Full employment, rising real wages, social security and 'a general change in the social climate' had eroded many managerial prerogatives. He nonetheless hoped co-operation would flourish outside the collective bargaining process; in particular, he suggested that workers should be given more opportunities to influence how their own tasks were allocated. Moreover, Crosland feared that incorporating the unions too closely within management would allow more disruptive – inevitably Communist – elements to usurp their role as the workers' representatives. Jay's outlook was similar and he opposed putting union officials on company boards, fearing officials would either suffer a conflict of loyalty or confuse the board's managerial function. However, he supported the election of employee representatives who were neither workers nor union officials. In this Jay echoed Albu's belief that worker representatives could 'ensure sanction for executive authority' and encourage employees to 'feel a direct ... responsibility for those who represent them in the making of management decisions'.[99]

During the first half of the 1960s some unions became more attracted to industrial democracy: it appears that affluence gave them the confidence to claim more than just higher wages.[100] Evidence submitted by the TUC to the Donovan Commission on Trade Unions and Employers' Associations in 1965 revealed their tentative interest. This was, however, an uneven conversion, with Jack Jones of the TGWU and Hugh Scanlon of the AEU taking the lead. Both supported the Institute for Workers' Control, established in 1964 by the Nottingham Labour activist Ken Coates, whose conferences attracted upwards of 500 people, although many attendees had sympathies well to Labour's left. Jones was the single most influential voice on this matter.[101] He emphasised how participation could not only make 'life worth living' on the factory floor but also help overcome unnecessary 'misunderstanding, resistance, low morale and suspicion'. Ultimately, Jones aimed to foster a series of 'self-governing communities', within which workers exerted full control. If apparently idealistic, Jones was hard-headed enough to reject any form of industrial democracy conducted directly by individual workers because that threatened the privileged position unions occupied within the workforce.

Not all unions were convinced: the leadership of the Electrical Trades Union remained firm adherents of the view that unions should concentrate on improving wages and conditions and leave management to managers.[102] In fact, it is possible that some union leaders who ostensibly supported industrial democracy saw it as no more than a means of increasing their ability to secure a more traditional objective: higher wages.[103]

Jack Jones' influence

Arguments about the merits of industrial democracy came to a head with the Wilson government's Iron and Steel Bill. This outlined Labour's plan to renationalise the steel industry but failed to make recommendations for involving workers in management, beyond consultation. Delegates at the 1965 Labour Party annual conference made their feelings clear and in response the NEC established a working party on industrial democracy.[104] This led to a report debated at the 1967 conference, which formed the basis for an NEC statement endorsed by conference the following year: many of its recommendations found their way into Castle's Industrial Relations Bill of 1969.

Before the debate on steel, the NEC had commissioned an investigation chaired by Mikardo into the port transport industry, which the government was committed to taking into public hands.[105] The object of Mikardo's Study Group, which counted Jones as a member, was to recommend what form state ownership should assume. As both men were well known critics of consultation, it came as no surprise when they proposed measures it was claimed would result in 'the injection of a new, radical element of industrial democracy'. The report argued that, for historical reasons, the dock unions – prominent among which was the TGWU – had unrivalled experience exercising joint authority with management and it proposed this should be extended to maintain harmony in a conflict-prone industry. In particular, the report recommended that a Group Operating Committee, to which managers would be responsible, should run each dock. This was described as a 'breakthrough' because sitting on the Committee would be representatives elected by the workforce, who would enjoy an unprecedented influence over discipline, safety, training, welfare and – most radically – wages.

While the Mikardo report justified its proposals in relation to the unique character of the ports, Jones, for one, believed they should be applied to other industries and was given the chance to influence that outcome when he was appointed chair of an NEC working party on industrial democracy.[106] The outward aim of this body was to make work a more satisfying experience, in the expectation that this would improve industrial relations. This would, of course, benefit everybody, including what was said to be an increasing number of employers interested in giving employees more responsibility. If treating workers as equals rather than subordinates gave them unprecedented autonomy, it would also help managers to exploit their 'untapped talent'.[107] In particular, the creation of mutual trust would help industry adapt to the consequences of technological change, something that otherwise might generate an insecure and strike-prone workforce. Thus, one of the purposes of reform was to reveal the compelling common interest that united both sides of

industry, by creating individuals 'with a widening range of social understanding, and a responsible and democratic approach to individual and
group problems'.

Most members of Jones' working party believed there was no limit
to how much managerial responsibility workers might exert. So far as
the Labour leadership was concerned there were some. Responding on
behalf of the NEC to the 1965 steel debate, White reaffirmed her view
that 'the tradition on which our trade union movement had grown up,
does not lend itself to workers' control'.[108] Reflecting his union's position
before Scanlon's election as President, the AEU official Bill Simpson
also feared too much democracy might imperil efficiency, whereas the
former should always be subordinated to this 'paramount factor'.[109]
Similarly, the MP Eric Moonman believed the rights claimed by workers
and managers were mutually exclusive and argued '[m]anagement must
manage', albeit supported by committees promoting greater worker
involvement.[110]

While one of its authors described the 1967 report as revolutionary,
its proposals were nonetheless justified in terms designed to appeal to
the gradualist strain in Labour thinking.[111] Hence, it recommended
industrial democracy be extended 'not by evolving new and complex
(and perhaps alien) structures, but by gradually increasing involvement
in a development of existing machinery … it would encourage a movement towards participation in democratic procedures; a natural
evolution rather than an attempt to conjure democracy out of the air'.
In concrete terms, this meant industrial democracy would proceed
through 'accredited representative[s] of working people': the unions.[112]
So far as Jones was concerned it meant stronger unions, and implied:
giving them the right to be recognised by any employer; granting them
access to confidential company information; increasing compensation
to workers faced with redundancy; and providing better training for
their representatives. Rather than needing separate consultative committees, industrial democracy would be expressed through the same
channel that dealt with wages. As Simpson noted, this meant consultation
would be linked to that basic union concern, so co-operation over a
whole range of matters could be made dependent on financial reward.[113]
While no specific form of industrial democracy was prescribed –
although Mikardo's scheme was cited as worthy of emulation – indicative examples significantly included giving unions responsibility for
distributing overtime and deciding on promotions.

Delegates reaching the rostrum during debates on industrial democracy held at the 1967 and 1968 conferences wanted full workers' control
of management and saw Jones' labours as an initial step towards that
end.[114] They were mostly sceptical about co-operation and partnership
with management, and criticised measures that did not lead to greater

union authority at the workplace. Jones appeared to sympathise with them, calling in 1968 for union representatives to 'invade the powers of the bureaucrats in industry' and limit the 'dictatorial and unilateral authority of management'.[115] How far conference reflected the views of the rest of the party is hard to say, as few CLPs debated the matter. While the 1967 NEC report was supposed to be the basis for party-wide consultations, Transport House received few comments.[116] If measured in column inches, *Tribune*'s interest was also limited. In addition, the 1968 debate was conducted over the incessant chatter of delegates, presumably talking about other matters, and the chair was forced to remind them of the subject's importance.[117]

The impact of Barbara Castle

Jones believed the government should implement the 1968 NEC statement without delay, in the first instance within the public sector.[118] Few advocates of workers' control were optimistic, for while Ken Coates welcomed the Jones report as a step in the right direction, he considered ministers were 'driving full speed in the opposite direction'.[119] This was not entirely accurate. Taking their lead from Crosland and Jay, most ministers opposed radical reform but were nonetheless willing to consider variations of, if not alternatives to, consultation. Moreover, as the Cabinet's greatest enthusiast for innovation, Barbara Castle, first as Minister of Transport and then First Minister of State at the DEP, pushed colleagues towards a serious consideration of industrial democracy.

Like Mikardo, Castle supported Bevan during the 1950s and wanted to 'forge ahead' with worker participation, to which end she regularly consulted Jones, although he thought she found his ideas too anarchistic.[120] As Minister of Transport, Castle nonetheless wanted to apply Mikardo's recommendations. She made it clear that her 'overriding consideration' was to 'give the individual dock worker … the feeling that his interests are being directly safeguarded by the presence of his representatives … at the meetings … where matters affecting his livelihood are being discussed'. Yet while she wanted to 'associate workers with management without handicapping management', employers' representatives opposed making managers answerable to bodies on which sat union officials.[121] Castle's Cabinet colleagues were also uncertain. Presumably because he did not want to antagonise the unions, Gunter agreed that worker participation should be a 'central feature' of the nationalised docks. However, he felt that it would be unwise to give employee representatives an influence over wage negotiations and proposed that each dock should merely have a consultative committee, albeit one with direct access to management. Michael Stewart at the

Department of Economic Affairs echoed Gunter's concern that union officials sitting on Group Operating Committees would be unable to assume a 'detached and dispassionate interest' over wages. Moreover, if they did acquire that outlook, the unions might then alienate their members, leaving the door open to unofficial strikes and far-left influence.[122]

In light of these comments, Castle decided against making any specific proposals for industrial democracy. Instead, she drafted some general principles favourable to increasing participation, in the hope they would be anodyne enough to pass Cabinet scrutiny but still allow the unions to use them to justify Mikardo-like experiments once the ports were nationalised. Yet, when the Ports Bill was finally published in November 1969, the wording was too vague for the unions. Their demand for an unequivocal promise that workers would play a managerial role was not unrelated to their belief that this would help them prevent the introduction of new labour-saving technologies. It was because he feared the unions would exploit any managerial function to prevent such innovation that the then Minister of Transport, Fred Mulley, refused to make legislation less obscure.[123] In the end, the Bill fell due to Labour's loss of power.

Although she was forced to make a tactical retreat on the docks, Castle tried to create a statutory framework for worker representation on the boards of state-owned industries under Ministry of Transport control, and was adamant that active union officials should be allowed to sit on these bodies.[124] She believed the established practice of appointing retired trade unionists with no experience of the industry on whose board they sat had done nothing to ensure workers were 'more closely identified with the policies adopted for the industry' and so might 'assume management habits of thought'. If the initial draft of Castle's proposals was anything to go by, her civil servants nonetheless feared the presence of union representatives would create conflicts of interest: in particular, it might allow them to influence wage negotiations from both sides of the table.[125] This echoed the view of leading board members and even that of some unionists, for the TUC's Nationalised Industries Committee received her proposals with some caution. Once again forced to rethink, Castle conceded that union representatives should not be involved in all board activity. When this did not go far enough for her detractors, rather than make immediate legislative proposals, Castle agreed to sponsor experimental schemes, in the hope that these would eventually generate support for her objective.[126]

In April 1968 Castle was moved from the Ministry of Transport. Her replacement, Richard Marsh, was hostile to any form of worker participation; indeed, Castle believed he had no 'feel for Socialist ideas at all'.[127] Marsh was certainly unwilling to allow union officials to sit on nationalised boards, as he was convinced they would inevitably adhere to union policy and so undermine managerial decision-making. This remained his view even after union officials conceded that full-time board members might relinquish their union posts while part-timers could stand aloof when wages were discussed. Even so, while Marsh thought consultative councils were the best means of promoting participation, he promised to do what Castle would have done, that is, draft the forthcoming Transport Bill in such a way as not to preclude experimentation.[128] He also commissioned a survey of British Rail employees' attitudes to industrial democracy, which, after numerous delays, began in March 1970 and so was concluded only after Labour had lost power. It is doubtful this would have led to radical action even had Wilson won re-election, for its conclusions, referred to above, were not encouraging.[129]

In place of shareholders?

Once installed at the DEP, Castle formulated a White Paper devoted to improving industrial relations, which she entitled *In Place of Strife*. Most union leaders and all the Labour left believed this represented Castle's desire to undermine workers' ability to hold strikes.[130] Wilson and his closest advisers were certainly concerned that, as his economic guru Thomas Balogh put it, the unions had become 'an irresponsible group who had to be dealt with'.[131] The Prime Minister consequently looked on Castle's proposals for compulsory strike ballots and the imposition of 'cooling off' periods before strikes could be held as ingenious devices to prevent unofficial disputes.

Yet, whatever might have been thought, Castle wanted to strengthen the unions rather than weaken them, and much of *In Place of Strife* was preoccupied with that aim.[132] In fact, one of her 'principal objectives' was to promote industrial democracy. Paragraph 49 was strongly influenced by the NEC's 1968 statement and endorsed the view that the best way to develop participation 'must be through a reform, extension and strengthening of collective bargaining' and the creation of a strong union movement. Castle saw this as fully endorsing the 'philosophic rightness' of allowing employees to influence decision-making.[133] The subsequent Bill consequently was to make it illegal for workers to be denied union membership or to be subject to discrimination once members; it also introduced the notion of 'unfair dismissal'. Employers were to be obliged to make available information considered relevant to wage bargaining. In addition, the Bill proposed regulating the position of shop stewards, by providing training and facilities to help them better perform their tasks; it also outlined plans to subsidise the training of both union officials and members, to enable them to participate more effectively. Most relevantly, Castle committed the government to undertake experiments involving placing worker representatives on the boards of nationalised industries.[134] Castle had only started consulting on what form these trials might take when Wilson announced the election date.[135]

One reason why experimentation was to take place initially in the public sector was that company law effectively prevented workers acquiring a managerial role outside it. Castle called for the law to be reformed. This the CBI inevitably opposed, as the existing statutes meant directors could be appointed only by shareholders rather than elected by workers, while all board members were obliged to accept collective responsibility and maintain the shareholders' interest. The Board of Trade, busy with other matters, echoed that view.[136] Yet there was some prospect of change, for, in 1967, when in charge of the Board, Jay had outlined his intention to introduce a systematic review of company law. In particular, he wanted to oversee the 'comparative rights and obligations of shareholders, directors, creditors, employees and the community as a whole'.[137] The Board in fact aimed to introduce legislation some time after the election; its proposals regarding company philosophy were informed by the findings of an NEC study group.[138] Quite how radical these would have been is uncertain. Lord Brown, Minister of State at the Board, marked out its possible limits by adamantly opposing the creation of elected worker directors, arguing on the familiar grounds that this would mean board business being dominated by surrogate wage negotiations.[139] Despite that, Labour's 1970 manifesto promised to reform company law and extend experiments in industrial democracy to the private sector.

Conclusion

As with those that follow, the main purpose of this chapter is to highlight the underlying reasons why the party embraced the policies it did, rather than to assess their impact. This was just as well, for at the time of leaving office Wilson's governments had made only a negligible impression on secondary education and industrial democracy.

The commitment to end segregated education was widely shared across the party, linking revisionist ministers to *Tribune*-reading activists; while the former advocated gradual progress and the latter urged immediate action, differences were limited to means, not ends. Thus, in explaining why only one-third of children were being taught in a comprehensive school by 1970, the Department of Education's limited powers should be taken into account. The failure to reform private education largely followed from the Cabinet's reluctance to confront the numerous practical and political problems raised by the issue at a time when Labour was already deeply unpopular. That the final official report into the issue was not produced until just before the 1970 general election was clearly a significant additional factor.

In contrast, no progress towards even the most modest forms of worker participation had been made as Labour ministers emptied their desks. There were, it is true, a dozen part-time 'worker directors' in the newly nationalised steel industry sitting on advisory regional boards. However, this initiative owed little to Labour ministers and was, in any case, widely criticised by advocates of industrial democracy as little more than glorified consultation.[140] Labour's lack of action was largely due to the fact that it was such a contentious issue within the party. The left wanted workers to exert at least co-determination with management; some even called for full workers' control. If most ministers (and some union leaders) were willing to enhance the means by which employees were consulted, they feared efficiency would be compromised if workers played a direct managerial role. How far each side of this argument was truly committed to reconciling workers and managers so that each might work together to advance the common interest is moot. Even so, largely due to the efforts of Barbara Castle, before the 1970 campaign the government was committed to introducing a number of experimental schemes that would have tested the nature of party members' intentions.

Notes

The place of publication is London unless otherwise specified.

1 Labour Party, *Towards Equality* (1956), pp. 3–4.
2 C. A. R. Crosland, *The Future of Socialism* (1956), pp. 105, 112–14.
3 House of Lords Record Office, Reginald Sorenson papers, Hist. Coll. 102/230, A backbencher's pilgrimage, 1968, p. 67.
4 Labour Party Archive (LPA), *Bagshot and Egham Clarion*, January 1965.
5 Labour, *Equality*, p. 14.
6 H. Gaitskell, 'The economic aims of the Labour Party', *Political Quarterly*, 26 (1956); C. A. R. Crosland, *The Conservative Enemy* (1962), pp. 173–4.
7 H. Gaitskell, 'Public ownership and equality', *Socialist Commentary*, June 1955, and 'Socialism and nationalisation', *Fabian Tract*, 300 (1956), p. 3.
8 See, in particular, L. Panitch, *Social Democracy and Industrial Militancy* (Cambridge, 1976).
9 *Report of the Sixty-Eighth Annual Conference of the Labour Party* (1969), p. 341.
10 Labour Party, *Let's Go with Labour for the New Britain* (1964), pp. 13–14; and Labour Party, *Time for Decision* (1966), pp. 15–16.
11 This account is based on M. Francis, *Ideas and Policies Under Labour 1945–1951* (Manchester, 1997), pp. 141–68.
12 D. Rubinstein and B. Simon, *The Evolution of the Comprehensive School* (1973), pp. 52–68.
13 M. Parkinson, 'The Labour Party and the organisation of secondary education', MA thesis, University of Manchester, 1968, pp. 183–95.
14 *Report of the Fifty-Seventh Annual Conference of the Labour Party* (1958), pp. 87–8.

15 LPA, Study Group on Education (SGE) papers, M. Stewart and M. Cole, Memorandum on Labour Party policy for education, Re. 161/May 1957.
16 Crosland, *Future*, p. 258; Labour, *Equality*, pp. 5–6.
17 *Report of the Sixty-Ninth Annual Conference of the Labour Party* (1970), pp. 91, 94.
18 London Metropolitan Archive (LMA), *London News*, April 1953.
19 LPA, *Abingdon Labour Party Constituency Digest*, August 1963.
20 British Library of Political and Economic Science (BLPES), North Kensington CLP papers, *North Kensington Labour Questionmaster*, June 1952 and September 1955.
21 SGE papers, minutes, 16 July 1957.
22 SGE papers, minutes, 19 December 1957, and Brief summary of the findings of the survey on educational attitudes, Re. 314/February 1958.
23 Bristol Record Office (BRO), Labour Party South West Region papers, 38423/43, *News-Sheet*, July 1964.
24 *Report of the Sixty-Sixth Annual Conference of the Labour Party* (1967), p. 124.
25 *Sixty-Seventh Annual Conference of Labour*, p. 231.
26 Modern Records Centre (MRC), Warwick and Leamington Spa CLP papers, MSS 133, Box 10, *Contact*, July/August and September/October 1966.
27 See, for example, D. Marsden, 'Politicians, equality and comprehensives', in P. Townsend and N. Bosanquet (eds), *Labour and Inequality* (1972).
28 S. Crosland, *Tony Crosland* (1982), p. 148.
29 SGE papers, minutes, 16 July 1957 and 29 January 1958.
30 Public Record Office (PRO), ED 207/22, A. Crosland, Draft note for the Prime Minister, October 1967.
31 *Sunday Telegraph*, 19 October 1969.
32 Crosland, *Conservative*, p. 174.
33 K. O. Morgan, *Labour in Power, 1945–1951* (Oxford, 1985), pp. 177–9; Francis, *Ideas*, pp. 159–63.
34 *Report of the Fifty-Second Annual Conference of the Labour Party* (1953), pp. 172–3.
35 Crosland, *Conservative*, pp. 180–1.
36 SGE papers, minutes, 11 December 1957.
37 SGE papers, Report of weekend conference on education, 7/9 February 1958, Re. 323/February 1958; Crosland, *Conservative*, p. 180.
38 SGE papers, Brief summary of the findings of the survey on educational attitudes, Re. 314/February 1958.
39 SGE papers, minutes, 19 February 1958.
40 Stewart and Cole, Memorandum.
41 Labour Party, *Signposts for the Sixties* (1961), pp. 31–2.
42 *Report of the Sixtieth Annual Conference of the Labour Party* (1961), p. 136.
43 PRO, PREM 13/2069, Mitchell to Cockerill, 17 May 1965, and Mitchell to Litton, 18 May 1965.
44 PRO, CAB 129/123, Public schools, Memorandum by the Secretary of State for Education and Science, C(65)155; Editorial, 'The politics of education', *Socialist Commentary*, February 1966; Crosland, *Crosland*, p. 149.
45 *Sixty-Sixth Annual Conference of Labour*, pp. 133–4.
46 J. Rae, *The Public School Revolution* (1981), pp. 38–46.
47 PREM 13/2069, Trend to Wilson, 17 July 1968; CAB 129/138, Public Schools Commission: First Report, C(68)86; CAB 128/43, 18 July 1968; T. Benn, *Office Without Power. Diaries 1968–72* (1988), p. 91.
48 *Sixty-Seventh Annual Conference of Labour*, pp. 235–6, 240.

49 A. Goodwin, 'Education without privilege', *Socialist Commentary*, May 1970.
50 *Sixty-Ninth Annual Conference of Labour*, p. 99.
51 B. Castle, *The Castle Diaries, 1964–1976* (1990), p. 34.
52 I. Mikardo, 'Trade unions in a full employment economy', in R. H. S. Crossman (ed.), *New Fabian Essays* (1952), pp. 143–4, 147–8; Crosland, *Conservative*, p. 219.
53 *Edinburgh Evening News*, 29 November 1962.
54 PREM 13/403, Note of a meeting held at Downing Street, 26 October 1964; PREM 13/978, Notes of the proceedings of the National Conference on Productivity, 27 September 1966. For more on the importance of productivity, see J. Tomlinson, *The Labour Governments 1964–70. Vol. 3: Economic Policy* (Manchester, 2004), chapter 8.
55 D. E. Butler and A. King, *The British General Election of 1964* (1965), pp. 115–16; PREM 13/606.
56 PREM 13/786, The Communist party and the threatened railway strike, 22 February 1966.
57 PREM 13/1847, Record of a meeting between H. Wilson and R. Gunter, 29 November 1967.
58 PREM 13/1847, Text of ministerial broadcast by R. Gunter, 3 December 1967.
59 PREM 13/607, Mitchell to McIndoe, 10 June 1965.
60 P. Foot, 'The seamen's struggle', in R. Blackburn and A. Cockburn (eds), *The Incompatibles: Trade Union Militancy and the Consensus* (Harmondsworth, 1967); and K. Coates, *The Crisis of British Socialism* (Nottingham, 1971), pp. 133–42. For a more measured view, see K. Thorpe, 'The "juggernaught method": the 1966 state of emergency and the Wilson government's response to the seamen's strike', *Twentieth Century British History*, 12:4 (2001).
61 CAB 130/465, Minute of meeting with the Executive Committee of the National Union of Seamen, 13 May 1966.
62 CAB 130/465, Minute of meeting with the Finance and General Purposes Committee of the TUC, 14 June 1966; PREM 13/1228, Note of a meeting held at 10 Downing Street, 9 June 1966.
63 J. McIlroy, 'Note on the Communist Party and industrial politics', in J. McIlroy, N. Fishman and A. Campbell (eds), *British Trade Unions and Industrial Politics. Volume II* (Aldershot, 1999), p. 241.
64 T. Benn, *Out of the Wilderness. Diaries, 1963–67* (1987), p. 436.
65 PREM 13/1228, Note of a meeting between H. Wilson and D. Rusk, 10 June 1966, and Note of a meeting between H. Wilson and E. Heath, 21 June 1966; H. Wilson, *The Labour Government, 1964–70* (Harmondsworth, 1971), p. 308.
66 PRO, LAB 43/535, The industrial situation, 30 April 1969.
67 PRO, BT 298/263, Lord Brown, Points to be considered for the Second and Third Companies Acts, 29 July 1967.
68 PREM 13/402, Note of meeting between the Prime Minister and representatives of the motor industry, 3 September 1965.
69 H. Scanlon, 'The role of militancy', *New Left Review*, 46 (1967), pp. 5, 15.
70 L. Minkin, *The Labour Party Conference* (1978), pp. 88–90.
71 D. Weakliem, 'Class consciousness and political change: voting and political attitudes in the British working class, 1964–1970', *American Sociological Review*, 58:3 (1993), pp. 385–90.
72 Lambeth Archives, Clapham CLP papers, IV/156/2/5, Clapham Central women's section minutes, 2 October 1957.

73 *Report of the Forty-Third National Conference of Labour Women* (1966), p. 18.
74 *Report of the Fortieth National Conference of Labour Women* (1963), p. 37.
75 *Tribune*, 11 March and 27 June 1966.
76 LPA, Ian Mikardo/Jo Richardson papers, Box 5, Tribune Group minutes, 8 November 1968, E. Heffer, Role of the group and its future work.
77 *Tribune*, 14 February 1969.
78 Castle, *Diaries*, p. 231.
79 Mikardo/Richardson papers, Box 5, Tribune Group minutes, 21 April 1969.
80 This account is based on Essex County Record Office, Chigwell and Ongar CLP papers, D/Z 84/3, 8023 GMC minutes, 23 March and 27 June 1966, 26 July and 27 November 1967, 23 June 1969.
81 Warwick and Leamington Spa CLP papers, MSS 133, Box 1, GMC minutes, 19 September 1968.
82 National Library of Scotland, Edinburgh South CLP papers, Dep. 203/4, GMC minutes, 28 July and 27 October 1966.
83 J. Torode, 'What is industrial democracy?', *Socialist Commentary* (July 1967), p. 30.
84 K. Coates, 'Democracy and workers' control', in P. Anderson (ed.), *Towards Socialism* (1965), pp. 294–5; Scanlon, 'Militancy', pp. 9–10; K. Coates and T. Topham, 'The Labour Party's plans for industrial democracy', *Institute for Workers' Control Pamphlet No. 5* (Nottingham, 1968).
85 J. Edmonds, 'The worker', in B. Lapping and G. Radice (eds), *More Power to the People* (1968), pp. 39–40; PRO, MT 87/224, Tavistock Institute Inquiry into Worker Participation in Decision-Making in British Railways. Summary of findings and Worker Participation in British Railways Steering Group minutes, 9 August 1971.
86 J. H. Goldthorpe, D. Lockwood, F. Bechhofer and J. Platt, *The Affluent Worker: Industrial Attitudes and Behaviour* (Cambridge, 1968), pp. 108–9.
87 *The Times*, 29 July 1968.
88 LAB 10/2994, Minutes of Working Party on Workers' Attitudes and Industrial Efficiency, 26 June 1964; LAB 10/3061, Heron to Clucas and Marre, 17 April 1967.
89 R. Currie, *Industrial Politics* (Oxford, 1979), pp. 157–64.
90 E. White, 'Workers' control?', *Fabian Society Challenge Series Pamphlet No. 4* (1949), p. 27.
91 J. Tomlinson, *Democratic Socialism and Economic Policy* (Cambridge, 1997), pp. 117–23; Francis, *Ideas*, pp. 78–83.
92 A. Albu, 'The organisation of industry', in Crossman, *New Fabian*, pp. 129–30.
93 Labour, *Equality*, pp. 9–10.
94 LPA, Judith Hart papers, Section 1, File 1 (ii), speech to selection meeting, Lanark, 1957.
95 A. Bevan, *In Place of Fear* (1952), pp. 102–3.
96 C. Jenkins, 'The retreat from industrial democracy', *Focus*, 5 (1956), p. 15.
97 H. Jenkins, R. Lewis, G. Southgate and W. Wolfgang, 'The red sixties', *Victory for Socialism Pamphlet* (1957), pp. 10–11.
98 Crosland, *Conservative*, pp. 217–27; D. Jay, *Socialism in the New Society* (1962), pp. 325–33.
99 Albu, 'Industry', pp. 136–7.
100 H. Scanlon, 'The way forward for workers' control', *Institute for Workers' Control, Pamphlet No. 1* (Nottingham, 1968); Coates, 'Democracy', pp. 304–5.
101 J. Jones, 'The right to participate – key to industrial progress', *TGWU Pamphlet* (1970).
102 Torode, 'Industrial democracy', pp. 30–1.

103 Edmonds, 'The worker', p. 38; Currie, *Industrial*, pp. 224–7.
104 *Report of the Sixty-Fourth Annual Conference of the Labour Party* (1965), pp. 252–6.
105 Labour Party, *Report of the Port Transport Study Group* (1966); J. Jones, *Union Man* (1986), p. 174.
106 Unless otherwise stated this section is based on Labour Party, *Industrial Democracy* (1967), and *Sixty-Seventh Annual Conference of Labour*, pp. 344–7.
107 LPA, Industrial Democracy Working Party (IDWP) papers, Proposed conference on industrial democracy, Res. 13/June 1966.
108 *Sixty-Third Annual Conference of Labour*, pp. 255–6.
109 IDWP papers, W. Simpson, Industrial democracy, Re. 28/July 1966.
110 *Guardian*, 22 July 1966.
111 Institute for Workers' Control, *Report of the 5th National Conference on Workers' Control and Democracy* (Nottingham, 1967), p. 27.
112 IDWP papers, J. Jones, Action points on industrial democracy, Re. 105/March 1967.
113 *Sixty-Seventh Annual Conference of Labour*, pp. 160–1.
114 *Ibid.*, pp. 156–7.
115 *Ibid.*, p. 158.
116 IDWP papers, Industrial democracy. A draft action programme, Re. 49/February 1968.
117 *Sixty-Seventh Annual Conference of Labour*, p. 157.
118 *Ibid.*, pp. 158, 347; Labour, *Industrial Democracy*, p. 13.
119 Coates, *Socialism*, pp. 197–8.
120 Castle, *Diaries*, p. 206; Jones, *Union*, p. 193.
121 LAB 10/3061, Minutes of meeting to discuss workers' participation in the nationalised ports, 30 January 1967; LAB 10/3061, Castle to Stewart, 8 March 1967.
122 LAB 10/3061, Gunter to Castle, 21 March 1967; Stewart to Castle, 31 March 1967; Castle to Stewart, 11 May 1967.
123 J. Horner, *Studies in Industrial Democracy* (1974), pp. 146–7, 153–4; MT 87/222, 'Ports Bill. Meeting with the TUC', 20 January 1970; *Guardian*, 17 March 1970.
124 MT 87/145, Workers' participation, 13 February 1968.
125 MT 87/145, Worker representation on the boards of nationalised transport industries, February 1968; Scott-Malden to Heaton, 16 February 1968.
126 MT 87/160, Note of minister's meeting, 5 March 1968; Note of B. Castle's meeting with Sir R. Wilson and H. C. Johnson, 15 March 1968; Note of minister's meeting with the Nationalised Industries Committee of the TUC, 25 March 1968.
127 Castle, *Diaries*, p. 248.
128 MT 87/200, Woodcock to Marsh, 8 April 1968; Note of R. Marsh meeting with the Nationalised Industries Committee of TUC, 10 May 1968; Note of R. Marsh meeting with A. Kitson, 16 May 1968.
129 MT 87/223; MT 87/224, Worker Participation in British Railways Steering Group minutes, 9 August 1971.
130 Jones, *Union*, p. 207; *Tribune*, 10 January 1969.
131 Benn, *Office*, pp. 122–3.
132 Castle, *Diaries*, p. 296.
133 LAB 43/558, Castle to Shore, 15 January 1970; LAB 10/3445, Castle to Burgh, 30 January 1969.
134 LAB 43/558, The NEC statement on industrial democracy and the relevant provisions in the industrial relations legislation, January 1970.

135 LAB 10/3445, Appointment of workers' representatives to the boards of public and private undertakings – discussion document, 5 March 1970.

136 LAB 10/3445, Bayliss to Mason, 1 April 1969, Brownsport to Simons, 14 May 1969.

137 LAB 28/396.

138 BT 298/263, Peck to Jardine *et al.*, 18 October 1967.

139 Brown, Points to be considered.

140 T. K. Jones, 'Employee directors in the British Steel Corporation', in C. Balfour (ed.), *Participation in Industry* (1973).

5

Appealing to women

Some months before the 1959 general election, Labour's keenest women activists were told by one of their leading lights that they needed to accommodate 'a new generation, with new habits, new interests, and new reactions to the political problems of the day'.[1] The result in October appeared to confirm her analysis, as many observers believed a significant cause of Labour's defeat was its rejection by younger, affluent female voters.

If the problem appeared acute in the late 1950s, the party had always found it hard to convince women to vote Labour at the same rate as men. Historians explain this 'gender gap' by suggesting that, as a male-dominated organisation, Labour's perception of its overall purpose meant it did not take women's discrete interests seriously.[2] In contrast, the Conservatives are considered to have been more willing and able to focus on matters relating to women's prevailing home-making role.[3] As outlined in Chapter 3, however, Labour's 1959 campaign gave domestic issues some prominence. So far as Gallup was concerned, the gender gap nearly halved compared with 1955, so that only 5 per cent more men than women supported the party (see Table 3.1, p. 63). During the 1960s Transport House endeavoured to make Labour more attractive to young wives and mothers, such that in 1964 Harold Wilson claimed he would return Labour to power on the back of a 'women's crusade'.[4] Paradoxically, the gender gap actually doubled between 1959 and 1964 and stood at 8 per cent in 1966.

Despite official strategy, most male members continued to think their party's main purpose remained that of improving the position of male manual workers. But so did many female activists. Delegates to the 1959 national conference of Labour women had spent little time discussing consumer issues; instead, speeches were dominated by the spectre of rising *male* unemployment.[5] If the party's union connection encouraged this emphasis, it was also because such women were mostly members of households whose welfare relied on a husband's continued employment. So far as they were concerned, despite the increasing importance of domestic consumption and the rising number of wives entering paid employment, women as a whole remained dependent on male bread-winners.

This chapter first outlines the place of women in the party at the start of the 1960s, to locate subsequent events in their proper context. It focuses on Labour's response to women's changing place in society by looking at how officials promoted a variety of organisational reforms designed to increase the number of younger female members. The chapter then discusses Labour's efforts to come to terms with the per-ceived need to address gender inequality in the later part of the decade, especially with regard to equal pay. It does not dispute the predominant view that Labour was largely run by – and to some extent for – men, something which was also true of most other civil institutions during this period, including the Conservative Party. However, it seeks to stress the often obscured fact that, while much keener to promote equal pay than the leadership, Labour's women activists were in other respects broadly content with the party's emphases. Indeed, so far as attempts to increase the party's appeal to younger working wives and mothers were concerned, they often proved to be an impediment. Furthermore, Labour's women also blamed members of their own sex as much as or more than men for inequalities feminists would subsequently deem to be the result of 'patriarchy'.

Labour's women

While issued with a different-coloured membership card – which some thought denoted their second-class status – women could participate in the party just like men. They also had an additional means of working within Labour's ranks, which granted them, should they desire it, a separate voice. Thus, by 1965, 85 per cent of constituencies had at least one women's section. Apart from giving women a distinct platform – they could send representatives to meetings of the constituency's general management committee (GMC) – women's sections were meant to reflect their particular interests.[6] To encourage the growth of sections, each region was allotted a women's organiser, who operated under the direc-tion of the Chief Women's Officer (CWO), based in Transport House. To co-ordinate activities, sections in more than one constituency were gathered together into constituency committees within urban districts and federations in counties. These appointed delegates to regional women's advisory councils, which, in turn, sent representatives to the National Labour Women's Advisory Council (NLWAC), serviced by the CWO's department, which also organised the annual national conference of Labour women. The function of the NLWAC was, as its title implied,

Table 5.1 Labour's official female membership, 1960–70

	Official figure	*Percentage of membership*
1960	330,608	41.8
1961	316,054	42.1
1962	322,883	42.1
1963	349,707	42.1
1964	351,206	42.3
1965	341,601	41.8
1966	320,971	41.4
1967	306,437	41.8
1968	299,357	42.7
1969	292,800	43.0
1970	285,901	41.4

Table 2.1 (p. 43) gives total party membership.
Source: Labour Party conference reports, 1960–70.

to advise the National Executive Committee (NEC) on matters of importance to female members. Five members of the NEC were elected by
party conference from a women-only list, as a consequence of which
they owed their places to the unions rather than the support of other
women. While the NEC was under no obligation to heed their lobbying,
women at least had the chance to make their collective voice heard.

According to official figures, in 1960 there were 330,608 female party
members, accounting for 41.8 per cent of the total, a proportion that
hardly varied during the decade (see Table 5.1). In the unlikely event
these figures reflected reality, women were under-represented, a feature
that became much more pronounced higher up the party hierarchy.
Thus, in late 1950s Manchester, only one-quarter of ward secretaries
were women.[7] During the 1960s the proportion of female constituency
Labour party (CLP) secretaries and delegates to annual conference
remained steady, at 15–20 per cent. The extent of their lack of presence
varied across the country, although everywhere it was striking. In rural
areas, where Labour had never done well, female secretaries were rare,
but that was also the case in most industrial counties.[8] The position was
even worse in the Commons. In 1959 only thirty-six women stood as
parliamentary candidates, a mere 5.8 per cent of the total: the number
elected came to a paltry thirteen. Women Labour MPs continued to be
a tiny minority and while the 1966 landslide saw their number reach
the dizzy height of nineteen (or 5.2 per cent), in 1970 this fell to ten.
During the course of the 1964–70 governments there were never more
than six female junior ministers, while their representation around the
Cabinet table was mostly limited to Barbara Castle, although Judith
Hart joined her in 1968.

Despite this, the 1955 Wilson report on party organisation (see Chapter 2) claimed women supplied the majority of CLP volunteers; and Brixton's agent declared in 1956 that, 'if one of our active lady members has a baby we begin to get nervous about the ward organisation'.[9] Responsibilities were, however, generally allocated on the basis of conventional gender roles, which led some to complain that women were confined to catering for, and cleaning up after, male-dominated meetings. That a significant number of activists were married to each other clearly influenced matters.[10] Labour husbands and wives related to one another in the party as they did at home and domestic relationships largely reflected established gender norms. Thus, during the 1959 campaign, most women in Southall placed leaflets into envelopes, while safely seated in party offices, while their men-folk took to the streets.[11] Similarly, during the 1960s, Bristol South women supplied only one-fifth of the CLP's membership fee collectors.[12]

By no means were all female activists frustrated by this clearly gendered division of labour; some appeared to see it as part of their 'natural' lot. For instance, those in Brecon were annoyed after a member of the constituency's executive committee (EC) complained about a dirty party room. Their anger was, however, not due to his assumption that their job was to clean the room, but because they had not been informed earlier that it required attention.[13] There were, nonetheless, some occasions when women members asserted themselves. Most famously, Castle owed her position as a Blackburn MP after 1945 to them threatening to stop making tea for CLP meetings unless one of their kind was short-listed for consideration as a parliamentary candidate.[14] More prosaically, women on Llanelli's GMC cast their own modest version of the block vote to maximise female representation on its EC.[15] When one leading female activist was not selected as a candidate for local office in Swansea, she went so far as to stand as an independent. Owing to a collective frustration with their ward's lack of regard for the women's section, eleven other female activists supported her campaign.[16]

If nothing else, the range of issues discussed by at least some sections was impressive. In Bradford South during 1958, for example, women debated home safety, local landmarks, 'problem' families, welfare, a member's Mediterranean cruise and Labour's new leisure policy.[17] In the same year, those in Clapham talked about local government, rents, the Soviet Union, the work of magistrates, local elections, delinquent children and education. To make them more agreeable, as well as discussions the Clapham meetings featured raffles, performances of short plays or games of 'housey-housey'.[18] In contrast, other sections were almost entirely preoccupied with raising money for the CLP, through jumble sales and summer fetes.[19] Whatever they did, sections reflected the interests of those full-time housewives who generally attended meetings.

Table 5.2 Women's section delegates attending the national conference of Labour women, 1960–70

	Number of sections	Number of section delegates at conference	Percentage of sections sending delegates
1960	–	398	–
1961	1,564	358	22.9
1962	1,580	330	20.1
1963	1,613	461	28.6
1964	1,640	478	29.1
1965	1,660	438	26.4
1966	1,646	300	18.2
1967	1,603	333	20.8
1968	1,541	313	20.3
1969	1,420	286	20.1
1970	1,373	221	16.1

Note: After 1963 each section was entitled to send a delegate; before this, representation was based on constituency (i.e. groups of sections).
Source: *Reports of the National Conferences of Labour Women*, 1960–70.

Even so, while in the Grimsby women's section there were women 'who really enjoy being housewives' and believed a 'happy home should be our first aim', even they did not go as far as Morden members, who dedicated one gathering to a washing machine demonstration, to which they brought dirty clothes.[20] It is deceptively easy to denigrate the modesty of these activities. Some nonetheless argued – as did the South West Region's women's organiser – that less 'politically minded' women required sections.[21] They gave them the chance to learn about society, gain an insight into political issues and provided a platform to campaign on matters about which they cared. As one participant recalled, sections gave those 'too nervous' to attend meetings dominated by men the chance to build confidence so they might eventually become more directly involved in the wider party.[22]

Even more than wards and CLPs, women's sections were predominantly parochial in orientation. At least one-third did not take a copy of the monthly journal produced by Transport House, *Labour Woman*, whose circulation hovered around 10,000 during the 1960s.[23] Most failed to send delegates to their own national conference: it was a rare year that saw more than 20 per cent represented (see Table 5.2). This might have been partly due to lack of funds but was probably mainly accountable to the older age of many Labour women. Since the early 1950s the party had lost younger female members to paid employment, while even part-time work reduced the hours previously committed housewives with children could devote to the cause.[24] Thus, by the late 1960s, members of the women's section in Hammersmith North had an average age of seventy-two, while those in Oxford were too frail to attend meetings held in the city centre.[25] One regional advisory council was even described in 1966 by its former secretary as serving 'little useful purpose, political or otherwise except keeping the older Labour women together occasionally – it's the Mother's Union of the Labour Party'.[26]

Reforming the organisation

By the start of the 1960s, some in Transport House, such as Len Williams, the National Agent, believed there was no need for women to have their own 'political kindergarten', as they had largely achieved equality.[27] For similar reasons, the 1968 Simpson report on party organisation (see Chapter 2) recommended that those NEC seats reserved for women should be redistributed among the unions and constituencies. Like Williams, Simpson believed Labour women could stand on their own two feet without special assistance, although delegates to the Labour women's conference were less confident.[28] Simpson's proposal was rejected, possibly because it threatened to enhance the voice of the left on the NEC rather than because of NLWAC representations.[29] In 1961 the CWO's department was subsumed within that of the National Agent and while the title of Chief Women's Organiser remained, as did the regional women's organisers, post-holders ceased to act independently of male officials. Some on the NLWAC were convinced this was due to a desire to place women under the authority of 'Men Organisers'. Reformers nonetheless claimed change would ensure everybody in the party took raising female membership seriously, but agreed Labour should still cater for women's 'special interests'.[30]

It was not just men who doubted the efficacy of Labour's separate women's organisation. Some women, usually younger and more educated than most, had long called for its abolition, if only because members of the sections lacked what they considered to be an adequate interest in politics. In the late 1940s, for example, one critic described her north London section as a 'cross between a rummage sale and a tea-party'.[31] Some middle-class CLPs, such as Bristol West, even thought sections prevented women's integration into party life. As neighbouring Bristol North West's agent stated, 'modern woman' refused to be 'segregated' and was not prepared to 'sit back and be regarded as a useful adjunct to the Party making tea'. Instead, she wanted 'to play a full part in the Movement, a "man's" part'.[32]

In 1967 the women's conference debated a motion that advocated its own abolition, tabled in the belief that this would allow women to participate in the party on equal terms with men. Those who drafted the motion thought there were no 'subjects which were particularly suitable for women to deal with': men and women 'were equally concerned with all matters because they lived in the same world and their basic problems were the same'. The overwhelming majority present nonetheless considered the conference remained the only occasion on which women's problems could gain a proper hearing. As one put it, Labour was the 'most masculine dominated and masculine orientated movement' she had ever encountered.[33] A similar motion was debated the following year; it was moved by a young delegate who declared that, to those of her generation, sections appeared to serve 'no apparent purpose [other] than to bring together like minded people for pleasant, if rather aimless social occasions'.[34] While this view was again rejected, some continued to imagine that the very existence of women's sections perpetuated discrimination, as they gave some men the excuse they needed to deny women a proper say in the party as a whole.[35]

Despite these challenges, the prevailing view among those 300 or so women who attended their national conference during the late 1960s was that, as one put it, women were 'equal but different'. They still required a separate organisation because their 'unique function', as the NLWAC later had it, that of child-bearing, placed them at an inherent disadvantage. Thus, while Labour was unable to overcome the social consequences of biology, it should still cater for difference. Consequently, while most women preferred to be treated as individuals rather than 'women', they still needed 'preferential treatment'.[36]

Attracting younger women

It was never thought that encouraging younger women into the party would be easy. They were widely considered 'too busy to think much about politics' and would first have to be persuaded that their interests were indeed 'political', and only then that Labour membership could advance them.[37] Moreover, as one activist noted, those working outside the home, or looking after their family full-time, wanted to be 'lifted out of themselves' and did not 'want to read correspondence and discuss political issues all night'.[38] Sections were consequently asked to streamline routine business. As Mary Sutherland, Labour's long-standing CWO until she retired in 1961, declared, 'it is more important to double our membership and double attendances at meetings than to insist that every member shall discuss items of business'.[39] With that object in mind, women were urged to experiment with more appealing social activities, such as sherry parties and theatre trips.[40]

It would have surprised some critics that women's sections needed to enhance their social side. In any case, such was the target group's

Learning Resources

presumed resistance to formal political activity that officials' emphasis lay more on encouraging Labour women to pursue 'informal' activities outside the section structure, such as luncheon, dinner and supper clubs, coffee circles, 'young mums' clubs and neighbourhood groups.[41] The overt purpose of these initiatives was to bring Labour women into contact with friends and neighbours so they might enjoy a 'pleasant social gathering'. Covertly, however, they were meant to develop into opportunities for 'useful political discussion and membership recruitment'.[42] Members were warned they might be forced to participate in 'idle gossip about this T.V. programme or that', so they could put Labour's case at an appropriate moment.[43] With this strategy of permeation in mind, a Middlesbrough activist went so far as to urge Labour women to 'get into any organisation, no matter what – they could go and talk tiddly-winks provided they got on to Labour policy in the end'.[44] Young mothers were pursued with particular zeal. In Bradford members converted a garage so it could house a playgroup and in Bletchley women ran a playgroup which, after three years, catered for 271 children. Women in Halesowen were so successful in attracting young mothers that meetings were overrun by noisy toddlers – it became difficult to discuss anything, let alone politics.[45]

Labour women were also urged to take up popular non-partisan issues to place themselves in a more attractive light; a national effort to raise money for Freedom from Hunger (devoted to helping developing nations) in 1963–4 had this as its object, while in Stirling women established a presence on a new housing estate by collecting for people with disabilities. In Ipswich they organised a retail price survey to demonstrate Labour's sympathy for housewives, something undoubtedly behind a national campaign promoting consumer protection during 1962–3.[46]

In spite of official exhortation, few sections were keen to encourage a greater role for young women.[47] There were too many, such as the one in Toxteth, Liverpool, where a dwindling band of the aged few occasionally noted the reluctance of youngsters to attend their afternoon get-togethers. Members did not think they could do much about this, and blamed it on the rising number of married women in paid work and the spread of television ownership. It is likely they believed that, if anybody was to blame for Labour's lack of younger female members, it was women themselves.[48] In truth, many established activists were too comfortable with their cosy gatherings – sharing gossip about old acquaintances and listening to the occasional educational talk – to want to change. Unfortunately, few twenty-somethings found 'housey-housey' an attractive prospect, while many others were, for work or domestic reasons, simply unable to attend afternoon meetings.

In trying to enthuse sections to recruit younger women, officials confronted a generational divide that reflected tensions evident on numerous working-class housing estates.[49] Many Labour women looked on their less mature, non-party counterparts as in need of instruction rather than the indulgence of a glass of sherry. Like the archetypal matriarch in 'traditional' proletarian communities, Labour women expected to be listened to and learnt from.[50] At least some lacked sympathy for the plight of those to whom they were meant to appeal. Women in Grimsby, for example, were sceptical about whether young mothers should go out to work and believed that 'nothing, however good it may be, is as good as a mother's care'.[51] Young women were also, according to the MP Lena Jeger, that part of the population 'most careless of its rights of franchise and citizenship' and the 'laziest of all groups in doing their duty at the polls'.[52]

This rift was revealed most clearly during women's conference debates on consumer protection. While all speakers favoured increasing help and advice, this was often presented as giving aid to naïve young wives, who, as one speaker put it, did not have the 'guts' to shut the door in the face of predatory door-to-door salespeople and 'tell them where to get off'. After hearing various tales of women buying shoddy goods, another declaimed, 'what gullible people women were', and stated that those buying goods on hire purchase were also 'playing the Tory game'. A further speaker wondered 'what kind of fools and mugs housewives were'; she considered it impossible to protect some from their own foolishness.[53] One even wondered, possibly thinking of fellow Labour women as the prototype, 'what had become of the wise housewives of the past, who had known exactly what a shilling meant'. Even the fact that 'modern food … was not worth eating' was partly women's own fault, for they bought frozen food because it was quick and easy to cook.[54] That those few youngsters attending conference usually confirmed this picture did not help. As one said, she belonged to that 'deluded generation' who thought unemployment could never happen to them and who had 'bought their washing machines and their tellys, egged on to live right up to their income'.[55]

In light of this hostility, some officials came to believe it necessary to devise a new organisation, just for younger women.[56] Raising similar concerns generated by Tony Benn's Citizens for Labour (see Chapter 3), the NEC initially turned down the request of reformers in Buckingham to allow the Socialist Women's Circle to affiliate to their CLP. The Circle was organised by party activists; while its mostly non-partisan members mainly engaged in its social activities, they helped with electoral work when required. Despite this, the NEC believed such women should join sections and become fully integrated into the party.[57] The promotion of women's councils in the late 1960s marked a dramatic change of tack, being – contrary to officials' claims – an attempt to reduce the influence of elderly stalwarts based in sections.[58] These councils were to assume the co-ordinating role formerly performed by constituency committees, federations and advisory councils, bodies that only reflected section opinion. Councils would represent non-members who belonged to those 'informal' bodies – such as luncheon clubs and neighbourhood groups – established after 1959. Officials hoped this new 'outward looking structure' would finally enable the party to pursue more non-partisan 'community' activities and finally bridge the gap between Labour women and those active in less overtly political groups.[59]

Labour women and feminism

When Maureen Colquhoun entered the Commons in 1974, she claimed to find no 'feminist' women Labour MPs. If several sought to improve their sisters' lives, she claimed none wanted to dismantle the 'patriarchal society' – if only because they had not heard of the term.[60] That 'patriarchy' had no purchase among Labour's female MPs should have come as no surprise to Colquhoun, who had attended women's conferences during the 1960s. While activists supported greater equality, few believed male and female interests were inherently in conflict.[61] Hence, reflecting the majority position, Sutherland rejected the notion of an 'identity of the sexes', on the basis that the genders performed different but complementary roles, with women's key responsibility lying in the home.[62]

Some historians have stated that, for much of the post-war period, there was little evidence of a clear 'ideology of gender' among Labour's female activists, with the 1950s and 1960s being described as the 'nadir of women's equal rights' in the party.[63] That is going too far, as some at least believed male prejudice impeded the development of full gender equality, in Labour's ranks as much as anywhere else. One delegate to the women's conference, for example, said men considered women capable only of 'making tea, etc., trotting round streets and sitting in committee rooms'; a second claimed they only paid 'lip-service' to equal rights; men, another complained, 'simply did not want women to have equality'.[64] How far sections believed male prejudice prevented women assuming a prominent role in the party was measured by a survey conducted during 1968 to discover what they thought about women's position in public life. Leaders on the NLWAC expressed some alarm at the 'reasonableness' of the outlook revealed and accused sections of complacency. The survey indicated that, if Labour women were aware that male bigotry was one cause of women's modest public profile, most believed it was largely due to women's own shortcomings. They also reportedly neither expected nor even desired a substantial change in female under-representation; most apparently merely requested men's 'respect'.[65] In certain CLPs, respect would have been welcome: in at least one Yorkshire mining constituency, male members were said to react to female contributions to debate with 'amused tolerance'.[66]

It was a very rare constituency party that thought it necessary actively to promote women candidates. Largely middle-class Bristol North West was one of the few. In 1968 its GMC aimed to 'groom' women to ensure every ward was represented by at least one female Labour councillor.[67] For the most part, rather than reform the party's procedures to challenge the imbalance between men and women, the latter were exhorted to push themselves forward to beat men at their own game. Doris Fisher, one of the few women returned to the Commons in 1970, considered the basic reason for their under-representation was that politics was a 'tough, rough business where very often feelings are hurt'. Many women were, she judged, 'personally sensitive', so did not wish to enter the fray: Fisher advised them to 'adopt a "thick skin"'. Her words echoed those of a councillor who suggested women needed to acquire the 'skin of a rhinoceros' and 'show the men they were equally capable of conducting the country's affairs'.[68]

Others argued that 'men were not the ogres women made them out to be', and claimed that the 'biggest enemies of women were women themselves', as they were often biased in favour of male candidates. It was the minister Peggy Herbison who said that because 'too many women electors were against having women in politics', they should accept 'a great deal of the responsibility' for their own under-representation.[69] The NLWAC believed women in general 'disliked female managers, courted male patronage, rather than male competition, and when patronized by men accepted it without complaint'.[70] Ultimately, one activist argued, 'women themselves were responsible for most of the discrimination against their sex' because it 'began in the home where the small daughter was given the washing up to do while her brother was handed his fishing rod'.'Equality for women', it was said, 'began in the hearts of women themselves'.[71]

Studying discrimination

Despite this voluntaristic emphasis, as the decade drew to a close, some in the party became more conscious of the structural inequalities that distinguished the genders. On a superficial level, an increasing number of CLPs passed resolutions demanding that the 'archaic custom' of differently coloured membership cards be abandoned. East Ham North had been the first to make this proposal, in 1958, but it was only in 1970 that, despite the loss of a means of assessing how many women belonged to the party, the NEC agreed to issue a single style of membership card in future.[72]

More substantively, in July 1967 the NEC's Home Policy Sub-committee formed the Discrimination Against Women Study Group, charged with the aim of influencing policy.[73] In the end, the Group's output was so limited its impact was negligible, although its deliberations do illustrate how some of its leading members viewed the subject. The Group was drawn from the NEC and the Commons, as well as outside experts, and the importance attached to its deliberations was signified by the fact that Douglas Houghton was the chair. Houghton was an important figure, who had just left the Cabinet, who chaired the Parliamentary Labour Party and, in the wake of George Brown's final resignation, who was mooted as a possible deputy leader. More pertinently, Houghton had overseen a ministerial review of the social services and, as he put it, 'social security is mostly about women'.[74]

The Group's remit was ambitious – overly so, as it included a 'comprehensive study of the nature of discrimination against women', so that it could recommend policies that would help achieve equal rights. There was, from the outset, no question that women did suffer 'downright injustice'. Despite this, members rejected the 'standpoint of feminism' and instead proceeded on the basis that 'a country that designates any group, class, or sex as second class citizens will in the long run suffer by denying them a full contribution to society'. While agreeing about the reality of discrimination, the Group was divided over how to overcome it. Members' initial focus fell on tax, in particular the fact that wives were assessed as their husbands' dependants. As early as January 1968, Houghton suggested couples should be treated separately, as he considered the existing arrangement 'derogatory' to women's 'dignity as individuals'. Because some thought this would leave poorer families worse off, he did not prevail. The former minister Peggy Herbison even questioned why full-time housewives should be given the same social security benefits as men, given that they made fewer contributions, through their absence from paid employment. Women, she believed, 'could not expect both to have full social security rights and to opt out of contributions', her implication being that housewives should pay National Insurance. As Herbison told the 1968 national conference of Labour women, 'if women wanted equality they had also to accept the responsibilities of equality'.[75] On both subjects the Group found it hard to reach agreement and the tax question was unresolved when Wilson announced the date of the 1970 election.

An important by-product of the Group's work was Participation '69 (discussed in more detail in Chapter 8), which was a scheme meant to promote greater membership involvement in policy-making. The first subject used to test party opinion was women and social security, on which the Group had just produced an interim report. Members were asked for their thoughts on this in light of changing family relationships, which were said to be encouraging 'increasing independence and equality' for wives, while single mothers apparently accounted for a rising proportion of those in receipt of supplementary benefit. It was calculated that the opinions of 2,343 members were represented by the responses sent to Transport House. While these cannot be assumed to be representative, they give some indication of thinking in the wider party. Respondents overwhelmingly believed women should be treated the same as men when it came to tax, while there was little sense that unmarried mothers were less 'deserving' of benefits than their married equivalents. Some, however, disliked what they took to be the assumption behind the exercise, which, they believed, was that all women should be in paid employment. Leyland Trades Council, for example, stated that it was 'not conducive to good quality family life' for mothers of children under twelve to work outside the home.[76]

The Study Group had lost its way some time before this broad endorsement of its work. Reflecting its lack of direction, the last gathering before the 1970 election was presented with a historical analysis of female emancipation, which concluded that any discussion of women's social position should be preceded by an examination of their sexual relationships. For a body that had been in existence nearly two and half years, this was a bizarre time to consider first principles. Whether the Group's failure to come to firm conclusions about particular subjects was due to its original remit or a lack of consensus over detailed policy is not clear. Houghton's chairing certainly did not help: significantly, his earlier review of the social services was criticised for its production of overly detailed papers but lack of compelling general purpose, something that also characterised the Group's slight output.[77]

Labour women and working women

The Wilson governments introduced numerous pieces of legislation meant to improve women's lives, most obviously its 'permissive' reforms, which liberalised access to abortion and divorce. On the former issue in particular, while broadly in favour of reform, the party still faced a number of ways.[78] A delegate to the 1970 women's conference probably spoke for the majority when she declared that 'everyone should be thankful for a permissive society which threw open the doors and let out the fear of the unknown and let in the fresh air of commonsense'. She did not, however, speak for the Burnley delegate, who could not believe all those present fully supported the 1967 Abortion Act and whose concern with the supposed abuses to which it gave rise echoed that of some NLWAC members.[79]

So far as an increasing proportion of women were concerned, however, the most significant measure passed by the Labour administration was the 1970 Equal Pay Act. A series of articles published in *Labour Woman* before the 1959 election took as their theme 'women and the second industrial revolution' and outlined how the automation of production might affect them. The author correctly predicted there would be a rise in the number of jobs in the service industry, but erroneously believed this would not create a greater demand for female workers. Instead, she considered it probable that, as men's real wages rose through greater productivity, there would be less need for women to seek work outside the home. This, together with the wider availability of domestic labour-saving devices, led her to hope women would enjoy more leisure and so assume a more prominent public role.[80] As many women's sections were beginning to learn to their cost, women were already filling the expanding number of job vacancies caused by full employment. To meet this demand for female labour, some believed, women would have to be treated – or at least paid – the same as men. Yet, as late as 1969, Joyce Gould claimed on behalf of the NLWAC that they remained 'the slave labour of the 1960's' and 'waited for their Wilberforce to come and rescue them'.[81]

Labour women were in at least two minds over female employment. Some adhered to a belief in the hierarchy of need, so that, in 1959, a year when unemployment was thought to be on the rise, the women's conference debated a resolution demanding that employers made married female workers redundant before single women.[82] At their 1960 conference, Ron Hayward, who would become General Secretary of the Labour Party in 1969, informed delegates that if Labour had lost the previous general election because 'Jack was all right', Jack was in this happy state only because 'Mrs. Jack had a part-time job in order to maintain her family's standard of living'. Hayward's inference was clear: men should be paid enough so that their wives did not have to work. At least some women agreed, believing in 1964 that 'women only worked because they were desperate for the money'.[83] As one NLWAC speaker noted, 'the most important thing in the homes of the people was to have husbands and fathers working': a working wife was presumably either a luxury for the affluent or an unpleasant necessity for the poor.[84]

Women members also doubted whether it was proper for mothers, especially those with young children, to work. A survey of section thinking about the care of children revealed that most considered working mothers were entitled to expect child care. However, when the matter was debated, at least one speaker at the women's conference thought that, on this matter at least, too much was said about the rights of women, 'when in fact without hesitation or discussion the rights of the child should come first'.[85] When the 1969 women's conference called for more nursery schools, one delegate reported that her section believed employers should not be allowed to employ mothers with children under five, unless they supplied proper child care facilities. Another speaker went further and stated that unless a woman was in poverty she should stay at home during the first five years of her child's life. She asked:

> What was the matter with women today? They did not deserve to be mothers. If they could not sacrifice five years for their children before the children went to school they did not know what they were missing. They were missing the relationship between child and mother. It was no wonder there were so many child delinquents when that relationship was missing. Forget about the money ... and stay at home until the children go to school.[86]

For most, the ideal marriage remained one in which the wife stayed at home while the husband worked. Moreover, one contributor to *Labour Woman*, while bemoaning the 'double burden' of the working housewife, believed that, no matter how willing husbands might be, there remained domestic tasks 'which wives *must* shoulder'.[87]

The slow progress of equal pay

If some doubted that mothers with young children should join the labour force, they all believed that gender should not dictate pay: indeed, by 1966 the call for equal pay was described as the 'hardy annual' of the women's conference.[88] Labour had grappled with the issue for many decades. After the publication of a Royal Commission report on the subject in 1946, Clement Attlee's Cabinet declared that, while it was in favour in principle, the constraints imposed by post-war reconstruction meant it was impractical.[89] In 1953 the party conference reaffirmed Labour's belief in the 'principle of equal pay for equal work' and committed a future government to 'immediately implement' the policy – albeit only to government employees, to 'give a lead to industry generally'.[90] Individual Labour MPs did their best to further the cause during the years of Conservative rule. In 1954 Houghton introduced a Private Member's Bill that sought to achieve equal pay by altering contracts of service. He was supported by MPs from across the party's left–right divide, including Barbara Castle. During this period individual unions and the Trades Union Congress (TUC) also passed resolutions supportive of the measure.

As a result, Labour's 1964 manifesto promised to implement women's right to 'equal pay for equal work', a commitment reaffirmed in 1966.[91] Wilson's ministers were not, however, obliged to introduce equal pay immediately. At the 1963 party conference, the NEC indicated it would merely 'seek at an appropriate stage in its first term of office to consider ways and means of implementing' the policy.[92] Ray Gunter, Minister of Labour between 1964 and 1968, was merely adhering to policy when, in January 1965, he appointed a working party of civil servants, drawn from his ministry, the Department of Economic Affairs and the Treasury, to consider the matter. The subsequent report, presented in November, was cautious to say the least, in no small measure owing to the Treasury's preoccupation with rising labour costs. In the first instance, the working party recommended equal pay should come through agreement between government, the unions and employers, as it was deemed important to maintain the tradition of free collective bargaining. It also cautioned against implementing any measure while economic circumstances remained so uncertain. The authors were obviously not keen on equal pay and repeated many of the misgivings expressed by the earlier Royal Commission. Thus, they feared it would encourage full-time female workers to go part-time; that married men with dependants would be relatively worse off; and – contradicting the first objection – juvenile delinquency would rise through lack of a mother's presence in the home.[93]

Despite its obvious scepticism, Gunter used the report as the basis for separate – and leisurely – talks with the Confederation of British Industry (CBI) and TUC.[94] It was not until July 1966 that he convened a joint meeting with both bodies to agree a policy, something he must have known was unlikely. The TUC favoured the International Labour Organisation's definition of 'equal pay for work of equal value', while the CBI preferred the more restrictive European Economic Community's notion of 'equal pay for the same work', and neither side had moved from their original position since meeting the minister.[95] If Gunter appeared in no rush to reach an agreement, the CBI employed blatant delaying tactics. At their first meeting with the TUC, employers' representatives claimed they had no mandate to agree a policy, as the CBI had not formally determined its position. The CBI debated the issue only in 1968 and then claimed it would need another year before it could arrive at a definite policy. Even Ministry of Labour officials thought that a 'stately pace'.[96]

As a result, by the end of 1967 equal pay was as far away as it had ever been.[97] While Gunter tried to avoid responsibility, Labour women expressed frustration with his failure to deliver – although the NLWAC loyally defended the minister by stressing the complexity of the issue during a time of economic difficulty.[98] Gunter was informed of a particularly striking outburst at a trades union meeting in Newcastle upon Tyne (at the heart of a region with little known sympathy for feminism), which occurred during a debate on a resolution that called for the immediate introduction of equal pay:

The mover of the resolution complained in most bitter terms about the apparent lack of interest and inertia, from all responsible quarters. She very forcibly stated that women were not tied to be the 'law abiding' section of industry forever and a day, making reference to the fact, that the Engineering Industry in particular, had a backbone of women workers who could bring that industry to its knees.... Other delegates speaking in support, reflected the rising anger and impatience of women workers through this ever continuing delay.... They warned that they will no longer tolerate any longer the role of industries [*sic*] second class citizens, or accept being the means of cheap labour. They ... declared, that they were very seriously thinking of emulating the old Suffragettes, as an indication of their determination to achieve this objective.[99]

The impact of Barbara Castle (again)

Wilson sacked Gunter in April 1968 and subsumed his ministry into what became the Department for Employment and Productivity (DEP), at the head of which, and enjoying the prestigious title of First Secretary of State, was Barbara Castle. She initially echoed her predecessor's position on equal pay, claiming to favour the principle but stressing the practical problems regarding implementation. As the measure entailed a 'significant increase' in wages, Castle ruled it out while the country's economic problems persisted.[100] What seems to have encouraged Castle to revise this opinion was her responsibility for maintaining the government's incomes policy.[101] This meant the DEP was forced to intervene in numerous complicated pay disputes in which equal pay was at least tangentially raised. It was this experience, she subsequently claimed, which 'fired my determination to force the male chauvinists in the Treasury to accept the principle of equal pay' and made her realise that, despite their rhetoric, the unions did not take the issue seriously.

The most significant of these disputes was the one involving 190 sewing machinists who installed car interior upholstery at the Fords Dagenham plant.[102] In June 1968 these women went on strike believing they had been cheated by a job evaluation scheme, which they thought had not fairly graded their work. The scheme had taken months of tortuous negotiation to compile and involved a national joint council composed of the five unions with members in the factory. As the women complained only after the agreement had been signed, most unions were unwilling to address their concerns, as they feared the scheme would unravel as a result. The official inquiry into the dispute claimed the women were unconcerned with differentials between men and women on the same grade – and so did not call for equal pay. They were, however, unhappy about how their work as sewing machinists was graded in relation to other comparable occupations in the plant. The union representing most of the women endorsed this interpretation. Even so, some saw the matter otherwise. The Prime Minister received an anonymous note claiming to come from Dagenham which stated that 'we are fighting a great fight for equal pay for women ... we will force you to give us all equal pay, or strike with our unions' blessings, we're sorry for Fords, sorry for the men out of work, but more sorry for ourselves'. 'Give us what we want', the note demanded, 'not only us at Fords [but] all Women everywhere'.[103]

As the dispute held up vital car production, Castle tried to find a quick solution by intervening in person. She discovered that a shop steward had told the women there were two evaluation reports on their work, one of which (the one which allegedly favoured them) had been suppressed. This, Castle determined, was untrue and she convinced the women of it. Even so, to encourage an early return to work, the plant manager offered to reduce differentials between male and female workers on the machinists' grade. Ford had actually mooted this during negotiations but the unions rejected it because it entailed women under-taking shift work. As this could be squared with the government's prices and incomes legislation and would not force the collapse of the plant scheme, Castle approved the proposal, the women accepted it and the dispute ended.

The First Secretary was disappointed by the contribution of union representatives during the dispute. In her view some militants – par-ticularly those associated with the engineering union – indulged in 'deliberate mischief'. Although they were ostensibly acting in support of equal pay, they appeared only to want to undermine delicate wage agreements. Her low view of the unions was confirmed by another dis-pute, during the autumn of 1968. Engineering employers had agreed with unions led by Hugh Scanlon that male skilled workers should have their pay increased to £19 a week, even though Scanlon knew that women employees – already at the bottom of the industry's pay scale – would remain on just £13. Thus differentials between men and women would increase. Scanlon was denounced by a female member of his own negotiating team. As a result, he went back to the employers to demand more for women, only to be told no money was left. With a national strike in the offing, Castle became involved and persuaded the em-ployers to announce that, while they were willing to increase their offer to women workers, this could be done only if they reduced what had been put on the table for skilled men. Faced with the choice of reducing or increasing differentials, Scanlon accepted the original offer. Castle commented that, after this, she knew 'left to themselves the unions would never do anything serious about equal pay': government had to legislate.

In June the same year, Castle had wrung an important concession out of an embattled Chancellor of the Exchequer. Roy Jenkins faced defeat over an amendment to his Prices and Incomes Bill that had been tabled by Labour MPs led by Lena Jeger. This stipulated that settlements that included moves towards equal pay should be exempted from the provisions of the Bill. Jenkins feared this would undermine attempts to keep down wages, as any union worth its salt would exploit the loophole. Castle suggested that if he allowed her to announce that the government would implement statutory equal pay by 1975, the wind would be taken out of Jeger's sails without any immediate cost to the country. Grabbing hold of this lifeline, Jenkins agreed and his Bill was passed without the offending amendment.

While claiming the unions could not be trusted to win equal pay, Castle used the threat of industrial militancy to persuade ministerial sceptics that legislation was necessary. Certainly, DEP civil servants were unclear how they should present her case. According to one brief, Castle's initiative was meant to 'contain' union pressure for equal pay, while another indicated it was simply designed to 'make progress' to equal pay and made no mention of union pressure.[104] Even so, when Castle met the CBI to call an end to the talks initiated by Gunter over two years before, she waxed lyrical about the 'mounting pressure' for equal pay. It was, she claimed, to ensure that 'orderly progress' could be made towards what Castle identified as an inevitable end that action was now required.[105] When, in July 1969, Jenkins tried wriggle out of his earlier commitment and prevent the inclusion of equal pay in the Queen's Speech, she again cited militancy as an important influence on legislation. Castle told Cabinet they 'had run out of delaying excuses ... there would be a move to equal pay anyhow and it was far better that we should control it and get credit for it'. Giving legislation legal force only in 1975 was the 'maximum we could get away with'. More ominously, not to take a lead would mean trouble with the unions and the party: given the government's increasingly frosty relations with both, this argument could no longer be neutralised by the Treasury's line that equal pay was too expensive.[106]

A very quiet revolution

When finally debated in the Commons, equal pay had no enemies who were prepared to speak. Despite employers' hostility, the Conservatives decided not to oppose the measure, their own research having revealed that the majority of men and women supported it.[107] On the Labour side only Renee Short complained about how long it would take for equal pay to become a statutory requirement. Apart from that, even she was complimentary: the Bill was, Short said, an 'important landmark in women's emancipation'. Perhaps because of this lack of opposition, as the former minister Fred Lee noted, the Bill went through 'practically without a ripple' in the press. On its third and final reading the chamber was almost empty.[108]

If the introduction of equal pay provoked little open hostility, it generated only a grudging welcome. The NLWAC was 'not completely satisfied' with Castle's Bill, while the First Secretary was frustrated by the lifeless nature of the women's conference debate on the matter, even though it had just become law. She was more than a little annoyed by the response of fellow Labour women and tartly commented that it was 'another example of how our movement is so schooled in protest that it doesn't know how to celebrate victory'. This downbeat reaction was possibly due to the fact that, as Castle's deputy Harold Walked noted, the Bill marked only the 'end of the beginning' while, as she conceded, it was a 'long overdue piece of justice'.[109]

The final Act certainly left many issues unresolved and Castle was well aware of its limitations. It did not address women's unequal access to certain jobs and particular forms of training; on such matters the First Secretary admitted women would have to keep on pressing ministers.[110] With further progress on that front in mind, as the Bill reached its last stage, Castle asked DEP officials to investigate the possibility of legislating against discrimination in employment and training. True to form, her civil servants opposed an early initiative, owing to its apparent complexity.[111] Castle knew some would be disappointed that provision for equal pensions was also excluded from the legislation. She did her best, but had backed down in the face of the opposition of the Secretary of State for Social Security, Richard Crossman. Castle nonetheless kept options open by including in her Bill powers to deal with the matter sometime in the future.[112] Finally, she had wanted to abolish restrictions on the hours women could work, but considered the unions would oppose proposals of that sort. Castle meant to pursue this after equal pay had become a reality.[113]

Echoing the voluntaristic emphasis noted earlier, Castle stated that equal pay legislation would have a profound effect on society only if women's attitudes also changed. In particular, more should join a union, as they 'had no right to expect the full fruits of the Bill unless they bestirred themselves to assert their rights and to organise'. She was, Castle claimed, merely providing them with a legal framework, 'not a system of spoonfeeding', and so they 'must not leave it all to the Government'. Even Short believed the Bill would have come sooner had women workers been more militant; the problem was, she conceded, that not all women appeared to want equality.[114] As the NLWAC noted in 1968, many preferred 'a certain level of protection and discrimination, to an insecure freedom', such that opposition to divorce law reform, for example, was 'based less on an objection to easier divorce than on a concern for the social security of the wife divorced against her will'.[115]

Castle did not think the required change of attitude would come overnight. In particular, she believed women's lack of training was due less to problems of access and more to a 'fundamental problem of attitudes, including the attitude of women and girls themselves, of parents and others concerned with their career guidance and employment'. While something could be done about this through education, and the DEP itself was trying to change attitudes, 'we must expect that married women ... will continue to put family and home first and the job second; and what is more that society will expect this of them'. We have, she suggested, 'a long way to go to gain full public acceptance of the economic and social advantages of a workforce without divisions in responsibility and skill based on sex'.[116]

Conclusion

Given the detrimental influence the unions are thought to have had on Labour's attempt to appeal to women, it is ironic that the threat of industrial militancy helped Castle achieve equal pay. The critical role played by Castle in this process only adds to the paradox, for she had long avoided identifying with Labour's female wing, fearing, like fellow MP Jennie Lee, that would impede her advance in the wider party.[117] In fact, the introduction of equal pay legislation owed little to Labour women: the NLWAC was consulted only after the Bill was drafted and then the CWO was given just time enough to respond in a personal capacity.[118] If ineffectual in influencing policy, Labour's women's organisation was, as we have seen, no more proficient in boosting female party membership or support at the ballot box.

This chapter illustrates how far the contradictory impulses set in train by affluence were reflected in Labour's ranks. The party's female activists, who were mainly taken from an older generation of working-class housewives, could be severely critical of those young enough to be their daughters – and sometimes granddaughters. Few were prepared to change their ways to pander to those they thought should listen to counsel offered by older and wiser heads. While such activists looked on husbands and wives as partners, with the latter rightly performing a mainly nurturing role, they agreed the nature of this relationship should be more egalitarian and they supported equal pay. That it was only in the Wilson governments' final months that this latter matter was definitively addressed suggests that not everybody in the party – Ray Gunter and the unions in particular – looked on the subject with

the same kind of seriousness exhibited by women's conference delegates. Indeed, the delayed enactment of equal pay was seen as further
evidence of the party's lack of regard for women's interests. Yet, as the
concluding chapter suggests, the response of female voters at the 1970
general election indicates that the promise of an equal wage with men
was not as high on most women voters' lists of priorities as some of the
country's few feminists wished.

Notes

The place of publication is London unless otherwise specified.

1 *Report of the Thirty-Sixth National Conference of Labour Women* (1959), p. 9.
2 See, for example, A. Black and S. Brooke, 'The Labour Party, women, and
  the problem of gender, 1951–1966', *Journal of British Studies*, 36:4 (1997);
  and M. Francis, 'Labour and gender', in D. Tanner, P. Thane and N. Tiratsoo
  (eds), *Labour's First Century* (Cambridge, 2000).
3 I. Zweiniger-Bargielowska, 'Explaining the gender gap: the Conservative
  Party and the women's vote, 1945–1964', in M. Francis and I. Zweiniger-
  Bargielowska (eds), *The Conservatives and British Society, 1880–1990* (Cardiff,
  1996).
4 *Report of the Forty-First National Conference of Labour Women* (1964), p. 53.
5 *Thirty-Sixth Conference of Women*, pp. 10–12 and *passim*.
6 *Report of the Forty-Second National Conference of Labour Women* (1965), p. 4;
  'A women's section is formed', *Labour Woman*, 47:3 (1959), pp. 31–2.
7 J. M. Bochel, 'Activists in the Conservative and Labour parties. A study of
  ward secretaries in Manchester', MA thesis, University of Manchester (1965),
  p. 18.
8 This information is recorded in the annual reports of the party conference.
9 *Report of the Fifty-Fourth Annual Conference of the Labour Party* (1955), p. 69;
  Lambeth Archives, Brixton CLP papers, IV/156/1/3, GC minutes, 29
  February 1956.
10 Bochel, 'Activists', pp. 21, 35.
11 London Metropolitan Archive (LMA), Southall CLP papers, Acc 1267/57,
   agent's reports, Report of general election campaign 1959.
12 Bristol Record Office (BRO), Labour Party South West Region papers,
   38423/47, Bristol South, Annual reports for the years 1962/3–1969/70.
13 National Library of Wales (NLW), Brecon and Radnor CLP papers, 2,
   Brecon branch women's section minutes, 28 July 1970.
14 B. Castle, *Fighting All The Way* (1993), pp. 121–2.
15 NLW, Labour Party of Wales papers, file 126, Llanelli Federation of Labour
   Women's Advisory Council minutes, 3 May 1966; file 125, Llanelli Labour
   Women's Advisory Council aggregate minutes, 16 November 1966.
16 Labour Party Archive (LPA), National Executive Committee (NEC) Organisation Sub-Committee (OSC) minutes, 18 November 1958, Report of an
   enquiry, NAD/85/11/58.
17 West Yorkshire Archive, City of Bradford Labour Party papers, 60D84/2/4,
   Bradford South women's section minutes for 1958, *passim*.
18 Lambeth Archives, Clapham CLP papers, IV/156/2/5, Clapham Central
   women's section minutes for 1958, *passim*.

19 See, for example, Southall CLP papers, Acc. 1267/14, Glebe ward women's section minutes, 12 December 1958.
20 Humber ward section, 'Women and the second industrial revolution', *Labour Woman*, 49:9 (1959), p. 124; British Library of Political and Economic Science, Merton and Morden CLP papers, 3/7, Morden ward women's section minutes, 10 June 1962.
21 South West Region papers, 38423/49, regional women's officer reports, 24 and 30 September 1970.
22 H. Jenkins, *Rank and File* (1980), p. 107.
23 *Report of the Forty-Fourth National Conference of Labour Women* (1967), p. 26.
24 Essex County Record Office, EC of the Labour Party Eastern Region, minutes, D/Z 215/1, 9 February 1952; National Labour Women's Advisory Committee (NLWAC) minutes, 4 February 1960, Women's organisation and activities, pp. 1–2; *Report of the Forty-Fifth National Conference of Labour Women* (1968), p. 5.
25 LMA, Labour Party London Region papers, Acc 2417/H/36/7, Regional women's officer report, 19 October 1967; Modern Records Centre (MRC), Labour Party West Midlands Region papers, MSS6/3/1/368, organiser's report.
26 South West Region papers, 38423/20, Whiles to Cox, 4 May 1966.
27 *Report of the Thirty-Eighth National Conference of Labour Women* (1961), pp. 47–8.
28 *Report of the Sixty-Seventh Annual Conference of the Labour Party* (1968), pp. 119–28; *Report of the Forty-Sixth National Conference of Labour Women* (1969), pp. 35–6.
29 LPA, NEC minutes, 23 April 1969, B. Lockwood, Forty-sixth national conference of Labour women, NAD/W49/4/69.
30 NLWAC minutes, 2 June and 8 September 1960; NEC minutes, 23 March 1960, Interim report of the Salaries Sub-committee, pp. 8–10.
31 Tom Harrisson Mass-Observation Archive, Beveridge Social Services Survey, Box 2, File E, Interview with members of Park ward, North Tottenham, August 1947, and Report on Coleraine Labour Party women's section, Tottenham, August 1947.
32 BRO, Bristol West CLP papers, 38598/1/f, GMC minutes for 1968, *passim;* South West Region papers, 38423/46, North West Bristol CLP, Annual report 1966.
33 *Forty-Fourth Conference of Women*, pp. 33–7.
34 *Forty-Fifth Conference of Women*, p. 27.
35 *Report of the Forty-Seventh National Conference of Labour Women* (1970), p. 20.
36 *Forty-Fifth Conference of Women*, pp. 25–7; Labour Party, *Women and the Labour Party* (1971), pp. 3, 7, 9.
37 Labour Party, *Is This a Portrait of You?* (1961), and *Don't Let Men Make All The Decisions!* (1965).
38 *Report of the Fortieth National Conference of Labour Women* (1963), p. 38.
39 NLWAC minutes, 4 February 1960, Women's organisation and activities, pp. 3–4; 'Editor's letter', *Labour Woman*, 48:2 (1960), p. 14; 'Editor's letter', *Labour Woman*, 48:10 (1960), p. 118.
40 D. M. Loftus, 'A new look for Labour women', *Labour Organiser*, 39:458 (1960), pp. 150–2.
41 *Forty-First Conference of Women*, p. 3; *Forty-Second Conference of Women*, p. 3.
42 *Fortieth Conference of Women*, p. 4.
43 K. Butler, 'More about that new look', *Labour Organiser*, 39:460 (1960), pp. 187–8.
44 *Forty-First Conference of Women*, p. 28.

136   *Fielding*

45 *Forty-Sixth Conference of Women*, p. 18; R. Vincenzi, 'Playgroup', *Labour Woman*, 60:7 (1970), p. 140; West Midlands Region papers, MSS 6/3/1/289, 364, organisers' reports.
46 *Thirty-Eighth Conference of Women*, p. 49; *Fortieth Conference of Women*, pp. 29–31; *Forty-Third Conference of Women*, p. 4.
47 'Editor's letter', *Labour Woman*, 48:10 (1960), p. 118; NLWAC minutes, 3 November 1960.
48 Merseyside Records Office, Toxteth CLP papers, 331 TLP/3, West Toxteth women's section minutes, 3 October 1959, 17 May, 23 and 30 October 1960.
49 P. Wilmott, *The Evolution of a Community* (1963), pp. 71–2.
50 M. Young and P. Wilmott, *Family and Kinship in East London* (Harmondsworth, 1986), pp. 49–50, 56.
51 Humber ward section, 'Women', p. 124.
52 London papers, Acc 2417/B/76/3/6, *Clarion*, 42:1 (1963).
53 *Report of the Thirty-Seventh National Conference of Labour Women* (1960), pp. 14–16.
54 *Forty-First Conference of Women*, p. 47.
55 *Fortieth Conference of Women*, pp. 12, 16.
56 West Midlands Region papers, MSS 6/3/1/350, organiser's reports; *Forty-Third Conference of Women*, p. 38.
57 OSC minutes, 19 July and 13 December 1966.
58 *Report of the Sixty-Seventh Annual Conference of the Labour Party* (1968), p. 371; *Forty-Seventh Conference of Women*, pp. 4–5.
59 *Forty-Seventh Conference of Women*, pp. 1–5; *Forty-Sixth Conference of Women*, pp. 30, 34; NLWAC minutes, Outside contacts, 12 December 1969, NAD/W/114/12/69.
60 M. Colquhoun, *A Woman in the House* (Brighton, 1980), pp. 10–11.
61 Labour Party, *Women and the Labour Party* (1971), p. 4.
62 *Thirty-Seventh Conference of Women*, pp. 44–5.
63 C. Collette, '"Daughters of the Newer Eve": the labour movement and women', in J. Fyrth (ed.), *Labour's Promised Land?* (1995), pp. 47–9; *idem*, 'Questions of gender: Labour and women', in B. Brivati and R. Heffernan (eds), *The Labour Party. A Centenary History* (2000), p. 410.
64 *Forty-Third Conference of Women*, pp. 37–8; *Forty-Fifth Conference of Women*, p. 34.
65 Labour Party, *Discrimination Against Women* (1968), p. 20; *Forty-Fifth National Conference of Women*, pp. 29–30, 36.
66 N. Dennis, F. Henriques and C. Slaughter, *Coal Is Our Life* (1969), p. 165.
67 South West Region papers, 38423/18/2, Quarterly report – September 1967.
68 D. Fisher, 'Why not you?', *Labour Woman*, 60:8 (1970), pp. 154–5; *Forty-Fourth Conference of Women*, pp. 30–1.
69 *Forty-Fifth Conference of Women*, pp. 30–2.
70 Labour, *Discrimination*, p. 6.
71 *Forty-Fifth Conference of Women*, pp. 35–6.
72 OSC minutes, 17 July 1958; 17 January 1967, Resolutions, NAD/15/1/67; 18 March 1969, Resolutions, NAD/40/3/69; 15 April 1969, Resolutions, NAD/54/4/69; 7 December 1970, Resolutions, NAD/84/12/70.
73 Unless otherwise stated, this account is based on LPA, Discrimination Against Women Study Group papers.
74 *New Statesman*, 9 June 1967.
75 *Forty-Fifth Conference of Women*, p. 31.
76 MRC, Handsworth CLP papers, MSS 8/5/21, Labour Party Research Department, Participation '69. Women and social security: a short report, *Information Papers*, No. 50, February 1970.

77 R. Crossman, *The Diaries of a Cabinet Minister. Volume II* (1977), p. 668.
78 For more on this see P. Thompson, 'Labour's "Gannex conscience"? Politics and popular attitudes to the "permissive society"', in R. Coopey, S. Fielding and N. Tirasoo (eds), *The Wilson Governments, 1964–70* (1993).
79 *Forty-Seventh Conference of Women*, pp. 64–7; NLWAC minutes, 12 December 1970.
80 G. Colman, 'Women as citizens', *Labour Woman*, 47:2 (1959), pp. 19, 26; 'Women as wage-earners', *Labour Woman*, 47:3 (1959), pp. 33, 40; and 'Women as housewives', *Labour Woman*, 47:4 (1959), pp. 47–8.
81 *Forty-Sixth Conference of Women*, p. 22.
82 *Thirty-Sixth Conference of Women*, pp. 22–3.
83 *Thirty-Seventh Conference of Women*, p. 7; *Forty-First Conference of Women*, pp. 18–19.
84 *Forty-First Conference of Women*, p. 15.
85 *Forty-Third Conference of Women*, pp. 28–32.
86 *Forty-Sixth Conference of Women*, pp. 24–5.
87 MGH, 'Working wives', *Labour Woman*, 48:3 (1960), p. 27. Emphasis added.
88 *Forty-Third Conference of Women*, p. 18.
89 J. Tomlinson, *Democratic Socialism and Economic Policy* (Cambridge, 1997), pp. 199–203.
90 Labour Party, *Challenge to Britain* (1953), p. 29.
91 Labour Party, *Let's Go with Labour for the New Britain* (1964), p. 10, and *Time for Decision* (1966), p. 14.
92 *Report of the Sixty-Second Annual Conference of the Labour Party* (1963), pp. 262–3.
93 Public Record Office (PRO), LAB 10/2382, Draft report of working party on equal pay, July 1965; LAB 10/2514, Report of working party on equal pay, n.d. (but November 1965); LAB 10/2529, Johnston to Garcia, 28 July 1965, and Johnston to Maston, 13 August 1965.
94 LAB 10/2582, Ministerial Committee on Economic Development, 24 January 1966, and Equal pay. Memorandum by the Minister of Labour, 14 January 1966.
95 LAB 10/2582, Brief for Parliamentary Secretary, Joint meeting with the TUC and CBI on equal pay, 18 July 1966; Note for the record, equal pay, 6 May 1966; and note for the record, equal pay, 25 April 1966.
96 LAB 10/2878, Draft note of a joint meeting with representatives of the TUC and CBI on equal pay, 18 July 1966; LAB 10/3291, Memo by N. Singleton, 3 January 1968.
97 LAB 10/2878, Press notice on equal pay, 7 December 1967; LAB 10/3131, Equal pay, note of a meeting between Mr. Hattersley and representatives of the CBI and the TUC, 7 December 1967.
98 *Forty-Fourth Conference of Women*, pp. 74–5, 77–8.
99 LAB 10/2396, General Secretary, Newcastle and District Trades Council to Gunter, 9 November 1967.
100 LAB 10/2396, Castle to the Secretary, Battersea Labour Party, n.d. (but April 1968).
101 Unless otherwise stated, the following account is based on B. Castle, *The Castle Diaries, 1964–76* (1990), pp. 233, 235, 238–9, 265–8, 353–4, 357–8, 400, 402; and Castle, *Fighting*, pp. 409–12, 427.
102 For background to the dispute, see *Report of a Court of Inquiry under Sir Jack Stamp into a dispute concerning sewing machinists employed by the Ford Motor Company Limited* (August 1968, Cmnd 3749).
103 PRO, PREM 13/2412, letter to Wilson, June 1968.

104 LAB 10/2878, Equal pay, brief for the First Secretary for a meeting with the TUC on 31 July 1968 to discuss a phased programme for the introduction of equal pay; LAB 10/3310, Equal pay, brief for the First Secretary for a meeting with the TUC on 31 July to discuss a phased programme for the introduction of equal pay.

105 LAB 10/2878, Note for the record, equal pay – meeting with the CBI, 23 July 1968.

106 LAB 43/544, Equal pay, memorandum by the First Secretary of State and Secretary of State for Employment and Productivity', n.d.

107 Bodleian Library, Conservative Party Archive (CPA), CCO 180/33/1/1, ORC, A survey of women's interests and problems, March 1968.

108 *Parliamentary Debates (Hansard), 5th Series, Volume 800, House of Commons Official Report, Session 1969–70*, columns 753, 759–60, 762.

109 *Ibid.*, columns 754, 771.

110 *Forty-Fourth Conference of Women*, pp. 73–4; *Forty-Seventh Conference of Women*, pp. 14–16; M. Rendel, 'How equal pay works', *Labour Woman*, 60:4 (1970), pp. 65–6.

111 LAB 43/568, Press notice of speech to Women's Consultative Committee, 25 November 1969, and letter, Castle to Wilson, 25 March 1970; LAB 43/577, Memo from D. B. Smith, 23 April 1970.

112 LAB 111/11, Crossman to Castle, 25 February 1970; Shackleton to Castle, 9 March 1970; Note of meeting between the First Secretary and the TUC Employment Development Policy Committee, 11 May 1970; Treatment of pension rights under the Equal Pay Bill, 13 May 1970; Draft paper for the Social Services Committee, treatment of pension rights under the Equal Pay Bill, 13 May 1970.

113 LAB 43/545, Smith to Barnes, 25 September 1969.

114 *Hansard, 5th Series, Volume 800, Session 1969–70*, columns 770–2, 775; *Thirty-Ninth Conference of Women*, p. 18; *Forty-First Conference of Women*, p. 34; *Forty-Seventh Conference of Women*, p.19.

115 Labour, *Discrimination*, p. 5.

116 LAB 43/568, Press notice for speech to Women's Consultative Committee, 25 November 1969; Castle to Wilson, 25 March 1970.

117 P. Hollis, *Jennie Lee. A Life* (Oxford, 1997).

118 NLWAC minutes, 12 December 1969.

6

Integrating black immigrants

When in 1961 the Conservatives introduced a Bill to reduce the number of black members of the Commonwealth settling in Britain, Hugh Gaitskell attacked them with impressive moral force.[1] Their proposals contradicted Labour's adherence to both the free movement of British subjects within the Commonwealth and, more importantly, its commitment to racial equality. Conventional wisdom has it that after Gaitskell's death Labour abandoned his principled position because it alienated prejudiced white working-class voters. Hence, in 1965 Harold Wilson's government further tightened controls and in 1968 it prevented large numbers of Kenyan Asians entering the country. While two Race Relations Acts, meant to discourage discrimination based on colour, accompanied these measures, most authorities consider them palliatives, drafted to salve Labour's troubled conscience as ministers adhered to an essentially racist immigration policy.[2]

While in 1960 their party formally embraced a universal 'brotherhood', something the 1964–70 governments supposedly betrayed, many working-class activists nonetheless followed majority white opinion in their suspicion of black immigrants. For them, restricting black entry contradicted no principle because, so far as they were concerned, Labour's compelling purpose was to defend the material interests of the indigenous (and implicitly white) proletariat – that is, people like themselves. Given that immigration appeared to threaten workers' access to housing and jobs, the obvious solution seemed to be to reduce the numbers of black people entering the country, especially as (their Commonwealth status notwithstanding) they did not form part of the 'British way of life'. As suggested in Chapter 1, this outlook was informed by a historically entrenched colour prejudice, for white immigrants far outnumbered black immigrants, but it would be simplistic to describe it as racist. Numerous surveys suggested that much white antipathy was conditional; those in the party who took its commitment to brotherhood seriously dearly hoped that this was true. Thus, a regular columnist in *Socialist Commentary* argued it was not immigrants' colour that antagonised

139

many Britons as much as their customs – although the customs of black immigrants would be more readily obvious as a result of skin colour.[3] This implied that most whites could be educated out of their malign perceptions. However, before whites could be encouraged to look on blacks in a more positive light, the leadership came to believe government had to stem immigration to reassure them that neither their standard of living nor their established way of life was imperilled. At the same time, the new settlers needed to be encouraged to accept much of their hosts' culture – although quite how much was subject to debate. By the time Labour entered office in 1964, the leadership therefore considered that, as famously articulated by the MP Roy Hattersley: 'Integration without control is impossible, but control without integration is indefensible'.[4] In this way, Wilson and colleagues hoped to square the party's adherence to equality with the fact that many of their own members and potential supporters saw black immigration as a threat.

This chapter assesses Labour's byzantine response to the issue. Many members thought the growing presence of black immigrants in Britain's towns and cities was problematic. Moreover, the presumed dire electoral implications of rising numbers of black people encouraged party leaders to support controls to appease prejudice. However, consistent with Labour's commitment to equality, ministers also promoted measures that challenged white opinion, while some activists and officials enthusiastically advanced the policy of integration. Overall, however, black immigration was an issue Labour was ill prepared to address and one many wished would disappear as quickly as possible. As one of the party's few non-white activists rightly stated, the arrival of thousands of West Indians, Pakistanis and Indians provoked 'an all pervasive sense of embarrassment' in its ranks.[5]

Colour and the Commonwealth

During a 1948 Labour Party annual conference debate on racial discrimination, one delegate asked: if socialism 'does not mean that common men can live together decently and live together as brothers, I ask you what does it mean?'[6] Before the 1950s, however, practical expressions of the party's commitment to racial equality were largely confined to support for anti-colonialism, an issue that preoccupied a minority of activists throughout the post-war period.[7] Thus, in 1960 the National Executive Committee (NEC) supported a boycott of South African goods to protest against apartheid. Some constituency Labour parties (CLPs) took this campaign seriously: even in cash-strapped Glasgow Maryhill activists distributed 4,000 bills, held public meetings and hired a van to tour the city.[8]

The growth of black immigration meant that, during the 1950s, racial equality became more of a domestic issue and in 1953 activists in Brixton, an area of early West Indian settlement, established a committee to combat discrimination.[9] Throughout the decade, other CLPs expressed opposition to colour prejudice, while the NEC's Commonwealth Sub-committee supported attempts to make certain manifestations of prejudice illegal.[10] During 1957–8, 94 per cent of ward secretaries in Manchester opposed discrimination based on colour.[11] This commitment was confirmed in 1960, when, as a consequence of Gaitskell's updating of the party's aims, Labour declared its 'central ideal' to be 'the brotherhood of man'; underlined its opposition to 'discrimination on grounds of race, colour or creed'; and stated its adherence to the belief that 'men should accord to one another equal consideration and status in recognition of the fundamental dignity of man'.[12] So far as Gaitskell was concerned, racial equality was a principle like no other. As he told a BBC television interviewer in November 1959:

> If you were to say to me, 'Really we've got to accept the colour bar, because you'll never get into power if you don't', I should say, 'Well, in not very polite language, Go to hell ... that's absolutely against my principles.... But if you say to me 'I think your argument for nationalising the machine tool industry is rather weak', I would say, 'Well, I'll discuss that with you'.[13]

Wilson appeared to be of like mind. Within minutes of telling the 1962 conference that Labour was 'a moral crusade or it is nothing', he asserted that to 'attack a man because of his race, or because of his colour' was 'utterly repugnant to every Socialist'.[14]

For many, colour differences obscured that which united all human beings. As the Cabinet minister Judith Hart put it, everybody should 'recognise and admit their own humanity and decency – which tells them that a child is a child, a man is a man', so that 'whatever his colour may be, he is one of them, sharing the same fears and the same hopes for a better society and a better life'.[15] While she was on the left, Hart's perspective was the same as that of the revisionist Roy Jenkins: when he was Home Secretary, Jenkins claimed there was 'no overall rational basis for resentment' of black immigration, something he believed originated in 'personal inadequacy', 'fear and ignorance'.[16] While not discounting the psychological element, others on the left, like the MP Ian Mikardo, stressed the influence of material deprivation on attitudes. Mikardo thought most whites objected to black settlement because they had to compete for scarce resources: once there were enough jobs and houses, hostility would largely disappear.[17] This perspective was also embraced by more right-wing figures: deputy leader George Brown criticised Conservative restrictions for not addressing the 'real problems' associated with immigration, by which he meant the lack of resources in areas of black settlement.[18]

To some, the Commonwealth was the most tangible expression of Britain's commitment to racial harmony; Labour's 1959 manifesto even claimed Attlee's creation of the Commonwealth was his 'supreme achievement'.[19] As the NEC reaffirmed after the 1958 Notting Hill riots, the Commonwealth was 'the greatest multi-racial association the world has ever known', which enjoyed a 'unique opportunity to create racial understanding, confidence, and co-operation'. Thus, as Britain lay at the heart of the Commonwealth, it was imperative all its citizens be able to enter the country freely: attempts to restrict movement on a racial basis would destroy it.[20] Indeed, it was partly because he believed in the progressive possibilities of the Commonwealth that Gaitskell turned his back on Britain's entry into the European Economic Community.[21] If Wilson's later application to join the Community indicated that, by the end of the 1960s, the leadership no longer thought the Commonwealth able to play a decisive international role, others considered it could still exert a useful influence. The NEC's 1968 Study Group on Immigration discussed establishing a multilateral policy for migration within the Commonwealth, based on the needs of member states. By co-ordinating population flows on a non-discriminatory basis, they hoped it might yet set an important example to the world.[22]

'First contact'

Attlee's Cabinet did not believe its 1948 Nationality Act would encourage black immigration; if they had, ministers may well have had second thoughts.[23] While fearing that large numbers of unskilled black settlers would disrupt society, they thought those who came to Britain on the *Empire Windrush* in 1948 were just straws in the wind. Having considered controls, ministers dismissed them as unnecessary.

The early 1950s nonetheless saw increasing numbers of blacks arrive in Britain, particularly London. Labour officials in the capital gave every impression of wishing the immigrants would go away, while they did their best to calm white fears. An article in Labour's *London News* entitled 'Coloured Folk Prove Law-Abiding' claimed there were fewer West Indians than there might superficially appear to be: poor housing meant they spent much of their time on the streets, giving the *impression* of greater numbers. White readers were presumably meant to draw comfort from the assertion that most wanted to return home eventually.[24] Other than to issue reassuring statements, there did not appear much else Labour could do. When the London party investigated the 'problem of coloured people' in the middle of the decade, it ran through various possible solutions but rejected them all. Controls were considered 'repugnant', while dictating immigrants' place of settlement once they had arrived in Britain – so as to alleviate pressure on local resources – was thought discriminatory unless also applied to whites. The only answer appeared to be the creation of a prosperous West Indies, for there would then be no reason to emigrate, a viewpoint later endorsed by the NEC.[25]

By the late 1950s it was, however, apparent that most immigrants would not be returning home, as the economic development of the Commonwealth was at best a long-term project. Attention was consequently increasingly focused on the position of black settlers in Britain's cities and during 1957 Labour's Commonwealth Officer contacted CLPs in areas with large immigrant populations to assess the situation. His researches revealed a complex and difficult situation.[26] Some parties noted the hostility of 'the more backward section' of the working class, a category that included some Labour members. A few CLPs, such as South Paddington, reported their attempts to tackle prejudice by challenging instances of discrimination in pubs, clubs and dance halls. Elsewhere, however, immigrants were criticised for finding trouble where none existed.

By this time, white tenants were inundating parties in the capital with complaints that black landlords were driving them out of their homes and replacing them with immigrants who were prepared to live in overcrowded conditions for higher rents. David Pitt, Labour's West Indian-born parliamentary candidate for Hampstead in 1959, believed critics of black landlords were prejudiced, as they did not attack their white counterparts with the same vigour.[27] While the issue was used to legitimise a racist viewpoint, even CLPs with exemplary records opposing prejudice believed most complaints were justified. This is not necessarily evidence of their own racism: the secretary of Islington North CLP herself experienced 'coloured Landlord trouble' but claimed that did not mean she thought badly of all immigrants.[28] Yet, no matter how far prejudice distorted reality, activists were faced with a thorny dilemma. The secretary of Vauxhall CLP in south London warned that Labour members could no longer:

> blind ourselves to the fact that the present housing conditions, difference of standards and fear of possible unemployment are bound to have some effect. It is because we are so anxious to avoid this that we feel that a more realistic attitude should be adopted to what is undoubtedly becoming an increasing problem, and that not only should sympathy and understanding be extended to black immigrants, but attention should be paid to the natural reactions of working-class white people under present circumstances. Failure to realise this may have the very results which we, as Socialists, are so anxious to avoid.[29]

An uncertain principle

Gaitskell's forceful condemnation of the Commonwealth Immigration Bill appeared to be enthusiastically supported by the wider party, in particular by left-inclined CLPs that had hitherto been critical of his leadership. It has even been suggested that Gaitskell opposed the Conservatives with such vigour to restore unity to ranks recently divided over clause four and nuclear disarmament.[30]

If Labour's adherence to unrestricted immigration pleased some, it did not, however, enjoy universal support. After leaving office in 1951, the party leadership steered well clear of discussing controls, but more humble members did raise the issue. The Sheffield MP John Hynd was one of the more prominent advocates of regulated entry. Assuming the rural background of most black immigrants meant they were unsuited to industrial work, he suggested prospective settlers should be advised about what awaited them in Britain, in the hope that this would discourage most.[31] Although they expressed sympathy for the immigrants' plight, a number of London MPs and councillors still advocated controls, in order to take account of the anxieties of 'our own people' in relation to housing.[32] Economic slowdowns were often the occasion for CLPs to call for regulation.[33] Even in Rawtenstall, Lancashire, where immigration was insignificant, local trade unionists considered that, during a time of rising unemployment, it was wrong 'that these people should be allowed to come into the country without let or hindrance'. The reply to this from the local MP and leading left-wing parliamentarian, Anthony Greenwood, was equivocal at best. Given Britain's place at the head of the Commonwealth, he felt restrictions were inappropriate but conceded black immigration was 'one of the most difficult problems that we have to face', given difficulties associated with employment, health and 'social relationships'.[34]

While the NEC reaffirmed Labour's support for unrestricted entry after the 1958 riots in London and Nottingham, reactions to the disturbances showed how far members disagreed over the best response. MPs George Rogers and James Harrison, who respectively represented the areas concerned, called for controls – along with a variety of other measures meant to protect the 'British way of life'.[35] Rogers enjoyed his executive committee's support, as its members believed racial tension originated from immigrants aggravating local housing shortages. Hence, it advocated a 'wider dispersal of incomers' to ease the pressure; failing that, there should be a 'slowing down of the flow of immigrants'.[36] The wider North Kensington party was, however, divided and advocates of unrestricted entry refused to work for Rogers in the 1959 general election.[37] Yet support for 'dispersal' stretched much further than North Kensington. If earlier dismissed by the London party, *Socialist*

Commentary and Pitt advanced it even while opposing controls.[38] In fact, as late as 1967, the left-inclined Selly Oak general management committee (GMC) proposed dispersing Birmingham's immigrant population across the city as part of its programme to reduce discrimination.[39]

Behind Gaitskell, therefore, stood a party anything but united against controls; and while there were many reasons for this difference of opinion, one in particular stands out. As the 1961 Immigration Bill was debated in Westminster, two-thirds of GMC delegates in London's working-class dockside constituency of Bermondsey came out in support of restriction. In contrast, activists in the capital's more middle-class CLPs, such as South Kensington and Fulham, opposed the measure in similar proportions.[40] This does not necessarily mean proletarian activists were more likely to be racist, but it does point to the possible significance of more conditional – material – factors. After Notting Hill, members of the GMC in well heeled St Marylebone declared they were prepared to 'undergo temporary hardship' to ensure blacks enjoyed equal access to housing, employment and welfare. It was unclear what 'hardship' meant to a party counting Lord and Lady Lucan as activists.[41] Moreover, if ensuring racial equality was a question of whites foregoing material comfort for the benefit of others, less well placed Labour members believed that imperilled working-class interests. As remarked by a leading Labour council representative in Deptford, where by the mid-1960s just under 10 per cent of the population was black, '[i]mmigration has dragged us back twenty years … it's all right to talk about brotherhood of man, but our first job is to defend the gains we fought for here'.[42] Similarly, the labour movement, Nottingham North MP James Harrison stated, 'had fought for years for better conditions for the working class' and he was determined not to allow those he asserted had 'lower standards of housing and wages' to undermine them.[43] Finally, George Pargiter, MP for Southall, where Indian settlers accounted for about 10 per cent of residents in the early 1960s, called for a ban on immigration – to his constituency at least – and claimed that, in the first instance, 'we are entitled to look after our own people'.[44]

Integration

It was already something of a cliché in London Labour circles when, after Notting Hill, Pitt declared that the only way to avoid further tension was the 'full integration of Negroes into our life'.[45] Even so, although 'integration' became national policy in 1962, it remained uncertain what, in practice, the term implied. In 1965 the immigration specialist Nicholas Deakin tried to clarify the matter for *Socialist Commentary* readers. Integration, he stated, was a reciprocal process in which immigrants adapted to the receiving society; the majority, in turn, should tolerate 'certain distinct persistent religious and cultural patterns' and not expect settlers totally to abandon their way of life, as that would amount to 'assimilation'.[46] Deakin's definition still left matters open to dispute, for the balance of any agreement between host and immigrant was not prescribed. Moreover, when referring to 'integration' many Labour members continued to mean 'assimilation' or, at least, as *Socialist Commentary* had put it some years before Deakin's piece, that newcomers should discard practices that 'disturb the English community'.[47] That this was a widespread view was confirmed by a 1968 survey of local representatives in Nottingham, which found that the overwhelming majority of Labour councillors (like their Conservative counterparts) thought integration a homogenising process in which immigrants would fully adhere to the 'British way of life'.[48] It is impossible to be sure how many believed colour rather than culture defined this way of life. That it could be conceived of in purely cultural terms was suggested by the West Indian Pitt's reference to 'our life'. Yet even those keen to promote a positive response to blacks betrayed their obsession with colour. A *London News* article intended to promote Pitt's candidature in Hampstead went so far as to describe him as 'this whitest of black men' and a 'unique combination of red and black', whose face was difficult to see in the dark.[49]

According to its 1962 formulation, Labour believed integration was a reciprocal process that encompassed: educating whites about the Commonwealth and the realities of immigration; outlawing discrimination against blacks in public places; and alleviating competition for housing in areas of greatest settlement.[50] It also emphasised voluntary initiatives – like Willesden's International Friendship Council – that encouraged communication between black and white, and hoped the latter would accept the former as 'ordinary neighbours, work-mates and friends'. If whites were presumed to have things to learn, immigrants apparently had most to come to terms with, for they should not only be advised about access to housing and employment but also taught about the British way of life and urged not to indulge in activities, like holding noisy parties, that might antagonise white neighbours.

As a member of the NEC, Wilson urged conference delegates in 1962 to take integration seriously. Transport House expected CLPs to play a vital role by: helping immigrants get on the electoral roll; taking up cases of discrimination; promoting contact between black and white; and increasing the number of black members.[51] Some had pursued these activities from the earliest days of immigration, although their record was not encouraging. In 1953 Brixton CLP expressed its desire to welcome West Indian settlers by establishing a colour sub-committee, one of whose members was supposed to be an immigrant. Unfortunately, no such person was found and the initiative ran into the ground, so that as late as 1964 Brixton could claim only twenty black members.[52] If in Brixton Labour appeared to meet with immigrants' indifference, elsewhere the problem lay in the party's own ranks. In Coventry, during the late 1950s, officials encouraged the participation of Indian residents in the party. The borough secretary wrote to the President of the Indian Workers' Association (IWA), which was already affiliated to the party locally, to encourage him to send representatives to meetings. When one subsequently arrived, a white delegate made 'unfortunate personal remarks', for which the secretary apologised and indicated that the delegate had 'upset us probably infinitely more than yourself'.[53]

So few blacks belonged to parties in London in the late 1950s that Jim Raisin, Labour's organiser in the capital, made the fairly desperate proposal that, as West Indian men outnumbered women, CLPs should encourage the latter to join as a ruse to increase the formers' participation.[54] After Notting Hill, the party in London devoted more systematic thought to the subject and suggested CLPs should enrol a small number of immigrants to liaise with their peers. While conceding this meant 'recognising that coloured people are "different"', officials hoped the policy would be a temporary expedient that would merely hasten the time when immigrants could enter the party on the same basis as whites.[55] This approach was eventually adopted across the country and was thought especially helpful in the case of Asian immigrants, who often had poor English language skills.[56] Despite the good intentions, this tactic had the effect of keeping white activists apart from black voters and putting black members at some distance from white voters. This was, however, not always the case: in Dulwich pairs of black and white activists approached immigrant and non-immigrant alike.[57]

As the Coventry episode indicates, not all members favoured integration: that some held a 'very deep prejudice' against immigrants was reluctantly recognised.[58] During the early 1960s, the Bradford East CLP suffered a rapid fall in membership and, while numerous expedients were employed to reverse the decline, no attempt was made to recruit from the expanding Pakistani population, which accounted for nearly 12 per cent of the population by 1966. Indeed, when one immigrant asked to join he was accepted only after the CLP won a community leader's assurance that his application would not be the first of many.[59] The reasoning behind such hostility was revealed by one account of attitudes in an unnamed city with a large Asian population. There an activist recalled that, in the early 1960s, a few Indians had joined the CLP, but 'when they started coming to meetings they wanted to talk about Indian affairs, and a lot of our members walked out … they said "If they're coming, we're going. It's bad enough living with them next door, we don't want them here as well"'. Despite this, members welcomed the services of an intermediary, in this case an anglicised Indian doctor, as he promised to mobilise immigrants without making members suffer the discomfort of having Indians attend gatherings.[60] Thus, what was meant to be the first step towards integration was employed as a means of avoiding that very end. A similar situation was evident in the Birmingham constituency of Sparkbrook, whose combined West Indian and Asian population amounted to about 8 per cent of residents by the early 1960s. Despite this, Labour membership was almost wholly white, in fact largely Irish in origin. While discrimination was not overtly practised, it was clear immigrants were unwelcome, although during the 1964 campaign intermediaries were used to rally black Labour voters.[61]

As might be expected, the national picture was uneven. In accordance with Labour policy, in 1965 members in Flint East, north Wales, took up the case of a man of West Indian descent who had been prevented from buying a house on a new estate because the developer feared he would deter white clients.[62] Activists organised a meeting on the 'colour question', which their agent hoped would 'help both sides face the issues realistically'. Such faith in the power of fact was revealing, as was how the local MP Eirene White described the thwarted house purchaser. He was, she pointed out, a second-generation West Indian who had served in the Royal Navy, was married to an English woman and employed in skilled work. In other words, apart from being black, he adhered to conventional notions of the 'British way of life' and was just like any other respectable member of the community. Labour's willingness to advance his case may also have been due to the fact that immigration was insignificant in the constituency: together with the victim's background, this meant few locals considered their own way of life under threat.

In London, matters were much more contentious. In response to Rogers' support for the deportation of some disreputable blacks, alderman Nat Marock, leader of Lambeth Borough Council, claimed that the West Indian population was in fact 'clean, sober and industrious'. They were not much different in behaviour to the rest of the community and any peculiar habits, traditions, ways of eating or cooking were, he asserted, very much their own business.[63] Rogers nonetheless claimed some settlers were 'bad types' and were associated with all-night parties, prostitution and exploitative landlords: they deserved to be deported.[64] If Rogers claimed to judge immigrants on the basis of behaviour rather than colour, Marock clearly considered this a fine – even non-existent – distinction.

Similar divisions were exposed during the early 1960s in Southall, where activists were at odds over how to respond to Indian settlement. At a disputatious meeting held to discuss the issue, most municipal representatives complained there were too many immigrants locally. One even suggested that Indians threatened to 'colonise' some areas. If most agreed the pressure of numbers on housing was a key issue, immigrants' behaviour also seemed critical to some. According to one representative, their 'immorality' was striking, while another thought religious differences meant it would be impossible to educate them into 'our way of life'. Others disagreed and claimed religion irrelevant. In May 1963 John Millwood, of Transport House's Research Department, explained Labour policy to a largely irate audience; he presented it in a manner presumably meant to appease them. The purpose of integration, he assured the audience, was to 'fit these coloured people in, and to [get them] living up to the standards of our way of life'. This was certainly the view of Southall's MP: George Pargiter believed Sikhs should abandon their turbans and dietary laws, for only then might they be 'absorbed into our way of life'. He even declared they had to 'conform to our ways and standards, if they wish[ed] to be treated as part of the community'.[65]

The road to restriction

Despite Gaitskell's support for unrestricted Commonwealth immigration, controls proved extremely popular with the public. By the time the Commonwealth Immigration Act received royal assent in 1962, even the Labour leader recognised the electoral need to embrace some form of limitation. Moreover, as we have seen, so far as the wider party was concerned, Gaitskell's original position was something of an aberration.

Given the state of voter opinion, Labour officials had long thought that allowing immigration to become a topic of open debate – which in 1961–2 it most certainly was – could only help those wishing to profit from prejudice. When the Fascist Oswald Mosley proposed standing in North Kensington in 1959, Raisin believed it best to ignore him.[66] If some activists wanted to affirm their opposition to discrimination, those in places such as Bradford were less distressed; as one councillor there suggested, '[t]he least said about the issue the better'.[67] The extent of popular bigotry meant many in the party feared that if immigration became a point of open contention between the parties, Labour could only lose. Grass-roots Conservatives were, after all, not shy of exploiting the issue.[68] Fenner Brockway believed he nearly lost Eton and Slough in 1959 because opposing canvassers claimed he was responsible for bringing immigrants into the constituency. Some thought Labour in Brixton suffered a huge swing to their opponents after a Conservative whispering campaign alleged the local MP, Marcus Lipton, gave immigrants special help to secure housing.[69]

Some survey evidence indicates that, in the 1964 general election, immigration made little impact nationally on voter loyalties, which suggests that Labour's embrace of controls had eliminated it as a contentious issue.[70] Local perceptions were rather different. If party policy had changed, Labour leaders were too embarrassed to draw voters' attention to it, a reluctance that frustrated those fighting marginal seats. In Dulwich, the agent claimed large numbers of long-standing supporters were considering voting Conservative in the belief that only they advocated limitation.[71] The Conservatives certainly thought Labour remained vulnerable on the issue, especially in the West Midlands.[72] Smethwick, near Birmingham, gave that view credibility, as Patrick Gordon Walker lost the seat after a swing to the Conservatives of 7.2 per cent – compared with a national movement to Labour of 3.5 per cent. Few doubted the Conservative candidate, Peter Griffiths, had exploited hostility to the local Asian population: Wilson was so disgusted by the tenor of his campaign he described Griffiths as a 'Parliamentary leper'.[73] Many Labour members shared his anger, but one *Tribune* correspondent, who claimed to be an activist from nearby Walsall, defended Griffiths against charges of racism. Arguing that one could be a socialist and oppose black immigration, he claimed the Conservative candidate made sense to those living near immigrants' 'smell, noise and filth'.[74] As a later Leeds correspondent asserted of fellow members' reaction to black settlers, they did 'not enjoy having anybody living next door who cannot be understood and whose prejudices were not theirs', 'who themselves tend to prefer their own kind of people, and are not as serviceable neighbours as those who lived there before'.[75]

As the new Prime Minister wrote to the Archbishop of Canterbury after his attack on Griffiths, the 'backlash' against immigration, as evidenced by Smethwick, was too strong to ignore. Unless 'dealt with head on', Wilson predicted, 'I am afraid that it will foul our politics ... for a very considerable period of time'. He then outlined the need for legislation to outlaw racial intolerance and other efforts to promote integration – but not to restrict immigration.[76] In fact, most now believed some form of further limitation had to be imposed to appease the public. Wilson hoped that tightening up known means of evading the 1962 Act would reduce the flow of immigrants without recourse to parliamentary action.[77] His Home Secretary, Sir Frank Soskice, however, argued the Act still allowed what voters would consider too many to enter Britain legitimately. Initially looking on dispersal with favour, Soskice nonetheless knew of no legal means to prevent new immigrants living in areas of established settlement. Thus, appreciating most Cabinet colleagues would be 'understandably very uneasy about my proposals', he thought there was no alternative to the 'extremely invidious' introduction of further controls. To soften the blow, Soskice proposed a 'package deal' that combined restriction with legislation to ensure those allowed to enter the country were treated as 'first and not second-class citizens'.

The Cabinet accepted Soskice's case with little enthusiasm. The Midlands MP Richard Crossman, who believed restriction was the only way to prevent further situations like that in Smethwick, described the meeting that finalised the details of the Home Secretary's proposals as 'desultory [and] unhappy'.[78] Yet, by this point, even Reginald Sorenson, who as an MP during the 1950s had drafted anti-discrimination legislation and considered colour prejudice 'the most inane and scientifically baseless of all our traditional aversions', thought the case against more controls was fuelled by 'intoxicated idealism'.[79] In contrast, H. A. Alavi, a Pakistani Labour activist, believed that as restriction pandered to racism it would merely promote its growth.[80] Yet even some who argued that Labour should stand firm in the hope this would eventually overcome white prejudice accepted the party would lose votes in the short term.[81]

Promoting integration

In March 1965 Wilson informed the Commons that, while his government planned to reduce immigration, it would also take steps to ensure that once they were in the country new settlers were treated as full citizens. He proposed legislating to prohibit incitement to racial hatred but placed most emphasis on encouraging conciliation through a Race Relations Board.[82] Wilson also announced that Maurice Foley, a junior minister at the Department of Economic Affairs (DEA), would promote activities to advance integration.

Foley based his work on the proposition that Britain was already a 'multi-racial society' and, as immigrants and their children had already established roots, it was 'no use pretending they will go back'.[83] Recognising prejudice was rife, he believed only a small minority of whites were 'strongly prejudiced', while many more were 'slightly prejudiced' or 'simply suspicious of newcomers', particularly if they competed for scarce resources. Through government policy the latter group could be pushed towards deeper hostility or greater acceptance. The problem was not, however, all one way: Asian immigrants in particular were 'introvert and cutting themselves off from the community' and so had to change their ways.[84] Despite the dual nature of the problem, Foley believed the main emphasis should be the education of immigrants in 'our standards of hygiene and our social customs', although he did not want them to be forced to become 'ersatz Englishmen'.[85] If integration granted immigrants rights it also gave them responsibilities, although too often the latter were never explained. Consequently, Foley claimed it was understandable if people uprooted from 'rural primitive societies' tipped rubbish out of bedroom windows because they had not been told that the council collected refuse every week.

Foley was a junior minister with a small staff trying to coordinate the work of powerful ministries and local authorities that were, he complained, largely uninterested in his work.[86] He received no support from the Home Office. Soskice might have devised the 'package deal' but was reluctant to promote integration himself: that was why it became the DEA's responsibility. While committed to anti-discrimination legislation, Soskice wanted it to be of the narrowest possible scope and resisted pressure from colleagues to look into prejudice in housing, as he considered that would force government into 'difficult and controversial matters'.[87] This minimalist approach was not without support: Ray Gunter at the Ministry of Labour believed legislation would 'produce more difficulties than it solves'.[88] Thus, lacking Home Office backing, Foley could only urge Gunter's officials to inform employers 'that in the sort of multi-racial society that had come to stay ... equality of opportunity in matters of employment was in the national interest'.[89] As a result, the 1965 Race Relations Act was criticised for what it did not do, although, whatever its limitations, it did constitute the first legal challenge to white prejudice – and that with Labour's re-election in the offing.

Once Roy Jenkins became Home Secretary towards the end of 1965, the tone of government policy became less mealy-mouthed. He ensured integration became part of the Home Office remit by having Foley moved from the DEA. Jenkins articulated a definition of integration that was rather more positive than Foley's by stressing not just the reality but also the legitimacy of cultural diversity. He even talked of immigrants' constructive contribution to British life, something Soskice never did.[90] This shift of emphasis at the top was, however, not necessarily registered at constituency level. In Bedford, for example, where during the later 1960s at least 4 per cent of the population were black, activists remained divided.[91] When one GMC delegate suggested that immigrants did not receive their fair share of council housing, he was informed that if he said that in public 'there would not be one Labour Councillor left', a warning met with shouts of agreement. Even so, during a later debate, some suggested whites should be more tolerant and immigrants might even be able to teach the majority 'good habits'. However, others thought blacks needed to adhere fully to the dominant culture: as one delegate put it, 'he didn't see why we should accept their ways as it was our country'. Going further than everybody else, one speaker claimed:

> we might just as well give the whole damn country to the Blacks as they would get it in the end anyway. Before long we would have a Black king on the throne and then it would be God help us! The poor old white man might just as well emigrate and leave the place to them ... this Black menace had ruined our towns and forced the whites out of them. The best thing we could do would be to send the whole damn lot back to where they came from!

A subsequent discussion revealed some GMC delegates even thought rising unemployment was mainly due to this 'black invasion'.

Oblivious to these sentiments, Jenkins wanted to extend the Race Relations Act. One of his main concerns was to ensure the full integration of immigrants' children, who, as Jenkins' adviser Anthony Lester informed the 1967 Labour Party conference, 'will be as English as you or I, as British as you or I, and the only difference will be the colour of their skin'.[92] Without action to tackle discrimination in employment and housing, it was feared an alienated second generation would emerge, one stuck in badly paid jobs and forced to remain in American-style ghettoes. Civil strife would be the only result.[93] By the time legislation was ready, Jenkins had swapped jobs with the Chancellor, James Callaghan, someone whom he considered a 'reactionary' on immigration.[94] The new Home Secretary certainly thought some of the Bill's provisions would be difficult to enforce. Yet, in spite of his reputation, Callaghan fought hard against colleagues who tried to exclude housing from the Bill because of their fear of an adverse voter reaction.[95]

Equality at work

Apart from housing, the 1968 Race Relations Act broke new ground by subjecting the workplace to anti-discriminatory legislation. Prejudice in employment was a difficult issue for Labour, as it implicated many of its union supporters. Foley hoped the unions would promote integration by selecting immigrants as branch officials; the Birmingham borough party had also exhorted local unions to ensure black school-leavers suffered no prejudice in securing work.[96] More often than not, however, trade unionists appeared to be less the solution and more part of the problem. Foley and others believed this was due to fears that immigrants would accept lower wages and so threaten white jobs.[97] While there was no hard evidence to prove immigration reduced labour costs, Wilson's economic adviser, Thomas Balogh, counselled the Prime Minister against controls because he thought it did.[98] True or not, during the 1963 Deptford by-election Labour canvassers told voters that the Conservative government had encouraged immigration during the 1950s for that very purpose.[99]

While discrimination at the workplace was widespread, many of the most prominent examples which first came to light were located in public transport. This was uncomfortable for activists because those workforces found guilty of prejudice were all well unionised and often administered by Labour councils.[100] Particularly on the buses, it was common for employees and managers jointly to restrict or even prohibit the employment of blacks and occasionally ensure they were paid less than white workers. This contradicted Trades Union Congress (TUC) policy, which in 1955 confirmed its opposition to 'colour prejudice wherever it may occur'.[101] It is not clear how seriously TUC officials took that pledge, but individual union leaderships were certainly reluctant to confront instances in which their local representatives and members were involved. In confronting racial inequality among workers, activists then often stood alone. In 1958 Coventry Council's controlling Labour Group tried to tackle discrimination on the buses after it received complaints from the IWA and met with the Transport and General Workers' Union branch concerned. This resulted in an acrimonious encounter, after which one unionist was described as 'more national than Socialist' (i.e. a Nazi) and the branch secretary threatened to withdraw support for Labour if the Group pushed the matter further.[102] Similar party–union conflicts occurred elsewhere: in Bristol equality among bus employees was achieved only after a personal intervention by Wilson.[103]

Although few denied the existence of workplace discrimination, Gunter led the Ministry of Labour in opposing employment being subject to legislation.[104] The Ministry did not ignore prejudice, as much time was spent encouraging managers to take on black workers – but officials believed they could not force the issue.[105] Yet they hardly showed much sympathy to the immigrants' plight: when Foley asked the Ministry to explain why many blacks could not find work that matched their qualifications, he was told the problem was exaggerated and in most cases blacks were themselves at fault.[106] Gunter also claimed employers were often only responding to their employees' prejudices in rejecting black workers, a view shared by Alice Bacon, one of Jenkins' junior ministers.[107] Indeed, a North Paddington Labour councillor had earlier maintained he would have employed immigrants in his business but for the objections of white staff.[108]

Despite its formal position, along with the Confederation of British Industry the TUC urged Jenkins not to make employment subject to his Bill. Fred Hayday of the General and Municipal Workers' Union believed legislation would 'prejudice the integration of immigrants' by transforming blacks into a 'special class'. The Building Workers' George Lowthian thought it would create 'a new kind of discrimination' by effectively guaranteeing immigrants employment. The unions feared legislation would make illegal workplace 'quotas', that is, informal agreements between employees and managers to limit the number of black workers. Leading unionists claimed quotas fostered integration by educating white workers about immigrants without threatening their jobs. The Ministry of Labour endorsed claims that too many blacks in one workplace would lead experienced whites to leave and generate discontent among those remaining.[109] As A. S. Jouhl of the IWA stated, even his organisation initially aimed only to achieve a 'fair proportion of white and other labour in factories', and implied that a quota of a maximum 25 per cent black workers in any one workplace was acceptable.[110] Given the weight of such opinion and the fact that the logic of arguments in favour of quotas echoed that of Labour's immigration policy in general, it was no surprise that the new Act endorsed the concept of a 'balance' between black and white employees. Even the MP Paul Rose, a critic of the limitations of both the 1965 and 1968 Acts, thought this formula satisfactory – so long as quotas were operated in good faith.[111]

Whatever its shortcomings, Labour's second Race Relations Act was welcomed by *Socialist Commentary* for further shifting government policy from promoting conformity among black immigrants to challenging white prejudice.[112] So far as Jenkins' advisers were concerned, the need to face up to Britain's 'white problem' was an important reason for the Act.[113] If, in Callaghan's hands, the Act was slightly more conservative than it might have been had Jenkins remained in control, this was because the new Home Secretary wanted to secure the maximum possible agreement and ensure change was permanent.[114] It still provoked the hostility of a substantial minority of whites: while opinion was split 53:36 per cent in favour of the general principle of preventing discrimination in housing and jobs, the balance shifted to 48:44 when the public was specifically asked whether refusing to employ someone on the grounds of colour should be made illegal; and became 44:45 when the question turned to selling or renting accommodation.[115]

Kenyan Asians

Enoch Powell spent much of his 'rivers of blood' speech of April 1968 (see Chapter 1) attacking Callaghan's proposals to regulate the housing market and implied they proved blacks were being treated better than whites. His rhetoric had the impact it did because, at the time, many expected the imminent arrival of thousands of Kenyan Asians. When Kenya became independent from Britain in 1963, those of Asian descent could apply for citizenship of the new country or retain their British status. Having been exempted from the 1962 Immigration Act, most plumped for the latter.[116] The implications of their choice became clear during the autumn of 1967, when the Kenyan government's 'Africanisation' policy threatened thousands of ethnic Asians with expropriation and forced them to flee the country. Jenkins calculated that 1.5 million holders of British passports around the world were exempted from the 1962 Act and, while he accepted that few would want to settle in Britain, 200,000 East African Asians might be forced to do so. While there were 'formidable' legal objections to the imposition of restrictions, Jenkins feared such an influx would inflame white attitudes. Thus, if immediate

action was not thought necessary, he asked for a slot in the government's programme should the need arise for him quickly to introduce
legislation to curtail the Asians' right of entry.[117]

Fortunately for Jenkins' reputation as a liberal, when the rate of
immigration from Kenya continued to rise – prompting fevered press
speculation about the final number of immigrants – it fell to Callaghan
to deal with it. His solution was not to deny Kenyan Asians their right
to settle but to create a limit of 1,500 per year on their entry. Callaghan
was, in effect, creating a queue, ostensibly to protect domestic race relations by ensuring unbearable pressure was not placed on areas of
already high immigrant settlement. The main motive behind the legislation was to prevent a white backlash. Few sitting round the Cabinet
table relished the policy but none put up much opposition. Even critics,
such as the Colonial Secretary, George Thomas, accepted that the flow
of Kenyan immigrants had to be reduced to 'manageable proportions'
to ensure the success of integration. Thus, so as to close down the ability
of East African Asians to enter the country at will, ministers extended
controls to citizens of the United Kingdom and colonies 'with no
substantial connection with this country'.[118] Ministers hoped this 'connection', defined as possession of a parent or grandparent born in
Britain, meant they would appear non-discriminatory, while in practice
they would be limiting only non-white entry.[119] Most, however, saw it for
what it was.

When Callaghan presented legislation to the Commons, he faced
severe opposition from Labour MPs. The junior minister David Owen
later recalled how he 'agonized' over how to vote, for, while appreciating the measure was 'undoubtedly racial in character', he feared that
without it violence would ensue. Thus, if principle dictated allowing
the Asians free entry, he still supported the government.[120] The Home
Office minister in charge of integration at this point, David Ennals, a
former president of the Anti-Apartheid Movement, tried his best to
forestall criticism from locally employed community liaison officers by
claiming ministers shared their 'anguish'. He asked them to understand
that they had been forced to choose between the harm that would be
done to individuals wanting to come to Britain and the damage black–
white relations would suffer if they were allowed free entry. Had
limitations not been imposed, Ennals argued, greater prejudice and discrimination would have been the result, for too many whites remained
inclined to racism.[121] Ennals did not convince many. Resolutions passed
by various community relations councils, funded by Whitehall to improve the position of immigrants, complained that blacks now believed
the government was also racist and so despaired of co-operating with
it.[122] *Tribune* declared the proposals surrendered to racism and asserted
that a government truly determined to counter prejudice would have

taken a firmer stand.[123] Some on the Labour left had a one-eyed view of matters. *Tribune* in particular was reluctant to criticise the Kenyan government, which was after all guilty of forcing thousands to leave the country of their birth. Indeed, while one contributor attacked Callaghan's restrictions as immoral he welcomed 'Africanisation' as an attack on privilege.[124]

Opinion surveys indicated that almost three-quarters of the public approved of the government's measures; two-thirds thought they did not go far enough.[125] This reaction gave some credibility to ministers' fears about what might have happened had they not restricted entry. While Tony Benn dismissed Powell's supporters as 'white trash' and Crossman thought they belonged to the 'illiterate industrial proletariat', Powell posed a real political danger.[126] He enjoyed a special resonance with many workers: after his speech and subsequent sacking from the Conservative front bench, thousands downed tools to express their support. His views were even shared by some of the country's leading trade unionists.[127] Although some instigators of these demonstrations had Fascist links or already held viscerally racist views, that was not true of most of those who followed. As Ennals recognised, Powell did not create such feelings, but his speech made them appear more legitimate.[128]

Labour was already in a weak electoral position at the time of the Kenyan Asian controversy, working-class voters having been alienated by the government's prices and incomes policies and an economic slowdown. This was not the best of times to challenge voters' deepest prejudices and fears about immigration.[129] Thus, in the immediate aftermath of Powell's speech, Wilson urged ministers to emphasise bipartisanship in race relations and to avoid attacking Powell personally.[130] In fact Callaghan went the other way and expressed support for voluntary repatriation, claiming he had restricted Asian immigration to address the disquiet expressed by pro-Powell strikers.[131]

Two weeks after Powell's speech, Wilson did rebut his claims, in a speech also delivered in Birmingham. There he strongly identified Labour as an anti-racist party but reasserted the government's position that, if the principle of racial equality was to be maintained, 'we must create the practical conditions in which these principles are acceptable to all our people, including those who day by day live their lives alongside immigrant communities'.[132] Hence, inner-city areas with greatest black settlement were given aid under the remit of the Urban Programme, launched not long after Wilson's speech. This comprised modest Treasury pump-priming to local authorities that embarked on approved projects to help areas of acute deprivation. Yet, because of fears that it might arouse white antagonism, the Programme was presented as an attempt to relieve poverty in general rather than to help immigrants in particular.[133]

Conclusion

Like his predecessor at the Home Office, Callaghan hoped the 1968 Race Relations Act would prevent second-generation immigrants becoming alienated from mainstream society.[134] Despite ensuring the Act broadly reflected Jenkins' concerns, however, Callaghan had a different understanding of how that end might be achieved, one probably closer to the views of most Labour members and voters. During the spring of 1968 the Cabinet established a Ministerial Committee on Immigration and Assimilation, the title of which undoubtedly indicated how some believed blacks born in Britain should relate to its 'way of life'.[135] As the Kenyan Asian crisis reached a climax, the Committee discussed a Home Office paper that reviewed the established policy of promoting a form of integration that did not compromise immigrants' 'cultural diversity'. Although the paper was written under his name, Callaghan questioned its assumptions and asked how far diversity should be permitted to develop; he noted that allowing Sikhs to wear beards and turbans at work aroused white resentment. The Home Secretary was especially concerned with what he termed the 'ineradicability of colour', for, unlike previous immigrant groups, even second-generation West Indians, Pakistanis and Indians 'could not be concealed' and thereby raised problems 'of an entirely new kind'. According to Crossman, only a minority on the Committee wanted 'the coloured communities to remain foreign', that is, to retain their cultural distinctiveness. The rest, led by Callaghan, sought their 'full integration or assimilation', so that they would effectively become 'little Englishmen' – presumably ministers hoped that they would then provoke less hostility.

If, under Callaghan's lead, government policy appeared to take a step back, elsewhere the party gave evidence of a greater sensitivity to the issue of colour. In 1957 the Cardiff party had claimed there was 'no marked evidence of discrimination' in the city, a highly unlikely statement given the existence of the mainly black district of Tiger Bay. Eleven years later, the same organisation dismissed the 'strong myth' that Cardiff was immune to racial problems and embraced the need to educate against prejudice in schools and combat discrimination at work.[136] By the late 1960s greater efforts were also being made to recruit black residents into the party. In Norwood, south London, for example, activists invited potential West Indian recruits to their homes to try to overcome doubts they might have about Labour. Having recruited 50 new black members, one ward in the constituency held a meeting every other month in the home of a West Indian member, to encourage the attendance of other immigrants.[137] *Tribune* also challenged the assumption that black immigrants would destroy the country's settled way of life; and if Britain became more 'cosmopolitan' as a result, that was a prospect some Tribune MPs appeared to welcome.[138]

The greater attention to and sympathy with issues relating to colour were, however, unevenly developed. In 1956 Leeds West CLP marked Charles Pannell's first five years in the Commons by holding an evening of entertainment during which one of the turns involved songs delivered by lady members dressed as 'nigger minstrels'.[139] Just over a decade later, contributors to *Tribune* condemned *The Black and White Minstrel Show* (watched on BBC television every week by millions) as a disgrace for portraying black people as second-class citizens.[140] David Ennals, the minister in charge of integration, claimed, however, that, having seen the programme, he could find no trace of prejudice in it.[141]

Notes

The place of publication is London unless otherwise specified.

1 Some of the material contained in this chapter has appeared in 'Brotherhood and the brothers: responses to "coloured" immigration in the British Labour Party, c. 1951–65', *Journal of Political Ideologies*, 3:1 (1998).
2 P. Fryer, *Staying Power. The History of Black People in Britain* (1984), p. 381.
3 Candidus, 'Coloured immigration', *Socialist Commentary*, March 1968.
4 Quoted in J. Solomos, *Race and Racism in Britain* (1993), p. 84.
5 Labour Party Archive (LPA), British-Asian Overseas Fellowship (BAOF) papers, Agendas 1953–63 Box, Circulars 1962–3 File, H. A. Alavi, Pakistani immigrants and the Labour Party, 21 February 1963.
6 *Report of the Forty-Seventh Annual Conference of the Labour Party* (1948), pp. 180–1.
7 S. Howe, *Anticolonialism in British Politics. The Left and the End of Empire, 1918–1964* (Oxford, 1993).
8 Mitchell Library, Glasgow Maryhill CLP papers, Minutes, 6 March 1960.
9 Lambeth Archives, Brixton CLP papers, IV/156/1/2, General management committee (GMC) minutes, 21 January 1953.
10 LPA, NEC, Commonwealth Sub-committee papers, Minutes, agenda and documents 1955–56 and 1957–62 Boxes, *passim*.
11 J. M. Bochel, 'Activists in the Conservative and Labour parties. A study of ward secretaries in Manchester', MA thesis, University of Manchester (1965), p. 151.
12 *Report of the Fifty-Ninth Annual Conference of the Labour Party* (1960), p. 12.
13 Quoted in B. Brivati, *Hugh Gaitskell* (1996), p. 344.
14 *Report of the Sixty-First Annual Conference of the Labour Party* (1962), pp. 180–1; P. Zeigler, *Wilson* (1993), pp. 173–5.
15 LPA, Judith Hart papers, Section 1, File 2, notes for speech written at time of the 1968 Race Relations Bill, and Section 10, File 10/4, speech at memorial for Martin Luther King, 22 May 1968.
16 R. Jenkins, *Essays and Speeches* (1967), pp. 269–70.
17 *Tribune*, 3 and 10 May 1968.
18 LPA, Race Relations and Immigration Collection (RRIC), Various subjects 1958–65 Box, press release of speech delivered 14 November 1961.
19 Labour Party, *Britain Belongs to You* (1959), p. 15.
20 Commonwealth Sub-committee papers, Minutes, agenda and documents

1957–62 Box, NEC statement on racial discrimination, 26 September 1958.

21 *Sixty-First Annual Conference of Labour*, pp. 161–2.

22 LPA, Study Group on Immigration papers, Commonwealth immigration, Re. 382/November 1968.

23 K. Paul, *Whitewashing Britain. Race and Citizenship in the Postwar Era* (Ithaca, 1997), pp. 111–21; R. Hansen, *Citizenship and Immigration in Post-war Britain* (Oxford, 2000), pp. 56–61.

24 London Metropolitan Archive (LMA), *London News*, April 1954.

25 LMA, Labour Party London Region papers, Acc 2417/G/6, *London Labour Party Annual Report 1955* (1956), pp. 11–14; *London News*, October 1955; Labour Party, *Racial Discrimination* (1958), pp. 4–5.

26 Unless otherwise stated, the following two paragraphs are based on correspondence in RRIC, Various subjects 1929–58 Box.

27 *Labour News*, January 1959.

28 London Region papers, Acc 2417/E/6/17, Correspondence between Kinchella and Raisin during August and September 1958.

29 RRIC, Various subjects 1929–58 Box, letter from Vauxhall CLP secretary, 26 February 1957.

30 I. Katznelson, *Black Men, White Cities. Race, Politics and Migration in the United States, 1900–30, and Britain, 1948–68* (Oxford, 1973), p. 136.

31 *Parliamentary Debates (Hansard), 5th Series, Volume 532, House of Commons Official Report, Session 1953–54*, columns 821–32.

32 *London News*, May 1954 and January 1955.

33 Commonwealth Sub-committee, Minutes, agenda and documents 1955–56 Box, Analysis of resolutions received from Labour parties and trade union branches, July and September 1956; and 1957–62 Box, Resolutions from Labour parties, July 1958.

34 Bodleian Library, Anthony Greenwood papers, MS.Eng.c.6300/3–6, Driver to Greenwood, 3 June 1958, and Greenwood to Driver, 9 June 1958.

35 E. Pilkington, *Beyond the Mother Country. West Indians and the Notting Hill White Riots* (1988), pp. 110–11, 133–4.

36 RRIC, Various subjects 1958–65 Box, Statement issued by executive committee on behalf of the North Kensington Labour Party, 11 September 1958.

37 London Region papers, Acc 2417/B/65, Election report – County of London, p. 9.

38 Editorial, *Socialist Commentary*, October 1958; Editorial, *Socialist Commentary*, December 1961, p. 14; *London News*, October 1958.

39 Modern Records Centre (MRC), Selly Oak CLP papers, MSS 1 1/33, 35, 40 and 50, GMC minutes, 14 December 1967, 8 February and 13 June 1968, and 13 April 1969.

40 J. E. Turner, *Labour's Doorstep Politics in London* (1978), pp. 180–1, 260–3, 274.

41 Westminster Archives, St Marylebone CLP papers, Acc 1390, GMC minutes, 29 May and 25 September 1957; Report of the executive committee (EC) to annual general meeting (AGM) held 24 February 1960; London Region papers, Acc 2417/E/6/29, Report of EC to St Marylebone AGM, 25 February 1959.

42 A. Sherman, 'Deptford', in N. Deakin (ed.), *Colour and the British Electorate 1964* (1965), pp. 109–11.

43 BAOF papers, minutes, Fellowship Committee, 1953–4, Council, 1955–60 Box, Secretary's report, 9 October 1958.

44 D. Woolcott, 'Southall', in Deakin, *Colour*, p. 46.
45 St Marylebone CLP papers, Acc 1390, *Labour Life*, October 1958, p. 4.
46 N. Deakin, 'Key to the immigrant problem', *Socialist Commentary*, February 1965, pp. 8–9.
47 *Socialist Commentary*, July 1961, p. 13.
48 Katznelson, *Black Men*, pp. 154–5.
49 *London News*, July 1958.
50 Labour Party, *The Integration of Immigrants* (1962).
51 *Sixty-First Annual Conference of Labour*, p. 239.
52 Brixton CLP papers, IV/156/1/2, GMC minutes, 21 January, 25 November 1953 and 28 July 1954; L. J. Sharpe, 'Brixton', in Deakin, *Colour*, p. 27.
53 MRC, Coventry Borough Labour Party papers, MSS 11/3/15/181, Ritchie to Young, 12 June 1958; MSS 11/3/15/420, Ritchie to Singh, 21 October 1958; and MSS 11/3/15/438, Ritchie to Wahid, 30 October 1958.
54 RRIC, Various subjects 1958–65 Box, J. W. Raisin, Racial disturbances in London, 11 September 1958.
55 London Region papers, Acc 2417/K/48, Working party on problems of coloured people. Draft interim report, 14 April 1959.
56 NEC, Organisation Sub-committee, 12 December 1962, Immigrants and the Labour party, Int/1961–2/26/Sup.
57 BAOF papers, Agendas, 1957–60 Box, Circulars 1962–3 File, Council minutes, 22 June 1963; London Region papers, Acc 2417/E/6/21, organiser's report; MRC, Labour Party East Midlands Region papers, MSS 9 3/20/288, organiser's report.
58 BAOF papers, Agendas 1957–60 Box, Circulars 1962–3 File, Tenth annual conference minutes, 22 June 1963.
59 West Yorkshire Archive, City of Bradford Labour Party papers, 60D84/3/1, Bradford East CLP minutes, 14 November and 12 December 1961; 60D84/5/2, Exchange ward minutes, 27 November 1961.
60 D. Davies, 'The colourless vote', *Socialist Commentary*, November 1966, p. 26.
61 J. Rex and R. Moore, *Race, Community and Conflict. A Study of Sparkbrook* (Oxford, 1967), pp. 47, 197–9, 208–11.
62 National Library of Wales (NLW), Eirene White papers, L/1/20 File, White to Brooks, 16 December 1965; *Chester Chronicle*, 12 December 1965; *Flintshire Leader*, 29 October 1965 and 12 December 1965.
63 *Labour News*, October 1958.
64 *Labour News*, November 1958.
65 LMA, Southall CLP papers, Acc 1267/73, immigration file, B. Wyatt, Report of special meeting called on immigration problems in Southall, 28 May 1963; Pargiter to Ayres, 30 March 1962; *New Statesman*, 8 May 1964.
66 London Region papers, Acc 2417/A/70/2, organiser's report.
67 London Region papers, Acc 2417/A/70/1, organiser's report; Acc 2417/B/65, Election report – County of London, p. 9; Acc 2417/E/6/19, organiser's report; Brixton CLP papers, IV/156/1/4, GMC minutes, 30 October 1964; M. Spiers, 'Bradford', in Deakin, *Colour*, p. 127.
68 Raisin, Racial disturbances.
69 BAOF papers, Agendas, 1957–60 Box, Circulars 1962–3 File, Committee on Integration, minutes, 27 June 1963; London Region papers, Acc 2417/A/70/4, organiser's report.
70 D. T. Studlar, 'Policy voting in Britain: the coloured immigration issue in the 1964, 1966 and 1970 general elections', *American Political Science Review*, 72:1 (1978).

71 Southwark Local Studies Library, Dulwich CLP papers, Box 390/7, Dunce to Barker, 5 October 1964.

72 Bodleian Library, Conservative Party Archive, CCO 180/11/2/1–5, Gallup survey of marginal seats in Birmingham, June 1964.

73 P. Griffiths, *A Question of Colour?* (1966), p. 225; Hansen, *Citizenship*, pp. 132–4.

74 *Tribune*, 1 July 1966.

75 *Tribune*, 29 March 1968.

76 Quoted in Zeigler, *Wilson*, p. 174.

77 This paragraph is based on: Public Record Office (PRO), PREM 13/382, Soskice to Wilson, 4 January 1965, and PRO, LAB 8/3003, Memorandum by the Secretary of State for the Home Department (draft), 6 January 1965.

78 R. Crossman, *The Diaries of a Cabinet Minister. Volume I* (1975), pp. 270–1, 299.

79 House of Lords Record Office (HLRO), Reginald Sorenson papers, Hist. Coll. 102/230, A backbencher's pilgrimage, pp. 346–7.

80 BAOF papers, General correspondence 1963–72 Box, Alavi, to secretary, 6 August 1965.

81 *Tribune*, 7 January 1966.

82 For more on this legislation, see Hansen, *Citizenship*, pp. 136–46.

83 Unless otherwise stated, this paragraph is based on *Daily Express*, 11 March; *Sun*, 11 March; *Guardian*, 5 April, 18, 21 and 24 May, 12 June, 6 August; *The Times*, 6 August; *Daily Telegraph*, 12 October 1965.

84 PREM 13/384, Foley to Wilson, n.d. (but November 1965).

85 PRO, CAB 165/263, Integration of Commonwealth immigrants, Record of meeting, 12 February 1965.

86 *Ibid.*

87 LAB 43/425, minute from Green, 4 January 1965; PREM 13/2314, Soskice to Wilson, 19 March 1965.

88 LAB 43/468, Memorandum for the ministers' talk with the Home Secretary and Chief Secretary on racial discrimination, 3 February 1967.

89 LAB 8/3109, draft minutes of meeting between Thornton, Foley and employment exchange managers, 16 November 1965.

90 Jenkins, *Essays*, pp. 267–70.

91 This account is based on British Library of Political and Economic Science, Bedford CLP papers, GMC minutes, 1 June and 12 October 1967, and 9 February 1968.

92 LPA, Race Relations Study Group papers, Race relations, Re. 119/April 1967, and minutes, 25 April 1967; *Report of the Sixty-Sixth Annual Conference of the Labour Party* (1967), p. 312.

93 Labour Party, *Race Relations* (1967), p. 29.

94 R. Crossman, *The Diaries of a Cabinet Minister. Volume II* (1977), p. 666.

95 CAB 128/42, Cabinet minutes, 21 December 1967; CAB 134/2859, Home Affairs Committee minutes, 5 January 1968.

96 *The Times*, 12 March 1965; Birmingham Public Library, Birmingham Borough Labour Party, Subject collection: Immigration questions, circular to all affiliated union branches, 1 January 1968.

97 *Sun*, 11 March 1965.

98 PREM 13/383, Balogh to Wilson, 5 July 1965; PREM 13/384, Balogh to Brown, 8 July 1965.

99 Sherman, 'Deptford', p. 114.

100 For examples of discrimination among bus crews, see J. A. G. Griffiths *et al.*, *Coloured Immigrants in Britain* (Oxford, 1960), pp. 219–23.

101 *Trades Union Congress Report 1955* (1955), p. 456.
102 Coventry Borough Labour Party papers, MSS 11/3/15/378, Singh to Ritchie, 1 October 1958; MSS 11/3/15/409, Locksley to Ritchie, 15 October 1958; and MSS 11/3/15/506, Locksley to Ritchie, 3 December 1958. For a survey of the unions' ambivalent reaction to black immigration, see K. Lunn, 'Complex encounters: trade unions, immigration and racism', in J. McIlroy, N. Fishman and A. Campbell (eds), *British Trade Unions and Industrial Politics. Volume II* (Aldershot, 1999).
103 RRIC, various subjects 1958–65 Box, Assistant organiser, East Midlands Region to Phillips, 11 September 1958; T. Benn, *Out of the Wilderness. Diaries, 1963–67* (1987), pp. 13–15; M. Dresser, 'The colour bar in Bristol', in R. Samuel (ed.), *Patriotism. Volume I* (1989), pp. 288–316.
104 LAB 43/425, Draft minute from Gunter to Gordon Walker, n.d. (but January 1965?).
105 See, for example, LAB 8/3067.
106 LAB 43/433, Correspondence between Foley and Thornton, 27 April, 18 June and 28 June 1965.
107 LAB 43/457, Bacon to Gunter, 19 August 1966; Gunter to Bacon, 8 September 1966.
108 RRIC, Various subjects 1929–58 Box, Secretary North Paddington CLP to Assistant Commonwealth Officer, 5 March 1957.
109 LAB 43/468, Note of a meeting, 10 May, 19 June and 21 June 1967.
110 *Guardian*, 11 June 1965.
111 *Tribune*, 1 March and 19 April 1968.
112 Editorial, 'Race and reason', *Socialist Commentary*, December 1969, p. 4.
113 A. Lester, 'Labour's white problem', *Socialist Commentary*, June 1966.
114 J. Callaghan, *Time and Chance* (1987), p. 269.
115 Institute of Race Relations, *Colour and Immigration in the United Kingdom, 1968* (1968), pp. 18–19.
116 For the background to this issue, see Hansen, *Citizenship*, pp. 157–60, 165–9.
117 CAB 134/2858, Asian immigration from East Africa, Memorandum by the Secretary of State for the Home Department, 17 October 1967; Crossman, *Diaries II*, p. 526.
118 CAB 128/43, Cabinet minutes, 15 and 22 February 1968.
119 CAB 130/322, Minutes of meeting to discuss voucher scheme, 20 October 1967.
120 D. Owen, *Time to Declare* (Harmondsworth, 1992), pp. 112–13.
121 HO 376/118, Ennals to all community liaison officers, 13 March 1968.
122 HO 376/118, Jones to Ennals, 15 March 1968; Guthrie to Ennals, 19 March 1968; Kumar to Ennals, 29 March 1968; Grubb to Ennals, 1 April 1968.
123 *Tribune*, 1 and 8 March 1968.
124 *Tribune*, 8 March 1968.
125 CAB 152/11.
126 T. Benn, *Office Without Power. Diaries, 1968–72* (1988), p. 60; R. Crossman, *Diaries of Cabinet Minister. Volume III* (1977), p. 29.
127 F. Lindrop, 'Racism and the working class: strikes in support of Enoch Powell in 1968', *Labour History Review*, 66:1 (2001); J. Jones, *Union Man* (1986), p. 197.
128 For the views of Heathrow Airport staff, see the statements contained in HO 223/107 and 108; for a security service report of the dockers, see PREM 13/2315, March of Smithfield market porters to the House of Commons on 24 April 1968 in support of Mr. Enoch Powell, MP, 24 April 1968, and

Demonstration of dockers against the race Relations Bill on 23 April 1968, 24 April 1968; *Daily Sketch*, 27 April 1968.

129 Crossman, *Diaries II*, p. 785.

130 PREM 13/2314, Hall's memo to all private secretaries, 23 and 24 April 1968.

131 CAB 152/11, transcript of *Panorama*, transmitted BBC1, 29 April 1968.

132 H. Wilson, *The Labour Government, 1964–70* (Harmondsworth, 1971), pp. 664–8.

133 CAB 152/112, The Urban Programme. Report on development and strategy, September 1969.

134 *News of the World*, 7 April 1968.

135 This account is based on CAB 134/2899, Ministerial Committee on Immigration and Assimilation, minutes, 10 April 1968, and Note by the Secretary of State for the Home Department, 9 April 1968; Crossman, *Diaries II*, pp. 773–4.

136 RRIC, Various subjects 1929–58 Box, Secretary Cardiff City Party to Assistant Commonwealth Officer, 15 February 1957; NLW, City of Cardiff Labour Party papers, A programme for Cardiff, n.d. (but 1968).

137 *Labour Organiser*, 49:564 (1969), pp. 206–7.

138 *Tribune*, 26 April 1968; LPA, Ian Mikardo/Jo Richardson papers, Box 5, Tribune Group minutes, 28 October–16 December 1970 File, statement on racialism, n.d.

139 HLRO, Charles Pannell papers, Hist. Coll. 124/ W2, *Leeds Weekly Citizen*, 18 February 1956.

140 *Tribune*, 22 September 1967.

141 *Guardian*, 6 June 1967.

7

Instilling 'responsibility' in the young

If only for reasons of self-preservation, Labour was obliged to draw some young people into the party so they could eventually replace its elderly stalwarts.[1] Electoral logic also dictated that Labour had to ensure the support of at least a respectable proportion of what was an expanding number of voters. Consequently, the 1955 Wilson report on party organisation (see Chapter 2) expressed particular concern about the consequences of Labour's inability to interest youngsters in the party.[2] Many members were, however, uncertain about the purpose, manner and even merit of making a special appeal to the young. The 1960s began with commentators asserting that most young adults were materially satisfied and so inclined to Conservatism, but the decade ended with the impression that many young people had become alienated from society and embraced far-left causes. This shift in perceptions did not exactly help clarify thinking.

Those who have analysed Labour's attempt to win over the young tend to blame the party's apparent refusal to take their concerns seriously for its failure to do so.[3] They consider Labour's prescriptive notions of how the young should think and act inhibited its efforts. In particular, at the start of the decade the party's 'residual puritanism' is supposed to have prevented it evoking a positive response among purportedly hedonistic proletarians.[4] At the end of the 1960s, many believed the government's political caution had estranged middle-class students.[5] This chapter questions the exclusively 'supply-side' explanation of Labour's failure evident in such accounts. In fact, the party's various attempts to evoke a positive response among the young were usually based on a desire to engage with what was generally thought to be their interests. Before the 1959 general election, Labour established a Youth Commission, composed of progressive celebrities of the day like the footballer Jimmy Hill, which drafted proposals to meet the changing needs of the young. If this was principally meant to create favourable publicity, the creation of the Young Socialists in 1960 and the government's reduction of the voting age were more substantive initiatives. If neither made the party any more attractive to late adolescents and those in their twenties, it is unclear how far this was due to their flawed character or to the particular – and contradictory – inclinations of the young themselves. Both initiatives were certainly underpinned by the party's desire to instil 'responsibility' in the young, by which was meant their acceptance of Labour's own political assumptions. However, it is also true that most young people had long disparaged political activity of whatever kind; and those few who followed the path of budding revolutionaries, such as Tariq Ali, were implacably hostile to social democratic parties like Labour, whatever such parties said or did.

Labour's perception of youth

Towards the end of Clement Attlee's period in office, some of the party's leading younger members claimed Labour's 'most urgent' domestic problem was its deteriorating relationship with the country's youth. Most were judged 'unpolitical' and so biased 'towards the existing order ... and therefore towards conservatism'.[6] The reason for this was, a speaker at the 1948 Labour Party conference claimed, their lack of a memory of inter-war conditions. This meant, according to a later delegate, that to them 'the dole queue is not a reality but a historical fact' – and facts did convince as much as experience.[7] As already noted, many activists' personal familiarity with the inter-war years was critical to their appreciation of Labour's merits. When a Young Socialist told the 1964 national conference of Labour women that her generation 'did not want to hear about what went on in the thirties, they wanted to know what could be done now', she was rebuffed by a mature delegate from the North East, who stated, 'it was because of their experience in the thirties that many people had joined the Labour Party and fought so hard – a matter which ought not to be forgotten'.[8]

If the young lacked the necessary memory, their supposedly unthinking acceptance of full employment further distinguished them from activists. Hence, by the time of the 1959 Labour Party conference, it was a commonplace that, as one speaker put it, 'whether you like it or not', young people:

> have 'never had it so good.' Back in the thirties when we were young and fighting to get a job, at any hours, at any pay, we had something to strive and fight for. Today they get it easy: good wages, regular hours.... They have never had it so good, my friends, and it is not a damn bit of good telling them what we had to do in the twenties and thirties: they will either not believe it or tell you it is a dead duck.[9]

According to Vauxhall's agent, the widespread availability of well remunerated unskilled work had other implications that further detached adolescents from their parents' generation. In particular, the former were no longer 'subjected to discipline' at work, as they could easily find alternative employment, while the family had ceased to ensure conformity, because mothers were increasingly taking up part-time work outside the home.[10]

It was widely believed that, so far as working-class youngsters were concerned, the consequence of these changes was their weakening attachment to Labour; so dire was the problem, members in London reported that even their own children voted Conservative in 1959.[11] Affluence was thought to have affected younger members of the middle class in a rather different way. In 1955 the former Cabinet minister Hugh Dalton met with the MP Kenneth Younger and during their conversation Dalton spoke of their greater interest in 'Africans, Indians, etc'. Younger replied that, 'having done away with gross poverty' at home, the under-developed world was where their 'emotions now went'.[12]

Because of such changes in the outlook of some young people, a few activists believed greater regard should be shown to them. In 1962, the secretary of Brixton's Stockwell ward declared there was 'the BIG QUESTION for us to try and answer':

> How can we get the young people of today interested in politics. One part of the answer I think is for *us* to get interested in them, not keep on reliving the past, but to look forward to the future.... Let us listen to them and their ideas ... but at the same time point out where they are wrong and why without getting impatient with them because remember if we can encourage them to join the Party, as they get older they will be doing the same as we are trying to do today and that is to keep the party ALIVE.[13]

As Robert Sheldon, the defeated candidate for Manchester Withington, indicated to Labour's post-1959 election conference, the 'old methods' were no longer enough. He reported the establishment of a coffee-house – an innovation also favoured by the non-aligned Marxist New Left – in the centre of Manchester. The aim was to create an amenable venue for young people of vaguely left-wing sympathies to discuss the issues of the day, as the first step towards Labour membership.[14] In charge of the coffee-house was Paul Rose, who was later elected MP for Manchester Blackley in 1964 at the unusually young age of twenty-nine. He saw it as a means of sidestepping the party's unattractive wards and those older activists who, he claimed, resented 'the supposed in-gratitude of the younger generation' and objected to 'the sense of fun, the healthy iconoclasm and apparent self-confidence of the modern teenager'.[15] Rose, however, believed Labour had to do more than offer the young a chance to chat over a coffee. It needed to demonstrate its relevance by asserting that:

the world of football, cinema, skiffle, hiking, art and the Hallé Orchestra, is our world. The 'social hedgehogs' on the left who see no place for these things in the struggle for a better life are ill-equipped to represent youth.... There is no place for socialist 'squares' in the age of Humphrey Lyttleton, Aldermaston marches and Manchester United.[16]

This was something many were unwilling to do: they looked on what the MP Horace King described as 'cheap capitalist culture' as one of the means by which youngsters were corrupted.[17] As one 1956 pamphlet aimed at young people stated, spending money on clothes, going to football matches or having a drink were a 'kind of dope' that 'only keep you from thinking'.[18] Indeed, in the mid-1960s *Tribune*'s television critic identified a common assumption on the left that 'all pop music is trivial, decadent and in some undefined way – dangerous'.[19]

Even when trying to relate to the young's concerns, Labour often simply reiterated their need to adhere to its approach to politics. In time for the 1959 election, Transport House published 250,000 copies of *Hi!*, a broadsheet aimed at young workers, and employed in its production the popular writer Keith Waterhouse, to convince them of the importance of politics to their lives. Waterhouse claimed he came to appreciate that point after breaking his wrist, for the National Health Service was founded by 'those somewhat ridiculous, slightly pompous, earnest, plodding figures we call politicians'. Thus, Waterhouse asserted, 'politics is something that happens to everybody'.[20] On such occasions, especially when trying to communicate in what it imagined was the idiom of the young, Labour only reinforced its worthy image. As part of a regular 'Teenage Beat' column, the *East Ham South Citizen* stated that, in contrast to the Conservatives' 'old, dreary world of money-grabbing', Labour offered youth a 'clean, *wholesome* world'.[21]

Labour's problems became more acute later in the 1960s with the emergence of the 'counter-culture'. If young affluent workers passively rejected Labour, middle-class students at this time apparently took a more conscious leave of the party and society in general. Even the left-leaning Judith Hart, when Minister for Social Security, complained of the growing number of those refusing to take paid employment. This was, she claimed, 'causing me a very great deal of concern', as there were many, often from middle-class families, who 'say they are writers or disc jockeys – they pick themselves all sorts of esoteric occupations – and seem to think it quite right that they spend a considerable time without work'.[22]

The junior minister Shirley Williams thought the violent student protests that broke out across the West during 1968 meant irrational students threatened Labour's reformist strategy, based at it was on the application of reason.[23] Others, such as Doris Young, who chaired the

1970 women's conference, thought the young had something more positive to contribute. Yet, while praising the rising generation for its 'more direct, more impatient and more positive attitude to war and social equality', she feared this might lead them to abandon conventional politics. Young was also unsure whether their 'new protesting spirit' was the modern expression of Labour's own fight against social injustice or just 'materialistic and self-seeking'. Whatever its nature, she believed the party should acquire a 'deeper understanding and appreciation' of the young.[24] The revisionist MP John Mackintosh was similarly unclear what the generation gap represented. He thought those who joined Oxfam or War on Want shared his values, as they believed in steady 'progress'. However, he looked on the 'flower people and the freak outs' with despair because they rejected gradual improvement and established politics. If he did not condemn their values, Mackintosh admitted he could not understand them.[25]

Finally, and in complete contrast, were those, like the revisionist Cabinet minister Anthony Crosland, who questioned the reality of a significant generation gap, believing the concept was associated with a 'self-abusing attitude towards youth as a class'. If it did exist, he did not think it very wide, for various surveys suggested that, a few disgruntled students apart, the great majority of eighteen- to twenty-four-year-olds held political opinions very similar to those of their parents.[26] Crosland's colleague Richard Marsh was even more peremptory, feeling he could dismiss the violent demonstrations of 1968 because, as students 'just liked making trouble', their protests amounted to no more than 'intellectual masturbation'.[27]

The purpose of youth organisation

In 1935, the Labour League of Youth (LOY) claimed a membership of 25,000; it also enjoyed a fair degree of autonomy, having its own conference, an elected national committee and representation on the National Executive Committee (NEC). However, after falling victim to Communist 'entryism', in which members of that party masqueraded as Labour loyalists to promote their own programme, expulsions followed and the LOY was brought under strict NEC control. The LOY never recovered its inter-war position and by 1955 was moribund, at which point the NEC wound it up as a national body, although 200 or so constituency youth branches remained.

To ensure youth recruitment was still taken seriously, the NEC's Organisation Sub-committee formed a Youth Sub-committee and called on constituency Labour parties (CLPs) to appoint youth officers. This had little impact, even though for much of the 1960s nearly two-thirds

Table 7.1 Labour's youth and student organisations: numbers of branches, members and officers, 1955–70

	Youth			University students	
	Branches[a]	Members[b]	CLP youth officers	Clubs[c]	Members[b]
1955	237	–	–	40	–
1956	301	–	56	40	–
1957	275	–	147	–	–
1958	268	–	159	–	–
1959	262	–	173	–	–
1960	572	–	258	50	3,000
1961	721	–	344	–	5,000
1962	772	22,000	448	69	5,500
1963	769	–	459	83	5,644
1964	722	–	473	92	6,695
1965	605	–	386	99	7,000
1966	571	12,000	351	100	7,000
1967	576	–	401	–	–
1968	533	–	402	–	–
1969	386	–	348	–	–
1970	457	6,000	346	–	–

[a]Number of constituency youth branches, 1955–9, and branches of the Young Socialists, 1960 on.
[b]Estimated numbers – available for selected years only.
[c]After 1966 the National Executive Committee terminated its relationship with the National Association of Labour Student Organisations.
Source: Labour Party annual conference reports, 1955–70; Labour Party Archive, National Executive Committee Youth Sub-committee minutes, 17 September 1962, Summary of branch report forms, NAD/94/9/62, 22 June 1966, Report on organisation and activities, NC, 4 June 1966, and 7 July 1970, Summary of report forms, NC/10/JUN/70.

of CLPs claimed to have filled such a post (see Table 7.1). Many activists looked on youth organisation with considerable scepticism, partly due to memories of Communist infiltration, but mainly because they felt it would waste their limited time and money. Most local parties simply lacked suitable accommodation and adequate resources, and so could not compete with the better-placed Young Conservatives, let alone commercial leisure pursuits. In addition, those few young people who could be recruited were often associated with problems such as damaging property or misusing funds.[28] In addition, the majority of activists were themselves parents or even grandparents and did not sympathise with the preoccupations of youth. Such local gerontocracies were often irritated when young members played records on party premises and sometimes viewed their presence in the street as requiring police intervention.[29]

Even those who saw merit in supporting the organisation of youth disagreed over what form it should take: in particular, as early as 1946 there was what was described as the 'old problem of social versus political activities'.[30] This in turn was underpinned by the hoary question of whether Labour should aim to build an elite or a mass youth move-ment. Officially, Transport House wanted local branches to satisfy political and recreational interests, so they might generate both a small group of future activists and a greater number of firm Labour voters.[31] The problem, however, was that the few youngsters who took party activity at all seriously wanted to take it in an elitist – and overtly political – direction while the majority favoured social activities. Officers of the Bethnal Green LOY even disbanded their own branch in disgust at how little interest fellow members showed in political events.[32]

Those supporting the idea of a youth wing were at least united in the belief that its overall purpose should be, as George Brinham (chair of the Youth Sub-committee) confirmed, to 'train' the young 'to perform their civic responsibilities'.[33] Youth sections were described as 'chiefly for the purpose of developing the character and experience of their members to fit them for service in the Party'.[34] A corollary was that the young should subordinate themselves to their elders and betters: NEC member Percy Knight told the LOY they were 'enjoying the machine created by the pioneers', men such as himself, and it was their respon-sibility to leave it as they found it.[35] As Reg Underhill stated when Labour's Chief Youth Officer, if a branch did not see its 'real purpose to be that of strengthening the Labour Party', it was 'pointless'.[36]

While some thought the young would learn the Labour way simply by doing what they were told, others considered they required auton-omy to develop a sense of 'responsibility'. Given Communist infiltration and the post-war threat of Trotskyist entryism, the NEC was reluctant to concede too much freedom. Indeed, some of those who argued for greater independence were actually entryists, who believed it would allow them to manipulate the organisation better.[37] Nonetheless, most who campaigned for greater freedom did so from legitimate conviction, although they conceded that, if they were given a conference free of NEC control, young members would pass extremely radical resolutions. However, such 'a platform for ideas, a channel for grievances, would increase the responsibility of the younger members' because 'the only way to train for responsibility is to give opportunity for exercising responsibility'.[38] As the MP Richard Marsh (who was not at all left-wing) stated in 1959, a worthwhile youth movement would 'pass resolutions of no confidence in everybody on the platform, tell us what is wrong with the leadership of the Party and inform us how we can have the

Socialist revolution in the next 24 hours'. He was confident such angry young members would nonetheless conform in the end.[39]

The Young Socialists

The NEC decided to rescue Labour's youth movement from the limbo into which it had fallen and in April 1959 formed a working party to recommend action. This reported just after the party's performance at the general election had apparently illustrated its lack of appeal to younger voters.[40] Members gathered information from an eclectic range of sources, including other European social democratic parties and Stuart Hall of the New Left. In an indication of how resistant it feared the young had become to Labour, the committee thought that if the new body too closely identified with the party it would not attract many recruits. Members therefore favoured sponsoring an organisation with no direct ties to Labour but that was nonetheless committed to its 'progressive ideals'. This option was, however, abandoned, largely on grounds of cost, as it would have required a substantial professional staff. The revived movement – known as the Young Socialists (YS) and launched at the start of 1960 – had to operate from Transport House and be supervised by officials already overburdened with other responsibilities.

The working party believed that if the YS was to attract more young people than the LOY, it had to undertake social much more than political activities. While literature designed to appeal to prospective members indicated that one reason to join was the chance to express political views, most stress was put on the assertion that members knew how to have a good time. Companionship, especially with those of the opposite sex, was mentioned, as was the chance to join in team sports and a variety of other groups, including 'let's-just-sit-in-the-sun groups'.[41]

According to a series of internal surveys, the YS initially enjoyed some limited popular success but it quickly fell to levels that would have embarrassed the post-war LOY.[42] While YS membership stood at about 22,000 two years after its formation, by 1966 numbers had declined to 12,000 and by 1970 there were only 6,000. The number of local YS branches also fell, from a peak of nearly 800 in 1962 to under 400 by 1969 (see Table 7.1). Most members were men: in 1962, 62 per cent of branches reported having a majority of males while the 1970 survey suggested females accounted for only one-third of the total, appreciably less than in the adult party. According to an academic investigation in the early 1960s, like their Conservative and Liberal equivalents, most Young Socialists were the children of party supporters. Yet the YS appealed disproportionately to the offspring of middle-class Labour partisans, as members were equally divided between those whose parents were employed in manual and professional occupations.[43] Indeed, the organiser for the Northern Home Counties Region noted in 1967 that the YS had 'completely failed to bring any manual-type of workers to the fore'.[44] This failure was probably due to two main factors. First, few working-class youngsters questioned the status quo to the extent that political activity of any type appeared a sensible pastime.[45] Secondly, even had many young workers been so inclined, given the desultory state of Labour's machine in proletarian districts, few would have had the opportunity of joining a section. In the organisational black hole that was Glasgow, for example, it is unlikely that at any one time there were ever many more than fifty Young Socialists.[46]

In any case, right from the start, as one YS member from Surrey complained, most of those attracted to the movement belonged to the 'local left intelligentsia', who were unwilling to attract those not already immersed in political debate. Those most active in the YS were characterised as opposed to music being played at meetings, disgusted at the very mention of television and generally bearing a 'hatred of anything for the masses'.[47] As YS activists in Twickenham put it in 1967, theirs should be a mainly political movement: it 'would be worse than useless to have a mass membership based primarily on social activities', because the party needed to combat apathy, not accommodate it.[48] To make things worse, commitment often went hand in hand with equally unpopular cultural aspirations: YS members in Bristol South East were forced to listen to classical records supplied by their secretary, who hoped to 'entertain and/or educate' them.[49] Such efforts were rarely appreciated and officials did their best to curb the zeal of their young improvers. The St Ives YS had a relatively healthy membership of twenty-nine, sixteen of whom normally attended its weekly meetings. However, its secretary – a grammar school sixth-former headed for Oxbridge – worried its gatherings were purely social, so held a discussion meeting, to which only five turned up. While the South West Region's organiser sympathised with this young man's ambition, he made it clear that the first duty of the YS was to build a large membership – and that meant putting on social activities.[50]

The consequences of entryism

Despite arguments in favour of giving youngsters the freedom to become 'responsible', the YS was kept under firm NEC scrutiny through Bessie Braddock's chairing of the Youth Sub-committee, a woman described by Tony Benn as 'brutal and tactless and as out of touch as anyone could be' when it came to the young.[51] The YS was granted an annual conference with the right to discuss policy and elect a national committee, but Braddock's main concern was to prevent it falling into entryist hands. This did not, however, mean that officials demanded unquestioning loyalty: some claimed to welcome criticism, so long as it was the product of the 'honest opinions of loyal young Party members'.[52]

Despite Braddock, the YS was soon infiltrated by a variety of Trotskyist groups, pre-eminently Young Guard and Keep Left. They demanded greater autonomy for the YS, and in particular full editorial control of its journal, *New Advance*. These tactics were popular with many non-Trotskyists who wanted to be free of adult interference and helped leftists win representation at regional and national level, which, along with a noisy presence at conference, they used to promote their policies. Proscriptions, suspensions and expulsions as well as the disbanding of local YS branches followed, as the NEC tried to stem the tide. In 1965 it assumed even greater control and had to rename the YS the Labour Party Young Socialists (LPYS), owing to the appropriation of the former title by the Socialist Labour League. Many legitimate LPYS members complained that, after this, the atmosphere was infused with 'disillusion and disgust': without the return of some autonomy it was predicted that Labour's youth membership would continue to decline.[53] For a time, at least, the LPYS appeared clear of entryism, if only because most Trotskyists temporarily convinced themselves Labour was no longer worth taking over. This allowed the NEC to relax its grip and in 1968 the LPYS national committee was given control of *Left*, its renamed journal. The collapse of membership nonetheless continued apace.

One reason why entryists gained such a prominent position within the YS was that few others took its political role seriously. According to Labour's own surveys, no more than half its members attended section gatherings. Moreover, although every constituency section was part of an area federation that was meant to co-ordinate activity, if the Bristol area federation was typical, only a tiny handful attended federation meetings.[54] In addition, at the peak of its popularity, in 1961, only half of branches sent delegates to the YS conference, a proportion that fell during the decade.[55] Journals supposed to appeal to a YS audience also failed to generate readers: in 1961 *New Advance* reached its zenith when monthly circulation totalled 9,500; *Left* only ever enjoyed a maximum circulation of 6,000. In fact, the position was worse than the figures indicate, as many copies were bought by trade unions and CLPs to subsidise production costs.[56]

Only partly because of its Trotskyist cuckoos, YS members attending conferences quickly gained a reputation for far-leftism, although probably few rivalled the member who, when asked what item of news from 1963 made them really happy, replied: 'The death of Hugh Gaitskell'.[57] At its inaugural conference, only Gaitskell's resignation was demanded, albeit by two-thirds of delegates, while a motion calling for the national-isation of six major industries and the biggest 500 companies was carried almost unanimously.[58]

Entryism was especially developed in London: the region's 1963 youth conference was described by the capital's youth officer as 'mainly a battle between Young Guard and Keep Left, with the *bona fide* Young Socialist element wondering what the H— was going on'.[59] While assidu-ous in gaining national posts – six out of the eleven members of the YS national committee elected in 1964 were subsequently expelled – Trotskyists also enjoyed a significant local presence in the metropolis. During the mid-1960s, Hackney's YS was run for the benefit of entryists, whose main concern was to prevent it being taken over by other far-left factions. There, meetings would dispute arcane matters such as whether the Soviet Union was a 'degenerate workers' state' or 'state capitalist'. Not surprisingly, they were no more successful at recruiting working-class youngsters than were sections led by those embracing more main-stream views.[60]

In 1964, the National Agent, Sara Barker, blamed the spread of Trotskyism on older members' reluctance to supervise sections properly.[61] Whether through indolence or deliberate liberalism, some did let their youngsters run free. While not the victim of entryism, when the NEC investigated Putney in 1963, it discovered the YS was out of control. Of its sixty-one members, less than half were party members. It also pub-lished a journal, for which substantial sums were owed to the general management committee (GMC); according to investigators, this journal contained only articles that were critical of party policy and promoted views incompatible with Labour membership.[62]

Gaitskell loyalists briefly tried to counter leftist influence but nation-ally, at least, their efforts came to little. Locally, however, there were occasional instances in which Young Socialists challenged their older – and more radical – counterparts, often over unilateralism, an issue that saw the YS in Bristol South East and Stockport support the parlia-mentary leadership and oppose their GMCs.[63] Indeed, at the 1966 YS Eastern Region conference, one-third of delegates walked out when the left-wing MP and vocal critic of the Wilson government Stan Newens addressed the meeting.[64]

Other problems

Labour's attempt to establish a popular youth movement faced other problems, more mundane but no less intractable than entryism, pre-eminent among which was a high turnover of members. In Stroud, the constituency agent noted the existence of a two-year cycle in the life of

a section, which began when it was formed by like-minded contemporaries studying for their 'A' levels and ended as they left the area to
go to university or find work.[65] Sections were consequently formed and
reformed at a rapid rate; for example, during 1964 the South West
Region reported an overall decline of four sections to forty-five, but ten
of these had been established in the previous twelve months.[66]

Some felt this instability was due to the inexperience of Young
Socialists. The NEC had fixed the upper age limit at twenty-five years,
compared with thirty for the Young Conservatives and thirty-five for the
supposedly Young Liberals. Some called for those in their late twenties
to be allowed to remain, as they feared that in their absence the YS
would be 'a kind of tight trousered rock-club'.[67] Officials argued against
raising the limit because it would prevent teenagers from gaining know-
how, as older members would inevitably dominate proceedings.[68] Some
also believed that maintaining the age limit at twenty-five would keep
out the 'more experienced disruptionists' in the Trotskyist left, although
others thought a higher limit would prevent 'green' members from being
'easy prey to outside influence'.[69]

Possibly because of the lack of more mature influences, there were
many instances of youthful excess. In Warwick, the agent corroborated
damaging local press reports that YS members had scratched 'ban-the-
bomb' and other slogans on walls and furniture in their meeting place.[70]
Other sections were a constant source of concern, such as the one
established in Salford West during 1963 but suspended by the executive
committee (EC) soon after the 1964 general election. Youngsters fell
foul of that local party owing to their allegedly noisy meetings, dis-
orderly conduct, 'illegal literature' and unpaid bills, as well as the belief
that meetings were 'nothing more than an evening for dancing'. During
the campaign there were reports that 'hand bills were thrown all over
the streets and youths were running round and shouting and ranting in
a Riotous Manner'. At the meeting that suspended the organisation,
twenty YS members, practically its entire complement, refused to leave
the room and became abusive when asked to do so.[71] It was to avoid
such problems that the South West Region's youth organiser discouraged
one applicant joining the YS after the boy's own father had highlighted
his 'restlessness and irresponsibility'.[72]

Even when they adhered to the prescribed form of activity, some YS
members behaved in what can only be described as a puerile manner,
one that unconsciously parodied the adult party's often pompous
proceedings. The minutes for Bedford's youth section recorded the
following exchange during July 1968:

The secretary was asked if he had informed Mr Bayliss about the
meeting. When he answered to the negative Mr Luft called him a

Steaming Great Nellie. After considerable discussion Mr Luft reduced this to Steaming Little Nellie. Mr Harding still would not accept this and asked for the statement to be withdrawn. Mr Luft refused. Mr Harding threatened to resign but Mr Luft still refused. After the chairman pleading [*sic*] with Mr Luft he withdrew the remark verbally. We then went on to ordinary business.[73]

By no means was all YS activity so troublesome or juvenile. The section in the south London constituency of Merton and Morden was something of a success, at least for a few years in the early 1960s, and gives an insight into the assumptions of those few non-Trotskyists who took youth organisation seriously.[74] Members picketed shops selling South African goods; supported Oxfam; and were keen unilateralists. Visits were proposed to the Farnborough air show, London airport, the *Daily Herald* printing works, the House of Commons, the Royal Mint, a Cadbury's factory, the Mermaid theatre, a planetarium and Sadler's Wells theatre. Talks by outside speakers tackled an eclectic range of subjects, including spiritualism (which involved a demonstration by a clairvoyant), humanism, road safety and the probation service. Members also participated in folk singing, rambling and listening to pop records. Numbers were small, however – speakers sometimes had an audience of only six. Moreover, members' lack of commitment to everyday party work was illustrated when the section executive held a 'surprise evening' to entice more than the usual number to attend a gathering. The 'surprise', it turned out, was a night of canvassing, a ruse that aroused much resentment among those who had turned up expecting something rather more exciting.

The student revolt

If members' attitude to maintaining formal links with the young was at best unresolved, they were even more diffident about university students – not least because, according to one observer, most regarded 'student politics as merely a youthful game' in which participants were still 'groping their way' to socialism.[75] In 1947 the NEC supported the formation of the National Association of Labour Student Organisations (NALSO) only after intensive lobbying from established university Labour clubs. The NEC resisted student proposals to build a closer relationship and restricted itself to giving NALSO financial support on the condition that its officers, and those of its affiliates, belonged to the party.[76]

While NALSO boosted the political careers of a few individuals, such as Roy Hattersley, the extent to which it helped the party is moot. Even a generous estimate suggests no more – and probably far fewer – than

5 per cent of students ever belonged to a Labour club, which by 1965 meant about 7,000 (see Table 7.1).[77] By the mid-1960s these clubs were swamped by far-left students, who voted at NALSO's 1966 conference to free officers from the obligation of Labour membership. In response, the NEC terminated its relationship, although links with clubs still loyal to Transport House were maintained. The key issue behind this estrangement was Wilson's reluctance to criticise the escalating US intervention in South Vietnam. The Vietnam War both lent credibility to revolutionaries like Tariq Ali, who was prominent in the campaign to oppose it, and afforded at least some coherence to their otherwise disparate critique of the status quo. Student disgust at Labour's failure to condemn US actions also led to numerous encounters between ministers and protestors on campus: at best the former were mocked or pointedly disregarded by their tormentors; at worst a variety of objects were hurled in their general direction.[78] Labour politicians were unused to such behaviour. The party's candidate in the 1967 Cambridge by-election even welcomed the absence of undergraduates at one of his meetings because 'they make such a row'.[79]

Unlike affluent working-class teenagers, student radicals at least had an overt political perspective, albeit one articulated in a form many found disturbing. Some leading members of the Labour Party reflected on the questions posed by the student revolt of the late 1960s, thinking it indicative of a widespread discontent with authority. Even so, along with the thirty-three-year-old MP Paul Rose, the Cabinet Minister Richard Crossman remained bemused, sensing an insuperable barrier between those up to their mid-twenties and others just a few years older.[80] Hart spoke of her 'immense approval' of the greater involvement of students in universities, colleges and sixth forms in the administration of their affairs. While student participation shocked some, their participation in curriculum development and teaching she believed 'must surely be right'.[81] Not surprisingly, given the number of young university staff sitting on it, Bristol West's GMC discussed student power with some sympathy, one speaker indicating that the very purpose of higher education should be radically re-examined.[82] Even venerable figures like the newly elevated peer Reginald Sorenson considered the student rebellion to be 'stimulated by a vital search for finer values'. Sorenson nonetheless wanted them to articulate their case with a greater sense of 'responsibility', which meant working through the existing political system.[83] The writer of an editorial for the *Socialist Commentary* was particularly disturbed by the reluctance of 'practical idealists' to identify with the party.[84] The author believed they would once have joined Labour and helped it reform the established order, but their alienation from parliamentary democracy was such that they now looked on violent methods with favour. While the editorial considered Labour's basic social democratic outlook as relevant as ever, its writer believed the party still needed to address some of the issues students raised, in particular the remoteness of decision-making and the pointlessness of much political activity.

The students' lack of 'responsibility' upset Cabinet ministers, and led Wilson and colleagues to view their protests as primarily a law and order issue. Crossman feared democracy was coming to an end, and concluded: 'we should have no hesitation in dealing with these people who were destroying free speech'. This approach depressed the likes of Benn and Barbara Castle, although even the latter referred to the existence of 'thugs' among a majority who expressed genuine grievances.[85] This reaction did not derive just from generational differences. Labour loyalists at King's College, London, stated the party differed from student revolutionaries, as it believed in reform from within, not destruction from without. To students still committed to Labour's way of thinking, 1968 was a disastrous year, in which 'frustrations exploded into violence and irresponsible language' and challenged the legitimacy of existing political structures.[86]

Even the most apparently conservative of voices, the Home Secretary, James Callaghan, took student opinions seriously. Callaghan was clearly irritated by the extremes of the protest movement, and he described Ali as a 'spoilt, rich, playboy'.[87] When faced with the prospect of a violent anti-Vietnam War march through London in October 1968, to follow up the Gosvenor Square riot earlier in the year, he still sought to balance the need to thwart the 'hooligans' intent on violence and the need to protect the right to demonstrate in peace.[88] Callaghan later allowed the controversial German student leader Rudi Dutschke into the country and arranged a meeting, during which he tried to persuade Dutschke of the merits of the reformist politics practised by Labour.[89]

Events at the London School of Economics (LSE) during the early part of 1969 seemed to bring student problems to a head. The director of the LSE, Walter Adams, was a former Rhodesian official whose links with apartheid did him no favours; nor did his refusal to reform the LSE's system of governance, which denied students a voice. After a series of disruptions, Adams took the unprecedented step of temporarily closing down the institution. Edward Short, the Secretary of State for Education, was assured that only a small minority of LSE students wanted to end academic freedom and establish a revolutionary base. Thus he considered deporting those American students said to be at the heart of the problem and thought about dismissing up to 300 students.[90] Short was particularly worried about the 'great impatience' with students evident among party members and the public at large, and was 'deeply concerned' about the possibility of a right-wing 'anti-student anti-intellectual backlash'. He did not, however, endorse LSE officials unreservedly and – unlike some hard-line administrators – saw merit in students winning representation on decision-making bodies.[91] To that end, he wanted an inquiry into how the LSE should modernise its constitution after matters had calmed down.[92]

When he spoke in a Commons debate on the universities in January 1969, Short nonetheless wanted to make a 'hard hitting attack' that would verbally 'clobber' those causing trouble at the LSE. He did this with Wilson's full backing, for the Prime Minister 'was getting a bit fed up with this troublesome minority' and had also noted the public's annoyance with those upon whom large amounts of their taxes were spent.[93] If he was consequently cast as an authoritarian, Short noted that the 'chaos and violence of student protest, rightly understood and rightly used, could raise the whole quality of our democracy'. 'Schools and universities must', he asserted, 'get young people to take the responsibilities of citizenship by abandoning authoritarianism and involving them in government and decision-making'.[94]

The student protests put ministers in an uncomfortable position, one many believed was analogous to that experienced by 1920s Weimar social democrats, caught between reactionary defenders of the status quo and revolutionaries intent on tearing the system down. As the Labour chair of the LSE students' union pointed out, while the authorities had been provocative, the existence of 'dedicated American agitators' was undoubted. In proposing that both sides negotiate a settlement, Labour found itself preaching reason to two extremes uninterested in compromise.[95]

Tribune and the revolutionaries

Although Wilson's Cabinet was unwilling openly to criticise US actions in Vietnam, the same was not true of the Labour left, who, on the face of it, were in a good position to appeal to student radicals. *Tribune* welcomed the Parisian May events as 'the greatest achievement of any west European labour movement since the war' and criticised Short's intervention in the LSE dispute as indicative of a 'plain, old-fashioned fear of the unknown'.[96] In the wider party, while Chelsea's left-inclined GMC described Wilson's administration as 'semi-socialist', it thought students only a 'little irresponsible' in their methods. Like the revisionist *Socialist Commentary*, the GMC believed the students' desire to be more directly involved in decision-making should be emulated rather than condemned.[97] Bedford GMC even passed a resolution in support of the Sorbonne students, although the secretary was unable to pass on news of this vote, as he did not have their address.[98]

By the time of Labour's 1966 re-election there was, moreover, a sense that if it was to exert real pressure on the leadership, the Tribune Group of MPs should look beyond the Commons. David Kerr noted the 'widespread evangelical mood which today finds expression through CND or OXFAM or Voluntary Service Organisation', wherein lay 'an untapped well of Socialism'. To access this latent support, Kerr believed MPs should focus on policies that promised to bridge the gap between the West and less developed nations.[99] *Tribune* correspondent Illtyd Harrington even thought the 'gentle anarchism' evident at a 'happening love-in' held in London's Roundhouse was at least preferable to the 'commercially stimulated viscous antagonism of Mods and Rockers' of a few years earlier. If the young had moved away from conventional politics, he stated, it was still possible to enthuse them with new ventures like community work. If this suggested that some at least were open to the concerns preoccupying young radicals, most remained convinced the young were estranged from Labour for a familiar reason: the government's failure to transform society through greater state control of the economy.[100] If their analysis was antiquated, so was the proposed solution. In June 1968 an array of union leaders and dissident MPs launched the Socialist Charter, which aimed to strengthen their perspective within the party, establish links with those outside and so encourage Wilson to 'return to [the] socialist principles' from which he had departed after 1964.[101] As some commented at the time, the Charter bore the hallmarks of the earlier Keep Left, Bevanite and Victory for Socialism campaigns – which was not surprising, as the personnel were much the same.[102]

Even those who believed the political situation in the late 1960s was drastically different to that of the recent past did not figure they should change their tactics. Towards the end of 1968, Eric Heffer told a gathering of Tribune MPs that the new-found influence of the revolutionary left meant the 'whole tone and flavour of the protest movement has changed'. In particular, they should not think the Vietnam Solidarity Campaign (VSC) comparable to the old Campaign for Nuclear Disarmament (CND).[103] Most of those who formed CND were long-standing left-liberal figures; they saw their purpose as influencing Labour policy, a disposition reinforced by the presence of prominent members of the Labour left on unilateralist demonstrations. This culminated in the 1960 Labour conference voting for a unilateral policy, although that proved a short-lived triumph as Gaitskell won the support of delegates at the 1961 conference to reverse the decision.[104] Heffer recognised that the young revolutionaries did not want to influence Labour to achieve their ends – as one of their aims was to destroy the party. He nonetheless proposed meeting with VSC leaders to encourage them to put their energies into changing, not attacking, Labour. While even some left-wing MPs believed their party was finished as a radical force, most believed socialism could come only through a Labour government, so it was pointless trying to replace it with an ideologically purer alternative. Not all Tribune MPs believed they should engage with the radicals. For example, like many in the Cabinet, Sid Bidwell thought the VSC needed to be told in no uncertain terms that it was 'idiotic to advocate violence'; others feared their clashes with authority would only create a right-wing backlash. Hence, while Michael Foot supported establishing links with the VSC he also proposed going out to the universities and 'putting the view that young people should come inside the Party'.[105]

Tribune subsequently gave a platform to New Left figures, like John Saville, who had some influence over young radicals, in the hope of opening a dialogue. In January 1969 Foot and Heffer even participated in what was grandiloquently described as the 'debate of the decade' with Bob Rowthorne and Tariq Ali of the revolutionary bi-monthly *Black Dwarf*. During the course of an evening in which debate gave way to the acrimonious assertion of mutually contradictory positions, Foot tried to persuade his detractors that Labour was not an enemy of socialism. Echoing the analogies of his more mainstream parliamentary colleagues, Foot warned that this sort of outlook had led to Fascism in Germany. There was, he argued, merit in seeing Labour as 'one of the arenas' in which socialism could be advanced, as it remained possible the party would be finally transformed into an organisation fully committed to radical change. Citing the CND marches of the late 1950s, Foot claimed extra-parliamentary action had its place but needed to be directed towards achieving change within parliament and through Labour.[106] In its essentials, his argument was no different to the one advanced by the likes of Callaghan and it persuaded few (if any) revolutionaries, who saw CND as less a prototypical example of extra-parliamentary action and more a pathetic failure.[107] Ali, in particular, continued to view the Labour left as a well meaning but ineffectual force wholly incapable of transforming the party into a truly anti-capitalist body.[108]

Enfranchising the young

During 1967 and 1968 the Cabinet minister Lord Longford surveyed those services national and local government provided for young people to see how they might be improved. Longford subsequently resigned, in protest at the post-devaluation delay to raising the school-leaving age from fifteen to sixteen. Longford's idiosyncratic approach in any case meant his investigations were unlikely to generate a coherent set of proposals. A brief report was nonetheless produced after he left government, its main points being that youth services should be the responsibility of a senior Cabinet minister and a public inquiry be established with the aim of producing a 'new charter for young people'.[109]

Longford's investigations were one of a number of initiatives undertaken by the government to ensure ministers at least appeared to take
the interests of the young seriously. As one civil servant noted, although
it was 'amorphous and diffuse', the report on the peer's researches indicated that, at a time when the young population is 'growing, is armed
with much financial power and is very assertive', more serious attention
had to be given to their needs.[110] To further signify that, Wilson made
Judith Hart responsible for tackling 'all problems of youth' when he
promoted her to Paymaster General in 1968.[111] Hart tried to make sense
of Longford's work, although she found it 'very disappointing'.[112] She
at least brought to her task a positive disposition, even if it bordered on
the patronising – she declared at one point that all young people were
'absolutely marvellous'. Hart optimistically believed generational conflict was largely a problem of 'communication' and thought her task was
to open a 'channel' between the young and authority. As she considered
that a good place to start in her endeavours would be to consult the
eminently respectable members of the British Youth Council, it is no
wonder Hart achieved little.[113] Her senior officials approached the
subject with great reserve: one, taking his cue from surveys that suggested nearly 80 per cent of students were 'satisfied with life', rejected
the very existence of a 'youth problem'. Hart, finally, was also confronted by the Education Department, which thought it had primary
responsibility for youth-related matters. It is no wonder that when Peter
Shore succeeded Hart as Paymaster General he prudently refused to
accept the youth brief.[114]

The most significant piece of legislation to affect young people introduced during 1964–70 had nothing to do with Hart: it was the reduction
of the voting age from twenty-one to eighteen. This originated in Labour's
desire to remain relevant to the affluent society but was passed in the
hope of domesticating the student revolt. Lowering the voting age was
not unprecedented, as in the wake of the First World War anybody serving in uniform was allowed to exercise the franchise. A 1944 Speaker's
conference had, however, rejected permanently reducing the voting age
to eighteen and, when two Communist MPs revived the proposal four
years later, Chuter Ede, Attlee's Home Secretary, demurred.

By the late 1950s Labour opinion was more open to reform. The
1959 Youth Commission supported lowering the voting age, on the
basis that it was possible to be married with children and living in a
home of one's home by eighteen. Increasing the representation of young
people, the Commission asserted, also meant democracy would benefit
from their 'vigour and impatience' while – possibly more importantly –
they should acquire a greater sense of responsibility.[115] Labour's 1959
manifesto nonetheless remained shy of the matter, and stated only that
a Gaitskell government would consider lowering the voting age after

consulting with other parties. The party's election defeat gave the issue more impetus; for example, the revisionist Douglas Jay thought Labour's support for votes at eighteen would help identify it as 'modern'. Even so, Labour leaders did not wish to take up the matter during the run-up to the 1964 election, so that when the YS national committee wanted a commitment placed in the manifesto, the NEC refused.[116]

Once in power, Labour established the Latey Commission to consider reducing the legal age of majority, which also stood at twenty-one. In addition, ministers invoked a Speaker's conference to look into various matters, including the voting age. Neither body had reported by the time Labour stood for re-election, but the party's submission to the latter made its position absolutely clear. It echoed the Youth Commission's conclusion that lowering the voting age to eighteen would be 'just and logical', something underlined in the 1966 manifesto.[117]

Latey published his findings in the summer of 1967. He recommended that the age of majority should fall to eighteen, and this was a popular proposal; the Lord Chancellor consequently recommended that Cabinet accept his report and proceed to legislation.[118] In discussion, Michael Stewart noted that, if ministers accepted Latey's proposals, 'it would be difficult to resist the conclusion that the voting age should be similarly reduced', a view echoed by others round the Cabinet table. Not everybody agreed; some even questioned Latey's own proposals, although in the end Cabinet accepted them.[119] In any case, ministers could not alter the voting age until the Speaker's conference had concluded its business and precedent suggested that, as it reflected opinion at Westminster, they had to accept its recommendations.[120] When the conference voted decisively to reduce the voting age – but only to twenty – ministers were therefore faced with a dilemma.

Cabinet discussed the matter in May 1968 – an interesting month to debate votes for students.[121] Ministers were divided, as there was no compelling evidence of a public demand for change: even many of those due to be enfranchised did not appear over-keen. A Gallup poll taken in 1967 showed that 30 per cent of eighteen- to twenty-year-olds opposed lowering the voting age, although 56 per cent did support it.[122] It was the Cabinet's youngest member, Richard Marsh, who took the strongest position against change, arguing ministers 'must have gone absolutely mad' if they thought 'the working class wanted students to be enfranchised'. Marsh's position was echoed by the Welsh and Scottish Secretaries, who worried that reducing the voting age would help the nationalists. Others suggested the revolutionary left would also benefit. Stewart nonetheless adhered to his earlier view that the young had literally 'grown into' the legal rights conceded by Latey and it was therefore only logical they should be granted their political equivalent. Indeed, said one minister, 'to accept that they were capable of responsible political behaviour should do much to correct the growing sense of social alienation which undoubtedly lay at the root of some of the more extreme manifestations of youthful insubordination which had recently attracted public attention'. Some hoped reduction 'would widen the field for political pressures to be put on the student population'. So intense was the disagreement that the Prime Minister was forced to defer a final decision to a later meeting. By then, clear evidence had been produced that the public supported votes for eighteen-year-olds. Some now claimed events in Paris meant it was even more important to 'give young people an increased sense of responsibility'.

In finally agreeing to support reduction to eighteen the Cabinet took something of an electoral leap in the dark, one – as the likes of Marsh suggested – not universally supported in the party. The veteran MP George Strauss was certainly an opponent, as he feared the measure would 'inject into elections an immature, unstable and irresponsible element'.[123] Labour's Assistant National Agent Reg Underhill thought the new voters constituted an unknown factor, given that large numbers would probably abstain at elections.[124] The Chief Whip reported that only two-thirds of MPs favoured reduction: he had hoped the issue could have been made subject to a free vote but such was MPs' antipathy that he proposed placing it under a 'firm' two-line whip.[125] Accordingly, legislation was passed in time for eighteen-year-olds to vote in the 1970 election.

Conclusion

By the time Labour sought re-election in 1970 the student revolt had died down. Comparisons with Weimar Germany were no longer aired and Crossman could give vent to his relief that such an 'infantile' movement, one 'imbecile in its anarchism and bogus leftism', had apparently bitten the dust.[126] This did not mean the 'youth problem' had disappeared. In 1970, Labour's candidate for Kingston stated that the young still needed to be made to see that they were 'enjoying a false freedom, namely the freedom of doing what they like'. He went on to state that:

> Instead of youth's exploitation and perversion by entrepreneurs and the mass media what they require is firm but loving guidance. They need to be subjected to positive direction, to learn the value of self-discipline, to be shown the heights which a human spirit can reach, to be taught to appreciate the excellence of our heritage, the opportunities of service to the community.[127]

With only 6,000 members, the LPYS was in no position to exert an influence. Some nonetheless hoped that, by extending the franchise,

Labour had, in the words of a broadsheet aimed at new voters, enabled them to take their 'full place in politics'. As Les Huckfield, at twenty-seven years old the party's youngest MP, wrote: youngsters currently formed 'the most articulate, idealistic and educated generation the world has ever had', one hitherto 'forced to express itself in the language of protest, on the streets'. By lowering the voting age, Huckfield concluded, Labour had 'brought them into the legislative process'.[128]

It is questionable how many wanted to be incorporated into the political system. The record of the LPYS and earlier LOY suggested a small and declining minority wanted to adhere to Labour's own model of participation. As outlined at the start of the chapter, the party's failure to establish a viable youth wing has been blamed on its own lack of consideration for the interests of young people. The chapter went on to outline how members addressed the need to evoke a more positive response and the assumptions that underpinned their perceptions of the problem. The party broadly wanted to induce the young into what was considered appropriate political conduct. While some viewed the young's concerns as worthy of serious consideration, Labour's general approach implied they required its guidance before they could become political actors in their own right. The extent to which this outlook was embedded in ideology as much as generational experience should have come as little surprise to readers of earlier chapters.

Notes

The place of publication is London unless otherwise specified.

1 Some of the material contained in this chapter has appeared in 'The Labour Party and the recruitment of the young, 1945–70', in G. Orsina and G. Quagliariello (eds), *La Formazione della classe politica in Europa (1945–1956)* (Rome, 2000).

2 *Report of the Fifty-Fourth Annual Conference of the Labour Party* (1955), p. 70.

3 Z. Layton-Henry, 'Labour's lost youth', *Journal of Contemporary History*, 11 (1976); A. Thorpe, *A History of the British Labour Party* (1997), p. 176.

4 N. Tiratsoo, *Reconstruction, Affluence and Labour Politics. Coventry 1945–60* (1990), pp. 94–7; P. Abrams and A. Little, 'The young activist in British politics', *British Journal of Sociology*, 16:4 (1965), p. 320.

5 A. Arblaster, 'Student militancy and the collapse of reformism', in R. Miliband and J. Saville (eds), *Socialist Register 1970* (1970), pp. 143–4.

6 Labour Party Archive (LPA), Morgan Phillips papers, GS/YS/29, Box 6, Young Socialists File, The Labour Party and youth, September 1950.

7 *Report of the Forty-Seventh Annual Conference of the Labour Party* (1948), p. 113; *Report of the Forty-Ninth Annual Conference of the Labour Party* (1950), p. 152.

8 *Report of the Forty-First National Conference of Labour Women* (1964), pp. 19–20.

9 *Report of the Fifty-Eighth Annual Conference of the Labour Party* (1959), p. 94.

10 London Metropolitan Archive (LMA), *London News*, April 1954.

11 LMA, Labour Party London Region papers, Acc 2417/B/65, Election report – County of London.

12 B. Pimlott (ed.), *The Political Diary of Hugh Dalton, 1918–40, 1945–50* (1986), pp. 620–1.
13 Lambeth Archives, Brixton CLP papers, IV/156/1/9, Stockwell ward minutes, 24 January 1962.
14 *Fifty-Eighth Annual Conference of Labour*, p. 92.
15 *Labour Organiser*, 39:452 (1960), pp. 32–3.
16 P. Rose, 'Manchester Left Club on youth', *New Left Review*, 1 (1960), pp. 70–1.
17 *Report of the Sixtieth Annual Conference of the Labour Party* (1961), p. 130.
18 Labour Party, *Take It From Here* (1956), p. 3–4.
19 *Tribune*, 9 September 1966.
20 Labour Party, *Hi!* (1958).
21 LPA, *East Ham South Citizen*, December 1960, emphasis added.
22 *Daily Telegraph*, 2 February 1968.
23 National Library of Wales, Eirene White papers, L/3/8 File, S. Williams, The challenge of irrationality, n.d. (but 1969).
24 *Report of the Forty-Seventh National Conference of Labour Women* (1970), p. 13.
25 National Library of Scotland, John P. Mackintosh papers, Dep 323/44/2, Politics and the generation gap, n.d. (but *c*. 1968).
26 A. Crosland, 'A social democratic Britain', *Fabian Tract*, 404 (1970), p. 12.
27 T. Benn, *Office Without Power. Diaries, 1968–72* (1988), p. 151.
28 LPA, NEC Organisation Sub-committee (OSC) minutes, 14 April 1959, 'Youth', NAD/98/12/59.
29 *Report of the Fifty-Ninth Annual Conference of the Labour Party* (1960), pp. 243–4; Southwark Local Studies Library, Bermondsey CLP papers, Tunnel ward minutes, 11 September 1951; Working Class Movement Library, Salford East CLP papers, Trinity ward minutes, 5 March 1958.
30 *Young Socialist*, August 1946.
31 *Young Socialist*, July 1946.
32 Bancroft Library, Bethnal Green CLP papers, TH/8488, GMC minutes, 24 January 1952.
33 *Fifty-Eighth Annual Conference of Labour*, pp. 90, 97–8.
34 LMA, J. W. Raisin papers, Acc 2783/JWR/OA/2, The organisation of young people within the Labour Party, London Labour Party agents' conference, 26–28 November 1957.
35 *Report of the Fifty-Second Annual Conference of the Labour Party* (1953), p. 197.
36 *Labour Organiser*, 45:522 (1966), p. 30.
37 *Fifty-Second Annual Conference of Labour*, p. 196. The speaker, Pat Wall, was a prominent Militant member in the 1980s.
38 Phillips papers, The Labour party and youth.
39 *Fifty-Eighth Annual Conference of Labour*, p. 94.
40 This account is based on OSC minutes, 4 January 1960, Report and recommendations of the Youth Working Party, NAD/98/12/59, and Launching the Young Socialists, NAD/91/11/59.
41 Labour Party, *Let's Go!* (1960).
42 LPA, NEC Youth Sub-committee (YSC) minutes, 17 September 1962, Summary of branch report forms, NAD/94/9/62; 22 June 1966, Report on organisation and activities, NC 4, June 1966; and 7 July 1970, Summary of report forms, NC/10/JUN/70.
43 Abrams and Little, 'Young activist', p. 330.
44 Raisin papers, Acc 2783/JWR/ORG/67/103, organiser's report.
45 See the description of the young 'rebel' in P. Willmott, *Adolescent Boys of East London* (Harmondsworth, 1969), pp. 173–6.

46 OSC minutes, 14 February 1961, Enquiry into party organization in Glasgow, NAD/21/2/61, and 18 February 1969, Enquiry into party organization in Glasgow.

47 YSC minutes, 27 April 1960, Martin to Gaitskell, NAD/26/4/60.

48 London Region papers, Acc 2417/H/49, C. Bramhall, Twickenham Labour Party Young Socialists, n.d. (but August 1967).

49 Bristol Record Office (BRO), Bristol South East CLP papers, 39035/47, Young Socialist minutes, 27 January 1961.

50 BRO, Labour Party South West Region papers, 38423/53, Assistant Regional Organiser's report, 27 May 1960.

51 T. Benn, *Out of the Wilderness. Diaries 1963–67* (1987), p. 39.

52 YSC minutes, 13 December 1965, Young Socialists' national conference, 1965. Chief Officer's report, NAD/163/12/65.

53 *Tribune*, 28 October 1966 and 20 October 1967.

54 Bristol South East papers, 39035/47, Young Socialist minutes, V. Willcox, Report on area federation meeting of Friday 26 August 1961.

55 YSC minutes, 13 December 1965, Young Socialists' national conference, 1965, Chief Officer's report, NAD/163/12/65; LPA, NEC minutes, 26 April 1967, Young Socialists' national conference, 1967, Chief Officer's report, NAD/53/4/67.

56 YSC minutes, 13 December 1965, Young Socialists' national conference 1965, Chief Officer's report, NAD/10/1/67.

57 Abrams and Little, 'Young activist', p. 328.

58 M. Rustin, 'Young socialists', *New Left Review*, 9 (1961), pp. 52–3; YSC minutes, 10 April 1961, First annual conference of the Young Socialists, NAD/38/4/61.

59 London Region papers, Acc 2417/G/59, Regional Youth Officer's report, 2 March 1963.

60 S. Rowbotham, *Promise of a Dream. Remembering the Sixties* (Harmondsworth, 2000), pp. 88–94.

61 London Region papers, Acc 2417/G/56, Summary of agents' meeting, 2 December 1964.

62 OSC minutes, 11 November 1963, Report of an enquiry ..., NAD/99/12/63.

63 OSC minutes, 19 September 1961, Activities of organisations formed to influence Labour Party policy, NAD/91/9/61; Bristol South East CLP papers, 39035/47, Young Socialist minutes, 1 November 1960 and 3 January 1961; Stockport Local Heritage Library, Stockport Central CLP papers, B/MM/3/3, minutes, 22 November 1960, 26 January and 22 June 1961.

64 *Tribune*, 30 September 1966.

65 South West Region papers, 38423/18/5, Stroud Labour Party agent's reports, October and December 1968.

66 South West Region papers, 38423/25, Report of the Young Socialists in the South Western Region to the fourth annual meeting (1964).

67 *New Advance*, January 1961.

68 YSC minutes, 10 May 1965, Report on the Young Socialists' organisation, NAD/63/5/65; 26 May 1965, Report on the Young Socialists, NAD/63/5/65.

69 YSC minutes, 10 May 1965, Resolutions, NAD/64/5/65.

70 Modern Records Centre, Warwick and Leamington Spa CLP papers, MSS 133, Box 1, Executive Committee (EC) minutes, 15 August 1962.

71 Salford Archives, Salford West CLP papers, EC minutes, 11 February, 14 April and 10 November 1964; 9 February, 11 April 1965.

72 South West Region papers, 38423/53, organiser's report.

73 British Library of Political and Economic Science (BLPES), Bedford CLP papers, Youth Section minutes, 24 July 1968.

74 BLPES, Merton and Morden CLP papers, 2/1–4, Merton and Morden Young Socialists minutes, 1959–65, *passim*.

75 YSC minutes, 13 February 1961, Summary of report submitted by Nigel Harris re activity in training and technical colleges, NAD/4/1/61; 15 May 1969, Consultations with Labour students, NAD/56/5/69.

76 Phillips papers, GS/NALSO/1,NALSO file, Hyde to Phillips, 29 April 1949.

77 Figures for student numbers are taken from A. H. Halsey, 'Higher education', in A. H. Halsey (ed.), *Trends in British Society Since 1900* (1972), p. 206.

78 E. Pearce, 'The gentle art of protest', *Socialist Commentary*, August 1965; J. Young, 'Britain and "LBJ's war", 1964–68', *Cold War History*, 2:3 (2002), p. 77.

79 *New Statesman*, 15 September 1967.

80 R. Crossman, *Diaries of a Cabinet Minister. Volume III* (1977), pp. 60, 239.

81 LPA, Judith Hart papers, Section 10, File: Hart 10/5, speech in Poole, 22 May 1969.

82 BRO, Bristol West CLP papers, GMC minutes, 38598/1/g, 2 January 1969.

83 House of Lords Record Office, Reginald Sorenson papers, Hist. Coll. 102/230, A backbencher's pilgrimage, 1968, pp. 395–6, 398–400.

84 Editorials, *Socialist Commentary*, October 1968 and March 1969.

85 Benn, *Office Without Power*, pp. 247–9.

86 London Region papers, Acc 2417/H/72, *King's Left*, January 1968 and January 1969.

87 *The Times*, 17 June 1968.

88 *Daily Telegraph*, 19 October 1968.

89 K. O. Morgan, *Callaghan. A Life* (Oxford, 1997), p. 317.

90 Public Record Office (PRO), ED 188/340, Note for the record, 27 January 1969.

91 ED 188/340, Note for the record, 31 January 1969.

92 ED 188/340, Note for the record, 4 February 1969; memo from Weaver to Short, 14 February 1969.

93 PRO, PREM 13/2787, Note for the record, 28 January 1969.

94 *Daily Express*, 17 February 1969.

95 *Tribune*, 14 March 1969.

96 *Tribune*, 24 November 1967; 19 April and 7 June 1968; and 7 February 1969.

97 LMA, Greater London Labour Party papers (unsorted), *Chelsea Labour News*, April 1968.

98 Bedford papers, GMC minutes, 23 May and 6 June 1968.

99 *Tribune*, 22 April 1966.

100 *Tribune*, 20 October 1967.

101 *Daily Telegraph*, 6 June 1968.

102 LPA, Ian Mikardo/Jo Richardson papers, Box 4, File: Tribune Group. Papers on the left, *c.* 1968, T. Fletcher, Some thoughts on the organisation of the left, n.d. (but November 1967).

103 The subsequent account is based on Mikardo/Richardson papers, Box 5, File: Tribune Group minutes, 8 November 1968, E. Heffer, Role of the group and its future work, n.d.

104 R. Taylor, 'The Labour Party and CND', in R. Taylor and N. Young (eds), *Campaigns for Peace. British Peace Movements in the Twentieth Century* (Manchester, 1987).

105 Mikardo/Richardson papers, Box 5, File: Tribune Group minutes, 9 December 1968, statement on Powellism, n.d.
106 *Tribune*, 14 February 1969.
107 R. Hinden, 'Left, further left and protest left', *Socialist Commentary*, October 1968, p. 9; J. Jupp, 'Children of affluence', *Socialist Commentary*, June 1969, p. 30.
108 T. Ali, 'The extra-parliamentary opposition', in T. Ali (ed.), *New Revolutionaries. Left Opposition* (1969), pp. 69–70.
109 PRO, CAB 151/72, Conclusions and recommendations, n.d.
110 CAB 151/72, Odgers to Crossman, 20 November 1968.
111 *Parliamentary Debates (Hansard), 5th Series, Volume 773, House of Commons Official Report, Session 1968–9*, columns 1526–7.
112 CAB 151/72, Hart to Wilson, 12 December 1968; Crossman to Hart, 29 October 1968.
113 *Scottish Daily Mail*, 19 October 1968; CAB 151/67, Youth, 3 February 1970.
114 CAB 151/67, Jardine to Moss, 28 May, Jardine to Shore, 13 October and Jardine to Shore, 20 November 1969.
115 Labour Party, *The Younger Generation. Report of the Labour Party Youth Commission* (1959), pp. 43–4.
116 OSC minutes, 18 September 1963.
117 OSC minutes, 8 December 1965, Lowering of the voting age to 18.
118 CAB 134/2858, Age of majority, memorandum by the Lord Chancellor, 18 September 1967; CAB 129/133, Age of majority, C(67)164.
119 CAB 128/42, 2 November 1967; CAB 128/43, 22 February 1968.
120 CAB 129/135, The age of majority, C(63)32; CAB 134/2859, Home Affairs Committee, 2 February 1968.
121 This account is based on Benn, *Office*, pp. 68–9; Crossman, *Diaries III*, pp. 65, 92–3; CAB 128/43, 16 and 30 May 1968; CAB 129/137, Electoral reform, C(68)74.
122 CAB 134/2860, Possible reduction in voting age from 12–18, memorandum by the Lord President of the Council, 2 November 1967.
123 PRO, HO 328/63, Strauss to Callaghan, 29 July 1968, Callaghan to Strauss, 30 August 1968.
124 *Labour Organiser*, 48:554 (1969), p. 6.
125 CAB 128/43, 29 October 1968.
126 Crossman, *Diaries III*, pp. 298–9, 384–5.
127 LPA, *Richmond and Barnes Clarion*, April 1970.
128 Labour Party, *Youth Voice* (1970).

8

Engaging with participation

Most contemporaries dismissed Labour's attempts to accommodate demands for government to promote greater popular access to decision-making. Those on the New Left presumed the Cabinet opposed greater involvement in the political process; such critics adhered to Ralph Miliband's contention that the leadership was devoted to the parliamentary system and implacably hostile to those who challenged the constitutional status quo.[1] Censure was not, however, restricted to the far left. The backbench MP John Mackintosh was one of an increasing number of younger revisionists who were unhappy with their government's apparent lack of interest in redistributing power from Whitehall. As one of that number, David Marquand, later claimed, they questioned the assumption 'that outcome was all and process irrelevant', and began to consider that social democracy should be about political as much as economic and social equality.[2] Thus, Mackintosh believed ministers were captive to a Fabian tradition committed to the 'conviction that well-educated well-disposed people' working in London were 'more likely to be right and impartial than the more remote and backward inhabitants of the provinces'.[3]

Harold Wilson was definitely conservative when it came to constitutional matters.[4] Owing to their conception of electoral politics, most of Labour's leaders saw the party's main purpose as improving voters' material conditions. The number of individuals involved in deciding how to achieve this outcome and the means by which they did so were considered second-order matters. Thus, in 1964 and 1966, consideration of how to enhance popular influence on decision-making was brief, vague and placed towards the end of the party's manifestos. What is more, proposals to reform government were framed by the need to enhance its ability to further economic growth. Yet, if increasing efficiency rather than democracy was to the fore, there was still talk of 'humanising' government and establishing a 'true partnership' between people and parliament.[5] By the end of the decade, these thoughts had been expanded and given greater salience. The National Executive Committee

191

(NEC) issued two strategic statements – *Progress and Change* (1968) and *Agenda for a Generation* (1969) – that emphasised the need to make the country's institutions more accountable. The NEC recognised that 'man will not live by [economic] growth alone' and accepted that post-war expansion had been achieved at the cost of creating an over-centralised state. Warning that there was no easy solution to this problem, the NEC nonetheless called for a 'fresh look at our concept of representative democracy'.[6]

This was not just a question of rhetoric. By the time they left office, ministers had introduced numerous reforms and fostered an impressive collection of reports and Royal Commissions, part of whose purpose was to augment the individual's influence over those decisions that most affected their lives. Within Westminster, Select Committees and a Parliamentary Commissioner had been introduced to help MPs challenge the executive. There had also been an abortive attempt to reform the House of Lords. In addition, ministers had commissioned the Redcliffe-Maud and Wheatley reports into local government; the former mooted the creation of regional councils. The government also passed the 1968 Town and Country Planning Act and subsequently issued the Skeffington report, which gave the public an unprecedented say in planning. Finally, the Cabinet approved the formation of the Crowther-Hunt Commission and charged it with putting the constitution under the microscope, with a particular eye on exploring the merits of devolving power to Scotland, Wales and the English regions.

This chapter assesses the party's response to demands for greater participation – bearing in mind the uncertainties over both the nature of what it meant exactly and how many wanted to be involved – by first examining Labour's historical attitude to the subject. It then outlines how ministers responded to its emergence as a live issue during the late 1960s, and in particular highlights Judith Hart's thinking, as she was the minister briefly in charge of the matter. The chapter then looks at those areas where increasing participation was at least discussed, such as planning, devolution, and community development. The chapter finally turns to the matter of participation within the Labour Party itself.

Labour, the individual and the state

From the start, Labour sought to use the existing parliamentary system to achieve what it could for its constituents. Yet, while the party had an instrumental view of politics, not all its members were devotees of parliament. Labour's history in fact reveals a fitful interest in constitutional reform and direct forms of representation.[7] Thus, before 1914 the party was host to debates about the merits of referenda, proportional representation, abolition of the Lords and Home Rule for Wales and Scotland.

Some hoped to promote political participation because they thought it inherent to the building of socialism. They lost out, however, to the Fabian view, that it was safer for an elite to manipulate the existing system towards progressive ends. The likes of Ramsay MacDonald feared allowing the masses to do more than just vote for the party they wished to hold office would, in the short run, hamper reform. They judged the public's opinions to be unpredictable and often reactionary.[8]

Even so, during the 1920s Labour remained committed to improving the efficiency of the parliamentary system and MacDonald's 1929–31 government tried to introduce a form of proportional representation (the alternative vote) for general elections.[9] Although Labour briefly advocated abolishing the Lords, during the 1930s, the leadership maintained its broad acceptance of the political order. In relation to the alternatives then offered by Communism and Fascism, Westminster did not appear too bad. In addition, Labour became an enthusiast for the state ownership of much of the economy and subjecting what remained in private hands to centralised planning. This would entail a massive increase in the power of government. However, there was little sense that new forms of accountability or involvement were required. While they were not oblivious to the possibility that the state might encroach on individual liberties, Labour thinkers generally believed that, as the future member of Wilson's Cabinet Douglas Jay famously wrote, in certain instances, 'the gentleman in Whitehall really does know better what is good for the people than the people know themselves'.[10]

The Second World War confirmed Labour's faith in extending the state while maintaining the existing political system: the ease with which the post-war Attlee government implemented its programme further reinforced that view.[11] Even the doyen of the Labour left, Aneurin Bevan, praised the unwritten nature of the British constitution because it allowed legislators to define the limits of their own authority.[12] Others on the left accepted the parliamentary order with less enthusiasm. While Hugh Jenkins, who would become an MP in 1964, doubted that ballot box democracy would bring about socialism, he admitted he did not know of any better system.[13] In contrast, in 1968 Michael Foot echoed Bevan's outlook when he indicated that, so far as the left was concerned, the real problem was not the character of parliament but the failure of Labour ministers to place a greater share of the economy under its supervision through nationalisation.[14]

Attlee's ministers believed the enlightened few could achieve progressive ends through their manipulation of an enhanced state machine operating within the established political system. Not all of them, however, thought this would be sufficient to transform society fully: to achieve that, the people had to become more involved. As the supposed arch-pragmatist Herbert Morrison declared in 1948:

Ballot box democracy, where people go and vote – if they can be bothered and persuaded and shoved around to go and vote – every few years and do nothing in between, is out of date. We must have an active, living democracy in our country and we must whip up our citizens to their responsibilities.

This vision, however, essentially assumed 'responsible' citizens would join Labour and conform to the party's version of socialism.[15] In this regard, at least, left and right were united: left-inclined bodies such as Victory for Socialism took it for granted that socialism could occur only through the party, rather than through the actions of agencies independent of it.[16]

Be that as it may, revisionist thinking helped ensure that, after the mid-1950s, Labour at least nodded towards pluralism, although this reflected long-standing concerns about the dangers posed by unaccountable public bureaucracies.[17] The 1956 policy document *Personal Freedom* claimed that while Labour believed certain forms of individualism harmed the collective interest, it did not seek to create 'an all-powerful State or excessive centralisation'. Instead, it believed 'many important decisions and activities should be left to voluntary and local effort'. Given the expansion of welfare provision, contact with any number of public authorities had, however, become commonplace. Labour declared its determination that these should never 'degenerate into irresponsible bureaucracies'. Yet the proposed remedies were superficial, which was probably inevitable given the assertion that Britain enjoyed 'the most efficient, incorruptible and "non-political" Civil Service in the world'.[18] Not everybody thought this went far enough: MP Fred Willey, in particular, believed more needed to be done to promote 'responsible participation' and ensure the state 'continues to serve the individual', rather than the reverse.[19]

Labour therefore entered the 1960s armed with a particular vision of 'participation'. Members were confident that a centralised state run through Westminster would allow the party to achieve greater growth and a better redistribution of wealth. Some, however, were concerned that not enough citizens were active within the polity and that the state might be too domineering. Hope more than experience suggested that fully functioning local Labour parties in conjunction with a 'modernised' form of government would solve this problem.

Attitudes to participation

Some in the leadership certainly considered that demands for greater participation should not be taken too seriously. One of Wilson's favoured conversational themes at the time of the 1966 election was that the public was 'bored' with politics and wanted him to be their 'doctor who looked after the difficulties so that it could go on playing tennis'.[20] Wilson's first Chief Whip, Edward Short, concurred, and considered most voters were 'just ordinary, decent folks whose first thought about every government is how it will affect them and their families': they were not 'high-minded citizens' with broad horizons.[21] This sentiment was not confined to the leadership: it was a union delegate to the 1970 Labour Party conference who thought it 'a lot of bunkum' that anyone was denied the right to participate, as people could easily join their union and constituency Labour party.[22]

Others, if sceptical, were not wholly dismissive. Anthony Crosland considered 'participation' a 'hideously abused word' and believed only a small minority of the population wanted to influence decision-making – and most of these, being middle class, were hostile to Labour. The rest, he claimed:

> prefer to lead a full family life and cultivate their gardens. And a good thing too. For if we believe in socialism as a means of increasing personal freedom and the range of choice, we do not necessarily want a busy bustling society in which everyone is politically active, and fussing around in an interfering and responsible manner, and herding us all into participating groups. The threat to privacy and freedom would be intolerable.

Despite this, Crosland hoped his 1970 White Paper on local government reorganisation would encourage manual workers to become more active in local affairs.[23]

If Crosland was more positive about participation than he initially appeared, even those looking on the subject with more obvious sympathy agreed that only a few wanted to be active. Nor did they imagine that accommodating demands for participation required established authorities to transform themselves fundamentally. Mackintosh, for example, thought that most people simply wanted recourse to a 'clear system of accountability' and was confident that if authorities were more open in their procedures, although they might still irritate, they would at least not alienate.[24] On the other hand, while Labour's 1969 *Agenda for a Generation* advocated individuals' 'right to be consulted about, and to influence, particular decisions which affect their daily lives', it also claimed that some decisions would still have to be taken centrally and free from local influence.[25] There were, therefore, thought to be many practical limits to participation: those of popular interest, technical knowledge and ability, as well as the need to ensure decision-making was not unduly delayed and efficiency compromised.[26] This meant that most Labour reformers focused on the immediate and local rather than national matters.

While many of his colleagues also expressed their views on participation, it was the Minister for Technology, Tony Benn, who made the
issue his own, through a series of speeches that laid the foundation for
his post-1970 role as leader of the Labour left.[27] In the early 1960s,
Benn helped establish an early example of participation, the New Bristol
Group. This body sought to mobilise citizens from diverse political
backgrounds interested in promoting public debates about a variety of
local issues.[28] Significantly, however, it was in 1968, the year of Parisian
student unrest and massive Labour unpopularity, that Benn systematic-
ally considered the challenge posed by new demands for participation.

Benn started from the proposition that the electorate was better
educated and more self-confident than ever. This fostered a 'political
individualism' that could not be fully accommodated by conventional
political organisations and so gave rise to pressure groups that
challenged the parties' legitimacy.[29] People, he believed, were no longer
'prepared to have policy handed down from on high'; instead, they
sought 'a greater say and greater voice' than allowed by the parliamentary system. The perception was that people were being 'kicked
around' by those in authority and this alienation gave rise to Welsh and
Scottish nationalism, student radicalism and union militancy. Yet such
forces were hostile to government only because they had been denied
expression within it: most just wanted to 'participate constructively' and
win 'responsibility'.

Benn's proposals were, all things considered, fairly modest. First,
ministers needed to recognise the electorate's intelligence and so foster
a 'higher level of argument'. Politicians should tell the truth and present
the full complexity of the choices to be made. Election campaigns, in
addition, had to stop being 'vast marketing operations, with the voters
cast in the role of consumers looking for bargain offers that give the
most for the least' and instead should be the occasion for 'solemn
choices'. Moreover, while the parties still had to give leadership, they
needed to involve voters in decision-making. As he explained to the
Prime Minister, he should not be 'Dr Wilson' but become a teacher who
encouraged the people to achieve things themselves.

Benn secondly proposed that Labour should find new ways of
allowing voters to influence policy-making. For example, he invited his
Bristol constituents to write to him about selected issues so he could
assess opinion – although he refused to be bound by the results. More
ambitiously, Benn looked forward to the time when people could press
a button in their homes and participate in referenda on matters of principle. Thirdly, he wanted voters to enjoy easier access to information
and to that end supported moves to televise the Commons. Fourthly,
greater access to television airtime should be given to voluntary bodies,
like consumer groups, so they could present their views to a wider

audience. Finally, Benn supported ceding power to the regions: before the Troubles, he believed Northern Ireland proved that the devolution of industrial policy could be economically advantageous, because local politicians better knew how to deploy resources than Whitehall.

Benn's intervention generated a largely negative response within the party. Some MPs resented his 'thinking out loud', while Wilson claimed he compromised collective responsibility by appearing to criticise government policy. Others, like Michael Stewart, claimed their Cabinet colleague had just 'dressed up a lot of old ideas as if they were new', while Judith Hart thought Benn's proposals 'too safe and dull'. Still more ministers, like John Stonehouse, looked on his notions as irresponsible and deprecated 'the current vogue of attacking institutions as though they were mainly to blame for the maladies that we suffer'. Yet, in their irritation, critics failed to notice that Benn's proposals were meant to help Labour 'lead back into the system of peaceful political change' those forces that he supposed were now operating outside it. In other words, he wanted to alter the established political system in a variety of modest ways in order to domesticate the supposed threat posed by strikers, students, nationalists and the like.

Trendy Judith's Green Paper

Benn did not have ministerial responsibility to promote participation. As one of her leading officials resentfully put it, the Prime Minister had 'publicly saddled' Judith Hart with that job when she was promoted to Paymaster General in October 1968.[30] Hart's task was met with cynicism by the right-wing press, with the *Daily Mail* referring to her as '"trendy" Judith'.[31] Apart from journalistic scorn, she faced other disadvantages. In particular, with mounting by-election and municipal losses, 1968 was not the best of times for a Labour minister to show faith in the people's judgement. As Hart stated before her elevation, a Labour government was 'by its nature, a two-way process', in which 'we demand ideals and sense of purpose both from ourselves and from the community'. Given that, she believed ministers were 'entitled to a little more of both from the people than we are getting at this moment'.[32] Hart also faced scepticism in her own department, where one senior official observed that ministers should look on participation as they would on virtue: 'they must always be in favour of it, and maximise it, provided the price is not too high!'[33]

Despite all that, Hart set about drafting some proposals.[34] Reformers were, she claimed, presented with 'the most exciting opportunity open to us for 20 years to inject whatever new patterns and institutions we believe best to meet individual and community needs into a democratic

system suffering, perhaps, from a little hardening of the arteries'. Echoing the Seebohm report on social services, Hart believed the post-war
welfare state had created a new situation. At one time, income had
determined the quality of an individual's health care and education,
but the expansion of welfare provision meant this was now determined
by government. Unfortunately, public institutions had 'failed to satisfy
many of the people for whom they existed' and were 'totally inadequate'
in their 'provision for user-participation'. Thus, pressure groups had
grown up to represent consumers, who were better educated, free of
the threat of poverty and willing to focus their energies on achieving
'direct involvement'. Rather conveniently, the Paymaster stated that, as
parliament was reforming itself, she would focus on the 'peripheral area
of our democratic structure', by which she meant 'town halls, education
committees, nationalised industries, [and] local offices of government
bodies'. What Hart termed the 'built-in unresponsiveness of outdated
and inadequate institutions' had to be overcome and new patterns discovered, 'which not merely permit but invite and encourage effective
participation'.

Informed by this analysis, Hart wrote a Green Paper during the
spring of 1969.[35] Like many others in the party, she believed few craved
more involvement in decision-making but thought a larger number
wanted to participate in working out the implications of agreed policies
for their own communities. To that end, Hart proposed creating neighbourhood councils that would operate below established councils. These
would also be smaller than the local councils proposed by Redcliffe-
Maud's investigation of local government (referred to below), as they
would fit into areas smaller than existing municipal wards. They would:
enjoy the right to be consulted by council officials, who could be called
to attend meetings; have access to relevant information; and be able to
nominate representatives to public bodies.

Hart's draft contained many grey areas, but in particular the exact
nature of the relationship between a neighbourhood council and higher
bodies was not spelt out. Moreover, while she wanted neighbourhood
councils to represent an 'organic community', defining such an entity
proved hard. Hart nonetheless passed her document to the Prime
Minister for comment, with a mind to publishing a final version in the
autumn. Wilson, however, had already told Hart the time was not ripe
for concrete proposals and he was 'noticeably unenthusiastic' about her
work.[36] In fact, the Prime Minister was unimpressed by his Paymaster's
overall performance – he described her as 'just a prattling woman who
had done absolutely nothing'.[37] For her pains, Hart was moved to the
Ministry of Overseas Development in October 1969 and the Green
Paper was not heard of again.

Participation in planning

One criticism of the demand for more participation was that it was too vague. Hart believed Labour's proposals to enhance the public's ability to influence planning showed that participation 'can have a practical application in at least one important field'.[38] The 1968 Town and Country Planning Act gave the public the chance to make representations that authorities had to take into account at a much earlier stage than hitherto. With no little hyperbole, this stipulation was described by Arthur Skeffington, a junior minister at the Ministry of Housing and Local Government, as 'a new Magna Carta in planning'.[39]

The Committee on Public Participation in Planning, chaired by Skeffington, was established to determine how authorities should facilitate expression of the public's new voice and published its recommendations in July 1969. While Skeffington underlined how important it was that the public enjoyed adequate means of influencing planning, he still believed responsible authorities should retain the final say. His proposals were aimed at directing the people's talents into 'constructive channels', so that planning could be 'collaborative and friendly' and allow people and planners to realise they were on the same side.[40] Skeffington's proposals nonetheless proved contentious, in particular those relating to the creation of community forums and the appointment of community development officers. The object of the former was to gather together local voluntary associations to help them present their views; the role of the latter was to mobilise the opinions of individuals belonging to no formal organisation – which in practice meant helping working-class residents make a case.

The Skeffington report was written in such a way as to win over authorities sceptical of the need for greater participation.[41] Despite this, many remained opposed and, while not all were against the forums, they were almost universally hostile to development officers. The London Boroughs Association, for example, believed the latter were superfluous, thinking 'the individual's right not to comment should be accepted', while the Urban District Council Association argued that 'if it is to be genuine and of real value', participation 'must be voluntary and not induced'.[42] In contrast, most voluntary organisations welcomed the report: the National Federation of Women's Institutes considered Skeffington had created 'opportunities for intelligent and constructive comment [that] would help and overcome public apathy'.[43] Hart was especially enthusiastic about development officers and wanted their function extended, so they could promote community development 'as an active and positive function'.[44]

Ministers found it difficult to take account of such contradictory comments when constructing a circular to be issued to planning authorities.

Officials were still grappling with the task when Labour lost power. They had, however, prepared a draft that ceded most ground to Skeffington's critics, as neither forums nor development officers were made obligatory. Authorities were instead expected to take steps to ensure they consulted a cross-section of the public about any proposal; how this was to be achieved was left to them.[45] This was undoubtedly a step back from what had been promised: if the 1968 Act still represented a new Magna Carta, King John had regained many of his powers.

Responding to nationalism

Some Labour members reacted to the post-1966 by-election successes of the Scottish National Party (SNP) and Plaid Cymru by suggesting the party should embrace legislative devolution. Given that the likes of Keir Hardie had supported Home Rule, advocates claimed they were just 'reaffirming' a 'basic Labour policy' that had been temporarily cast aside.[46] A few argued that limited self-government was consistent with democratic socialism, as it would promote participation in decision-making and develop responsibility.[47] Others, however, looked on any measure that threatened to break up the United Kingdom as, at best, eccentric. Even Benn (albeit in 1967) argued that, as satellites could circumnavigate the earth in ninety minutes, it was 'a little odd to press for further disintegration of government'.[48]

Appeasing nationalist sentiment was, moreover, viewed with suspicion, for nationalism was considered an irrational and ultimately violent force, the very antithesis of enlightened democratic socialism. Thus, in 1959 activists in the Labour–Liberal marginal seat of Merioneth were most exercised not by their closest rival but by Plaid's 'wild dreams'.[49] After 1966, Labour's rhetoric became more vituperative but undoubtedly reflected genuine concern. Arthur Woodburn, Attlee's Secretary of State for Scotland, pronounced the SNP guilty of 'race hatred' and, drawing parallels with the Nazis, asserted that if nationalists achieved their end, they would spark a civil war.[50] When extremists set off bombs in Wales, one regional official considered this vindicated similar fears, and described such acts as the inevitable result of Plaid's purportedly hysterical language.[51] There was, in addition, the suspicion that once the British labour movement was fragmented into national units, it would be seriously weakened. As the party's Scottish Council put it in 1969, Labour's 'strength lies in unity; a unity which transcends the narrow limits of prejudice and nationalism, and reaches out towards a Democratic Socialist Commonwealth'.[52]

The essential basis for Labour's case in favour of the Union was economic. For example, the centralised policies pursued by the Attlee government were credited with rescuing Scotland and Wales from mass unemployment. Many outside England saw salvation in the further con- centration of economic power in the hands of the British state and then enhancing their influence within the Whitehall machine that ran it. Certainly, before 1966, economic criteria were the only ones that appeared to exert any force. Thus, during the 1950s, the Welsh Regional Council of Labour rejected calls for a separate parliament but supported the case for a Secretary of State on the grounds that while the former would harm prosperity in the principality, the latter would have the opposite effect.[53] Similar considerations led Labour's Scottish Council to reject a devolved legislature. Forced to clarify its position in 1958, it asserted that while centralisation had not eliminated all Scotland's prob- lems, those that remained would 'best be solved by socialist planning on a United Kingdom scale'. Citing the view of the Scottish TUC (STUC), it argued that 'economic security remains the primary factor for the Scottish people' and that could be achieved only if they remained fully integrated within the British economy and properly represented at Westminster.[54]

Given this frame of reference, it was not surprising that many saw nationalist success as a reflection of how the government's economic policies were hurting voters. The cuts in spending and insistence on wage restraint after July 1966 were widely resented across the United Kingdom, which saw unemployment rise, particularly in industrial Wales and Scotland. In England, it was argued, disaffected voters turned to the Conservatives, but elsewhere they used the nationalists to vent their feelings. Given the supposedly negative nature of SNP and Plaid support, once the government's policies began to work it would, as one minister put it, 'evaporate'. It was therefore unnecessary to address the issue of constitutional change; indeed, given that it would only encourage nationalists, such a course was dangerous.[55]

Others were not so confident that nationalist support would dis- appear – but agreed its rise reflected problems general to the United Kingdom. In arguing for Scottish legislative devolution during the late 1950s, Mackintosh proceeded from the assumption that all Britons wanted to control the expanded post-war state bureaucracy. His solution was to create a number of elected sub-parliaments, to bring government closer to the people; these would enjoy responsibility for most internal issues, leaving Westminster to deal with economic planning, defence and foreign policy. Labour's 1967 Hamilton by-election defeat was due, he believed, to the fact that this feeling of 'remoteness' from govern- ment had not yet been addressed.[56]

Some did think the rise of nationalism said something specific about the situation in Wales and Scotland. Even so, while they did not make the connection, much of their analysis was applicable to other parts of industrial Britain, where Labour also enjoyed a virtual monopoly of elected office. Gwilym Prys Davies, the party's candidate in the 1966 Carmarthen by-election, believed Labour representatives had alienated the young – presumed to be a core nationalist constituency – because they had become the 'new conservatives'. Labour in Wales, he stated, was merely committed to maintaining the status quo.[57] Adopting a slightly different tack, James Griffiths, Welsh Secretary of State during 1964–6, came to a similar conclusion. He believed rising unemployment had created a sense of helplessness among established Labour voters, although Griffiths also accepted that the party no longer represented the kind of idealistic cause to which he supposed the young were attracted. Thus, like Prys Davies, Griffiths thought Labour needed to embrace a 'constructive alternative' to independence or was 'doomed to disappear' in the principality.[58] In Scotland as much as in Wales, one of Labour's most intractable problems was that it had held on to power in many local authorities for a number of generations: the party's municipal record was hardly unblemished, while accustomed electoral success bred complacency and a frail organisation – most especially in Glasgow.[59]

While some were exercised by how to respond to nationalism, it would be wrong to imagine Labour's predicament appeared acute to everybody. During the later 1950s, it was unsurprising that Edinburgh Fabians did not think devolution or independence important enough to devote even one of their many speaker meetings to.[60] More unexpectedly, Edinburgh South's general management committee (GMC) entirely disregarded the question of Scottish government throughout the 1960s. The one time constitutional change figured on its agenda was when members asked Edinburgh City Party to counter SNP propaganda.[61] More generally, immediately before the Hamilton by-election only one resolution on Scottish government was submitted to the 1967 Scottish party conference. In contrast, in 1968 ten such resolutions – albeit out of seventy-two – were submitted. Of these, however, only two favoured a devolved legislature, while a further two simply wanted nationalist arguments refuted. The remainder just called for greater administrative devolution, such as holding meetings of the Grand Committee in Edinburgh and moving more civil servants north of the border. As they submitted only one resolution on the topic in 1969, presumably most members' interest had by then been exhausted.[62] Measured in terms of resolutions submitted to their conference, Welsh activists were more concerned with rising unemployment; in comparison, Cardiff's relationship with Westminster was insignificant.[63]

This lack of interest suited the Scottish Council executive, which was reluctant to amend the approach outlined in 1958.[64] The Hamilton reverse forced the hierarchy to promise to consider the question 'anew', although this resulted in a simple reiteration of policy. After the un-precedented – if still limited – interest shown at the 1968 Scottish party conference, support for further administrative devolution was mooted and the matter was placed in the hands of a sub-committee. If this was not a delaying tactic it looked like one, for members took eighteen months to decide that any type of elected legislature was unwise. As a concession to new thinking, however, they supported local government reform and called for the powers of the Scottish Office to be enhanced. Even these modest proposals appeared dangerous to many Scots MPs.[65]

Those advocating a new relationship with Westminster despaired of such thinking. Mackintosh was no friend of nationalism and had long argued that an elected assembly for Scotland would be a bulwark against it. Such an arrangement, he argued, would be efficient and meet the democratic needs of the people, while Scots MPs could still play a full part in debating national economic issues. Regionalism would also be a fillip to Labour's wider ambitions, for voters would never support a radical reduction of inequality if they believed government was run by a remote bureaucracy which did not have their interests at heart.[66] The end of the 1960s saw the revisionist Mackintosh joined by others drawn from the party's left, like the MP Alex Eadie and future MP Jim Sillars, who took a firm line against independence but who nonetheless endorsed the establishment of regional authorities.[67] Yet even advocates of a devolved Scottish parliament accepted that prosperity depended on 'socialist planning for the whole of Britain'.[68] Activists in Edinburgh even justified a parliament on the grounds that it would rebuild public 'respect' for government, and suggested devolution was a 'natural' evolution of existing arrangements.[69] Despite their moderation, these voices nonetheless remained on the periphery of the Scottish debate.

In Wales matters were more dynamic, if only because the principality lacked the same degree of autonomy long enjoyed by Scotland. Labour entered the 1959 campaign committed to creating a Welsh Office, and made good this promise in 1964. The Secretary of State for Wales, how-ever, enjoyed fewer powers than the Scottish counterpart, something that rankled with many, who continued to push for additional powers short of devolution. In particular, they called for the Welsh Economic Council to assume more responsibility and even for it to be directly elected, a view endorsed by Cledwyn Hughes, Secretary of State during 1966–8.[70] While its recommendations were watered down, the study group established by the Welsh party to investigate the machinery of government favoured creating an elected parliament that would share responsibility for economic planning with Westminster.[71] The appoint-ment of George Thomas as Secretary of State in 1968 indicated that Downing Street did not welcome such thinking. Instead of dallying with constitutional matters, Thomas focused his attention on ensuring the

the Department of Economic Affairs, leading lights in the North East considered elected regional government 'essential'. Using economic arguments in a way contrary to that employed in Scotland, they claimed that if their region was to overcome its many problems, it needed greater responsibility for planning. Although they still believed central government should retain overall control of planning, they argued that its detailed application could be the job of assemblies accountable to the voters. Autonomy, of course, had its limits and it was thought taxation should not be levied at the regional level – if only because it would leave the troubled North East even poorer.[75] Indicative of divisions few in the national leadership wanted to expose, members in the affluent West Midlands also wanted an elected regional council – but one armed with the power to levy income tax.[76]

Federalism, however, faced formidable opposition outside the Cabinet, in the form of most trade unions. They believed devolution would undermine disadvantaged regions, as it would expose the extent to which Westminster redistributed wealth from the better-off areas to the poorest. Thus, while it might increase democracy, federalism would exacerbate Britain's uneven economic development.[77]

Despite everything, Labour's formal attitude to devolution did not much change during 1964–70. There was support for measures, such as the 1967 Welsh Language Act, that accommodated cultural difference. However, many in Wales feared a devolved parliament with legislative powers would undermine the ability of Welsh MPs to influence Whitehall and so harm the national interest.[78] In Scotland, the issue moved an even shorter distance: echoing the views of the party's Scottish Council, the chair of Edinburgh West CLP claimed that only one factor would revive Labour's fortunes north of the border: economic recovery.[79]

Reforming local government

The slow progress of the Redcliffe-Maud Commission on the Reform of Local Government in England, as well as of other investigations into the situation in Wales and Scotland, was one legitimate reason why ministers were unwilling to allow discussion of federalism to develop too quickly. The commission was known to be considering regional government, although it was taking its time: it sat for over three years and its report was not published until June 1969. The commission was Wilson's response to concern about the relevance of local government, for when Attlee nationalised utilities such as gas and water, then created a National Health Service, he stole many of the municipal authorities' responsibilities. It is no wonder that, by the mid-1960s, most local contests provoked the participation of little more than one-third of the electorate.

Introducing the Redcliffe-Maud report, the Prime Minister rightly described it as recommending the 'most far-reaching reorganisation of local government the country has ever seen'. Wilson particularly welcomed its proposals to rationalise a confusing array of bodies, something he hoped would create more effective authorities. He also correctly predicted that some of the report's proposals would be contentious, although he did not say this would be especially true in his own party.[80] While the Commission raised the possibility of regional government and suggested new means by which people might participate at the grass roots, Redcliffe-Maud was seen as further centralising power and as being interested in efficient rather than democratic administration.[81]

The report's main recommendation was to create three tiers of administrative responsibility. It proposed that England (excluding London) should have its current 1,200 elected bodies replaced by just sixty-one, all but three of which would have exclusive responsibility for services. Given their size, Birmingham, Manchester and Liverpool were granted metropolitan status, which meant they would share service provision with a number of smaller councils. These sixty-one bodies were each to appoint some of their members – and co-opt a smaller number of outside experts – to eight provincial councils. Wheatley made similar proposals for regional government in Scotland. Building on the Department of Economic Affairs' regional economic planning councils, their main role was to lie in economic planning and development. Below these two layers, Redcliffe-Maud suggested a third, composed of local councils of various sizes with limited and mostly undefined responsibilities.

Labour was divided over the report. Wilson was attracted to the creation of newer, fewer and (he presumed) more efficient local authorities. However, George Thomson, whom the Prime Minister charged with assessing party opinion, detected a 'depressingly conservative response' among councillors and activists. Not only did they fear for their own prospects as a result of the boundary changes required by reform, but they had also become attached to administrative units with venerable traditions, and opposed their abolition. Crosland similarly noted that the proposed reduction of councillors – numbers were set to drop from 32,000 to 7,000 – caused 'dismay' within the ranks. Given their influence in CLPs, Thomson warned the Prime Minister that he needed to take full account of councillors' views when drafting legislation. Transport House was consequently persuaded to arrange a series of regional conferences designed to win over critics.[82]

Such was the concern in Bristol West, its GMC devoted two meetings to the subject, which confirmed Labour activists' largely critical response to Redcliffe-Maud. The future MP Michael Cocks feared rural areas would enjoy undue weight in the provincial councils and so loosen Labour's already precarious grip on local government in the South West.

He also believed the report 'had an air of Civil Service thinking about it', inasmuch as it gave too much power to chief executives and appointed members, as opposed to elected representatives. Some called for municipal authorities to be reshaped to allow people to participate actively, believing it was better to have more democracy even if was at the cost of efficiency. Paradoxically, however, Cocks did not want Whitehall to give up too much power to the provincial councils, as he feared the quality of services would then vary across the country – an understandable fear for a Labour activist in a region where the Conservatives were likely to dominate. In the end, the GMC agreed to support a motion that rejected the report on the grounds that it would concentrate power in too few hands.[83]

Labour's 1969 conference revealed that many activists believed the report sacrificed democracy 'on the altar of efficiency'. If applied, they feared a worsening of the 'apathy and feeling of cynicism felt by many people, the feeling of remoteness that the elector has to even his town or civic hall'. The provincial councils would be undemocratic, the unitary authorities too big and local councils toothless.[84] Those 1,000 members who attended Labour's eight regional conferences held on the subject during October generally supported that view. Given the earlier discussion on devolution, it will be no surprise that their overwhelming view was that provincial councils should be directly elected. Especially from the North and the West Midlands came the call to be granted legislative powers. Members were also sceptical about the proposed local councils and regarded them as functionless sounding boards for local opinion. If they were to be more than that, their powers needed to be defined and enhanced.[85]

As the minister responsible for local government, and latterly participation, Crosland had his own doubts about Redcliffe-Maud. His White Paper, published in February 1970, reflected some of those misgivings.[86] In particular, Crosland appeared only too happy to wait for the Crowther-Hunt Commission to report before pronouncing on provincial councils. Possibly influenced by Hart's abortive Green Paper, he nonetheless made some concrete proposals with regard to local councils, suggesting they should be created throughout all unitary areas – although in metropolitan districts these should come into being only if demanded by residents. Although he was unwilling to give them responsibility for providing services, Crosland ensured they could play a part in their administration. More generally, he presented the White Paper as giving authorities greater freedom from central government. While they would have to conform to certain national policies – such as the introduction of comprehensive education – they would be free of detailed supervision in a variety of areas and enjoy unprecedented financial autonomy.[87]

The Community Development Programme

While usually thought of as a flawed experiment in welfare provision, the Community Development Programme (CDP) also indicated how far ministers were willing to recast the relationship between individual and state.[88] It was not a Labour scheme but originated in the work of the Home Office Children's Department and was largely the initiative of Derek Morrell, an official described by Crossman as 'of quite unusual administrative drive combined with a mystical imagination'.[89] Yet the fact that the CDP saw the light of day showed how far the government – even conservative figures like James Callaghan – was willing to sponsor innovation.

The essential aim of the CDP was to discover new ways of meeting the needs of those apparently suffering from 'multiple deprivation' and so dependent on the welfare state. It was thought such groups remained trapped in poverty partly because welfare agencies had failed to co-ordinate their efforts, so the CDP relied on an inter-service team, including local and national bodies. Most innovative, however, was its stress on the need to involve the poor in guiding the project and ensuring welfare providers actually met their needs.[90] As Crossman put it, the CDP would help the poor 'stand more on their own in the future by their own efforts, without having to rely so much on external support', as it would encourage 'mutual help and voluntary effort' within local communities.[91] Thus, while an example of state intervention, its purpose was to empower the poor and help them 'exercise more control over their lives'.[92]

Callaghan launched the scheme in January 1969. It was meant to embrace twelve pilot areas, each of which would enjoy a generous degree of autonomy from Whitehall, to allow them to reflect residents' self-defined interests. In the spring, four councils were invited to participate, the object being to have another four up and running by October 1970. However, by the time Labour left office only two projects – Liverpool and Coventry – were properly established and it was not until Wilson was back in power in 1974 that the target number of projects was met.[93] One reason for delay was the reluctance of most local authorities, for, while mostly funded from a £20 million budget, each project still required some municipal expenditure. Local officials were also afraid of giving away too much control; Coventry's Director of Education, for example, predicted 'permanent instability' if too much store was put in residents' opinions. Finally, consultations with council officials, local agency representatives and, especially, residents had to be protracted to ensure each side fully co-operated.[94] In particular, determining who represented the 'community' proved problematic. In Liverpool, the influential Catholic Church-dominated Scotland Road

Residents Association claimed to speak for locals, but officials doubted that.[95] In Coventry's Hillfields district there were three neighbourhood organisations but the CDP director thought co-opting them would smack of a nominal form of 'community' involvement. However, he appreciated that picking those he considered best suited to the task was also unsatisfactory.[96]

The election of a Conservative government in June 1970 did not help the development of the CDP and resulted in the project being shifted from its original administrative home. This compounded problems associated with high levels of personnel turnover and unwieldy steering groups that appeared to find decision-making traumatic. Moreover, from the outset, the principle on which the CDP was based had been criticised by those influenced by 'radical' sociology. Even the academic charged with co-ordinating CDP research believed the assumption that the poor could be helped to improve their position within the existing system was a 'shibboleth of liberal society in decline'.[97] Others praised its aims but considered that, without any conflict between deprived communities and the state, the poor would never achieve improvement. Despite the intention to help the poor help themselves, these detractors considered it was based on a patronising 'missionary approach'.[98] Many social workers employed by the projects adhered to these views and refashioned – or Callaghan believed misused – them to suit their own agendas. If such attempts to radicalise the poor failed to improve their lives, they nonetheless gave CDP employees a base from which they could transform inner-city CLPs during the 1970s.[99] Thus, two years after all twelve projects had been finally established, the CDP was closed down and dubbed a dismal failure, even by progressive Labour figures such as the Home Office minister Alex Lyon.[100]

A participatory party?

Despite the assumptions of many in the party, it was uncertain how far CLPs were the best means of fostering wider political participation. Most working-class members exhibited what some considered a 'natural quietism', in that they rarely challenged even representatives who went against their wishes. Others believed there was so little evidence of members making any impact on government policy that party democracy was a myth.[101] Activists were certainly frustrated by Wilson's refusal to take heed of conference; as one noted in 1969, CLPs contained those 'who work like hell for the Labour Party to keep it financially sound [but] … who frankly are ignored on so many occasions when the question of policy has to be discussed'.[102] At least some ministers believed this the proper state of affairs. Short, for one, believed the NEC – and presumably the party as a whole – should confine itself to acting as the government's 'cheerleader'. Wilson's own conception of consulting members was limited to attending meetings, where he would listen to activists' complaints, then sign autographs.[103]

If the party's internal procedures were problematic, by the end of the decade an increasing number were concerned that many CLPs were 'claustrophobic and inward-looking' and so unable to give voice to local residents.[104] They needed, it was said, to involve themselves more closely in community action and help build 'a more effective grass roots social democracy'. Members should become involved in every aspect of society, 'right down to the ordinary, everyday things of ordinary people's every-day lives'. MP and NEC member Tom Bradley stated that local parties should support tenants' associations, so that residents could appreciate that Labour would 'fight with them, not just for higher wages and better conditions, but for a cleaner, more civilised environment and for a say in how hospitals, schools and factories are run'. Some were more inter-ested than others in exploring these possibilities. Labour-controlled Sheffield Council was one of the few to form a committee on which sat members of the Housing Committee and tenants' groups, which had the power to recommend action.[105]

Transport House had always appreciated that a healthy organisation required an informed and enthusiastic membership. In the late 1960s, officials sought new means to overcome members' ignorance of policy and alienation from policy-making.[106] Even old hands such as the regional organiser Jim Raisin believed Labour required a 'genuinely democratic structure'.[107] With that in mind, in 1969 the Home Policy Sub-committee recommended a scheme, referred to as Participation '69, that involved circulating a background document to local organisations along with a questionnaire to be submitted to the NEC. According to one critical observer, this was 'the first new approach to party democ-racy since 1918'.[108] Even so, if its main purpose was to give members a more direct say in policy-making, officials hoped it would also enlighten them as to the difficult decisions faced by ministers and so create a greater degree of empathy for their leaders.[109]

The first topic selected for discussion was women and social security. Armed with members' responses, the NEC proposed to brief MPs in time for a forthcoming Commons debate on the issue. A discussion document and questionnaire were duly despatched to 2,000 local parties, women's sections, Young Socialist branches and affiliated unions, who were all urged to debate the subject. The response was rather dis-appointing. Only 198 questionnaires were returned by the deadline, although over 250 were eventually submitted; it was calculated that 2,343 individuals had taken part in discussions. The NEC nonetheless considered this a helpful first step in a procedure it wanted to become an established feature of policy-making. Discussion of the second topic – economic equality – was, however, disrupted by the 1970 election campaign and the documents were never circulated to members.[110]

Conclusion

Labour's 1970 manifesto devoted five pages to policies designed to make Britain an 'active democracy' and announced how seriously the party took the need to 'infuse a democratic element into the increasingly complex institutions which dominate our lives'.[111] While it is usually unwise to place much credence in the contents of a manifesto, it would be churlish to dismiss this as constituting no more than a rhetorical shift. Although Labour's response to demands for greater participation was more ambivalent and limited than some wanted, its engagement was much more positive than often supposed.

It would still be fair to stress how far the party had not moved and the extent to which any shift in position was the result of ministers' desire to appease apparently powerful electoral forces. Thus, despite Labour ministers' 'pious words', by 1970 Mackintosh considered Britain remained one of the most centralised of industrial societies.[112] Labour's was an open-ended legacy, one consisting of a generous number of Royal Commissions, reports, experimental projects and White Papers, but comparatively little substantive change. At least some of this was deliberate: for many ministers, investigating the 'facts' was preferable to tackling tricky issues head on. The likes of Wilson were largely uninterested in changing the process, being preoccupied with manipulating the existing mechanics of decision-making. Even so, the Prime Minister still gave colleagues limited scope to develop ideas that echoed radical opinion outside government.

Change in this matter, above all others, was protracted – possibly inevitably so – and Labour in office had taken but a few faltering steps by June 1970. As Judith Hart warned in relation to the Skeffington report, even after some reform the people 'will continue to show the irrationality and ingratitude which is their right as citizens'. Moreover, 'for a long time all that will be possible to demonstrate as a result of the whole effort will be a little more understanding and give and take here and there'. However, at least there might be 'a willingness on the part of the authorities to take the public into their confidence rather more fully and at an earlier stage than hitherto'.[113] As Hart was an enthusiast for innovation, it is no wonder that many others, inherently sceptical about the need for change, preferred to cling to the familiar ways of doing politics rather than take such a leap into the dark.

Notes

The place of publication is London unless otherwise specified.

1 R. Williams (ed.), *May Day Manifesto 1968* (Harmondsworth, 1968), pp. 143–50; R. Miliband, *Parliamentary Socialism* (1972), p. 13.

2 D. Marquand, 'Reaching for the levers', *Times Literary Supplement*, 11 April 1997.

3 National Library of Scotland (NLS), John P. Mackintosh papers, Dep. 323/231, Democracy and the devolution of power, n.d. (but late 1960s).

4 See, for example, H. Wilson, *The Governance of Britain* (1977).

5 Labour Party, *Let's Go With Labour for the New Britain* (1964), pp. 22–3; Labour Party, *Time for Decision* (1966), pp. 18–19.

6 *Report of the Sixty-Seventh Annual Conference of the Labour Party* (1968), pp. 340–2.

7 M. Taylor, 'Labour and the constitution', in D. Tanner, P. Thane and N. Tiratsoo (eds), *Labour's First Century* (Cambridge, 2000).

8 L. Barrow and I. Bullock, *Democratic Ideas and the British Labour Movement, 1880–1914* (Cambridge, 1996).

9 P. Joyce, *Realignment of the Left? A History of the Relationship Between the Liberal Democrat and Labour Parties* (1999), pp. 70–2; N. Riddell, *Labour in Crisis. The Second Labour Government, 1929–31* (Manchester, 1999), pp. 137–9.

10 D. Jay, The *Socialist Case* (1947), p. 258.

11 S. Fielding, P. Thompson and N. Tiratsoo, *'England Arise!' The Labour Party and Popular Politics in 1940s Britain* (Manchester, 1995), pp. 86–8.

12 A. Bevan, *In Place of Fear* (1952), pp. 100–2.

13 British Library of Political and Economic Science, Hugh Jenkins papers, 6/9, Socialism, democracy and the Labour Party, n.d. (but 1955).

14 M. Foot, 'Credo of the Labour left – interview', *New Left Review*, 49 (1968), pp. 28–9.

15 S. Fielding, 'Labourism in the 1940s', *Twentieth Century British History*, 3:2 (1992), pp. 145–7.

16 H. Jenkins and W. Wolfgang, 'Tho' cowards flinch', *Victory for Socialism Pamphlet* (1956).

17 W. B. Gwyn, 'The Labour Party and the threat of bureaucracy', *Political Studies*, 29 (1971).

18 Labour Party, *Personal Freedom* (1956), pp. 7–9, 11–12.

19 London Metropolitan Archive (LMA), *London News*, July 1956.

20 T. Benn, *Out of the Wilderness. Diaries, 1963–67* (1987), p. 422.

21 E. Short, *Whip to Wilson* (1989), p. 110.

22 *Report of the Sixty-Ninth Annual Conference of the Labour Party* (1970), p. 277.

23 A. Crosland, 'A social democratic Britain', *Fabian Tract*, 404 (1970), pp. 12–15; *The Times*, 25 September 1970.

24 Mackintosh papers, Democracy.

25 *Report of the Sixty-Eighth Annual Conference of the Labour Party* (1969), pp. 388–9.

26 Editorial, 'Participation', *Socialist Commentary*, December 1968.

27 For more on Benn during this period, see L. Panitch and C. Leys, *The End of Parliamentary Socialism* (1997), pp. 39–65.

28 For more on the Group's activities, see Bristol Record Office (BRO), Bristol South East CLP papers, 39035/146, New Bristol Group, *Output 1962/63* (Bristol, 1963), *Output 1963/64* (Bristol, 1964) and *Output 3* (Bristol, 1966).

29 This account is based on: T. Benn, *Office Without Power. Diaries, 1968–72*

(1988), pp. 59, 67–8, 73, 81, 107–13, 122; *The Times*, 19 April and 13 May; *Guardian*, 23 March, 10 June and 6 November; *Observer*, 26 May; *Daily Telegraph*, 6 November 1968.

30 Public Record Office (PRO), CAB 151/58, R. Jardine, Participation, 3 December 1969.

31 *Daily Mail*, 18 October 1968.

32 Labour Party Archive (LPA), Judith Hart papers, File Hart 10/4, Section 10, Speech to rally of Sudbury and Woodbridge CLP, 18 May 1968.

33 CAB 151/57, Jardine to Barnes, 17 August 1969; CAB 151/58, Jardine, Participation.

34 The following two paragraphs are based on CAB 151/57, Speech to the Council of Social Services, in *Survey of British and Commonwealth Affairs*, 10 (October 1969), and Notes on participation, February 1969; CAB 151/58, Notes for speech to the Council of Social Services, 19 September 1969; Hart papers, File Hart 10/4, Section 10, Speech to London conference, 9 June 1968; Benn, *Office*, p. 121.

35 CAB 151/57, R. Jardine, Note for record, Local councils, n.d.; Outline of Green Paper on participation; Hart papers, Section 12, File 13, R. Jardine, Note for record, n.d.

36 PRO, PREM 13/2713, Note of a meeting between the Prime Minister and the Paymaster General, 24 March 1969; CAB 151/58, Barnes to Jardine, 25 November 1969; CAB 151/58, Jardine, Participation.

37 Benn, *Office*, p. 193.

38 CAB 151/63, Hart to Greenwood, 10 July 1969.

39 CAB 151/63, Press release for speech by A. Skeffington, 17 September 1969.

40 PRO, HLG 120/1045, Press release for a speech by A. Skeffington, 23 September 1968; CAB 151/63, Press release for Skeffington.

41 HLG 136/274, Sub-committee on public participation, Note of first meeting, 29 May 1968.

42 For these and other responses, see HLG 136/308.

43 HLG 136/309, Witall to Corrie, 26 January 1970.

44 CAB 151/63, Hart to Greenwood, 10 July 1969.

45 PRO, AT 35/51, Public participation circular (revised draft), 12 June 1970.

46 *Sixty-Seventh Annual Conference of Labour*, p. 174.

47 National Library of Wales (NLW), Labour Party of Wales papers, file 106, G. D. Purnell, Notes for study group, Reform of machinery of government, Socialist attitude to government, n.d. (but 1969).

48 NLW, MS 23699, f.118, Benn to Ifor Jones, 20 March 1967.

49 NLW, Merioneth CLP papers, Annual report and statement of accounts for the year ending 31 December 1959.

50 *Scotsman*, 22 February 1968; A. Woodburn, 'The rise of Scottish nationalism', *Socialist Commentary*, June 1968, p. 9; *Alloa Journal*, 15 November 1968.

51 NLW, Brynmor John papers, 19, G. Jones, Extremism in Wales, 3 July 1969.

52 Labour Party Scottish Council, *Scottish Government. Interim Report* (Glasgow, 1969), p. 23.

53 Welsh Regional Council of Labour, *Labour's Policy for Wales* (Cardiff, 1954), pp. 3–4; R. M. Jones and I. R. Jones, 'Labour and the nation', in D. Tanner, C. Williams and D. Hopkins (eds), *The Labour Party in Wales, 1900–2000* (Cardiff, 2000), pp. 249–52, 254–5.

54 M. Keating and D. Bleiman, *Labour and Scottish Nationalism* (1979), p. 146; M. Keating, 'The Labour Party in Scotland, 1951–1964', and F. Wood, 'Scottish Labour in government and opposition, 1964–79', in I. Donnachie, C. Harvie and I. S. Wood (eds), *Forward! Labour Politics in Scotland, 1888–*

1988 (Edinburgh, 1988), pp. 91–2, 97–8, 101; Labour Party Scottish Council, *Special Report on Scottish Government* (Glasgow, 1958), pp. 3, 11.

55 D. Douglas, 'The lessons of Pollock', *Socialist Commentary*, April 1967; and K. Morgan, 'Inaction for Wales', *Socialist Commentary*, June 1967; CAB 130/390, Minutes of meetings held to discuss devolution to Scotland and Wales, 18 July, 23 and 28 October 1968.

56 *Scotsman*, 27 April 1957; Mackintosh papers, Dep 323/47, Transcript from 'Ten o'clock', transmitted 3 November 1967, BBC Radio 4.

57 NLW, James Griffiths papers, C/3/14, G. Prys Davies, A memorandum on the political situation in Wales, 12 November 1967, pp. 1–2.

58 Griffiths papers, C/3/18, J. Griffiths, The political situation in Wales, October 1968.

59 J. Connell, 'Collapse in Scotland?', *Socialist Commentary*, January 1969.

60 NLS, Edinburgh Fabian Society papers, Acc 4977/15, *passim*.

61 NLS, Edinburgh South CLP papers, Dep 203/5, GMC minutes, 28 December 1967.

62 Labour Party Scottish Council, *Report of the Executive Committee to the 52nd Annual Conference* (Glasgow, 1967), p. 77; *Report of the Executive Committee to the 53rd Annual Conference* (Glasgow, 1968), pp. 45–7; and *Report of the Executive Committee to the 54th Annual Conference* (Glasgow, 1969), p. 73.

63 Labour Party of Wales papers, Welsh Council of Labour papers, Executive committee minutes, 20 February 1967 and 13 May 1968.

64 This account is based on Mitchell Library, Scottish Labour Party papers, TD 1384/1/5, Scottish Council executive committee minutes, 16 December 1967, 13 January, 11 May and 14 September 1968, 13–14 September 1969, and 21 March 1970.

65 NLS, George Lawson papers, Acc 9588/65, Scottish Labour Group, Executive committee report for submission to group meeting, 5 March 1968, and Memo by G. Lawson and R. Buchanan, 11 December 1968.

66 Mackintosh papers, Democracy; *Scotsman*, 2 November 1963.

67 A. Eadie and J. Sillars, *Don't Butcher Scotland's Future* (Glasgow, 1969).

68 *Sixty-Seventh Annual Conference of Labour*, pp. 174–6.

69 PRO, HO 221/39, Evidence submitted by Edinburgh Central CLP to the Royal Commission on the Constitution, n.d. (but October 1968); HO 221/41, Memorandum of written evidence to the Commission on the Constitution by Edinburgh City Labour Party.

70 Labour Party of Wales papers, Welsh Council of Labour papers, Executive committee minutes, 20 November 1967 and 9 December 1968; CAB 134/2697, Minutes of the ministerial committee on devolution for Scotland and Wales, 13 March 1968.

71 Labour Party of Wales papers, File 106, Machinery of government, n.d. (but 1969).

72 This paragraph is based on NLS, Arthur Woodburn papers, Acc 7656/Box 1/File 1, Crossman to Woodburn, 10 November 1967; Griffiths papers, C/3/15, Crossman to Griffiths, 28 November 1967; CAB 130/390, Minutes of meetings held to discuss devolution to Scotland and Wales, 18 July, 23 and 28 October 1968; R. H. S. Crossman, *Diaries of a Cabinet Minister. Volume II* (1977), pp. 610–11.

73 K. O. Morgan, *Callaghan. A Life* (Oxford, 1997), pp. 361–2.

74 *Sixty-Seventh Annual Conference of Labour*, p. 184.

75 HO 221/176, Northern Regional Council of the Labour Party, Evidence for the Crowther Commission, n.d.; T. Dan Smith, *An Autobiography* (Newcastle upon Tyne, 1970), 86–107.

76 HLG 131/756, West Midlands Labour Party Working Party on Regional Government, Discussion paper, August 1969.
77 HO 221/99, Trades Union Congress, Observations submitted to the Commission on the Constitution, 3 February 1970.
78 HO 221/73, Evidence of the Labour Party in Wales to the Commission on the Constitution, 7 January 1970.
79 D. Leach, 'Scottish Labour in perspective', *Socialist Commentary*, March 1969; Wood, 'Scottish Labour', pp. 106–7; HO 221/142, The Government of Scotland, Evidence of the Labour Party in Scotland to the Commission on the Constitution, March 1970.
80 *Parliamentary Debates (Hansard), 5th Series, Volume 784, House of Commons Official Report, Session 1968–9*, columns 1461–4.
81 D. Regan, 'Start not end of a debate', *Socialist Commentary*, August 1969.
82 PREM 13/2763, Thomson to Wilson, 23 June, 30 July and 4 August 1969; PREM 13/2763, A. Crosland, Redcliffe-Maud: the options, October 1969.
83 BRO, Bristol West CLP papers, 38598/1/g, GMC minutes, 31 July and 25 September 1969.
84 *Sixty-Eighth Annual Conference of Labour*, pp. 152–4.
85 LPA, Regional and Local Government Advisory Committee (RLGAC) papers and minutes, 22 October 1969, Report of regional conferences on local government reform in England, Re. 522, October 1969, and Principles for local government reform in England, Re. 528, October 1969; *Sixty-Eighth Annual Conference of Labour*, pp. 149–64.
86 RLGAC papers, Local government reform in England: the White Paper and the National Executive Committee suggestions compared, Re. 588, February 1970.
87 A. Crosland, *Socialism Now* (1974), pp. 173–89.
88 A. H. Halsey, 'Government against poverty in school and community', in D. Wedderburn (ed.), *Poverty, Inequality and Class Structure* (Cambridge, 1974); R. Kraushaar, 'Policy without protest: the dilemma of organising for change in Britain', in M. Harloe (ed.), *New Perspectives in Urban Change and Conflict* (1981); M. Mayo, 'The history and early development of CDP', in R. Lees and G. Smith (eds), *Action-Research in Community Development* (1975).
89 CAB 165/665, Crossman to Wilson, 1 August 1968.
90 HO 291/1420, Working party on community development, Draft report to ministers, n.d.; PRO, BN 29/1392, Community Development Project departmental responsibility, n.d. (but October 1970), pp. 1–2.
91 CAB 152/111, Press release for speech by R. Crossman, 14 February 1969.
92 HO 389/12, Community Development Project, March 1970, p. 3.
93 BN 29/1392, Otton to Thomas, 5 October 1970.
94 BN 29/1345, Community development, Project progress report, July 1969, pp. 1–2; CAB 152/114, J. O. Bennington, Meeting with representatives of central and regional services, 13 April 1970, and CDP Central Steering Group minutes, 21 July 1970.
95 HO 389/12, J. Banks, Meeting in Liverpool, 17 April 1970.
96 HO 389/12, J. O. Bennington, Report of the Director of the Community Development Project, 5 March 1970.
97 Halsey, 'Government against poverty', p. 125.
98 *New Society*, 16 January and 20 March 1969.
99 J. Callaghan, *Time and Chance* (1987), pp. 237–9; J. Gyford, *The Politics of Local Socialism* (1985), pp. 26–36; Kraushaar, 'Policy without protest', p. 105.
100 A. Lyon, 'A Labour view', in M. Loney and M. Allen (eds), *The Crisis of the Inner City* (1979), pp. 23–4.

101 A. Barker, 'Participation in politics', in B. Lapping and G. Radice (eds), *More Power to the People. Young Fabian Essays on Democracy in Britain* (1968); I. Bing, 'New approaches to democracy', in I. Bing (ed.), 'The Labour Party. An organisational study', *Fabian Tract*, 407 (1971), p. 20.
102 *Sixty-Eighth Annual Conference of Labour*, p. 156.
103 Short, *Whip*, p. 112; Wilson, *Governance*, p. 202.
104 *Sixty-Ninth Annual Conference of Labour*, pp. 274–9.
105 RLGAC papers, Participation: a draft paper for the 1970 local government conference, Re. 545, November 1969; *Sixty-Ninth Annual Conference of Labour*, p. 275.
106 LPA, NEC minutes, Working party on political education, Report, 13 September 1967.
107 LMA, J. W. Raisin papers, Acc 2783/JWR/ORG/68/51 and 87, organiser's reports.
108 Bing, 'New approaches', p. 24.
109 *Sixty-Eighth Annual Conference of Labour*, pp. 29, 355–6; NEC Home Policy Sub-Committee minutes, 12 May 1969, Participation 1969, Re. 453, May 1969.
110 Modern Records Centre, Handsworth CLP papers, MSS 8/5/21, Labour Party Research Department, Participation '69, Women and social security: a short report, *Information Papers*, No. 50 February 1970; see also *Sixty-Ninth Annual Conference of Labour*, p. 37.
111 Labour Party, *Now Britain's Strong Let's Make It a Great Place to Live In* (1970), pp. 20–5.
112 Mackintosh papers, Dep 323/44/1, Democratic reform and economic planning, May 1966; and HO 221/84, J. P. Mackintosh, Evidence for the Crowther Commission, n.d.
113 CAB 151/63, Hart to Greenwood, 10 July 1969.

9

Conclusion. The 1970 general election

Labour lost the 1970 general election, ending what was then only the second time the party had held office backed by a comfortable Commons majority. Unlike Clement Attlee's 1945–51 administration, however, Wilson's had few positive achievements to its name. The consensus among the government's innumerable critics on the left was that this was a failure of will more than circumstance. As Ralph Miliband wrote, the government 'could have had all the support it required from trade unionists, had it been seen to be genuinely engaged in the creation of a society marked by greater social justice'. The point was, however, that the likes of Wilson were uninterested in promoting equality because they were preoccupied with maintaining the status quo.[1]

Regarding the concerns highlighted in this work, the government's detractors similarly claimed that, had they wanted to, ministers could have: promoted comprehensive education with greater enthusiasm; pursued a more radical version of industrial democracy; introduced equal pay for women far sooner; taken a firmer line against racism; been more accommodating to the concerns of youth; and promoted popular participation with less suspicion. While such matters did not all directly determine Labour's electoral fate, the party's failure to secure re-election suggests that it had not adequately come to terms with at least some of the cultural changes fostered by the 'Golden Age'. The picture was, however, not universally bleak. With that proposition it mind, this final chapter reviews how the party approached the 1970 campaign, assesses the result and accounts for Labour's response, one that set it down a path that led to the wilderness years of the 1980s.

'Selsdon man'

Despite the economic problems of the previous three years, Labour members saw in 1970 with some optimism. In January, Wilson went on the offensive after the Conservative shadow Cabinet held a weekend

217

conference at the Selsdon Park Hotel. This gathering was meant to imbue the Conservative's post-1966 policy review with some coherence, but the media created the impression that it marked a dramatic departure from post-war policy. Certainly, Edward Heath, the party's leader since 1965, wanted to introduce more economic competition, cut taxes, reform industrial relations through legislation, tackle 'law and order' and tighten immigration controls. Yet Heath did not seek fundamentally to alter the direction of policy set down in the 1940s and he remained committed to full employment.[2]

It nonetheless suited Wilson's purpose to stress the extent to which the Conservatives wanted to change tack. He sought to create an enemy that posed such a threat to the existing order he could rally Labour's most disenchanted supporters back to the cause. In following this defensive strategy, the Labour leader nonetheless marked out a genuine, if crudely drawn, distinction between the parties over the appropriate use of the state to secure collectively desirable ends. Wilson invented 'Selsdon man' to personify Heath's supposed new Conservatism, which, he alleged, had turned its back on the more consensual approach of Harold Macmillan. The Prime Minister declared Selsdon man was consumed by the 'atavistic desire to reverse the course of 25 years of social revolution' by proposing a 'wanton, calculated return to greater inequality' that substituted a 'free for all in place of the welfare state'. He apparently wanted to 'replace the compassionate society with the ruthless, pushing society', 'reject the society that has been created since the war, a civilised society in which the community, working through Government and Parliament, provides for the needs of the community, on the basis that everyone counts'.[3]

Wilson's Cabinet colleagues, Judith Hart among others, echoed his message, stressing the contrast between the parties. Grass-roots Conservatives were, she alleged, selecting 'rampaging Powellite near-fascists' as parliamentary candidates and so posed a 'threat to all our civilised social values'.[4] Even before the Selsdon Park meeting, ministers, including the normally temperate Edward Short, warned of the dangers of a 'massive lurch in society towards reaction'. While such a lurch was claimed to be embodied by Enoch Powell, it was also said to be generally evident in the defence of elitism, authoritarianism and racism, and in demands for capital and corporal punishment, the ending of the welfare state and a return to 'traditional' values in education.[5] As the chair of the spring 1970 national conference of Labour women told delegates, the choice before voters was clear: 'to keep in forward gear with Labour – or to go into reverse with the Tories'.[6]

On the eve of Roy Jenkins' April Budget, Wilson secretly decided to hold the general election in June, in the hope he would to steal a march on the Conservatives, as they were preparing for an October poll. During the following weeks, events seemed to confirm Wilson's decision. Opinion polls gave Labour a lead for the first time in years; the party's by-election performances became less grim; and it made a satisfactory showing in the local elections. Most economic indicators were also positive: in particular, the balance of trade remained in the black. As is common with Prime Ministers, Wilson implicated leading party figures in his decision, just in case anything went wrong. Few expected it would. When Wilson went to ask the Queen to dissolve parliament, the vast majority of the Parliamentary Labour Party was keen for a June contest. Tony Benn was not alone in imagining Labour had secured a remarkably complete recovery in its fortunes; he described other Cabinet members as 'euphoric'.[7]

The Prime Minister's decision was made with little reference to the state of the party in the country, although at the end of April he did tip off the National Agent as to his intentions.[8] While by the spring it was thought members' morale had greatly improved since the previous autumn, many activists – especially trade unionists still resentful of wage controls and *In Place of Strife* – remained to be won back. A joint meeting in May of the Cabinet and National Executive Committee (NEC) was consequently warned by officials that, if a contest was held too early, it would be 'very much a "Do it Yourself campaign"'. Transport House wanted an autumn poll, to allow for the return of more activists and to give local parties time to relay their organisational foundations.[9] In line with the party's focus in 1964 and 1966, Wilson was confident he could deliver victory in 1970 by projecting an attractive personal image through the voters' television screens.

A revived organisation?

Labour's experience in the marginal constituency of Halifax typified that endured in many other parts of the country.[10] Immediately after winning the seat in 1966 the constituency Labour party (CLP) suffered a dramatic decline, so that, as early as the spring of 1967, it was short of both members and money. Activists became increasingly disenchanted: price rises, Common Market entry negotiations, devaluation of the pound and prescription charges were all criticised at meetings of the general management committee (GMC). A resolution demanding that ministers 'cease their numerous deviations from socialist policy', in order to 'preserve the fast dwindling solidarity within the Socialist party', was defeated only through the chair's casting vote. By early 1968, members who remained on the books retreated into inactivity: meetings became inquorate; it proved impossible to find enough candidates to contest all wards in the local elections; and in the autumn the agent resigned to seek a constituency that could pay his salary. Loyalist speeches from the constituency MP, Edith Summerskill, which stressed Labour's support for the social services, cut little ice. Despite a few initiatives, such as a new bingo scheme to raise revenue and the introduction of coffee evenings to reach potential recruits, the party was falling apart. The CLP had even ceased to function as a social institution: in 1969 the annual flower show was cancelled.

If this experience was common enough, Halifax was unique in being able to rely on the expertise of Sara Barker, Labour's former National Agent, who settled in the town after her time at Transport House came to an end. When in January 1970 she offered her services, the GMC responded 'with acclamation'. Barker's survey of the CLP showed how dire the situation was: only four out of fifteen ward sections were functioning, and there were just ninety-eight paid-up members. The party would recover, she informed the GMC, only with the 'hearty co-operation of every Labour worker', and she concluded her address 'with an eloquent appeal for Socialist loyalty, for personal involvement in the life and service' of the party. Barker's efforts in the town revealed the possibilities but also limits to this venerable Labour voluntarism. During the spring, Barker conducted a remarkably energetic revival campaign. Through circulars, personal letters and home visits, existing ward organisations were urged to contact ex-members; where wards had disintegrated, Barker cajoled activists to re-establish them. As a result, by the time Wilson called the election on 18 May, the number of functioning ward sections had doubled and membership stood at 230. Yet the CLP was still judged to have 'literally no organisation to enable it to fight an election'. The position elsewhere was, if anything, even worse. The elderly activists of South East Bristol were taken so unawares by the election that they did not have enough envelopes in which to put their candidate's address.[11]

Once Wilson announced the election date, most gaps in the party's ranks were filled either by new faces or by activists who had left the fold after 1966. In London, at least, organisation and morale were thought comparable to those in 1964: as a senior organiser in the capital noted, it was 'the happiest election I have experienced and the enthusiasm was tremendous'. Some even optimistically imagined Wilson might have won if Labour had not peaked too soon.[12]

Wilson's personal campaign, the focus of the national party's efforts, was informed by his desire to appear confident and responsible: 'presidential' was the often-used term.[13] Inspired by the Queen's then novel practice of mingling with crowds, Wilson indulged in numerous 'walk-abouts', after which the Prime Minister visited local party offices to enthuse activists, which in practice meant delivering brief, banal speeches to tame audiences. There was, however, a bit more to Labour's campaign than smiles and sunshine. Wilson's basic proposition was that his government had been economically 'responsible', even at the risk of losing electoral support. Yet, as he informed those watching his last television broadcast of the campaign, economic strength was not an end in itself. 'The socialism I believe in', he stated, 'means above all using all our resources for making Britain a better place to live in and for a Labour government this means sharing prosperity in a way which is fair and just'. Thus poverty had to be rooted out and bad housing eradicated, while the social services, health provision and educational resources all had to be strengthened. 'It means, above all', he concluded, 'accepting that individual misfortune is not just a private concern but a community concern, that we are all members one of another'.[14]

Workers

Immediately before the poll, Wilson believed his stress on Selsdon man had decisively turned the tide against Heath.[15] Defeat therefore came as a massive shock and numerous short-term influences were blamed, in particular the publication of a bad set of trade figures. The England football team's three–two reverse at the hands of West Germany in the World Cup was even thought significant. To be fair, leading Conservatives were also unsure quite how they managed to beat Wilson.[16]

More substantively, the result was noteworthy in three respects. First, while representing a great recovery from Labour's nadir of 1967–8, at 43 per cent the party's share of votes cast was its lowest since before 1945. Secondly, at 4.7 per cent, the swing to the Conservatives was the largest post-war shift of support between the two parties. Finally, turnout fell to a post-1945 low of 71.4 per cent, from 75.8 per cent in 1966 – and a full 12 per cent less than in 1950. While there were a variety of possible causes for the last, contemporary analysts thought that, Selsdon man notwithstanding, many voters felt Labour and the Conservatives were just too similar to make voting necessary.[17]

As the weeks passed, an increasing number in the party were struck by the fact that a significant proportion of abstainers came from the 'traditional' working class, those whose support Labour had once taken for granted. The NEC elliptically conceded that Labour had 'failed to stir the enthusiasm, beliefs and interests of the voters' and lost 'that natural link through which people see in the Labour Party the expression of their own aspirations'.[18] Members of the Scottish Council were rather more direct; they believed Labour's campaign, with its focus on personality, had been the primary cause of a 'quiet and lifeless election'. They argued Labour should have presented itself as a 'fighting enthusiastic radical force', on the basis that this would have aroused working-class voters.[19] The implication for left-leaning activists was clear: as Salford

Table 9.1 The composition of the Labour vote, 1964–70

Category	1964	1966	1970	Difference, 1964–70
All	44.8	48.7	43.8	–1.0
AB (upper and professional middle class)	8.9	15.5	10.4	+1.5
C1 (lower middle class)	24.8	29.9	30.5	+5.7
C2 (skilled manual working class)	54.4	58.5	55.4	+1.0
DE (semi/unskilled working class)	59.1	65.2	57.3	–1.8
Men	48.3	52.4	47.3	–1.0
Women	41.7	45.4	40.6	–1.1

Source: D. Butler and A. King, *The British General Election of 1964* (1965), p. 296; D. Butler and A. King, *The British General Election of 1966* (1966), p. 264; and D. Butler and M. Pinto-Duschinsky, *The British General Election of 1970* (1971), p. 342.

East's executive committee concluded, Labour lost because Wilson had failed to carry out left-inspired and pro-union conference decisions. Voters saw little difference between the parties because Labour had not properly represented the workers' interests.[20]

Much party analysis read like a mirror image of that produced after 1959: Labour had apparently lost 'traditional' supporters while retaining much of its hold on 'younger couples in the newer housing areas' established in 1964 and 1966.[21] The impression from marginal constituencies such as Bristol North West was that, after 1966, Labour's problems were mainly located in areas in which council estates predominated, whereas matters were less troubling where private housing was common.[22] Experienced regional organisers like Jim Raisin even believed Labour's best hope was to cultivate those who first voted for the party in 1966, to compensate for the decline in working-class support.[23] Less impressionistic evidence from National Opinion Poll surveys suggests (see Table 9.1) that in 1970 Labour was indeed better represented among the middle class than in 1964, but enjoyed less support from unskilled and semi-skilled manual workers.

While one leading Labour woman blamed defeat on 'working class folly', in that normally loyal voters had been 'bemused and beguiled into voting Conservative', more humble female activists, albeit hardly left-wing ones, thought workers had abandoned the party because they 'had not been fairly dealt with' by the government.[24] This latter perspective prevailed at the party's conference in the autumn of 1970.[25] Especially in light of Heath's proposed industrial relations legislation, delegates argued that Labour should fall in line behind the unions and oppose what was described as the new Prime Minister's 'own special brand of maidenly lower middle class warfare'. Jack Jones was but the most eloquent exponent of the view that all the people's interests were best served by the actions of shopfloor militants free from government meddling. The union movement was, he declared, the 'shield and defender of workers everywhere'. Jones' speech brought NEC member and MP Walter Padley, no radical, to tears because Padley thought it summed up 'what it was all about – the class war'.[26]

In complete contrast, the revisionist John Mackintosh considered the conference 'a curious, muddled, rather sad affair', as defeat had encouraged 'a return to the womb, a retreat into primitive attitudes on the part of a large section of the Party', behind an unqualified defence of the unions.[27] If Mackintosh criticised the left for its conservatism, new thinking was hardly evident among the party's leading revisionists. Once the shock of defeat had passed, Tony Crosland produced a Fabian pamphlet, described as 'a coherent statement of democratic socialism for the 1970s'.[28] Yet Crosland merely concluded that *The Future of Socialism* remained relevant, meaning a 'clear reaffirmation of ideals' was all that was required. He simply reiterated his belief that growth was 'an essential condition of any significant allocation of resources', without which Labour could not promote equality. Consequently, a future Labour government would have to reject those Treasury orthodoxies that had thwarted the pursuit of growth during 1964–70. It would also have to apply an incomes policy, which meant overcoming union opposition. Very much as he had done immediately after 1959, Crosland stated that Labour should not be afraid of the latter course, for it was a 'broad-based, national people's party; [so] it must not be deterred from finding national solutions to national problems'.

Other revisionists, less restrained by leadership position, called for Labour to loosen its ties with the unions in particular and the working class in general. Even before defeat, Christopher Mayhew, who had resigned as one of Wilson's ministers, noted that many workers were deeply conservative on subjects such as black immigration, abortion and capital punishment, much more so than the middle class. Moreover, while Labour aimed to create a classless society, the unions upon whom it relied organised themselves exclusively on the basis of class, and so emphasised conflict over reconciliation.[29] In private Crosland, Roy Jenkins and Denis Healey, Labour's three most significant revisionists, echoed such thoughts, which had also been aired after 1959. They agreed it was necessary to 'minimise the Party role of the trades unions' and appeared to think they could rely on the CLPs to achieve that end, as activists were moving away from the left.[30] This betrayed a profound ignorance of grass-roots opinion, something that would not have mattered so much in the past, when Hugh Gaitskell could rely on the union block vote to neutralise leftist sentiment. However, having alienated the unions while in government and still managing to lose office, after 1970 the revisionists no longer controlled the levers of power in the party. In frustration Mayhew joined the Liberals in 1974; he was but the first of many to take leave of Labour.

Women

In February 1970, the ex-Cabinet minister Fred Lee wrote to Wilson to say that equal pay was a 'subject which properly put, can be political dynamite in bringing in the women's vote'.[31] According to survey evidence, however, in June women abandoned Labour at about the same rate as men, and that from a much lower base. The main reason for this shift was widely believed to be inflation, an issue the Conservatives exploited with alacrity: Heath had even declared the contest a 'shopping basket election'. Labour women certainly thought his promise to deal with rising prices 'at a stroke' played an important part in determining female affiliations.[32]

Labour's reaction to its failure with women was mixed. For their supposed susceptibility to Conservative propaganda, Lena Jeger criticised housewives for being 'politically less mature' than their husbands.[33] Barbara Castle, however, suggested Labour itself was largely to blame, if even working-class women believed that the party was too concerned to increase male wages to be bothered with keeping prices down.[34]

In any case, not all women responded to Labour's period in office in the same way. Data generated by the British Election Study suggest that between 1966 and 1970, compared to their male counterparts, women in the working class, as well as those under twenty-five and over sixty-four years of age, moved strongly against Labour (see Tables 9.2 and 9.3). However, women aged between twenty-five and sixty-four and those in the intermediate class moved relatively closer to the party. In crude terms, Labour did worst with young and old working-class women but better among white-collar, middle-aged women. It is possible to suggest why: the former group contained most full-time housewives – those in their twenties or thirties with children to care for and others over sixty drawing their pensions – while the latter included most of those in full- or part-time employment. Hence, if not quite 'dynamite', Labour's announcement regarding equal pay helped it retain the loyalties of women in work, while those whose main concern was with consumption were less impressed. Overall, however, prices rather than wages – that is, the domestic sphere rather than the workplace – continued to dominate most women's horizons.

Defeat only increased enthusiasm at Transport House for organisational change. From seventy-one in 1970, the number of women's councils

Table 9.2 Women and Labour voting, by social class and age, 1964–70

Category	1964	1966	1970	Difference, 1964–70
Social class				
Professional	17.2	19.8	23.4	+6.2
Intermediate	24.3	25.4	32.9	+8.6
Working class	63.4	68.1	53.2	–10.2
Age				
Under 25	57.2	64.2	51.9	–5.3
25–44	50.3	52.4	44.8	–5.5
45–64	42.2	48.2	43.5	+1.3
Above 64	44.5	50.3	29.3	–15.2

Source: I. Crewe, A. Fox and N. Day, *The British Electorate 1963–1992* (Cambridge, 1995), Table 1.14.

Table 9.3 Men and Labour voting, by social class and age, 1964–70

Category	1964	1966	1970	Difference, 1964–70
Social class				
Professional	17.1	20.0	25.3	+8.2
Intermediate	26.2	34.3	32.3	+6.1
Working class	65.0	70.1	60.7	–4.3
Age				
Under 25	45.5	50.3	52.3	+6.8
25–44	50.0	60.5	48.8	–1.2
45–64	46.2	51.4	45.8	–0.4
Above 64	45.6	49.2	44.4	–1.2

Source: I. Crewe, A. Fox and N. Day, *The British Electorate 1963–1992* (Cambridge, 1995), Table 1.14.

more than doubled a year later, by then being described as 'the main unit of women's organisation'.[35] This proved a severe emotional wrench for some stalwarts. At the last meeting of Flintshire and Denbighshire's advisory council, due to be replaced by a women's council, members spoke of nearly three decades of attendance and declared 'they would miss it very much', for the advisory council had been 'so dear to their hearts'. The long-standing secretary recorded that, as she wrote those minutes, 'I am not ashamed to say that I am wiping my tears away, thinking of happy years spent together, with these delegates'.[36] Despite the exit of such stalwarts from the scene, the new bodies failed to create many bridges to wider society but, as the 1970s progressed, did become the site for much more radical political activities.[37]

There is some evidence that Labour women were becoming slightly less tolerant of their accustomed place in the party, something which was brought to a head by the small number of female candidates selected to contest the 1970 election. The 1970 women's conference even discussed a resolution that called on the NEC to ensure future short-lists contained at least one woman. This was, however, remitted at the request of the National Labour Women's Advisory Council (NLWAC), which nonetheless promised to put the matter to the NEC, although delegates were warned CLPs would resent such a stipulation.[38] The NLWAC also established a sub-committee to look into the subject, but in the end it merely called on the NEC to ask CLPs to give greater consideration to the need to promote higher numbers of women candidates. This the NEC duly did, but few were optimistic that the exhortation would produce results and the emphasis remained on the need for a 'change of attitude' rather than structural reform.[39] It would take two decades before Labour forced CLPs to alter their selection procedures.

Black immigrants

Looking to the future, the young Neil Kinnock, candidate for a safe seat in 1970, told a pre-election gathering of Glamorgan Labour women that race relations would become as important to his generation as unemployment was in the 1930s.[40] It would have been surprising if many of Kinnock's audience wanted this prediction to come true for, just as they had been at the start of the 1960s, most Labour members – like the majority of their white compatriots – wanted the issue to disappear, by black immigrants becoming fully assimilated into the 'British way of life'.

While some party members exhibited a greater sensitivity to the issue than hitherto, Labour remained an imperfect means of promoting black integration; for example, only one non-white delegate attended the party's 1968 annual conference.[41] Moreover, at the start of the 1970s activists in places such as Nelson in Lancashire and Handsworth in Birmingham continued to treat immigrants as different to whites, and still relied on intermediaries to reach the former.[42] This suited white activists, as it won them black votes while maintaining the established character of their organisations; it also bolstered the prestige of those who liaised between Labour and their own communities. Few, however, now saw it as a way of advancing integration: it was instead employed as its substitute.

As the election approached, James Callaghan considered producing a White Paper to redefine British nationality so as to restrict immigration further. More for practical than principled reasons he abandoned the idea, only for Heath's government to take it up.[43] It would have been unusual for a Labour Home Secretary to take the initiative on this matter: the government had twice restricted black immigration but only because party leaders feared the state of public opinion meant they had no alternative. Partly because of Wilson's tightening of immigration, it was less salient in 1970 than in 1964. Yet, if Conservative and Labour leaderships managed to prevent most of their candidates referring to immigration on the hustings, this did not mean voters ignored it. A subsequent academic survey suggested that Enoch Powell's regular interventions after 1968 so encouraged the public to imagine Conservative policy was closer to their prejudices than was Labour that Heath won an extra 6.7 per cent of votes cast.[44] Fearing that very outcome, Wilson wanted to pay no attention to Powell, as he assumed any rebuttals would concentrate minds on a subject from which, given the state of opinion, Labour could only lose. He was therefore extremely annoyed when Benn reacted to Powell raising immigration during the campaign by publicly comparing his views to those the Nazis held about the Jews. While Benn thought the issue too important to ignore, his speech nonetheless brought little light to the subject.[45]

Labour selected only one black parliamentary candidate in 1970, that being David Pitt, who first stood for the party in 1959. This time he contested the fairly safe seat of Clapham rather than, as previously, the Conservative bastion of Hampstead. Pitt, however, suffered a massive swing to the Conservatives, of 10.8 per cent, one far greater than experienced in comparable constituencies, and so failed to retain the seat for Labour. As an indication either that the party had done too little to promote integration or of the ingrained nature of white prejudice, a significant number of the party's accustomed supporters clearly felt unable to vote for a black candidate.[46]

The young

Some in the party believed Labour had created a problem for itself when the government enfranchised eighteen-year-olds. Although the young might have been broadly sympathetic to progressive ends, it was not clear how many would vote: at best, they were an unknown quantity. As it transpired, in 1970 Labour won the support of just over half of voters under twenty-five; this was higher, if not dramatically so, than support registered among some older cohorts (see Tables 9.2 and 9.3). The extent to which this influenced the overall result must remain unknown, especially as fewer than two-thirds of potential new electors were registered to vote.[47]

Labour members' mistrust of the young, especially students, survived the events of 1968; it had, after all, long pre-dated them. Yet, as the party's National Youth Officer pleaded, activists should not write off students because of their far-left activities – if only because there were too many to ignore.[48] Since cutting its links with the National Association of Labour Student Organisations (NALSO), the NEC had not seen the need for another means of mobilising their support. To meet good this lack, Students for a Labour Victory (SLV) was established in 1970 – although that was largely the brainchild of Jack Straw, President of the Leeds Students Union, and Hugh Anderson, President of the Cambridge Union. They persuaded a reluctant NEC of the advantages of backing this nominally independent body.[49]

It was hoped that SLV would appeal to students' apparent desire to see ideals put before self-interest and, while noting that in that regard Labour had fallen short – especially over immigration and Vietnam – it was said to have some achievements to its credit. Moreover, given the Conservative alternative, Labour was presented as students' only hope of ever seeing their ideals put into practice.[50] Although it was disbanded shortly after Wilson lost office, SLV led to the establishment of the National Organisation of Labour Students in 1971 as a permanent successor to NALSO, although it is doubtful whether this new body made more of an impact than its predecessor.

Labour remained stumped by the conundrum posed by the young in general. Bristol South East's aged agent, Herbert Rogers, was but one activist who, after 1970, made the familiar assertion that 'Something must be done to educate and organise the young voter', as it was 'useless to expect an intelligent political reaction' from untutored eighteen-year-olds.[51] Many would have sympathised with Wilson when he reportedly dismissed one long-haired heckler during the campaign by stating that: 'You're too young to know anything'.[52] At the very least, these attitudes did not help Labour attract youngsters on a significant scale – and during the 1970s its youth wing would once again fall victim to a small band of far-left zealots, this time those organised by Militant Tendency.

Participation

While the decline in the proportion of those voting in June might be read as a sign of increasing alienation from the political system, by 1970 most contemporaries believed the problem of 'participation' had receded. Certainly, in Scotland and Wales the nationalist challenge had evaporated. In 1969 Labour held on to Glasgow Gorbals in a by-election against what was feared would be an insuperable challenge from the Scottish National Party; and the investiture of Prince Charles as Prince of Wales in the same year helped mobilise unionist opinion against Plaid Cymru. Apparently confirming voters' real feelings about independence from Westminster, the 1970 election saw the nationalist parties win only 11 per cent of votes cast in their respective countries.

More widely, however, Benn, whose speeches during 1968 had done much to highlight the need to reconnect the people to established politics, thought one cause of Labour's defeat had been its failure to address the concerns of those 'new citizens' who demanded more self-government.[53] His was not quite a lone voice. In 1969 an editorial in *Socialist Commentary*, reflecting the views of revisionists like Mackintosh, stated that student radicals had exposed real problems with representative democracy, in particular the remoteness of decision-making. Despite this, all the political parties, and Labour in particular, were 'geared to the traditional political process stemming from another era; their members seem to spend endless hours debating resolutions calling on the Government to do this or that, or condemning it for not doing the other – most of which is a futile exercise, altering nothing'. There was, it suggested, a pressing need to reconsider how the party related to society in light of its failure to make links with those 'practical idealists' among the young. However, the only concrete measure *Socialist Commentary* proposed was Benn's earlier (and by then frustrated) Citizens for Labour initiative.[54]

The loss of hitherto impregnable council majorities across the country during 1967 and 1968 had also forced some activists to rethink their relationship with the communities they hoped to serve. In 1967 Labour lost control of Salford City Council for the first time since 1945, and then failed to win it back the following year. This initially galvanised activists to criticise how they conducted politics locally. While many blamed government policy for the swing in Salford, it was nonetheless appreciated that their own organisation needed to be 'drastically overhauled' if it was ever to regain a majority. This sentiment led to the promise to create a 'new form of meeting' in wards, by cutting out routine and stressing political debate and the discussion of local issues.[55] Wards became more active than they had been for many years – running recruitment campaigns, distributing leaflets, organising petitions and holding public meetings – for they could openly oppose the shortcomings of what was now Conservative Council policy and exploit popular discontent over issues such as rehousing and traffic congestion. The party also became more involved with tenants' associations, bodies that in the past some had seen in threatening terms.[56]

The response to defeat in neighbouring Manchester was more muted. Nonetheless, even there the chair of Newton Heath ward considered the Labour Group of councillors should produce a 'Policy that the people want and not what they want them to have'.[57] Defeat also meant Ardwick ward revived its advice centre and ran it weekly – if only because the newly elected Conservative councillors did the same.[58] As the City of Cardiff Labour Party declared, the route back to power meant activists 'must start again with leaflets and knocking on doors and [holding] public meetings'. Labour 'must become a *Movement* and not just a collection of administrators', while wards should become more involved in their own communities by tackling problems themselves rather than simply reporting them to the relevant authority.[59]

The extent to which this meant reviving old – rather than creating new – ways of doing politics should be clear. Even so, Labour's 1970 manifesto highlighted to an unprecedented extent the party's desire to increase more direct participation in decision-making. Although participation was still considered a marginal issue by many, it had nonetheless started to shuffle in from the wings. The creation of the Crowther-Hunt Commission meant constitutional change remained alive and if the motives of Cabinet ministers like Callaghan for establishing this body can be questioned, there were, it should be recalled, others who hoped it would lead to a federal Britain.

Conclusion

This work has been underpinned by the assumption that Labour's generally unimpressive post-war electoral performances were not the inevitable result of cultural change. In line with much of what has been described as the 'new political history', the relationship between party and society has been interpreted as being determined by a combination of the peculiar circumstances in which Labour existed and the party's own understanding of and response to that context.[60] It was, therefore, at least possible that the party could have done better, had members more accurately identified the nature and meaning of change and responded in the appropriate manner. Some elements in the party did react much more positively than has usually been supposed but, overall, Labour hindered rather than helped itself. However, the dominant response to that failure, or at least Wilson's loss of office – the 'return to class' – was probably even more disastrous for the party's longer-term fortunes. But that is another story.

The book's main focus has been on what was said and done (and not done) within the Labour Party. This is not because, on its own, the party's internal culture explained its electoral fortunes. After all, Labour won one of its most famous victories, in 1966, despite a crumbling organisation; and the party lost in 1959 and 1970 for reasons more compelling than, for example, many members' hostility to the young. Instead, the work has concentrated on Labour's internal culture to promote a broader understanding of the post-war party, to demonstrate its possibilities and limitations at this particular moment in its history. One motive was quite basic. Little is known about this culture, which has led historians to make sweeping – and often inaccurate – generalisations about its character. If nothing else, therefore, this work should encourage a more empathetic appreciation of the party's plight: so far as Labour is concerned, it is time we understood a little more and condemned a little less. Moreover, ultimately, even if political scientists and historians cannot precisely measure its impact at any particular general election, Labour's internal culture played a significant part in what, at one point in the 1980s, looked like its terminal decline.

If Labour's inability to exploit change should no longer be seen as exclusively dictated by structural factors, this failure was, however, always likely. No party is able to interpret contemporary developments in a purely 'pragmatic' manner. As society is in constant flux – and in the 1960s that was especially the case – no one can hope to acquire a totally accurate knowledge of those capricious forces that shape this dynamic. Moreover, any picture of society a party may assemble can be viewed only through the inevitably distorting lens of its established ideological tradition, or 'discourse' if you will. Thus, readers should have been struck by how far Labour members – self-conscious reformers like Tony Benn as much as more conservative figures such as James Callaghan – looked on events via a framework constructed well before Clement Attlee became Prime Minister. This could be an optimistic outlook, being underpinned by the MacDonaldite confidence that most contemporary developments could be integrated within the party's wider purpose. It was, however, ultimately disabling, insofar as most assumed the party was under no obligation to change its nature to accommodate such developments better.

This reluctance to change the party in even some fairly modest ways was not informed just by political considerations, although some believed 'socialism' had achieved its least worst expression in the shape of the Labour Party. It was partly because members of any political party are unavoidably subject to society's prevailing cultural norms. These notions of how people should think and behave are, in fact, often more insidious in shaping perceptions than formal ideology, and can structure understandings of how a particular belief system may be made manifest at any one point in time. It is likely some readers were struck, for example, by contemporary claims that one could oppose black immigration and be a socialist. At the start of the twenty-first century this seems contradictory. Given a proper appreciation of the nature of British society during the 1960s, it should be understandable why to many – but not all – loyal Labour members it was an unremarkable proposition.

During the 'Golden Age' many established norms were attacked, albeit by a minority (although an articulate and loud one). This assault challenged not so much the ends of Labour politics as much as its means. With regard to the latter, party members believed socialism (however it was conceived) would come gradually as a result of conventional electoral work that focused on winning power at Westminster. While one object was to reconcile differences, the party would achieve this by largely basing itself on the support of a white, patriarchal working class, although remaining open to the help and guidance of enlightened members of the bourgeoisie. It was not exactly clear at the time how far those who criticised this strategy were harbingers of History or eccentrics soon to find a place in Posterity's dustbin. The Britain of 1970 was, after all, structurally very similar to that of 1960; if some keenly felt the impact of radical change, for others change was imperceptible. Therefore, party members' often sceptical response to criticism was at least understandable: if Labour's tradition generally pointed in the wrong direction at the time, the right road, to be fair, was never particularly clear.

When it came to arguments over cultural norms, Labour members broadly found themselves on one side of the argument, the one that favoured continuity – or at least incremental reform – over radical transformation. That so many were of the generation that remembered the 1930s and 1940s played a significant part here: theirs was a socialism of unemployment and austerity rather than affluence and freedom of expression. It was only in the years immediately following 1970 that party membership underwent a generational shift, when many of those who criticised the party in the 1960s tried to convert it to their way of doing politics.[61] The impact of these younger radicals and militant feminists on the party's electoral fortunes – one hesitates to lay all the blame for 1983 on their shoulders – suggests they hardly enjoyed a privileged insight into cultural change either.

In outlining Labour members' reaction to their party's defeat in 1970 it is, finally, striking how little their understanding of society had changed since the 1950s, perceptions that themselves harked back to the party's earliest days and before. The 'return to class' confirmed by the 1970 party conference was not an about-turn resulting from minds having been changed by experience. It was instead a question of the left, whose views had hitherto been sidelined, being able to assert themselves, thanks to unprecedented union support, over a parliamentary leadership still attached to an essentially (but apparently discredited) revisionist strategy. Those who, well before the 1959 general election, believed Labour's purpose was largely defined by representing the interests of mainly male-orientated unions could now exert an influence, along with the newly arrived younger radicals, over policy-making previously denied them. This they did with alacrity.[62]

In a similar vein, party officials noted that the 1970 campaign had exposed well known organisational deficiencies, principally a lack of money, of young and motivated activists as well as of experienced agents.[63] As of old, some considered these flaws could be overcome if the right evangelical spirit was allied to hard work in the constituencies. The former minister Arthur Skeffington was due to chair Labour's 1970 conference but, stricken by terminal illness, he was unable to preside. Skeffington had, however, written his chair's address, which Sir Harry Nicholas, the party's ineffectual General Secretary, read out to delegates as its mute author sat on the platform. Noting an apparent upsurge in enthusiasm for Labour immediately after the election, Skeffington, via Nicholas, appealed as follows:

> *This time*, comrades, we *must* tap that source of support. Every ward must have a membership drive. Try and get one or two collectors from among your new members. Organisation doesn't win elections but it helps! We need more members and more money, so that we can take full advantage of our next electoral opportunity.[64]

Skeffington was a dying man and his attachment to past methods was emotionally understandable; even so, both for him and for those who sat listening and agreeing with his words, time might as well have been standing still.

Notes

The place of publication is London unless otherwise specified.

1 *Marxism Today*, April 1982, p. 41.
2 J. Campbell, *Edward Heath. A Biography* (1993), pp. 263–72.
3 H. Wilson, *The Labour Government, 1964–70* (Harmondsworth, 1971), pp. 952–6.
4 Labour Party Archive (LPA), Judith Hart papers, Section 10, File Hart 10/6, Speech to the South West Region annual meeting, 14 March 1970.
5 *Guardian* and *The Times*, 9 April 1969.
6 *Report of the Forty-Seventh National Conference of Labour Women* (1970), p. 13.
7 T. Benn, *Office Without Power. Diaries, 1968–72* (1988), pp. 274, 277, 281; Wilson, *Government*, pp. 979–83; letter from J. Haines, *Sunday Telegraph*, 21 August 1994.
8 M. Williams, *Inside Number 10* (1975), p. 263.
9 LPA, NEC, Organisation Sub-committee minutes, 5 May 1970, Progress report on the pre-general election campaign, NAD/34/5/70.
10 This account is based upon Calderdale Archives, Halifax CLP papers, TU: 28/5 and 6, Executive committee (EC) and general management committee (GMC) minutes, 1967–71, *passim*.

11 Bristol Record Office, Labour Party South West Region papers, 38423/48, Regional organiser's report, 27 January 1970, and H. Rogers, Parliamentary election, 18 June 1970, South East Bristol, 14 July 1970.

12 LPA, NEC minutes, 24 June 1970, Interim organisational report on the general election, NAD/40/6/70, and 22 July 1970, General election 1970, Report by the General Secretary; London Metropolitan Archive (LMA), Greater London Labour Party papers (unsorted), J. S. Keys, Southern organising area report on the general election 1970, 23 June 1970, and L. Sims, Report to the National Agent on the general election as it related to Greater London, 25 June 1970, and W. A. Jones, Interim organisational report, London North, 6 June 1970.

13 Williams, *Number 10*, pp. 263–4; B. Pimlott, *Wilson* (1992), pp. 554–8; P. Zeigler, *Wilson* (1993), pp. 346–54.

14 Wilson, *Government*, pp. 988–9.

15 A. Alexander and A. Watkins, *The Making of the Prime Minister 1970* (1970), p. 152.

16 Boldleian Library, Conservative Party Archive, CCO 130/11/4/7, J. Douglas, The public opinion polls in the 1970 general election, 19 November 1970; *The Times*, 3 August 1970.

17 D. Butler and M. Pinto-Duschinsky, *The British General Election of 1970* (1971), pp. 342, 345–51, 386–93.

18 *Report of the Sixty-Ninth Annual Conference of the Labour Party* (1970), p. 324.

19 Mitchell Library, Scottish Labour Party papers, TD 1384/1/6, Scottish Council executive committee minutes, 17 October 1970.

20 Working Class Movement Library (WCML), Salford East CLP papers, EC minutes, 25 June 1970.

21 South West papers, 38423/48, Regional organiser's report, 27 January 1970, and H. Rogers, Parliamentary election, 18 June 1970, South East Bristol, 14 July 1970; and *Sixty-Ninth Annual Conference of Labour*, p. 6.

22 South West papers, 38423/18/2, Bristol North West CLP, Quarterly reports for June 1966, September 1967 and June 1968.

23 LMA, J. W. Raisin papers, Acc 2783/JWR/ORG/68/74, organiser's report.

24 *Report of the Forty-Eighth National Conference of Labour Women* (1971), p. 13; National Library of Wales (NLW), Brecon and Radnor CLP papers, 2, Brecon women's section minutes, 30 June 1970.

25 *Sixty-Ninth Annual Conference of Labour*, pp. 112–26.

26 Benn, *Office*, p. 306.

27 National Library of Scotland, John P. Mackintosh papers, Dep. 323//291, Jockeying for position, n.d. (but 1970).

28 A. Crosland, 'A social democratic Britain', *Fabian Tract*, 404 (1970).

29 C. Mayhew, *Party Games* (1969), pp. 94–5.

30 British Library of Political and Economic Science, Anthony Crosland papers, 4/13/21–3, Report of discussion, n.d. (but autumn 1970).

31 Public Record Office (PRO), LAB 43/568, Lee to Wilson, 10 February 1970.

32 *Forty-Seventh Conference of Women*, pp. 26–7; *Report of the Forty-Eighth National Conference of Labour Women* (1971), pp. 12–13; *Labour Woman*, 60:6 (1970), p. 103; Butler and Pinto-Duschinsky, *1970*, pp. 156–6, 221–3, 326.

33 'Labour must face challenges', *Labour Woman*, 60:6 (1970), p. 108.

34 *Sixty-Ninth Conference of Labour*, p. 125.

35 *Forty-Eighth Conference of Women*, p. 4.

36 NLW, Labour Party of Wales papers, 124, Flintshire and Denbighshire Labour Women's Advisory Council minutes, 18 March 1971.

37 See, for example, M. Creear, 'Gender, class and political activism in the

North West: Labour's women's organisation in the 1970s', *North West Labour History Journal*, 27 (2002).

38 *Forty-Seventh Conference of Women*, pp. 29–32.

39 LPA, National Labour Women's Advisory Committee (NLWAC) minutes, 12 December 1969, 21 July and 21 October 1970, 20 January 1971; *Forty-Eighth Conference of Women*, p. 51.

40 NLW, Labour Party of Wales papers, 121, East Glamorgan Labour Women's Advisory Council papers, Annual conference minutes, 21 February 1970.

41 *Report of the Sixty-Seventh Annual Conference of the Labour Party* (1968), p. 285.

42 WCML, Nelson and Colne CLP papers, Nelson Labour party minutes, 21 April 1970; Modern Records Centre, Handsworth CLP papers, MSS 8/4/1, Election of Fred Howell in Handsworth, 6 May 1971.

43 PRO, HO 376/126, Callaghan to Wilson, 18 February 1969; Commonwealth immigration meeting, 13 February 1969; Draft outline of White Paper on Commonwealth immigration and community relations, n.d.; and HO 344/285, Note of meeting, 31 July 1969.

44 D. T. Studlar, 'Policy voting in Britain: the coloured immigration issue in the 1964, 1966 and 1970 general elections', *American Political Science Review*, 72:1 (1978), p. 62.

45 Benn, *Office*, pp. 287–9.

46 Butler and Pinto-Duschinsky, *1970*, pp. 295, 341 and 408.

47 *Ibid.*, p. 263.

48 *Labour Organiser*, 49:571 (1970), p. 110.

49 LPA, NEC Youth Sub-committee (YSC) minutes, 14 January 1970, Report of working party on labour student organisation, NAD/11/1/70.

50 YSC minutes, Students for a Labour Victory, 10 March 1970.

51 South West Region papers, 38423/48, H. Rogers, Parliamentary election, 18 June 1970, South East Bristol, 14 July 1970.

52 Alexander and Watkins, *Prime Minister*, p. 153.

53 See his 'The new politics: a Socialist reconnaissance', reprinted in Benn, *Office*, pp. 507–8.

54 Editorial, *Socialist Commentary*, March 1969.

55 Salford Archives, Salford West CLP papers, GMC minutes, 21 September 1967; Salford East CLP papers, Trinity ward minutes, 2 November 1967.

56 Trinity ward minutes, 7 April 1960; Salford West CLP papers, GMC minutes, 19 October 1971; Salford East CLP papers, EC minutes, 2 July 1972.

57 Manchester Local Studies Library (MLSL), Newton Heath ward papers, M147, minutes, 19 May 1967.

58 MLSL, Ardwick ward papers, M435/1, minutes, 5 July and 11 September 1967.

59 NLW, City of Cardiff Labour Party papers, A programme for Cardiff, n.d. (but 1968).

60 L. Black, '"What kind of people are you?" Labour, the people and the new political history', in J. Callaghan, S. Fielding and S. Ludlam (eds), *Interpreting the Labour Party: Approaches to Labour Politics and History* (Manchester, 2004).

61 P. Whiteley, *The Labour Party in Crisis* (1983), pp. 53–80.

62 For more on the period after 1970, see M. Wickham-Jones, *Economic Strategy and the Labour Party* (1996).

63 NEC minutes, 24 June 1970, Interim organisational report on the general election, NAD/40/6/70.

64 *Sixty-Ninth Annual Conference of Labour*, p. 87. Emphasis in original.

Bibliography

Abbreviations used in bibliography and chapter notes

BLPES British Library of Political and Economic Science, London School of
       Economics
BPL Birmingham Public Library
BRO Bristol Record Office
ECRO Essex County Record Office, Colchester
HLRO House of Lords Record Office, Westminster
LMA London Metropolitan Archive
LPA Labour Party Archive, Manchester
MLSL Manchester Local Studies Library
MRC Modern Records Centre, University of Warwick
NLS National Library of Scotland, Edinburgh
NLW National Library of Wales, Aberystwyth
PRO Public Record Office, Kew
SLSL Southwark Local Studies Library
WCML Working Class Movement Library, Salford
WYA West Yorkshire Archives, Bradford

Official records

Government records (PRO)

AT 35	Department of Local Government and Regional Planning
BN 29	Ministry of Health
BT 298	Board of Trade
CAB 128, 129, 130, 134, 151, 152, 165	Cabinet Office
ED 188, 207	Ministry of Education
HLG 120, 131, 136	Ministry of Housing and Local Government
HO 221, 223, 291, 328, 344, 376, 389	Home Office
LAB 8, 10, 28, 43, 111	Ministry of Labour
MT 87	Ministry of Transport
PREM 13	Prime Minister's Office

Official publications

Hansard
Report of a Court of Inquiry under Sir Jack Stamp into a dispute concerning sewing machinists employed by the Ford Motor Company Limited (1968, Cmnd 3749)

Labour Party records

National records (LPA)

Discrimination Against Women Study Group papers
Industrial Democracy Working Party papers
National Executive Committee minutes
  Campaign Sub-committee minutes
  Commonwealth Sub-committee minutes
  Home Policy Sub-committee minutes
  National Labour Women's Advisory Committee minutes
  Organisation Sub-committee minutes
  Publicity and Political Education Sub-committee minutes
  Regional and Local Government Advisory Committee minutes
  Youth Sub-committee minutes
Race Relations and Immigration Collection
Race Relations Study Group papers
Study Group on Education papers
Study Group on Immigration papers
Youth Commission papers

Regional records

East Midlands, MRC
Eastern, ECRO
London/Greater London, LMA
Scotland, Mitchell Library, Glasgow
South West, BRO
Wales, NLW
West Midlands, MRC

Borough/city records

Birmingham Borough, BPL
Cardiff City, NLW
City of Bradford, WYA
Coventry Borough, MRC

Constituency records

Ashton-under-Lyne, Tameside Local Studies Library
Bedford, BLPES
Bermondsey, SLSL
Bethnal Green, Bancroft Library, Mile End

Birmingham Northfield, BPL
Bradford East, WYA
Brecon and Radnor, NLW
Bristol North West, BRO
Bristol South East, BRO
Bristol West, BRO
Brixton, Lambeth Archives
Cardiff South East, NLW
Carmarthen, NLW
Chigwell and Ongar, ECRO
Clapham, Lambeth Archives
Coventry North, MRC
Dulwich, SLSL
Edinburgh South, NLS
Glasgow Maryhill, Mitchell Library, Glasgow
Halifax, Calderdale Archives, Halifax
Handsworth, MRC
Ilford South, LMA
Leith, NLS
Maldon, ECRO
Merioneth, NLW
Merton and Morden, BLPES
Nelson and Colne, WCML
North Kensington, BLPES
Norwood, LMA
Poplar, Bancroft Library, Mile End
Rugby, MRC
Salford East, WCML
Salford West, Salford Archives
Selly Oak, MRC
Shoreditch and Finsbury, Hackney Archives
Southall, LMA
St Marylebone, Westminster Archives
Stockport Central, Stockport Local Heritage Library
Toxteth, Merseyside Records Office, Liverpool
Warwick and Leamington, MRC

Ward records

Ardwick, MLSL
Newton Heath, MLSL

Labour-related organisation records

British–Asian Overseas Fellowship papers, LPA
Edinburgh Fabian Society papers, NLS
Socialist Vanguard Group papers, MRC
Tribune Group papers, LPA

National Labour Party publications (LPA)

Reports of the annual conferences of the Labour Party
Reports of the national conferences of Labour women

Challenge to Britain (1953)
Personal Freedom (1956)
Take It From Here (1956)
Towards Equality (1956)
Hi! (1958)
Racial Discrimination (1958)
The Future Labour Offers You (1958)
Britain Belongs to You (1959)
Housewives' Choice (1959)
The Britain We Want (1959)
The Younger Generation. Report of the Labour Party Youth Commission (1959)
Let's Go! (1960)
Is This a Portrait of You? (1961)
Science and the Future of Britain (1961)
Signposts for the Sixties (1961)
The Integration of Immigrants (1962)
'Let's Go' Campaign Guide (1963)
Let's Have a Party That Will Get Things Done (1963)
Let's Go with Labour for the New Britain (1964)
Vote for Them (1964)
Don't Let Men Make All the Decisions! (1965)
Report of the Port Transport Study Group (1966)
Time for Decision (1966)
Industrial Democracy (1967)
Race Relations (1967)
Discrimination Against Women (1968)
Progress and Change (1968)
Agenda for a Generation (1969)
Now Britain's Strong Let's Make It a Great Place to Live In (1970)
Youth Voice (1970)
Women and the Labour Party (1971)

Regional Labour Party publications (LPA)

Labour Party Scottish Council, *Report of the Executive Committee to the 52nd Annual Conference* (Glasgow, 1967)
Labour Party Scottish Council, *Report of the Executive Committee to the 53rd Annual Conference* (Glasgow, 1968)
Labour Party Scottish Council, *Report of the Executive Committee to the 54th Annual Conference* (Glasgow, 1969)
Labour Party Scottish Council, *Scottish Government. Interim Report* (Glasgow, 1969)
Labour Party Scottish Council, *Special Report on Scottish Government* (Glasgow, 1958)
Welsh Regional Council of Labour, *Labour's Policy for Wales* (Cardiff, 1954)

National Labour periodicals (LPA)

Focus
Labour Organiser
Labour Woman
New Advance
Young Socialist

Local Labour periodicals

Abingdon Labour Party Constituency Digest, LPA
Bagshot and Egham Clarion, LPA
Barons Court Citizen, LPA
Chelsea Labour News, Greater London Region papers
Contact, Warwick and Leamington CLP papers
East Ham South Citizen, LPA
Huddersfield Citizen, LPA
King's Left, Greater London Region papers
Labour Life, St Marylebone CLP papers
Labour News (up to 1962 *London News*), London Region papers
Labour News. Journal of Yardley Constituency Labour Party, West Midlands Region
    papers
Leeds Weekly Citizen, Charles Pannell papers
London News (after 1962 *Labour News*), London Region papers
News-Sheet, South West Region papers
North Kensington Labour Questionmaster, North Kensington CLP papers
Richmond and Barnes Clarion, LPA
Romford, Hornchurch and Brentwood Labour Voice, LPA
Warrington and District Labour News, Warrington Local Studies Library

Labour-inclined periodicals

Focus, BLPES
Forward, LPA
Socialist Commentary, LPA
Tribune, LPA

Personal papers

George Brown, Bodleian Library, Oxford
Frank Cousins, MRC
Anthony Crosland, BLPES
Maurice Edelman, MRC
Bob Edwards, LPA
Ron Evans, NLW
Anthony Greenwood, Bodleian Library
James Griffiths, NLW
Judith Hart, LPA
Deian Hopkin, NLW
Emrys Hughes, NLS

Hugh Jenkins, BLPES
Brynmor John, NLW
George Lawson, NLS
John P. Mackintosh, NLS
Ian Mikardo/Jo Richardson, LPA
Charles Pannell, HLRO
Morgan Phillips, LPA
Cliff Protheroe, NLW
J. W. Raisin, LMA
Baron Shackleton, HLRO
Edgar Simpkins, BLPES
Reginald Sorenson, HLRO
Frank Soskice, HLRO
Eirene White, NLW
Arthur Woodburn, NLS

Other parties' records

Conservative Party Archive, Bodleian Library
   General elections, 1959–70 files
   Immigration, 1958–60, 1967–72 files
   Women, 1946–73, 1968 files
   Youth, 1960–75, 1966–73 files
Wood Green and Lower Tottenham Conservative Association, LMA

Scottish National Party, NLS

Other archives

Tom Harrisson Mass-Observation Archive, Beveridge Social Services Survey, University of Sussex

Autobiographies, memoirs and diaries

The place of publication is London unless otherwise specified.

Benn, T., *Out of the Wilderness. Diaries, 1963–67* (1987)
Benn, T., *Office Without Power. Diaries, 1968–72* (1988)
Benn, T., *Years of Hope. Diaries, Papers and Letters 1940–1962* (1994)
Callaghan, J., *Time and Chance* (1987)
Castle, B., *The Castle Diaries, 1964–1976* (1990)
Castle, B., *Fighting All The Way* (1993)
Colquhoun, M., *A Woman in the House* (Brighton, 1980)
Crossman, R., *The Diaries of a Cabinet Minister. Volume I* (1975)
Crossman, R., *The Diaries of a Cabinet Minister. Volume II* (1977)
Crossman, R., *The Diaries of Cabinet Minister. Volume III* (1977)
Jones, J., *Union Man* (1986)

Manning, L., *A Life for Education* (1970)
Morgan, J. (ed.), *The Backbench Diaries of Richard Crossman* (1981)
Owen, D., *Time to Declare* (Harmondsworth, 1992)
Pimlott, B. (ed.), *The Political Diary of Hugh Dalton, 1918–40, 1945–50* (1986)
Rowbotham, S., *Promise of a Dream. Remembering the Sixties* (Harmondsworth, 2000)
Short, E., *Whip to Wilson* (1989)
Smith, T. D., *An Autobiography* (Newcastle upon Tyne, 1970)
Williams, M., *Inside Number 10* (1975)
Wilson, H., *The Labour Government, 1964–70* (Harmondsworth, 1971)
Wilson, H., *The Governance of Britain* (1977)

Contemporary sources

Abrams, M., *The Teenage Consumer* (1959)
Abrams, M., 'Opinion polls and party propaganda', *Public Opinion Quarterly*, 28:1 (1964)
Abrams, M., R. Rose, and R. Hinden, *Must Labour Lose?* (Harmondsworth, 1960)
Abrams, P. and A. Little, 'The young activist in British politics', *British Journal of Sociology*, 16:4 (1965)
Albu, A., 'The organisation of industry', in R. H. S. Crossman (ed.), *New Fabian Essays* (1952)
Alexander, A. and A. Watkins, *The Making of the Prime Minister 1970* (1970)
Ali, T., 'The extra-parliamentary opposition', in T. Ali (ed.), *New Revolutionaries. Left Opposition* (1969)
Almond, G. A. and S. Verba, *The Civic Culture. Political Attitudes and Democracy in Five Nations* (Princeton, 1963)
Anderson, P., 'The left in the fifties', *New Left Review*, 29 (1965)
Arblaster, A., 'Student militancy and the collapse of reformism', in R. Miliband and J. Saville (eds), *Socialist Register 1970* (1970)
Arblaster, A., 'Participation: context and conflict', in G. Parry (ed.), *Participation in Politics* (Manchester, 1972)
Banton, M., *White and Coloured. The Behaviour of British People Towards Coloured Immigrants* (New Brunswick, 1960)
Barker, A., 'Participation in politics', in B. Lapping and G. Radice (eds), *More Power to the People. Young Fabian Essays on Democracy in Britain* (1968)
Bealey, F., J. Blondel and W. P. McCann, *Constituency Politics* (1965)
Benney, M., A. P. Gray and R. H. Pear, *How People Vote. A Study of Electoral Behaviour in Greenwich* (1956)
Bevan, A., *In Place of Fear* (1952)
Bing, I., 'New approaches to democracy', in I. Bing (ed.), 'The Labour Party. An organisational study', *Fabian Tract*, 407 (1971)
Birch, A.,H., *Small Town Politics* (Oxford, 1959)
Blackburn, R. and A. Cockburn (eds), *The Incompatibles: Trade Union Militancy and the Consensus* (Harmondsworth, 1967)
Blackstone, T., K. Gales, R. Hadley and W. Lewis, *Students in Conflict. LSE in 1967* (1970)
Blythe, R., *Akenfield* (Harmondsworth, 1969)
Bochel, J. M., 'Activists in the Conservative and Labour parties. A study of ward secretaries in Manchester', MA thesis, University of Manchester (1965)
Booker, C., *The Neophiliacs* (1969)

Budge, I. and D. W. Urwin, *Scottish Political Behaviour* (1966)

Butler, D. and A. King, *The British General Election of 1964* (1965)

Butler, D. and A. King, *The British General Election of 1966* (1966)

Butler, D. and M. Pinto-Duschinsky, *The British General Election of 1970* (1971)

Butler, D. and R. Rose, *The British General Election of 1959* (1960)

Butler, D. and D. Stokes, *Political Change in Britain* (Harmondsworth, 1971)

Coates, K., 'Democracy and workers' control', in P. Anderson (ed.), *Towards Socialism* (1965)

Coates, K., *The Crisis of British Socialism* (Nottingham, 1971)

Coates, K. and R. Silburn, *Poverty. The Forgotten Englishman* (Harmondsworth, 1970)

Coates, K. and T. Topham, 'The Labour Party's plans for industrial democracy', *Institute for Workers' Control Pamphlet No. 5* (Nottingham, 1968)

Crane, P., 'What's in a party image?', *Political Quarterly*, 30:3 (1959)

Crewe, I., A. Fox and N. Day, *The British Electorate 1963–1992* (Cambridge, 1995)

Crosland, C. A. R., 'The transition from capitalism', in R. H. S. Crossman (ed.), *New Fabian Essays* (1952)

Crosland, C. A. R., *The Future of Socialism* (1956)

Crosland, C. A. R., *The Conservative Enemy* (1962)

Crosland, A., 'A social democratic Britain', *Fabian Tract*, 404 (1970)

Crosland, A., *Socialism Now* (1974)

Crossman, R. H. S., *Planning for Freedom* (1965)

Dennis, N., F. Henriques and C. Slaughter, *Coal is Our Life* (1969)

Donnison, D. V. and D. E. G. Plowman, 'The functions of local Labour parties', *Political Studies*, 2:3 (1954)

Eadie, A. and J. Sillars, *Don't Butcher Scotland's Future* (Glasgow, 1969)

Edmonds, J., 'The worker', in B. Lapping and G. Radice (eds), *More Power to the People* (1968)

Fienburgh, W. and the Manchester Fabian Society, 'Put policy on the agenda', *Fabian Journal*, February 1952

Foot, M., 'Credo of the Labour left – interview', *New Left Review*, 49 (1968)

Foot, P., 'The seamen's struggle', in R. Blackburn and A, Cockburn (eds), *The Incompatibles: Trade Union Militancy and the Consensus* (Harmondsworth, 1967)

Fyvel, T. R., *The Troublemakers. Rebellious Youth in an Affluent Society* (New York, 1964)

Gaitskell, H., 'Socialism and nationalisation', *Fabian Tract*, 300 (1956)

Gaitskell, H., 'The economic aims of the Labour party', *Political Quarterly*, 26 (1956)

Gallup, G. H. *The Gallup International Public Opinion Polls. Great Britain, 1937–75. Volume I* (New York, 1976)

Glass, R., *Newcomers. The West Indians in London* (1960)

Goldthorpe, J. H., D. Lockwood, F. Bechhofer and J. Platt, *The Affluent Worker: Industrial Attitudes and Behaviour* (Cambridge, 1968)

Goldthorpe, J. H., D. Lockwood, F. Bechhofer and J. Platt, *The Affluent Worker in the Class Structure* (Cambridge, 1969)

Gould, J., '"Riverside": a Labour constituency, *Fabian Journal*, November 1954

Griffiths, J. A. G., *et al.*, *Coloured Immigrants in Britain* (Oxford, 1960)

Griffiths, P., *A Question of Colour?* (1966)

Hamilton, M. A., *The Labour Party Today* (1939)

Harrisson, T., *Britain Revisited* (1961)

Hill, C. S., *How Colour Prejudiced Is Britain?* (1965)

Hill, D. M., *Participating in Local Affairs* (Harmondsworth, 1970)

Hoggart, R., *The Uses of Literacy* (Harmondsworth, 1958)

Hoggart, R., *Speaking to Each Other. Volume I* (Harmondsworth, 1970)
Institute for Workers' Control, *Report of the 5th National Conference on Workers' Control and Democracy* (Nottingham, 1967)
Institute of Race Relations, *Colour and Immigration in the United Kingdom, 1968* (1968)
Jackson, B., *Working Class Community* (Harmondsworth, 1972)
Janosik, E. G., *Constituency Labour Parties in Britain* (1968)
Jay, D., *The Socialist Case* (1947)
Jay, D., *Socialism in the New Society* (1962)
Jenkins, H., *Rank and File* (1980)
Jenkins, H., R. Lewis, G. Southgate and W. Wolfgang, 'The red sixties', *Victory for Socialism Pamphlet* (1957)
Jenkins, H. and W. Wolfgang, 'Tho' cowards flinch', *Victory for Socialism Pamphlet* (1956)
Jenkins, R., *The Labour Case* (Harmondsworth, 1959)
Jenkins, R., *Essays and Speeches* (1967)
Jones, G. S., 'The meaning of the student revolt', in A. Cockburn and R. Blackburn, *Student Power* (Harmondsworth, 1969)
Jones, J., 'The right to participate – key to industrial progress', *TGWU Pamphlet* (1970)
Jupp, J., 'The discontents of youth', *Political Quarterly*, 40 (1969)
Kornhauser, W., *The Politics of Mass Society* (1960)
Lane, T. and K. Roberts, *Strike at Pilkingtons* (1971)
Levin, B., *The Pendulum Years* (1970)
Mayhew, C., *Party Games* (1969)
McKitterick, T. E. M., 'The membership of the party', *Political Quarterly*, 31 (1960)
Mikardo, I., 'Trade unions in a full employment economy', in R. H. S. Crossman (ed.), *New Fabian Essays* (1952)
New Bristol Group, *Output 1962/63* (Bristol, 1963)
New Bristol Group, *Output 1963/64* (Bristol, 1964)
New Bristol Group, *Output 3* (Bristol, 1966)
Nichols, T. and P. Armstrong, *Workers Divided. A Study in Shopfloor Politics* (1976)
Parkin, F., *Middle Class Radicalism* (Manchester, 1968)
Pateman, C., *Participation and Democratic Theory* (Cambridge, 1970)
Pearson, J. and G. Turner, *The Persuasion Industry* (1965)
Pelling, H., 'Then and now: popular attitudes since 1945', in his *Popular Politics and Society in Late Victorian Britain* (1968)
Rex, J. and R. Moore, *Race, Community and Conflict. A Study of Sparkbrook* (Oxford, 1967)
Rose, E. J. B., *Colour and Citizenship* (1969)
Rose, P., 'Manchester Left Club on youth', *New Left Review*, 1 (1960)
Rose, R., *Influencing Voters* (1967)
Rowbotham, S., 'The beginnings of women's liberation in Britain', in M. Wandor (ed.), *The Body Politic. Women's Liberation in Britain* (1972)
Rowland, C., 'Labour publicity', *Political Quarterly*, 31:3 (1960)
Rowntree, S. and G. R. Lavers, *Poverty and the Welfare State* (1951)
Rustin, M., 'Young Socialists', *New Left Review*, 9 (1961)
Samuel, R., 'Dr. Abrams and the end of politics', *New Left Review*, 5 (1960)
Scanlon, H., 'The role of militancy', *New Left Review*, 46 (1967)
Scanlon, H., 'The way forward for workers' control', *Institute for Workers' Control Pamphlet No. 1* (Nottingham, 1968)
Sharpe, L. J., 'Brixton', in N. Deakin (ed.), *Colour and the British Electorate 1964* (1965)

Sherman, A., 'Deptford', in N. Deakin (ed.), *Colour and the British Electorate 1964* (1965)

Shils, E. and M. Young, 'The meaning of the Coronation', *Sociological Review*, 1 (1953)

Shore, P., *The Real Nature of Conservatism* (1952)

Spiers, M., 'Bradford', in N. Deakin (ed.), *Colour and the British Electorate 1964* (1965)

Thompson, E. P. (ed.), *Warwick University Ltd* (Harmondsworth, 1970)

Titmus, R. M., *Income Distribution and Social Change* (1962)

Trenaman, J. and D. McQuail, *Television and the Political Image* (1961)

Watkins, A., 'Labour in power', in G. Kaufman (ed.), *The Left* (1966)

West, R., 'Campaign journal', *Encounter*, December 1964

Westergaard, J. H., 'Sociology: the myth of classlessness', in R. Blackburn (ed.), *Ideology in Social Science* (1972)

White, E., 'Workers' control?', *Fabian Society Challenge Series Pamphlet No. 4* (1949)

Williams, R. (ed.), *May Day Manifesto 1968* (Harmondsworth, 1968)

Wilmott, P., *The Evolution of a Community* (1963)

Willmott, P., *Adolescent Boys of East London* (Harmondsworth, 1969)

Wilson, H., *The New Britain* (Harmondsworth, 1964)

Woolcott, D., 'Southall', in N. Deakin (ed.), *Colour and the British Electorate 1964* (1965)

Young, M. and P. Wilmott, *Family and Kinship in East London* (Harmondsworth, 1957)

Young, M. and P. Wilmott, *The Symmetrical Family* (Harmondsworth, 1975)

Zweig, F., *The Worker in an Affluent Society* (1961)

Zweig, F., *The Student in the Age of Anxiety* (1963)

Secondary sources

Almond, G. A., 'The intellectual history of the civic culture concept', in G. A. Almond and S. Verba (eds), *The Civic Culture Revisited* (Boston, 1980)

Bain, G. S. and R. Price, 'Union growth: dimensions, determinants and density', in G. S. Bain (ed.), *Industrial Relations in Britain* (Oxford, 1983)

Ballaster, R., M. Beetham, E. Fraser and S. Hebra, *Women's Worlds. Ideology, Femininity and the Woman's Magazine* (1991)

Barrow, L. and I. Bullock, *Democratic Ideas and the British Labour Movement, 1880–1914* (Cambridge, 1996)

Baucher, D., *The Feminist Challenge. The Movement for Women's Liberation in Britain and the USA* (1983)

Beer, S. H., *Britain Against Itself* (1982)

Beer, S. H., 'Why study British politics?', *British Politics Group Newsletter*, 100 (2000)

Black, A. and S. Brooke, 'The Labour Party, women, and the problem of gender, 1951–1966', *Journal of British Studies*, 36:4 (1997)

Black, L., *The Political Culture of the Left in Affluent Britain, 1951–64* (2003)

Black, L., '"What kind of people are you?" Labour, the people and the new political history', in J. Callaghan, S. Fielding and S. Ludlam (eds), *Interpreting the Labour Party: Approaches to Labour Politics and History* (Manchester, 2004)

Bourke, J., *Working-Class Cultures in Britain, 1890–1960* (1994)

Brivati, B., *Hugh Gaitskell* (1996)

Brooke, S., 'The Conservative Party, immigration and national identity, 1948–1968', in M. Francis and I. Zweiniger-Bargielowska (eds), *The Conservatives and British Society, 1880–1990* (Cardiff, 1996)

Butler, D., *British General Elections Since 1945* (Oxford, 1989)

Byrne, P., 'The politics of the women's movement', *Parliamentary Affairs*, 49:1 (1996)

Campbell, J., *Edward Heath. A Biography* (1993)

Capet, A., 'Rediscovering the "rediscovery of poverty" in the 1950s', paper presented to the conference 'Affluent Britain?', Bristol University, May 2002

Cesarani, D. (ed.), *The Making of Modern Anglo-Jewry* (Oxford, 1990)

Cheetham, J., 'Immigration', in A. H. Halsey (ed.), *Trends in British Society Since 1900* (1972)

Clapson, M., *Invincible Green Suburbs, Brave New Towns* (Manchester, 1998)

Clarke, P., 'The social democratic theory of the class struggle', in J. Winter (ed.), *The Working Class in Modern British History* (Cambridge, 1983)

Clarke, P. F., *Liberals and Social Democrats* (Cambridge, 1978)

Coates, D., 'Labour governments: old constraints and new parameters', *New Left Review*, 291 (1996)

Coates, D. and L. Panitch, 'The continuing relevance of the Milibandian perspective', in J. Callaghan, S. Fielding and S. Ludlam (eds), *Interpreting the Labour Party: Approaches to Labour Politics and History* (Manchester, 2004)

Collette, C., '"Daughters of the Newer Eve": The labour movement and women', in J. Fyrth (ed.), *Labour's Promised Land?* (1995)

Collette, C., 'Questions of gender: Labour and women', in B. Brivati and R. Heffernan (eds), *The Labour Party. A Centenary History* (2000)

Conekin, B., F. Mort and C. Waters, 'Introduction', in B. Conekin, F. Mort and C. Waters (eds), *Moments of Modernity. Reconstructing Britain, 1945–1964* (1999)

Creear, M., 'Gender, class and political activism in the North West: Labour's women's organisation in the 1970s', *North West Labour History Journal*, 27 (2002)

Crosland, S., *Tony Crosland* (1982)

Currie, R., *Industrial Politics* (Oxford, 1979)

Davies, A. and S. Fielding (eds), *Workers' Worlds. Cultures and Communities in Manchester and Salford, 1880–1939* (Manchester, 1992)

Davis, J., 'Rents and race in 1960s London: new light on Rachmanism', *Twentieth Century British History*, 12:1 (2001)

Dresser, M., 'The colour bar in Bristol', in R. Samuel (ed.), *Patriotism. Volume I* (1989)

Fielding, S., '"Don't know and don't care": popular political attitudes in Labour's Britain, 1945–51', in N. Tiratsoo (ed.), *The Attlee Years* (1991)

Fielding, S., 'Labourism in the 1940s', *Twentieth Century British History*, 3:2 (1992)

Fielding, S., *Class and Ethnicity. Irish Catholics in England, 1880–1939* (Buckingham, 1993)

Fielding, S., '"White heat" and white collars: the evolution of "Wilsonism"', in R. Coopey, S. Fielding and N. Tiratsoo (eds), *The Wilson Governments, 1964–70* (1993)

Fielding, S., 'Brotherhood and the brothers: responses to "coloured" immigration in the British Labour party, c. 1951–65', *Journal of Political Ideologies*, 3:1 (1998)

Fielding, S., '"Labourism" and the British Labour Party', in the Collection de l'Ecole Francaise de Rome – 267, *Les Familles Politiques en Europe Occidentale au XXe Siecle* (Rome, 2000)

Fielding, S., 'The Labour party and the recruitment of the young, 1945–70', in G. Orsina and G. Quagliariello (eds), *La Formazione della classe politica in Europa (1945–1956)* (Rome, 2000)

Fielding, S., 'The "penny farthing machine" revisited: Labour Party members and participation in the 1950s and 1960s', in C. Pierson and S. Tormey (eds), *Politics at the Edge* (2000)

Fielding, S., 'Activists against "affluence": Labour party culture during the "Golden Age", c. 1950–1970', *Journal of British Studies*, 40:2 (2001)

Fielding, S., '"But westward, look, the land is bright!" Labour's revisionists and the imagining of America, c. 1945–64', in J. Hollowell (ed.), *Twentieth-Century Anglo-American Relations* (2001)

Fielding, S., '"New" Labour and the "new" labour history', *Mitteilungsblatt des Instituts fur soziale Bewegungen*, 28 (2002)

Fielding, S., P. Thompson and N. Tiratsoo, *'England Arise!' The Labour Party and Popular Politics in 1940s Britain* (Manchester, 1995)

Finch, J. and P. Summerfield, 'Social reconstruction and the emergence of companionate marriage, 1945–59', in D. Clark (ed.), *Marriage, Domestic Life and Social Change* (1991)

Foote, G., *The Labour Party's Political Thought* (1997)

Fowler, D., *The First Teenagers. The Lifestyle of Young Wage-Earners in Interwar Britain* (1995)

Francis, M., *Ideas and Policies Under Labour 1945–1951* (Manchester, 1997)

Francis, M., 'Labour and gender', in D. Tanner, P. Thane and N. Tiratsoo (eds), *Labour's First Century* (Cambridge, 2000)

Francis, M. and I. Zweiniger-Bargielowska (eds), *The Conservatives and British Society, 1880–1990* (Cardiff, 1996)

Fryer, P., *Staying Power. The History of Black People in Britain* (1984)

Gallup Poll, 'Voting behaviour in Britain, 1945–1974', in R. Rose (ed.), *Studies in British Politics* (1976)

Giddens, A., *Beyond Left and Right* (Cambridge, 1994)

Gilroy, P., *'There Ain't No Black in the Union Jack'. The Cultural Politics of Race and Nation* (1987)

Glennester, H., 'Education and inequality', in P. Townsend and N. Bosanquet (eds), *Labour and Inequality* (1972)

Goldthorpe, J. H., *Social Mobility and Class Structure in Modern Britain* (Oxford, 1980)

Graves, P., *Labour Women: Women in British Working-Class Politics, 1918–1939* (Cambridge, 1994)

Green, E. H. H., *The Crisis of Conservatism. The Politics, Economics and Ideology of the British Conservative Party, 1880–1914* (1995)

Green, E. H. H., 'The Conservative party, the state and the electorate', in J. Lawrence and M. Taylor (eds), *Party, State and Society* (Aldershot, 1997)

Gwyn, W. B., 'The Labour party and the threat of bureaucracy', *Political Studies*, 29 (1971)

Gyford, J., *The Politics of Local Socialism* (1985)

Hall, S. and T. Jefferson (eds), *Resistance Through Rituals* (1976)

Halsey, A. H., 'Higher education', in A. H. Halsey (ed.), *Trends in British Society Since 1900* (1972)

Halsey, A. H., 'Government against poverty in school and community', in D. Wedderburn (ed.), *Poverty, Inequality and Class Structure* (Cambridge, 1974)

Halsey, A. H., *Change in British Society* (Oxford, 1985)

Hansen, R., *Citizenship and Immigration in Post-war Britain* (Oxford, 2000)

Hatton T. J. and R. E. Bailey, 'Seebohm Rowntree and the postwar poverty puzzle', *Economic History Review*, 53:2 (2000)

Heath, A., R. Jowell and J. Curtice, *How Britain Votes* (Oxford, 1985)

Heath, A., R. Jowell, J. Curtice, G. Evans, J. Field and S. Witherspoon, *Understanding Political Change. The British Voter, 1964–87* (Oxford, 1991)

Heffer, S., *Like the Roman. The Life of Enoch Powell* (1999)

Hinton, J., '1945 and the Apathy School', *History Workshop*, 43 (1997)

Hobsbawm, E., 'The Labour aristocracy in nineteenth century Britain', in his *Labouring Men* (1964)

Hobsbawm, E., 'The formation of British working class culture', in his *Worlds of Labour* (1984)

Hobsbawm, E., 'The making of the working class, 1870–1914', in his *Worlds of Labour* (1984)

Hobsbawm, E., *Age of Extremes. The Short Twentieth Century 1914–1991* (1995)

Hollis, P., *Jennie Lee. A Life* (Oxford, 1997)

Holmes, C., *John Bull's Island. Immigration and British Society, 1871–1971* (1988)

Horner, J., *Studies in Industrial Democracy* (1974)

Howard, A., *Crossman. The Pursuit of Power* (1990)

Howarth, D., A. J. Norval and Y. Stavrakakis (eds), *Discourse Theory and Political Analysis* (Manchester, 2000)

Howe, S., *Anticolonialism in British Politics. The Left and the End of Empire, 1918–1964* (Oxford, 1993)

Inglehart, R., 'The silent revolution in Europe: intergenerational change in post-industrial societies', *American Political Science Review*, 65:4 (1971)

Inglehart, R., *The Silent Revolution. Changing Values and Political Styles Among Western Publics* (Princeton, 1977)

Jones, R. M. and I. R. Jones, 'Labour and the nation', in D. Tanner, C. Williams and D. Hopkins (eds), *The Labour Party in Wales, 1900–2000* (Cardiff, 2000)

Jones, T., *Remaking the Labour Party* (1996)

Jones, T. K., 'Employee directors in the British Steel Corporation', in C. Balfour (ed.), *Participation in Industry* (1973)

Joyce, P., *Realignment of the Left? A History of the Relationship Between the Liberal Democrat and Labour Parties* (1999)

Katznelson, I., *Black Men, White Cities. Race, Politics and Migration in the United States, 1900–30, and Britain, 1948–68* (Oxford, 1973)

Kavanagh, D., 'Political culture in Great Britain: the decline of the civic culture', in G. A. Almond and S. Verba (eds), *The Civic Culture Revisited* (Boston, 1980)

Keating, M., 'The Labour party in Scotland, 1951–1964', in I. Donnachie, C. Harvie and I. S. Wood (eds), *Forward! Labour Politics in Scotland, 1888–1988* (Edinburgh, 1988)

Keating, M. and D. Bleiman, *Labour and Scottish Nationalism* (1979)

Kitschelt, H., *The Transformation of European Social Democracy* (Cambridge, 1994)

Kraushaar, R., 'Policy without protest: the dilemma of organising for change in Britain', in M. Harloe (ed.), *New Perspectives in Urban Change and Conflict* (1981)

Lancaster, B., 'Who's a real Coventry kid? Migration into 20th century Coventry', in T. Mason and B. Lancaster (eds), *Life and Labour in a 20th Century City. The Experience of Coventry* (Coventry, 1986)

Lawrence, J., *Speaking for the People. Party, Language and Popular Politics in England, 1867–1914* (Cambridge, 1998)

Lawrence, J. and M. Taylor, 'Introduction', in J. Lawrence and M. Taylor (eds), *Party, State and Society* (Aldershot, 1997)

Layton-Henry, Z., 'Labour's lost youth', *Journal of Contemporary History*, 11 (1976)

Lewis, J., 'Myrdal, Klein, "Women's two roles" and postwar feminism, 1945–1960', in H. L. Smith (ed.), *British Feminism in the Twentieth Century* (Aldershot, 1990)

Lewis, J., 'From equality to liberation: contextualising the emergence of the Women's Liberation Movement', in B. Moore-Gilbert and J. Seed (eds), *Cultural Revolution? The Challenge of the Arts in the 1960s* (1992)

Lindrop, F., 'Racism and the working class: strikes in support of Enoch Powell in 1968', *Labour History Review*, 66:1 (2001)

Lunn, K., 'Complex encounters: trade unions, immigration and racism', in J. McIlroy, N. Fishman and A. Campbell (eds), *British Trade Unions and Industrial Politics. Volume II* (Aldershot, 1999)

Lyon, A., 'A Labour view', in M. Loney and M. Allen (eds), *The Crisis of the Inner City* (1979)

MacIntyre, S., *A Proletarian Science. Marxism in Britain, 1917–1933* (Cambridge, 1980)

Marquand, D., 'Reaching for the levers', *Times Literary Supplement*, 11 April 1997

Marsden, D., 'Politicians, equality and comprehensives', in P. Townsend and N. Bosanquet (eds), *Labour and Inequality* (1972)

Marwick, A., *The Sixties* (Oxford, 1998)

May, J. D., 'Opinion structure of political parties: the special law of curvilinear disparity', *Political Studies*, 21 (1973)

Mayo, M., 'The history and early development of CDP', in R. Lees and G. Smith (eds), *Action-Research in Community Development* (1975)

McClymont, G., '"A squalid raffle"? Labour, affluence and the introduction of Premium Bonds, 1956', paper presented to the conference 'Affluent Britain?', Bristol University, May 2002

McHugh, D., 'A "mass" party frustrated? The development of the Labour party in Manchester, 1918–31', PhD thesis, University of Salford (2001)

McIlroy, J., 'Note on the Communist party and industrial politics', in J. McIlroy, N. Fishman and A. Campbell (eds), *British Trade Unions and Industrial Politics. Volume II* (Aldershot, 1999)

McIlroy, J. and A. Campbell, 'The high tide of trade unionism: mapping industrial politics, 1964–79', in J. McIlroy, N. Fishman and A. Campbell (eds), *British Trade Unions and Industrial Politics. Volume II* (Aldershot, 1999)

McKenzie, J. M., *Propaganda and Empire. The Manipulation of British Public Opinion 1880–1960* (Manchester, 1984)

McKibbin, R., *The Ideologies of Class. Social Relations in Britain, 1880–1950* (Oxford, 1991)

McKibbin, R., *Classes and Cultures: England, 1918–51* (Oxford, 1998)

Miliband, R., 'Socialism and the myth of the golden past', in R. Miliband and J. Saville (eds), *Socialist Register 1964* (1964)

Miliband, R., *Parliamentary Socialism* (1972)

Miliband, R., 'Politics and poverty', in D. Wedderburn (ed.), *Poverty, Inequality and Class Structure* (Cambridge, 1974)

Miliband, R., 'A state of de-subordination', *British Journal of Sociology*, 29:4 (1978)

Minkin, L., *The Labour Party Conference* (1978)

Minkin, L., *The Contentious Alliance* (Edinburgh, 1992)

Morgan, K. O., *Rebirth of a Nation. Wales, 1880–1980* (Oxford, 1981)

Morgan, K. O., *Labour in Power, 1945–1951* (Oxford, 1984)

Morgan, K. O., *The People's Peace. British History 1945–1990* (Oxford, 1992)

Morgan, K. O., *Callaghan. A Life* (Oxford, 1997)

Mulgan, G., *Politics in an Antipolitical Age* (Cambridge, 1994)

Musgrove, F., *Ecstacy and Holiness. Counter Culture and the Open Society* (1974)

Osgerby, B., *Youth in Britain Since 1945* (Oxford, 1998)

Panitch, L., *Social Democracy and Industrial Militancy* (Cambridge, 1976)

Panitch, L. and C. Leys, *The End of Parliamentary Socialism* (1997)

Parkinson, M., 'The Labour party and the organisation of secondary education', MA thesis, University of Manchester (1968)

Paul, K., *Whitewashing Britain. Race and Citizenship in the Postwar Era* (Ithaca, 1997)

Pearson, G., *Hooligan. A History of Respectable Fears* (1983)

Pilkington, E., *Beyond the Mother Country. West Indians and the Notting Hill White Riots* (1988)

Pimlott, B., *Wilson* (1992)

Pugh, M., 'Domesticity and the decline of feminism, 1930–1950', in H. L. Smith (ed.), *British Feminism in the Twentieth Century* (Aldershot, 1990)

Rae, J., *The Public School Revolution* (1981)

Reid A. and E. Biagini (eds), *Currents of Radicalism. Popular Radicalism, Organized Labour and Party Politics in Britain, 1850–1914* (Cambridge, 1991)

Reynolds, D., *Rich Relations. The American Occupation of Britain, 1942–1945* (1995)

Richards, M. P. M. and B. J. Elliott, 'Sex and marriage in the 1960s and 1970s', in D. Clark (ed.), *Marriage, Domestic Life and Social Change* (1991)

Riddell, N., *Labour in Crisis. The Second Labour Government, 1929–31* (Manchester, 1999)

Roberts, E., *Women and Families. An Oral History, 1940–1970* (Oxford, 1995)

Rollett, C. and J. Parker, 'Population and family', in A. H. Halsey (ed.), *Trends in British Society Since 1900* (1972)

Rubinstein, D. and B. Simon, *The Evolution of the Comprehensive School* (1973)

Sampson, A., *Macmillan. A Study in Ambiguity* (Harmondsworth, 1968)

Samuel R. and G. S. Jones, 'The Labour party and social democracy', in R. Samuel and G. S. Jones (eds), *Culture, Ideology and Politics* (1982)

Sassoon, D., *One Hundred Years of Socialism* (1997)

Schwarz, B., 'Politics and rhetoric in the age of mass culture', *History Workshop Journal*, 46 (1998)

Seed, J., 'Hegemony postponed: the unravelling of the culture of consensus in Britain in the 1960s', in B. Moore-Gilbert and J. Seed (eds), *Cultural Revolution? The Challenge of the Arts in the 1960s* (1992)

Shaw, E., *Discipline and Discord in the Labour Party* (Manchester, 1988)

Sinfield, A., *Literature, Politics and Culture in Postwar Britain* (Oxford, 1989)

Solomos, J., *Race and Racism in Britain* (1993)

Spencer, I., 'World War Two and the making of multiracial Britain', in P. Kirkham and D. Thoms (eds), *War Culture. Social Change and Changing Experience in World War Two* (1995)

Studlar, D. T., 'British public opinion, colour issues and Enoch Powell: a longitudinal analysis', *British Journal of Political Science*, 4:3 (1974)

Studlar, D. T., 'Policy voting in Britain: the coloured immigration issue in the 1964, 1966 and 1970 general elections', *American Political Science Review*, 72:1 (1978)

Tanner, D., *Political Change and the Labour Party, 1900–1918* (Cambridge, 1990)

Taylor, M., 'Labour and the constitution', in D. Tanner, P. Thane and N. Tiratsoo (eds), *Labour's First Century* (Cambridge, 2000)

Taylor, R., 'The Labour party and CND', in R. Taylor and N. Young (eds), *Campaigns for Peace. British Peace Movements in the Twentieth Century* (Manchester, 1987)

Thane, P., 'Towards equal opportunities? Women in Britain since 1945', in T. Gourvish and A. O'Day (eds), *Britain Since 1945* (1991)

Thompson, E. P., *The Making of the English Working Class* (1963)

Thompson, P., 'Labour's "Gannex conscience"? Politics and popular attitudes to the "permissive society"', in R. Coopey, S. Fielding and N. Tirasoo (eds), *The Wilson Governments, 1964–70* (1993)

Thorpe, A., *A History of the British Labour Party* (1997)

Thorpe, K., 'The "juggernaught method": the 1966 state of emergency and the Wilson government's response to the seamen's strike', *Twentieth Century British History*, 12:4 (2001)

Tiratsoo, N., *Reconstruction, Affluence and Labour Politics. Coventry 1945–60* (1990)

Tiratsoo, N., 'Popular politics, affluence and the Labour party', in A. Gorst, L. Johnman and W. S. Lucas (eds), *Contemporary British History, 1931–61* (1991)

Tiratsoo, N. (ed.), *The Attlee Years* (1991)

Tomlinson, J., *Democratic Socialism and Economic Policy* (Cambridge, 1997)

Turner, J. E., *Labour's Doorstep Politics in London* (1978)

Vernon, J., *Politics and the People. A Study in English Political Culture, c. 1815–1867* (Cambridge, 1993)

Vernon, J., 'Notes towards an introduction', in J. Vernon (ed.), *Re-reading the Constitution. New Narratives in the Political History of England's Long Nineteenth Century* (Cambridge, 1996)

Waters, C., *British Socialists and the Politics of Popular Culture, 1884–1914* (Manchester, 1990)

Weakliem, D., 'Class consciousness and political change: voting and political attitudes in the British working class, 1964–1970', *American Sociological Review*, 58:3 (1993)

Weight, R., *Patriots. National Identity in Britain, 1940–2000* (2002)

Whiteley, P., *The Labour Party in Crisis* (1983)

Wickham-Jones, M., *Economic Strategy and the Labour Party* (1996)

Williams, P. M., *Hugh Gaitskell* (Oxford, 1982)

Williams, R., *The Long Revolution* (Harmondsworth, 1965)

Williams, R., *Keywords* (1976)

Wood, F., 'Scottish Labour in government and opposition, 1964–79', in I. Donnachie, C. Harvie and I. S. Wood (eds), *Forward! Labour Politics in Scotland, 1888–1988* (Edinburgh, 1988)

Wrigley, C., 'Trade unions, the government and the economy', in T. Gourvish and A. O'Day (eds), *Britain Since 1945* (1991)

Yeo, S., 'A new life: the religion of socialism in Britain, 1883–1896', *History Workshop Journal*, 4 (1977)

Young, J., 'Britain and "LBJ's war", 1964–68', *Cold War History*, 2:3 (2002)

Young, K., 'Orpington and the "Liberal revival"', in C. Cook and J. Ramsden (eds), *By-elections in British Politics* (1973)

Young, N., *An Infantile Disorder? The Crisis and Decline of the New Left* (1977)

Zeigler, P., *Wilson* (1993)

Zweiniger-Bargielowska, I., 'Explaining the gender gap: the Conservative Party and the women's vote, 1945–1964', in M. Francis and I. Zweiniger-Bargielowska (eds), *The Conservatives and British Society, 1880–1990* (Cardiff, 1996)

Index

Page references for tables are in *italics*.

abortion 125
Abrams, Mark 73, 75
Adams, Walter 17, 180
advertising 73
affluence 5, 7–9, 61–2
  accommodating 65–8
  criticising 68–72
Agenda for a Generation (Labour Party) 192, 195
Alavi, H. A. 151
Albu, Austen 99
Ali, Tariq 16, 166, 178, 182
Almond, Gabriel 3
Anderson, Hugh 228
Anderson, Perry 23
Asians 147–9, 151, 155–7, 158
ASLEF 94
Attlee, Clement 39, 68, 142, 205

Bacon, Alice 87, 92, 154
Balogh, Thomas 153
Banton, Michael 13–14
Barker, Sara 47, 75, 175, 220
Beer, Samuel 4, 20
Benn, Tony 53, 231
  1966 general election 80
  1970 general election 219
  on Braddock 173
  Citizens for Labour 74–5, 121
  devolution 200
  immigration 157, 227
  Newsom report 92
  participation 196–7, 229
  students 180
Bevan, Aneurin 99, 103, 193
Bidwell, Sid 182

Bing, Geoffrey 70
Birmingham 206
Black and White Minstrel Show (BBC) 159
black people
  1970 general election 226–7
  immigration 11–15, 139–40, 142–3, 144, 145
  integration 145–9
Booker, Christopher 4
Braddock, Bessie 65, 173–4
Bradley, Tom 210
Brinham, George 171
Britain Belongs to You (Labour Party) 64
Brockway, Fenner 149
Brown, George 141–2
Brown, Lord 95, 106

Callaghan, James 231
  Community Development Programme 208, 209
  devolution 204, 230
  immigration 153, 155, 156–7, 158, 227
  students 180, 182
Campaign for Nuclear Disarmament (CND) 16, 181
capitalism 65–6, 67, 69, 70
Castle, Barbara 115, 116
  equal pay 127, 129–31, 132–3, 224
  In Place of Strife (White Paper) 105–6
  industrial democracy 101, 103–5, 107
  industrial relations 94, 96, 97
  students 180
Charles, Prince 203–4, 229
Chief Women's Officer (CWO), Labour Party 114, 118

Citizens for Labour 74–5, 121, 229
civic culture 3–4, 5
class 86–7, 230, 232
  1970 general election 222–3
  and education 87–93
  and Labour Party 23, 72, *222*
  women *224*
  in workplace 93–9
  see also middle class; working class
clause four 66–7, 72, 73
CLPs *see* constituency Labour parties
Coates, Ken 100, 103
Cocks, Michael 206–7
Cole, Margaret 88, 91
Collins, Victor 53–4
Colquhoun, Maureen 122
Committee on Public Participation in
  Planning 192, 199–200, 211
Commonwealth 12, 13, 142, 144, 149
Commonwealth Immigration Act 1962
  13, 149
Communist Party (CP) 94, 95, 169,
  171
Community Development Programme
  (CDP) 192, 208–9
comprehensive education 88–90, 207,
  217
Confederation of British Industry (CBI)
  106, 128
Conservative Party
  1951 general election 68, 70
  1955 general election 69
  1959 general election 61–5, 71, 72
  1964 general election 79
  1970 general election 221, 224
  Community Development Programme
  209
  electoral support 20–1, *21*, 22
  equal pay 131
  history 25
  immigration 13, 15, 139, 141–2, 144,
  149, 150, 227
  policy review 217–18
  women 113
  young people 165, 167, 170, 176
constituency Labour parties (CLPs) 35–6,
  50
  membership *44*, 45, *45*, 47
  and participation 209–10
  recruitment 48
  and trade unions 37, 38–9
  women candidates 226
  young people 169–70, *170*

constitution, Labour Party 36
  clause four 66–7, 72, 73
constitutional change, in Britain 192–3,
  230
  see also devolution
Cousins, Frank 68, 70
Coventry 208, 209
crime 15
Crosland, Anthony
  1970 general election 223
  education 89–90, 91, 92, 93
  generation gap 169
  industrial democracy 99–100
  inequality 86
  local government 206, 207
  participation 195
  party image 72
  revisionism 65–6, 68, 70
Crossman, Richard
  Community Development Programme
  208
  devolution 204
  equal pensions 132
  'fighting socialist opposition' 71
  immigration 151, 157, 158
  science 76
  students 178, 179, 185
Crowther-Hunt Commission 192, 204,
  207, 230
cultural change 1–2, 3–5
  and Labour Party 23–4, 55–6, 230–3
culture 1

Daily Herald 70
Daily Mail 197
Daily Mirror 78
Dalton, Hugh 167
Davies, John 98
Deakin, Nicholas 145–6
democracy 211
  within Labour Party 209–11
  see also industrial democracy; participation
devolution 19–20, 192–3, 197, 200–5
discrimination
  race 13, 141, 143, 153–5, 158
  women 123–5
Discrimination Against Women Study
  Group, Labour Party 124–5
divorce 125, 133
dock workers 101, 103–4
Donnison, David 93
Donovan Commission 10, 100

Douglas-Home, Sir Alec 77
Durbin, Evan 65
Dutschke, Rudi 180

Eadie, Alex 203
East African Asians 155–7, 158
Ede, Chuter 183
Edelman, Maurice 72
education 106–7, 217
    comprehensive schools 87–90
    private 90–3
    within Labour Party 51–2
Education Act 1944 88
Empire Windrush 11, 12, 142
employment
    racial equality 152, 153–5
    women 9–10, 126–9
England
    local government 205–7
    regional government 204–5
England Arise! (Fielding, Thompson and
    Tiratsoo) 25–6
Ennals, David 156, 157, 159
entryism 169, 173–5
equal pay 10, 127–34, 217, 224
Equal Pay Act 1970 126, 131–2
European Economic Community (EEC)
    142

family, and Labour Party membership
    42
federalism 204–5
fellowship 42–3
feminism 10–11, 122–3
Fisher, Doris 123
Focus 174
Foley, Maurice 151–2, 153, 154
Foot, Michael 23, 68, 71, 77, 96, 182, 193
Fords 129–30
Freeman, John 22, 70
Future Labour Offers You, The (Labour
    Party) 63–4
Future of Socialism, The (Crosland) 65–6,
    223

Gaitskell, Hugh 22, 61
    1959 general election 61–2, 63, 65
    class 87
    education 91
    EEC 142
    immigration 149
    party image 73
    racial equality 139, 141, 144

revisionism 56, 66–8, 69
    unilateralism 181
    Young Socialists 174–5
general election 1950 *21*
general election 1951 *21*, 68, 70
general election 1955 *21*, 69
general election 1959 *21*, 61–5, 71, 72,
    77, 230–1
general election 1964 *21*, 61, 79–80
general election 1966 *21*, 61, 80–1, 230
general election 1970 *21*, 217, 230–1,
    233
    black immigrants 226–7
    participation 228–30
    party organisation 219–21
    timing 217–19
    women 224–6, *225*
    working class 221–4, *222*
    young people *225*, 227–8
general management committees (GMCs)
    35, 36
    trade unions 37, 38
generation gap 17–18, 168–9
Giddens, Anthony 5
Glasgow 48, *49*
Glasgow Gorbals 228–9
'Golden Age' 3, 217, 232
Goldthorpe, John 8, 98
Gould, Joyce 126
grant maintained schools 91, 92
Greenwood, Anthony 144
Griffiths, James 88, 202
Griffiths, Peter 150
Gunter, Ray
    Citizens for Labour 75
    equal pay 128, 131, 133–4
    Labour in the Sixties 76
    racial equality 152, 154
    trade unions 94, 95, 104

Halifax 219–20
Hamilton 201, 202
Hardie, Keir 200
Harrington, Illtyd 181
Harrison, James 144, 145
Hart, Judith 115
    on Conservative Party 218
    industrial democracy 99
    participation 192, 197–8, 199, 207,
        211
    racial equality 141
    young people 168, 178, 183
Harvey Spicers 93–4

Hattersley, Roy 140, 177
Hayday, Fred 154
Hayward, Ron 126
Healey, Denis 223
Heath, Anthony 22
Heath, Edward 21, 218, 222, 224
Heffer, Eric 181, 182
Herbison, Peggy 123, 124
Hi! (Labour Party) 168
Hill, Jimmy 165
Hobsbawm, Eric 3, 15, 21
Hoggart, Richard 16, 41
Houghton, Douglas 124, 125, 127
House of Commons 192
House of Lords 192, 193
housing, race discrimination 13, 143, 153
Huckfield, Les 186
Hughes, Cledwyn 203
Hynd, John 144

image 72–3, 75–9
immigration 11–15, 139–40, 142–3, 158–9
    and 1970 general election 226–7
    colour and the Commonwealth 140–2
    equality at work 153–5
    integration 145–9, 151–3
    Kenyan Asians 155–7
    restriction 149–51
    uncertain principle 144–5
Immigration Act 1962 145, 155
In Place of Fear (Bevan) 99
In Place of Strife (White Paper) 97, 105–6, 219
Indians 12, 147–9
industrial democracy 97–100, 106, 107, 217
    Castle's impact 103–5
    In Place of Strife 105–6
    Jack Jones' influence 101–3
Industrial Organiser (Labour Party) 38
industrial relations 8–9, 87, 93–5
    and equal pay 129–30
Industrial Relations Bill 1969 101
inflation 224
Inglehart, Ronald 3, 17, 18
Institute of Race Relations (IRR) 14
Institute for Workers' Control 100
integration, of immigrants 140, 145–9, 151–3, 158
Ireland 11, 12
Iron and Steel Bill 1965 101

Jay, Douglas 69, 99, 100, 106, 184, 193
Jeger, Lena 121, 131, 224
Jenkins, Hugh 193
Jenkins, Roy 64, 66
    equal pay 131
    immigration 141, 155–6, 158
    integration 152, 153, 154, 155
    trades unions 223
Jones, Gareth Stedman 27
Jones, Jack 95, 100, 101–3, 223
Jones, Tom 37
Jouhl, A. S. 154–5
Jupp, James 17

Keep Left 174, 175
Kenyan Asians 155–7, 158
Kerr, David 181
King, Horace 168
Kinnock, Neil 226
Kitschelt, Herbert 22
Klein, Viola 10
Knight, Percy 171

Labour in the Sixties (Labour Party) 76
Labour League of Youth (LOY) 169, 171, 172, 186
Labour Party
    1959 general election 61–5
    1964 general election 79–80
    1966 general election 80–1
    and affluence 65–72
    and change 22–4
    and class 86–7
    and cultural change 230–3
    as a cultural institution 53–5
    education 51–2
    electoral support 20–1, *21*, 22
    fellowship 42–3
    history 25–7
    image 72–3, 75–9
    membership 39–42, 43–5, *43*, *44*, *45*, *46*, 47–9, *49*
    organisation 35–7, 55, 73–5
    participation within 209–11
    professionalism 49–50
    Scotland and Wales 19–20
    and trade unions 37–9, 96–7
    women 113–18, *115*, *117*, 118–19, 133–4
    young people 165–72, *170*, 185–6
Labour Party Young Socialists (LPYS) 174, 185, 186
Labour Women 117

Latey Commission 184
Lavers, G. R. 7
Lawrence, Jon 21–2, 26
Lee, Fred 224
Lee, Jennie 133
Left 174
Leisure for Living (Labour Party) 64
Lester, Anthony 153
'Let's Go!' campaign 75–9
Levin, Bernard 4
Liberal Party
    1964 general election 79
    1966 general election 81
    Orpington 73
    young people 176
Liddle, Joan 24
Lipton, Marcus 149
Liverpool 206, 208–9
local government 192, 195, 205–7
    and devolution 204–5
    Hart's Green Paper 198
    participation 229–30
Lockwood, David 8, 98
London
    entryism 175
    immigration 13, 142–3
London Boroughs Association 199
London School of Economics (LSE) 17,
    180–1
Longford, Lord 182–3
Lowthian, George 154
Lyon, Alex 209

MacDonald, Ramsay 23, 193
Mackintosh, John 78, 169, 211, 223
    participation 191, 195, 201, 203,
    204
Macmillan, Harold 5, 218
    1959 general election 62, 63, 77
Manchester 167–8, 206, 229–30
Manning, Leah 70
Marock, Nat 148
Marquand, David 191
marriage 11
Marsh, Richard 104–5, 169, 171–2,
    184
Marwick, Arthur 3
Marx, Karl 27, 66
Maxwell, Robert 92
May, John 27
May Day 54–5
Mayhew, Christopher 223, 224
McKibbin, Ross 25

membership, of the Labour Party 43–5,
    43, 44, 45, 46, 47, 55
    age 41
    associate 74–5
    class 40–1
    fellowship 42–3
    ideal and reality 39–40
    recruitment 47–9, *49*
    women 41, 114–18, *115*, *117*, 119–22,
    123
men, occupational class *6*
middle class
    1964 general election 79
    1966 general election 81
    party membership 74–5
    students 16, 165, 168–9
    young people 167, 172–3
Mikardo, Ian 93, 99, 101, 103, 141
Miliband, Ralph 25, 191, 217
Militant Tendency 228
Miller, Millie 24
Millwood, John 149
modernity 4
Moonman, Eric 102
Morgan, Kenneth 4
Morrell, Derek 208
Morrison, Herbert 26, 39, 79, 193–4
Mosley, Oswald 149

National Association of Labour Student
    Organisations (NALSO) 177–8, 228
National Executive Committee (NEC)
    1970 general election 219, 221
    constituency section 35
    education 89, 90, 91, 92
    equal pay 127–8
    immigration 143
    industrial democracy 101–3, 105
    participation 191–2
    party democracy 210–11
    party image 75–6
    party membership 43, 48
    party organisation 36, 37, 74–5
    racial equality 141, 142
    South Africa 140
    students 177, 228
    trade unions 37, 38
    voting age 184
    women 114–15, 118, 121, 124–5, 226
    young people 169, 171, 172, 173,
    174, 175, 176
National Federation of Women's Insti-
    tutes 199

National Labour Women's Advisory Council (NLWAC) 114–15, 118, 119, 122, 123
  abortion 125
  equal pay 128, 132–3
  female employment 126
  women candidates 226
National Organisation of Labour Students 228
National Union of Railwaymen 94
National Union of Seamen (NUS) 94–5
nationalisation 66–7, 70–1, 72, 87, 98–9, 193
nationalism 19–20, 200–4
Nationality Act 1948 12, 142
New Advance 174
New Bristol Group 75, 196
Newens, Stan 175
Newsom, Sir John 92
Nicholas, Sir Harry 233
Northern Ireland 90, 197

opinion polls 22
  1959 general election 62–3
  1964 general election 79
  1970 general election 219, 222, *222*
  voting age 184
Orpington 73
Owen, David 156

Padley, Walter 223
Pakistanis 147
Pannell, Charles 72, 76, 159
Pargiter, George 145, 149
parliament 192–3
participation 18–20, 191–2, 211, 217
  1970 general election 228–30
  attitudes to 194–7
  Community Development Programme 208–9
  devolution 204–5
  Hart's Green Paper 197–8
  Labour, the individual and the state 192–4
  local government 205–7
  nationalism 200–4
  planning 199–200
  students 17, 178, 180–1
  within Labour Party 209–11
  see also industrial democracy
Participation '69 124–5, 210

party organisation 35–7, 55, 73–5
  1970 general election 219–21
  and participation 209–11
  women 118–19
  young people 169–77, *170*
Pelling, Henry 4
Personal Freedom (Labour Party) 194
Phillips, Morgan 65, 72, 73, 76
Pitt, David 143, 144–5, 146, 227
Plaid Cymru 19, 20, 200, 201, 229
planning 192, 199–200
Political Education Officers (PEOs), of the Labour Party 51
Politics of Democratic Socialism, The (Durbin) 65
popular participation *see* participation
port transport industry 101, 103–4
Ports Bill 104
poverty 7
Powell, Enoch 14–15, 155, 157, 218, 227
Prices and Incomes Bill 131
private education 90–3, 106–7
Progress and Change (Labour Party) 192
proportional representation 193
Prys Davies, Gwilym 202
public schools 90–2

race discrimination 13, 141, 143, 153–5, 158, 217
Race Relations Act 1965 139, 152, 153
Race Relations Act 1968 139, 153, 154–5, 158
Race Relations Board 151
Raisin, Jim 149, 222
  membership recruitment 43, 44, 48, 147
  party democracy 210
  party organisation 36–7, 38
Redcliffe-Maud Commission on the Reform of Local Government in England 192, 198, 204, 205–7
regional government 204–5, 206
Rents Act 1957 13
revisionism 65–8, 69–70, 77
  1970 general election 223–4
  class 87
  education 91
  participation 194, 229
Rogers, George 69, 144
Rogers, Herbert 228
Rose, Paul 155, 167–8, 178
Rose, Richard 22
Rowntree, Seebohm 7

Rowthorne, Bob 182
Royal Commission on Marriage and Divorce 9
Royal Commission on Population 12
Royal Commission on the Reform of Local Government in England 192, 198, 204, 205–7
Royal Commission on Trade Unions and Employers' Associations 10, 100

Salford 229
Samuel, Raphael 27
Sassoon, Donald 22
Saville, John 182
Scanlon, Hugh 95, 100, 130
science 76–7
Scotland 19–20, 200–1, 202–3
    1970 general election 228–9
    devolution 204, 205
    regional government 206
Scottish National Party (SNP) 19, 20, 200, 201, 228–9
Scottish TUC (STUC) 201
Seear, Nancy 10
'Selsdon man' 218, 221
Sheldon, Robert 167
Shils, Edward 3
Shore, Peter 76, 95, 183
Short, Edward 54, 92, 180–1, 195, 218
Short, Renee 131–2
Signposts for the Sixties (Labour Party) 76–7, 91–2
Sikhs 149, 158
Sillars, Jim 203
Simpson, Bill
    industrial democracy 102
    party organisation 36, 47, 50, 51, 118
Skeffington, Arthur 199, 233
Skeffington report 192, 199–200, 211
Smethwick 13, 14, 150
Smith, T. Dan 204
socialism 2, 23, 25–6, 231–2
    and participation 193–4
    revisionism 65–6
Socialist Charter 181
Socialist Commentary 66
    immigration 144–5 139–40, 145–6
    participation 229
    racial equality 155
    students 178–9
    voluntarism 49–50
Socialist Labour League 174

Socialist Women's Circle 121
Sorenson, Reginald 24, 69, 86, 151, 178
Soskice, Sir Frank 150–1, 152
South Africa 140
Stewart, Michael 88, 91, 92, 103–4, 184, 197
Stonehouse, John 197
Strauss, George 185
Straw, Jack 228
strikes 8–9, 87, 94–5
students 16–17, 165, 168–9, 177–80, 185
    1970 general election 228
    Labour Party membership *170*
    participation 229
    Tribune 180–2
Students for a Labour Victory (SLV) 228
Summerskill, Edith 220
Sun 80
Sutherland, Mary 71, 119, 122

Taylor, Miles 21–2
television 40, 69, 196–7
Thomas, George 156, 203–4
Thompson, Edward 25
Thompson, Peter 25–6
Thomson, George 206
Tiratsoo, Nick 9, 25–6
Towards Equality (Labour Party) 86–7, 88, 99
Town and Country Planning Act 1968 192, 199, 200
trade unions
    1970 general election 222–4
    devolution 205
    equal pay 127, 130, 131
    industrial democracy 98, 100, 101, 102–4
    industrial relations 94–5
    and Labour Party 23, 37–9, 74, 96–7, 217
    membership 8, 10
    racial equality 154
Trades Union Congress (TUC) 127, 128, 154
Transport Bill 105
Transport and General Workers' Union 154
Tribune
    immigration 150, 156–7, 158, 159
    industrial relations 96
    students 180–2
    youth culture 168
Trotskyism 174–5

Underhill, Reg 171, 185
United Dairies 94
universities 16, 17, 178, 180–1
    see also students
Urban District Council Association 199
Urban Programme 157

Verba, Sidney 3
Vernon, James 26
Victory for Socialism 194
Vietnam Solidarity Campaign (VSC) 16,
    17, 181–2
Vietnam War 16, 178, 180
voluntarism 49–50, 220
voting age 165, 183–6

Wales 19–20, 200–2, 203–4
    1970 general election 228, 229
    devolution 204, 205
Walked, Harold 132
Walker, Patrick Gordon 150
Waterhouse, Keith 168
Watkins, Alan 8–9
Welsh Language Act 1967 205
West Indians *see* black people
Wheatley report 192, 204
White, Eirene 65, 98–9, 102, 148
Willey, Fred 194
Williams, Len 44–5, 118
Williams, Raymond 1–2, 25
Williams, Shirley 168
Willis, Norman 86–7
Wilmott, Peter 11
Wilson, Des 18
Wilson, Harold
    1970 general election 217, 218–19,
        220–1
    class 87
    economy 80
    EEC 142
    immigration 150, 227
    industrial relations 93–5
    integration 146, 151
    local government 205, 206
    participation 191, 194–5, 197, 198,
        211
    party democracy 209, 210
    party image 76–8, 79
    party organisation 36, 38, 39, 42, 44,
        47–8, 50, 51, 116, 165
    racial equality 154, 157

scientific revolution ix, 61, 76
students 179, 180
Vietnam War 178
women 113
young people 228
women 9–11, 133–4
    1959 general election 64–5
    1964 general election 80
    1966 general election 81
    1970 general election 224–6, *225*
    discrimination 123–5
    employment 126–7
    equal pay 127–33, 217
    feminism 122–3
    in Labour Party 41, 78, 113–18, *115*,
        117, 118–22
    occupational class *6*
Woodburn, Arthur 24, 93, 200
working class 3
    1959 general election 63
    1964 general election 79–80
    1970 general election 221–4, *222*
    Labour Party membership 40–1, 44
    Labour vote 157
    transformation 5, *6*, 7–9
    women 10, 224
    young people 15–16, 167, 173
World Cup 221

Young, Doris 168–9
Young, Michael 3, 11
Young Conservatives 170, 176
Young Guard 174, 175
young people 15–18, 165–6, 185–6, 217
    1959 general election 64
    1964 general election 80
    1966 general election 81
    1970 general election *225*, 227–8
    enfranchisement 182–5
    Labour Party perception 166–9
    party organisation 169–72, *170*, 172–7
    students 177–82
    women 119–22
Young Socialists (YS) 165, 172–3
    entryism 173–5
    other problems 175–7
    voting age 184
Younger, Kenneth 167
Youth Commission 165, 183, 184

Zweig, Ferdynand 7

Learning Resources
Centre